Getting out

- A fielder catches your fair or foul ball before it touches the ground (unless it is a foul tip to the catcher with less than two strikes).
- You hit a foul tip (a ball caught by the catcher off your bat) for strike three.
- After hitting the ball, you or first base is tagged before you touch the base.
- The umpire calls three strikes during your at-bat (whether you swing or not).
- A ball that you hit fair hits your bat a second time while you are in fair territory.
- While running outside the foul lines, you obstruct a fielder's throw.
- You hit the ball with one or both feet outside the batter's box or step from one batter's box to another while the pitcher winds up.
- You obstruct the catcher from fielding or throwing.
- You run into your own fairly-batted ball while running from home to first base.

Getting on base

- You hit a fair ball that is not caught by a fielder before it touches the ground.
- You hit a fair ball that touches the ground and is caught by a fielder whose throw fails to beat you to a base.
- The umpire calls four pitches out of the strike zone during your at-bat.
- A pitch in the strike zone hits you without first touching your bat.
- The catcher obstructs your swing.
- You hit a fair ball beyond the playing field (for a home run).
- You hit a fair, catchable ball, but the fielder drops the ball, throws it away, and so on.
- A third strike skips past the catcher and you beat the throw to first.

The Positions

Abbreviation	Player
P	Pitcher
C	Catcher
1B	First baseman
2B	Second baseman
3B	Third baseman
SS	Shortstop
LF	Left fielder
CF	Center fielder
RF	Right fielder

American League lineups include a desig-nator hitter who bats for the pitcher without taking a defensive position in the field. DH is the abbreviation for that slot.

Baseball
For Dummies, 3rd Edition

Cheat Sheet

Getting out on the base paths

- You are on the same base with a teammate when the ball is alive (the second runner is out).
- You pass a preceding runner on the base paths.
- You miss a base and the defense notices it.
- A fielder tags you with a ball that is alive while you are off the base. (However, no one can tag you out if you overrun first base provided you return immediately to that bag without making a turn toward second.)
- Your teammate hits a ball that touches you in fair territory without it first touching or passing any fielder except the pitcher.
- In the judgment of the umpire, you hinder a fielder from making a play.
- A batted ball forces you to advance to another base and the fielder possessing the ball tags that base before you reach it.

Major league baseball "mosts" (since 1900)

Most Career Home Runs: 744, Henry Aaron (1954-1976)

Most Home Runs in a Season: 73, Barry Bonds (2001)

Most Runs Batted In (RBI) in a Season: 190, Hack Wilson, (1930)

Most Runs Scored in a Season: 177, Babe Ruth (1921)

Most Hits in a Season: 257, George Sisler (1920)

Most Consecutive Games Batting Safely: 56, Joe DiMaggio (1941)

Most Wins by a Pitcher in a Season: 41, Jack Chesbro (1904)

Most Saves in a Season: 57, Bobby Thigpen (1990)

Most Strikeouts in a Season: 383, Nolan Ryan (1973)

Highest On-Base Percentage in a Season: .582, Barry Bonds (2002)

Highest Slugging Average in a Season: .863, Barry Bonds (2001)

Highest Batting Average in a Season: .426, Napoleon Lajoie (1901)

Most Wins by a Team in a Season: 116, Chicago Cubs (1906), Seattle Mariners (2001)

Copyright © 2004 Wiley Publishing, Inc.
All rights reserved.
Item 7537-6.
For more information about Wiley Publishing, call 1-800-762-2974.

For Dummies: Bestselling Book Series for Beginners

Praise for Baseball For Dummies

"There may not be anyone alive who knows more about baseball than Joe Morgan."

> — Bob Costas, NBC Sports broadcaster

"Whether you are a first-day fan or a lifetime fan of baseball as I am, everyone can learn something from *Baseball For Dummies*. 'Little Joe' is truly Big Joe with this book."

> — Chris Berman, ESPN Sports broadcaster

"What Joe Morgan doesn't know about baseball is simply not worth knowing."

> — Jon Miller, ESPN Baseball commentator

"Joe Morgan knows baseball. In fact, he was one of the most intelligent players to ever play the game."

> — Sparky Anderson, three-time World Series winning manager

"Joe Morgan could hit singles, doubles, triples and home runs. This book is a grand slam."

> — Pete Rose, 1975 World Series Most Valuable Player, Cincinnati Reds

"*Baseball For Dummies* brings out the kid in every reader. A terrific book for people of all ages."

> — Fred Opper, coach at Fordham University

"NBC's Joe Morgan again showed himself a rare bird: an ex-jock with savvy and the ability to communicate it."

> — *People* magazine

by Joe Morgan with Richard Lally

Foreword by Sparky Anderson

WILEY

Wiley Publishing, Inc.

Baseball For Dummies,® 3rd Edition

Published by
Wiley Publishing, Inc.
111 River St.
Hoboken, NJ 07030-5774
www.wiley.com

WILEY

About the Author

Joe Morgan, one of six children born to Mr. and Mrs. Leonard (Ollie) Morgan, moved from Bonham, Texas, to Oakland at the age of 10 in 1954. His principal residence has been in the East Bay Area since that time. Joe was an active participant in sports and social programs at the Brookfield Community Center. He continued his education in the Peralta College District, attending Merritt College from 1961 to 1963 and graduating with honors and an AA degree. He also attended California State University at Hayward, earning a BS in Physical Education. Again, both scholastic and athletic honors were accorded him. Entering the ranks of professional baseball in 1963, Joe signed with the Houston Colt 45's. He participated with their farm club for approximately two seasons and became a regular player for the Astros in 1964. He was named National League Rookie of the Year in 1965, and his exceptional performance continued with the Astros until 1972 when he was traded to the Cincinnati Reds. He continued to be a dominant factor in the ranks of professional baseball throughout his career. Honors accorded him during this period are numerous. These honors include Most Valuable Player in the 1972 All-Star Game; Most Valuable Player in the National League in 1975 and 1976; the Commissioner's Award in 1976 for most votes by the fans for the All-Star Game; and the Comeback Player of the Year award in 1982. Before ending his career in 1984, Joe established a new career home-run record for a second baseman; played in a record 92 consecutive games without an error (by a second baseman); played in four World Series, winning two championships; played in seven League Championship Series; and established an All-Star record by playing in seven consecutive games with a hit. In addition, he won five Gold Glove Awards, played in ten All-Star Games, and recorded 692 stolen bases. These honors are clearly indicative of his great abilities. He was elected to the National Baseball Hall of Fame in 1990 on the first ballot.

Richard Lally's articles and columns on baseball, politics, boxing, business, the arts, and general sports have appeared in prestigious publications throughout the world. He is the author or co-author of nineteen books, including the baseball autobiography *The Wrong Stuff* written with Boston Red Sox pitching ace Bill Lee. The book enjoyed a long run on bestseller lists in the U.S. and Canada and was selected as part of Total Baseball's Ultimate Baseball Library.

Dedication

I want to dedicate this third edition of *Baseball For Dummies* to my father Leonard, who passed away on May 18, 2004. My dad taught me everything I know about baseball. He always stressed that I should devote myself to excelling in all facets of the sport, rather than trying to be the best in only one or two departments. One of his proudest moments came when I was voted the most complete player in the game. I couldn't have won that award without his guidance.

— Joe Morgan

Authors' Acknowledgements

Joe Morgan: I must express my gratitude to the entire Morgan family for their support and sacrifices when I was a player and their love that keeps me motivated today. Lisa, Angela, Ashley, Kelly — Dad loves you. I also want to thank all of my former teammates who were part of my learning experience about the greatest game in the world. What are friends for? They are there when you need a favor. Thank you Johnny Bench, Rusty Staub, Ken Caminiti, Bob Gibson, Ken Griffey, Sr., Barry Larkin, Harry Wendelstedt, Bill Lee, Derek Jeter, Keith Hernandez, and Willie McCovey. A special thanks to the man who taught me the real philosophy of managing, the great Sparky Anderson. The Cincinnati Reds 1976 team was the greatest team ever. Richard, you are a great partner. The Wild Bunch would have cleaned up Dodge City easier than Doc and the Earp brothers. Thanks to Wiley Publishing; your staff does a great job. Your turn, Richard.

Richard Lally: I want to first thank my partner, Joe Morgan, for bringing the same dedication and intelligence to this project that he brought to the field in every game he played. Mr. Morgan is Hall of Fame in everything he does, as well as being a grand fellow with great taste in westerns. (And remember, JM, if you ever want to take on Johnny Ringo and the Clantons, I'm your Huckleberry.) Joe's assistant, Lolita Aulston, kept us on track and on schedule. The staff at Wiley could not have been more supportive: Kathleen Cox, Natalie Harris, and Elizabeth Rea made this project a pleasant task. Mark Reiter, our ace literary agent, was a driving force behind the original book, and IMG's Sophia Siedner has been a constant source of encouragement and inspiration. We did not have a staff of researchers, but whenever data proved elusive, I was always able to turn to one of my gang of Usual Suspects: Billy Altman, Bill Shannon, Jim Gerard, Jordan Sprechman, Bill Daughtry, Rob Neyer, and John Collett (Our Man in the Ballparks). Messers. Shannon and Gerard, a pair of walking baseball databases, also doubled-checked our work to cut out any glitches. Willie Mays, Bob Gibson, Rusty Staub, Bill Lee, Sparky Anderson, Johnny Bench, Willie McCovey, Barry Larkin, Ken Caminiti, Ken Griffey, Sr., Derek Jeter, Keith Hernandez, and Harry Wendelstedt, our "all-star" team of advisors, could not have been more generous with their time and insights.

Every writer should be blessed with the friends and relatives who have encouraged me, many of them from the first time I picked up a pen. I thank and love them all: My brothers Joseph and Sean; my late parents Richard and Anne, who instilled in me my love for baseball; the late Brother Leo Richard, who taught me to dream in wide-screen Technicolor; Aunt Kathy; Uncle Tommy (if for no other reason than that he was miffed over being left out of the first edition's acknowledgments); the ever-alluring, violet-eyed Maria DiSimone ("Like you blend, pussycat?"); the estimable Natalie Ferrouw for her smoky voice and Barbara Stanwyck eyes; Barbara Bauer, who nurtured my love of the written word; the magical Eve Lederman, the best young writer in America and the second best second baseman I know; my pal for life Al Lombardo and his wife Cathy; the Kiam family; my buddy Charlie Ludlow ("Stay in the boat, young captain!"); Joyce Altman (who doesn't seem to mind when her husband Billy and I spend hours on the phone talking about this great game); Alan Flusser; Richard and Jessie Erlanger; Karl and Margrid Durr; Alecks, Michaela, Rasmus, Paulina, and Mathilda Budny; Robert Moss; W. Michael Gillespie; and Vesna, Jean, Joey ("You are definitely insane . . . sir!"), Gil, Roz, and Andy and the rest of my gang of renegades at Q Bistro in Forest Hills whose port and curried red snapper helped me keep body and soul intact throughout this project.

Publisher's Acknowledgments

We're proud of this book; please send us your comments through our Dummies online registration form located at www.dummies.com/register/.

Some of the people who helped bring this book to market include the following:

Acquisitions, Editorial, and Media Development

Project Editor: Natalie Faye Harris

(Previous Edition: Christine Meloy Beck, Joan Friedman)

Acquisitions Editor: Kathy Cox

(Previous Edition: Stacy S. Collins)

Copy Editor: Elizabeth Rea

(Previous Edition: Donna Frederick)

General Reviewer: Jim Gerard

Reprint Editor: Carmen Krikorian

Editorial Manager: Christine Meloy Beck

Editorial Assistants: Courtney Allen, Melissa Bennett

Cover Photos: ©Arthur Tilley/Getty Images/Taxi

Chapter Photos: National Baseball Hall of Fame Library, Cooperstown, NY

Cartoons: Rich Tennant, www.the5thwave.com

Composition

Project Coordinator: Maridee Ennis

Layout and Graphics: Denny Hager, Joyce Haughey, Stephanie D. Jumper, Michael Kruzil, Barry Offringa, Lynsey Osborn, Mary Gillot Virgin

Proofreaders: Brian H. Walls, TECHBOOKS Production Services

Indexer: TECHBOOKS Production Services

Publishing and Editorial for Consumer Dummies

    Diane Graves Steele, Vice President and Publisher, Consumer Dummies

    Joyce Pepple, Acquisitions Director, Consumer Dummies

    Kristin A. Cocks, Product Development Director, Consumer Dummies

    Michael Spring, Vice President and Publisher, Travel

    Brice Gosnell, Associate Publisher, Travel

    Kelly Regan, Editorial Director, Travel

Publishing for Technology Dummies

    Andy Cummings, Vice President and Publisher, Dummies Technology/General User

Composition Services

    Gerry Fahey, Vice President of Production Services

    Debbie Stailey, Director of Composition Services

Contents at a Glance

Table of Contents

· ·

Chapter 12: There Are Tricks to This Game: Coaching 261

Chapter 13: Men in Blue: Umpiring Like a Professional 267

Chapter 14: Major-League Baseball 273

Chapter 15: Off-the-Field Baseball Jobs and How to Snag Them 277

Foreword

Joe Morgan ("The Little Man," as I like to call him) knows baseball. In fact, he was one of the most intelligent players to ever play the game. And I should know, I had the distinct pleasure to know and work with Joe for more than two decades. During my years as the manager of the Cincinnati Reds, Joe was an incredible ball player — not just because of his Hall of Fame abilities but because of his genuine love of the game. Joe was an unselfish player with a healthy respect for the rich history and tradition of baseball. His first priority was always the team; he never tried to selfishly pad his individual statistics. I love and respect Joe for his giving attitude, and he is universally respected by both his peers and baseball fans worldwide.

Now, Joe gives back to the game through this grand slam of a book, *Baseball For Dummies.* (I even helped out with a chapter or two.) Joe explains the game with insight and down-to-earth information so that anyone can understand and appreciate the game. I'm so glad Joe had the opportunity to share his vast baseball knowledge. His gift for understanding baseball and people sets him apart from the "average Joe."

Joe continues to give back to the game through his expert analysis and commentary and, of course, through *Baseball For Dummies.*

Joe was a very special player who turned out to be a total person.

Sparky Anderson, major-league manager (two teams) for more than 26 years and three-time World Series winning manager

Introduction

· ·

*W*elcome to *Baseball For Dummies,* 3rd Edition, a book dedicated to the proposition that no one's education is complete unless it includes a thorough grounding in the principles of the greatest sport ever created. This book is much like a baseball game: orderly but spontaneous, filled with nuance and surprise, and packed to the brim with fun. We hope you enjoy reading it as much as we enjoyed writing it.

About This Book

We wrote this book to appeal to fans of every level, from the novice who just recently purchased his first pack of baseball cards to the loyalist who has been sitting in the same seat at the ballpark since the Coolidge administration. Whether you participate on the field or just watch, our mission is to increase your baseball pleasure by a factor of ten.

As a spectator, you'll have an easier time watching and appreciating baseball's finer points after you finish our book. You will not only know what the players on the field are doing, but you'll also know why they are doing it. If an extraterrestrial dropped out of the skies, we would hope it could read *Baseball For Dummies,* 3rd Edition, today and attend its first baseball game tomorrow without experiencing any confusion.

If you're a player, there isn't any component of your game that can't be elevated by studying this volume. Pitching, hitting, fielding, and baserunning — we cover it all with the aid of some of the game's legendary players. It doesn't matter if you're taking your first cuts in Little League or already sitting in a big-league dugout; you can find something in this book to make you a better player.

Why You Need This Book

Novices need *Baseball For Dummies,* 3rd Edition, because no other book can offer you such a comprehensive introduction to the national pastime. You're going to discover things about baseball that many die-hard fans still haven't learned. Do you know how the great outfielders are able to get a good jump on the ball? Where the first baseman should stand to receive a cutoff throw?

How many stitches are in a baseball and who manufactures bats that meet major-league standards? You can find the answers to these and many more questions within these pages. And if you already know a lot about the sport, you're about to learn a good deal more. This book is chock-full of inside tips and insights that you rarely encounter anywhere below the professional ranks.

To be honest, we believe that all human beings need this book because baseball is part of our genetic destiny. Archaeologists have unearthed evidence linking bat-and-ball games to our prehistoric ancestors. What compelled them to start smacking around a tiny sphere with a stick? No one knows for certain, but our guess is they did it because there was no television — no *Oprah,* no *Sopranos,* and no reruns of *Seinfeld.* What were the Cro-Magnons to do with all their leisure time? Cavemen would swing clubs to slay the odd raptor and throw stones to bring down an occasional pterodactyl. So it was a natural leap to utilize these talents for a less daunting sport.

Ever since the prehistoric days, the urge to strike round objects with a stick or club has been encrypted in our DNA. You can't escape it. Try suppressing this drive, and there's no telling how much damage you can do to yourself. (*Ripley's Believe It or Not* has reported cases of spontaneous combustion in which people burst into flames for no apparent reason. We think those people would still be alive today if they had only played a game of catch every few weeks.) So we offer this book to you as a kind of public service. Utilize it to find a safe release for your primordial urges.

How to Use This Book

You may use this book any way you like. Read it from cover to cover or just pick a section and dive in. If you're a novice, you may want to read the glossary first (or at least refer to it often) so you can understand the language we use. Then read Chapters 1 through 3 for an understanding of baseball's rules. If you're a more advanced player or coach, you may want to start with Part II to improve various aspects of your game. We designed this book so that you never have to read any chapter or part in its entirety; you can often find many short paragraphs that can stand alone as minichapters. And Joe's Part of Tens chapters should appeal both to longtime fans and to those of you who are just learning the difference between a slider and a curve.

How This Book Is Organized

In each chapter, we start with the basics and build from there. For example, when Joe discusses hitting, we begin by advising you on what sort of bat you should use. Next, we focus on your grip, and then gradually we add all the other elements of a perfect swing until you're slashing line drives all over the field. Whenever we think a point needs further clarification, we cross-reference the appropriate chapter so you can immediately get any additional information you may need.

Part I: Getting Started (Before Your First At-Bat)

This is a baseball and this is a bat — yes, the book is that basic at the start. First, we give you a little history to tell you how baseball began. Then we review the rules so you won't commit any *faux pas* on or off the field, such as running the bases in the wrong direction. Because you can't take the field without the proper equipment, we also identify the tools of the trade, tell you where to acquire them, and show you how to take care of your bats, balls, and gloves so they can take care of you.

Part II: Taking Your Swings — How to Play the Game

In this part, we help you shape up your game so you look like a pro no matter what your level of play. First, we get you into baseball shape. When you finish your workout, you'll be able to chew horsehide (it's terrific with a nice Bordeaux) and spit split-fingered fastballs. Next, a group of major leaguers joins us to improve every facet of your game. We smooth the kinks out of your swing so you can maximize your bat speed to hit for power and average. Would you rather take a turn on the mound? We can add some zip to your fastball and show you how to throw a major-league curve. Fielding? You'll discover the proper way to turn a double play and catch a pop foul. And you'll never again get your feet tangled while chasing a fly ball hit over your head. (If you think a lot of major-league outfielders won't be reading that section, you haven't seen a game lately.) For coaches and players, we include a playbook that reveals baseball's basic defensive alignments at a glance. No extra charge; we just threw it in as a bonus.

Part III: From Little League to the Major Leagues: Organized Baseball

In this part, we take you through every level of professional and amateur ball to impart some sense of where the game is played and how it is run. We also bring in future Hall of Fame skipper Sparky Anderson for some tips on managing. And we even show you some basic baseball math so that you won't be at a loss the next time your friends ask you to calculate their OBPS (don't worry, you'll find out what that is soon enough).

Part IV: We Don't Care if We Ever Get Back: A Spectator's Guide

If you'd rather watch than play, this is the section for you. In this part, you discover how to follow the game as a spectator, where to find game coverage in various media, and — best of all — how to keep score. You also get an analysis of all the major-league parks with an eye toward how they affect player and team performances. Want a little more involvement without going onto the field? We devote a whole chapter to fantasy baseball.

Part V: The Part of Tens

It wouldn't be a *For Dummies* book without this part. Joe's all-time all-star team will give you a taste of baseball history, and you can use our lists of current players as miniscouting reports. The rest is just interesting stuff we thought you should know.

Part VI: Appendixes

You can't understand the game if you don't understand its language. Our glossary in Appendix A broadens your baseball vocabulary. Appendix B is a contact list for the major baseball organizations around the world.

Icons Used in This Book

Talk like this and the folks in the bleachers will have no trouble understanding you.

This icon cues you to some "must have" books to start or enhance your baseball library.

This icon signals tips from the Hall of Famer himself.

This icon gives you valuable information that can prevent you from making a bonehead play on or off the field.

This icon alerts you to sage advice from the greats of the game, signals an insight that can enhance your baseball viewing (whether you are in the stadium or in front of the TV), and alerts you to advice that comes from a coach and can be passed on by a coach.

Beware! This icon warns you that a situation can be dangerous.

Part I
Getting Started (Before Your First At-Bat)

ALEXANDER CARTWRIGHT, A NEW YORK BANK TELLER, INVENTS BASEBALL

©RICHTENNANT

...and then all the bats will have these little chains on them so players don't just walk off the field with them.

In this part . . .

A father of one of the authors was a Marine drill instructor, who told him that the secret to succeeding in anything was to "have clear objectives." In this part, we start by describing baseball's objectives (to make sure you don't go wandering around the base paths during a game). We also tell you where to get the best balls, bats, and gloves — so you'll not only play like a pro, you'll also be geared up like one. We then share some of the rules that give baseball its structure.

Chapter 1

What Is Baseball?

For those of you who still believe that Abner Doubleday invented baseball in Cooperstown, New York, we bring you a line from the gangster movie *Donnie Brasco:* "Fuhgedaboudit!" Abner didn't invent nuttin'. No one person actually conceived of the sport. Baseball evolved from earlier bat and ball games including town ball, rounders, and one o'cat. Although there's no denying that the English game of cricket was also an influence, baseball is as singular an American art form as jazz. (Although during the early 1960s, the Soviet Union claimed baseball was a Russian creation. We should note, however, that Soviets were also taking credit back then for the invention of the telephone, the electric light, Wite-Out, and — well, you get the idea.)

The Roots of the Game

If anyone invented baseball, it was Alexander Joy Cartwright. This gentleman bank teller founded the New York Knickerbockers, America's first organized baseball team, in 1842. Three years after that, Cartwright formulated the sport's first codified rules (which included three strikes per out and three outs per half-inning). Cartwright's game included a pitching mound that was only 45 feet from home plate and base paths spaced 75 feet apart. Baseball's lawmakers have altered these distances while modifying other rules over the years.

The pitcher's mound is now 60 feet from home, and the bases now sit 90 feet apart. But the bank teller's guidelines remain the basis of the modern sport. If a time machine were to transport Cartwright to a present-day major-league ballpark, it would only take him an inning or two to acclimate himself to the action on the field. That's because the most fundamental aspects of the game haven't changed since Cartwright's Knickerbockers first suited up. Most importantly, the objective of a baseball game is still for a team to win its game by outscoring its opponent.

The Structure of the Game

In the major leagues, a game is divided into nine units of play called *innings*. (Almost all leagues play nine-inning games, except some youth leagues that play only five to seven innings.) An inning consists of a turn at-bat and three outs for each team. Visiting teams bat in the first half (called the *top*) of an inning; home teams bat in the second half (called the *bottom*) of the inning.

While one club (the offensive team) is at-bat, the other (the defensive team) plays in the field. Nine players compose each team's lineup. The defensive team consists of the pitcher, catcher, first baseman, second baseman, third baseman, shortstop, left fielder, center fielder, and right fielder. Check out Figure 1-1 of the playing field to see the basic positions for each of the defensive players. (Table 1-1 gives you the abbreviations for these players.)

Table 1-1	The Players
Abbreviation	*Player*
P	Pitcher
C	Catcher
1B	First baseman
2B	Second baseman
3B	Third baseman
SS	Shortstop
LF	Left fielder
CF	Center fielder
RF	Right fielder

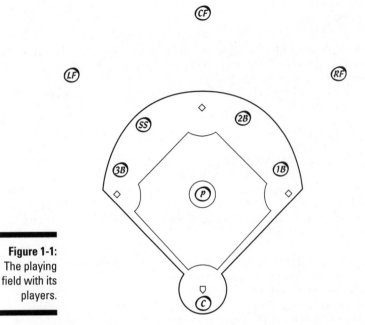

Figure 1-1:
The playing
field with its
players.

When nine isn't really nine

Many baseball games are finished before the completion of nine full innings. If
the home team leads after the top of the ninth, it wins the game without taking
its turn at-bat in the bottom of that inning. The home team can also win the
game in less than nine if it scores the winning run during the final frame. For
example, the New York Mets come to bat in the bottom of the ninth inning of
a game against the Florida Marlins. The Marlins lead 3–2. With two men out,
Mets second baseman Jose Reyes hits a two-run homer off Marlins starter
Josh Beckett. New York wins 4–3. The game is over even though the two teams
combined for only 8⅔ innings. (Remember, a team doesn't complete an inning
until it makes the third out.)

This example illustrates a difference between baseball and other major team
sports. Either team can win a game that ends in regulation time in football
(four quarters), basketball (four quarters), and hockey (three periods). In baseball, the home team can never win any game that lasts the full nine innings
(except in the event of a forfeit).

Extra innings

Games that are tied after nine innings go into *extra innings*. The two opponents play until they complete an extra inning with the visiting team ahead or until the home team scores the winning run.

The Playing Field

Baseball is played on a level field divided into an infield and an outfield. The infield (also known as the *diamond*) must be a square 90 feet (27.45 meters) on each side. Home plate sits at one corner of the square, and the three bases rest at the other corners. Moving counterclockwise from home, you see first base, second base, and third base.

Base lines run from home plate to first base, as well as from home to third. Base lines also extend from first base to second and from second to third. However, only the base lines extending from home to first and home to third are marked by white chalk. The lanes connecting the bases are the base paths. Runners must stay within them while traveling around the diamond. Should a runner step out of the base path to elude a tag, the umpire can call him out.

Foul lines extend from the first-base and third-base lines and run straight to the outfield walls. The section of the outfield beyond first base is called *right field,* the outfield section behind second base and shortstop is *center field,* and the outfield section beyond third base is *left field.*

Coaches pass on advice to players from the *coach's boxes,* the chalk rectangles in foul territory near first and third. When the players are not on the field, they sit in shelters in foul territory called *dugouts.* Between the dugout and home plate is the *on-deck circle,* where the next hitter awaits his turn at-bat. (See Figure 1-2.)

Major league rules require the distance from home plate to the nearest fence or wall in fair territory to be at least 250 feet (76 meters). Home plate must be a 17-inch (43-centimeter) square with two of its corners removed to leave a 17-inch edge, two 8½-inch (21.5-centimeter) adjacent sides, and two 12-inch (30.5-centimeter) sides angled to a point. The result is a five-sided slab of white rubber. A regulation pitching rubber is a 24-x-6-inch (61-x-15.5-centimeter) rectangle made of white rubber, set in the middle of the diamond 60 feet, 6 inches (18.4 meters) from the rear of home plate. (See Figure 1-3.)

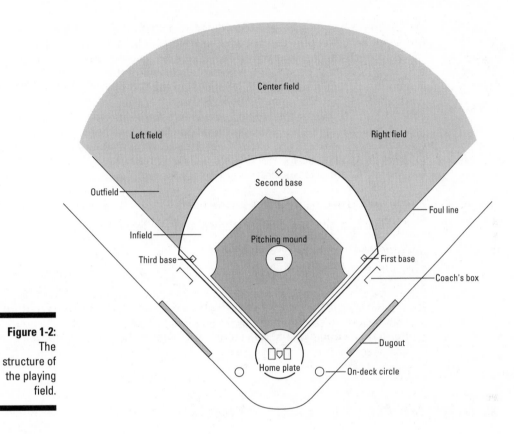

Figure 1-2:
The
structure of
the playing
field.

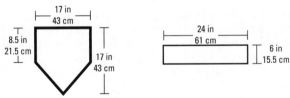

Figure 1-3:
Home plate
and the
pitching
rubber.

The Action of Play

The pitcher is the player who stands at the middle of the infield diamond
on the hill called the *mound,* where the pitching rubber is located. He throws
the baseball toward the catcher, a teammate who squats behind home plate.
When the pitcher throws the ball to the batter at home plate, he is said to be
delivering a pitch.

Each batter comes to the plate according to a specific order (the batting order or *lineup*) designated by the manager or head coach. The opposing team's batter (hitter) stands in one of two batter's boxes on either side of home plate. If he's right-handed, he stands in the box to the left of the plate (as viewed from behind). If he's left-handed, he stands in the box to the right of the plate. As the ball reaches the home plate area, the batter tries to hit it with a club called a *bat*. The batter tries to hit the ball into *fair territory* — that part of the playing field between the first- and third-base lines, from home base to the outfield fences — where it is either *fielded* (caught) for an out or drops in safely for a *base hit*. (We describe the various ways a batter makes an out or reaches base safely in Chapter 3.) A hit can take four forms:

- A *single* delivers the batter to first base.
- A *double* is hit far enough that the batter reaches second base.
- A *triple* gets the batter to third base.
- A *home run* means the batter circles all three bases and touches home plate for a run.

Home runs usually travel over the outfield fence in fair territory. If a batter hits a ball that stays on the field, but he is able to circle the bases and touch home before he can be called out, he has hit an *inside-the-park home run*.

Coming Home (Eventually)

Players score runs by getting on base and then moving around (and tagging) all three bases in order before crossing home plate. They must reach home before the offensive team tallies three outs in its half of the inning. When a club's hitters make three outs, its half-inning ends. Then it takes the field (moves to defense) and the opposing team comes to bat. (Chapter 3 has all the details on how an out is made.)

Game called because of . . .

Umpires can *call* (end) games because of inclement weather, power outages, earthquakes (don't laugh — a tremor postponed the 1989 World Series between Oakland and San Francisco), a disciplinary action (a mob of fans runs on the field and refuses to vacate; no matter which team is ahead, the umpire forfeits the game in favor of the visiting club), or some other event that renders play impossible or dangerous. To be an *official game* (one that counts as a win or a loss in the league standings), the two teams must play at least five full innings. Exceptions to this rule occur whenever the top of the fifth concludes with the home team ahead or if the home team scores the winning run during that fifth frame.

You can advance on the bases (move from first to second, second to third, or third to home) at any time, but you do so at your own peril. If you're off base when a member of the defensive team (a *fielder*) tags you with the ball, you are out. The exception to this occurs when the umpire calls "Time" (timeout). At that moment, the ball is considered dead. You may step off base without being put out, but you may not advance. Umpires may call time at the request of either team, when an injury occurs, or if some circumstance threatens the flow of the game (for instance, a cat running across the field).

The People in Charge

In professional baseball, *managers* are the team leaders. (At some other levels, such as college baseball, this person may be referred to as the head coach.) Managers plot strategy and decide which team members play which positions. They also determine a club's batting order.

Managers have assistants, called *coaches,* who help them train and discipline the team. Managers also use the first- and third-base coaches to pass along instructions to players through a series of signs. In recent years it has become fashionable for managers to employ a dugout coach. This coach is usually a savvy baseball veteran with whom the manager plots strategy throughout the game.

Umpires and Official Scorers

On-field officials known as *umpires* enforce the rules of play. In the Major Leagues, four umpires — one for each base and home plate — are assigned to each game. They decide whether a batted ball is fair or foul and whether a player is safe or out. The home-plate umpire also calls balls and strikes during the pitcher-batter confrontation. Umpires have complete authority over the game. They can eject anyone from the field who violates the rules of conduct. (See Chapter 13 for more information about umpires.) All professional games also have *official scorers.* The league hires these people to record on a scorecard all the events that take place on the field during a game. (See Chapter 16 for scoring information.) Scorers can't overrule an umpire, nor can they affect the outcome of a game. They do, however, often rule on whether a batted ball should be labeled a hit or an error for the official record. (In high school and college games, the home team provides a scorer, who usually consults with the visiting team scorekeeper on a close call.)

Baseball's Hall of Fame

To learn more about the history and evolution of this great game, there's only one place to visit: the National Baseball Hall of Fame and Museum in Cooperstown, New York. The museum has over 6,500 artifacts, including examples of the earliest bats, balls, and gloves. Many of the exhibits are interactive. The Hall's library and archives boast the world's most comprehensive collection of printed baseball matter, including box scores from the late 1800s.

The Hall of Fame gallery is this institution's Valhalla, the place where baseball's immortals are commemorated in bronze. Members of the Baseball Writers Association of America elect honorees from a list of players with ten years or more of major-league service. All candidates must be retired from baseball for at least five years before they can be considered for induction. Every two years, the Hall of Fame Veterans Committee votes for managers, pioneers of the sport, baseball executives, umpires, players from the Negro Leagues, and players who missed election their first time through the Baseball Writers Association of America voting process. A candidate must collect 75 percent of all ballots cast by either the writers or the Veterans Committee to earn a plaque in the gallery.

The Hall reserves the right to exclude anyone who is on baseball's ineligible list — for example, Pete Rose or Joe Jackson — from its ballots. Players on the ineligible list are disqualified from holding jobs with any major-league teams. Rose was ruled ineligible because he bet on baseball games. Though deceased, Jackson's name remains on the ineligible list because he actively participated in a conspiracy with gamblers and seven Chicago White Sox teammates to deliberately lose the 1919 World Series.

At various times of the year, the Hall of Fame also showcases special temporary exhibits. Recently it opened the Barry Halper Gallery, a showcase for a vast array of memorabilia — it includes such rare items as a camelhair overcoat formerly

worn by one George Herman (Babe) Ruth — that Mr. Halper had previously displayed in the basement of his New Jersey home. The gallery also hosts traveling exhibits on a revolving schedule.

You can get ticket, schedule, and exhibit information for the Hall by calling 607-547-7200 or visiting its Web site at `www.baseballhallof fame.org`.

The Strike Zone

Pitchers try to throw the ball through a *strike zone,* an imaginary box that, according to the rules, is the width of home plate and extends from the bottom of the batter's kneecap to the uniform letters across his chest (see Figure 1-4). Any pitch that passes through the strike zone without being struck by the batter is a strike — provided that the umpire calls it a strike, that is. (See the nearby sidebar "Baseball's strike zone controversy.")

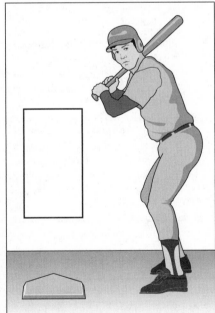

Figure 1-4:
The strike zone.

Pitches outside the strike zone are called *balls,* as long as a batter doesn't swing at them. If a batter does swing at a ball outside the strike zone and misses it, he registers a strike, regardless of where the pitcher threw the ball.

JOE SAYS

Baseball's strike zone controversy

Major league baseball's official rule book defines the strike zone as "that area over home plate, the upper limit of which is a horizontal line at the mid-point between the top of the shoulders and the top of the uniform pants, and the lower level is a line at the hollow beneath the knee cap. The strike zone shall be determined from the batter's stance as the batter is prepared to swing at the pitched ball." Seems pretty clear, doesn't it? If a pitch is over the plate and arrives between a batter's knees and the team letters across his chest, it should be a strike, right? Only if the umpire enforces the rule as it's written, which few arbiters do. Almost every umpire in the big leagues brings his own interpretation of the strike zone to each game. So-called "pitcher's umps" call strikes on pitches that barely share the same zip code as home plate. Other umps demonstrate a clear bias toward the hitter.

As long as these arbiters consistently call the same zone for both sides, pitchers and hitters can function. However, some umpires have elastic zones that seem to change from batter to batter. It's impossible to adapt to their idio-syncrasies.

In 1999, Sandy Alderson, major-league base-ball's director of operations, tried to create a uniform strike zone by issuing a directive that required all umpires to call balls and strikes by the rule book. In his memo, Alderson declared, "the upper limit of the strike zone will extend *two inches above the top of the uniform pants.*" Alderson's interpretation further confused mat-ters because it clearly contradicted the existing rules. Though some umpires altered their strike zones, most of them refused to follow the direc-tive; they continued to call balls and strikes as they had in the past. The disagreement over what constitutes balls and strikes heightened the long-standing tensions between team owners and the umpires union. The strike zone continues to be a hot debate, and it might not be resolved for many seasons to come.

Hitters and pitchers who are extremely disci-plined can influence an umpire by demonstrat-ing a thorough knowledge of the strike zone. Because umpires realize that players like Barry Bonds, Jason Giambi, Jamie Moyer, and Greg Maddux know the zone so well, they tend to concentrate more whenever one of these craftsmen is at work. However, if a pitcher is consistently wild or a batter comes to the plate swinging at anything, umpires generally call the close pitches against that player.

BASEBALL SPEAK

During an at-bat, if a batter tallies three strikes before the pitcher throws four balls, the umpire declares the batter out. If the pitcher throws four balls (which the batter doesn't swing at) before registering three strikes, the umpire awards the batter a *walk* — a trip to first base.

HEADS UP

If a batter hits a pitch into foul territory (no matter where the batter makes contact with the ball, in or out of the strike zone), it counts as a strike against him. The only exception to this rule occurs when a batter has tallied two strikes; at that point, he can foul balls off indefinitely without any of them counting as third strikes. (Just to make things more confusing, the foul tip rule is an exception to this exception; check Appendix A for an explanation of the foul tip rule.)

Chapter 2

Suiting Up: Equipment

*W*hen Pittsburgh Pirates shortstop Dick Groat was hitting his way to a batting title and MVP award in 1960, his manager Danny Murtaugh claimed, "Groat could hit .300 using a piece of barbed wire as a bat." Perhaps Groat could, but no one expects you to attempt that feat. When you take the field, you should take along the best equipment available. You don't need to spend vast sums to purchase top-quality accessories as long as you know what to look for and where to find it. Hence, as the late sportscaster Howard Cosell would say, this chapter tells it like it is.

Choosing Your Weapons: Balls, Bats, and Gloves

Unless you're under ten years old, buy equipment that meets all the major-league specifications. Equipment licensed by a reputable body such as Major League Baseball, the NCAA, or the Little League offers you some quality assurances.

In this section, we show you how to shop for the basic tools you need in order to play the game effectively and keep yourself protected both on the field and in the batter's box. With the right ball, bat, and glove, your chances of success on the playing field can increase dramatically.

Baseballs that last (and last and last . . .)

To be considered major league, a baseball must

- Have a circumference between 9 and 9¼ inches (22.9cm and 23.5cm) (Some youth league balls may be slightly smaller.)
- Weigh between 5 and 5¼ ounces (141.8g and 148.8g)
- Have an outer covering constructed from two pieces of white horsehide or cowhide stitched together with red thread
- Have a cork core surrounded by two layers of rubber and wrapped in yarn

Figure 2-1 shows a standard major-league baseball.

Figure 2-1:
A standard baseball.

You don't have to go to your local sporting goods store armed with a tape measure, scale, and scalpel (for filleting the ball to check its innards) to make sure you're buying a baseball that conforms to major-league standards. Rawlings (866-660-4151, www.rawlings.com) is the only company licensed by both major leagues to manufacture their official baseballs. So if you buy one of their balls, you know you're getting the genuine article. Rawlings' major-league baseballs carry the designation "Official Baseball of the American (or National) League" and are signed by the commissioner of baseball. You can buy first-rate baseballs that other companies manufacture, but you have no way of knowing whether these products are of major-league quality.

If you plan to lose a lot of balls bashing homers during batting practice, you may want to invest in a bagful of Rawlings' new Recreational Play baseballs. Constructed of synthetic leather with a rubber center, these balls have the same weight and dimensions as the official league balls at a fraction of the cost.

Reducing injuries with innovative baseballs

Many baseball-playing youngsters live in fear of being struck by a batted or thrown ball. Likewise, many parents fret while watching their children face live pitching for the first time. To ease such fears, Worth, Inc. manufactures Sof-Dot Reduced Injury Factor (RIF) baseballs — softer balls that reduce the peak force of impact, lessening the chance of serious injury. Although slightly spongier, a RIF ball has the exact size and weight of a regulation baseball, giving children a realistic training tool that reduces the chance of head trauma by as much as 70 percent.

Worth manufactures three types of RIF baseballs with varying injury protection:

✔ **Level 1,** the softest of the three, is recommended for players age 5–7 or as a training ball for all ages.

✔ **Level 5,** a medium-firm ball, is recommended for players age 8–10.

✔ **Level 10,** the firmest RIF baseball, is recommended for players age 11 and up.

You can find Worth's RIF baseballs at many sporting goods stores; check www.worthsports.com for the Worth dealer nearest you.

Rawlings tests its baseballs by injecting them into an air gun and firing them against a wall nearly nine yards away. To pass muster with the company's ballologists (yes, we made that word up), the hurtled sphere must rebound at 51.4 to 54.6 percent of its original velocity. Other machines roll each ball for 15 seconds to ensure roundness.

A ball whose insides are poorly wrapped rapidly becomes misshapen with use. If your baseball is poorly stitched or constructed from inferior leather, it will fall apart. Avoid balls made with synthetic leather wrapped around a core of hard plastic. This kind of ball makes a good toy or first ball for a toddler, but if you're a young adult or older, you'll tear its cover off in one good afternoon of batting practice. The toy balls are also so light that you risk throwing out your arm if you use one for a serious game of catch.

Want to rip a few line drives inside a gymnasium during the dead of winter? Several companies manufacture balls with nylon covers and cloth centers so your best line drives won't shatter any windows. Honing your batting eye after dusk? Shop for orange-colored baseballs — a brainchild of Charlie Finley, the late, innovative owner of the Oakland A's — specifically designed for nighttime play. And for those of you who like to play through rain delays, Worth Sporting Goods (www.worthsports.com) makes the 3DX100, a wool-wound ball with a waterproof core.

Bats that really swing

Although pro players are required to use wooden bats, many people prefer the power that aluminum can offer. In this section, we cover how to buy a bat that will last, how to care for it after you've made your purchase, and what to expect if you choose the metal version rather than your standard lumber.

Professional wood

A major-league bat must be a single, round piece of solid wood, no more than 2¾ inches (7 centimeters) in diameter at its thickest point and no more than 42 inches (1.06 meters) long. Figure 2-2 shows what a standard bat looks like.

Figure 2-2:
A standard
baseball
bat.

Choose a bat that you can swing comfortably with control and speed (see Chapter 5 for more details), but also look for one that will last. Bats made of white ash have greater durability than bats constructed from less dense woods. When you choose a bat, look for one with a wide grain, the mark of an aged wood. These bats are more resistant to breaking, denting, chipping, or flaking than bats made from less mature wood.

Hillerich & Bradsby (800-282-2287, www.slugger.com), the official bat manufacturer for major-league baseball, makes the Louisville Slugger, a bat that remains the bludgeon of choice among major-league hitters. Their new TPX Pro Composite features barrel grooves filled with resin to impart greater durability for those teams that don't want broken bats breaking their budgets. Former batting champion and Hall of Famer George Brett owns Brett Brothers Bats (509-891-6435, www.brettbats.com), which produces a laminated ash bat with what the company has dubbed a *boa constrictor handle*. Laminating increases the wood's durability, and the boa handle decreases the likelihood that your bat will come flying out of your hands during a particularly strenuous plate appearance. Martial arts buffs might be in the market for their lethal-sounding Bamboo Dragon, a bat constructed with a bamboo core and a maple exterior.

For the color-coordinated among you, Glomar Enterprises (714-871-5956, www.glomarbats.com) sells a customized white ash bat that you can have stained in your favorite hue and with your name printed on the middle line of the barrel. Hoosier (800-228-3787, www.hoosierbat.com) manufactures an ultradurable bat made of three types of glued wood: ash for the handle, maple for the barrel, and hickory at the *sweet spot* (a spot four to eight inches from the end of the barrel, where the ball can be hit most solidly). Former big-league pitcher Bill Lee will handcraft a bat for you on his lathe if you e-mail him for prices and specifications (spaceman@vtlink.net).

Powerful aluminum

Aluminum bats are currently popular in many levels of nonprofessional base-ball. The choice of aluminum over wood is largely an economic one. Most non-pro leagues find that the cost of regularly replacing broken wooden bats can bust their budgets.

Hitters love aluminum bats because they're hollow and light yet they have more hitting mass than heavier wooden bats. This combination enables the hitter to generate greater bat speed and power. Balls that are routine outs when struck by a wooden bat are out of the park when launched by aluminum.

An aluminum bat's *sweet spot,* the launching point for so many base hits, is twice the size of that found on a wooden bat. Pitchers dislike these war clubs for obvious reasons.

Aluminum bats have a longer game-life than wooden models, but they aren't immortal. After 600 hits or so, metal fatigue becomes a factor.

If your league insists that you use an aluminum bat, buy one that rings or lightly vibrates when you strike its barrel on something hard. Bats that don't ring have no hitting life left in them.

Other batting options

Ceramic and graphite bats are the new kids on the block. They have the dura-bility of the aluminum bats but are closer in weight/mass ratio to wooden bats, so they don't give hitters an unfair advantage over pitchers. Their price, how-ever, can be prohibitive: Top-of-the-line models can cost as much as $280.

Gloves that fit the job

Major-league baseball rules regulate the size of gloves at each position. Most leagues for young adults and older players adhere to these directives. (In Chapter 7 you can find out how to choose a glove for the position that you want to play.)

Caring for your wood bat

Eddie Collins, a Hall of Fame second baseman with the Chicago White Sox and Philadelphia A's, reportedly kept his bats stored in a manure pile during the off-season to ensure their freshness. (When we told that to our resident left-handed sage Bill Lee, he quipped, "Well, at least Eddie knew no one would steal them.") We're not suggesting you do anything quite so exotic to keep your wooden bats in the swing of things (and won't your teammates be thankful). Instead, perform the following maintenance:

✔ Clean your bat with rubbing alcohol every day, especially if you cover its handle with pine tar. Cleansing prevents pine tar and dirt buildup.

✔ Keep the bat away from dampness. Absorbed moisture adds weight to your bat, which is why Ted Williams never, ever placed his bats on wet ground. If your bat gets wet, dry it off immediately and rub it with linseed oil.

✔ *Bone* your bat to maintain its hard surface. Rub it hard along the grain using another bat or a smooth piece of bone (any kind of thick bone will do — a thick steak bone or a turkey leg bone works great).

✔ Store your bats vertically, barrel down, in a dry place.

Catchers' mitts can be no more than 38 inches (96.5 centimeters) in circumference and no more than 15½ inches (39.4 centimeters) from bottom to top. The webbing should be no more than 7 inches (17.8 centimeters) across the top. It should also extend for no more than 6 inches (15.2 centimeters) to the base of the thumb.

The first baseman's mitt must be no longer than 12 inches (30.5 centimeters) from top to bottom and no more than 8 inches (20.3 centimeters) wide across the palm. The web of this mitt — which can be a lacing, a lacing through leather tunnels, or an extension of the palm with lacing — cannot exceed 5 inches (12.7 centimeters) from top to base or 4 inches (10.2 centimeters) in width.

Pitchers' and other fielders' gloves must not measure more than 12 inches (30.5 centimeters) long from the base to the tip of any one of the four fingers and no more than 7¾ inches (19.7 centimeters) wide. If you work on the mound, your opportunity to make a fashion statement is limited: Pitchers' gloves must be a solid color other than white or gray (which could serve as camouflage for the ball).

All major-league gloves and mitts are made of leather. Children can get by with using vinyl gloves and plastic balls, but when you're playing serious baseball, leather is the only way to go. Pick a glove that conforms to the major-league standards and fits your hand comfortably. Gloves with open webbings allow you to watch the ball until you catch it, which is always a good thing. You don't have that advantage with closed-web gloves, which are also more difficult to break in (though if you're a pitcher, you need the closed webbing to better hide your pitches).

Major-league baseball licenses Wilson Team Sports (800-428-0548, www. wilson.com) to manufacture fielding gloves (see Figure 2-3). The Wilson SOG series features a slip-on glove that shapes itself to the player's hand without the use of straps or other adjustments, a real hi-tech breakthrough. Akadema, Inc. (973-772-7669, www.akademapro.com) produces gloves with names straight out of the latest sci-fi flick. The Reptilian-Mantis series includes the Praying Mantis Catcher's mitt whose features include a patent-pending Stress Wedge to soften the impact of your pitcher's most blazing fastball. The craftspeople at Barraza BBG, Inc. (877-753-2552, www.barrazapro.com) will customize a glove for you that fits like, well, a glove.

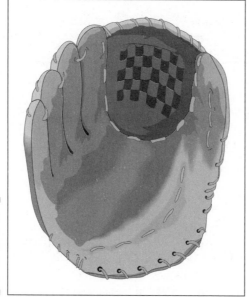

Figure 2-3: A left-handed fielder's glove.

Ballplayers didn't always wear gloves to capture scorching line drives. During the sport's early days, athletes bravely fielded their positions barehanded. It wasn't until 1869 that Doug Allison, a catcher for the Cincinnati Red Stockings, set up behind the plate wearing a mitt (for which Joe's teammate, Hall of Fame backstop Johnny Bench, would be eternally grateful). Allison's leather accessory, however, didn't become all the rage until the mid 1880s, when a livelier, faster-moving baseball finally convinced players that they needed some padding to keep their digits intact.

Caring for your leather glove

The best way to break in a leather glove is to play catch with it frequently. You can also make it more pliable by rubbing it with linseed oil, saddle soap, or — here's a Helpful Hint from Heloise — shaving cream (though you may want to avoid shaving gels, which tend to dry out quickly). If your glove gets wet, let it dry naturally. Placing it on a radiator or some other heat-producer cracks the leather. When your glove is idle, place a ball in its pocket, and then tie the glove closed with a leather strap or wrap a rubber band around it to maintain its catching shape.

Shodding Yourself Like a Pro

Most nonprofessional players give little thought to their shoes; they just put on whatever they can. In fact, standard baseball shoes are no longer obligatory for many pro players. I've seen Frank Thomas hit in tennis shoes. But I'm a traditionalist in this area. I believe you should buy a light shoe with metal spikes so that you can get maximum traction in the batter's box and on the base paths. (Slipping in the batter's box, on the bases, or in the field could cost your team a ballgame.) If you don't want to wear spikes, at least get shoes with rubber cleats so you can grip the playing surface as you run.

Your shoes should fit properly and offer your feet adequate support; otherwise you risk damaging the connective tissue in your lower legs. Choose a sturdy shoe with support that runs its entire length. Because your shoes stretch with use, choose a pair that fits snugly when you first wear them.

Adidas (800-4AD-IDAS, www.adidas.com) and Nike (503-671-6453, www.nike.com) produce reliable spikes (the shodding of choice when you're playing on natural grass) and rubber cleats (preferably worn on artificial turf).

Equipping Yourself for Safety

Baseball is not as limb-threatening as football, with its 300-pound human condominiums hurtling themselves into each other. However, you do face some risk of injury whenever you step onto the baseball field. You can minimize the chances of getting hurt by buying the proper protective equipment.

Catchers' gear

Besides their gloves, catchers have to wear the traditional tools of ignorance to survive behind the plate (as shown in Figure 2-4):

- ✔ Chest protector
- ✔ Mask
- ✔ Shin guards
- ✔ Protective helmet
- ✔ Throat guard
- ✔ Neck protector

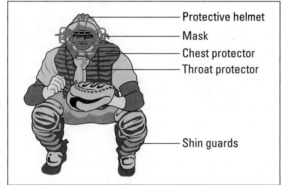

Protective helmet
Mask
Chest protector
Throat protector

Shin guards

Figure 2-4: The catcher's equipment.

If these items are of questionable quality, you're jeopardizing your health every time you drop into your crouch. Diamond Sports (562-598-9717, www.diamond-sports.com) produces major-league-quality catcher's gear, including a chest protector with an ergonomic shoulder design that alleviates stress on the upper body.

Batting helmets

Major-league rules require hitters to wear batting helmets with at least one earflap (protecting the side facing the pitcher). Anytime you go to bat against live pitching without wearing a batting helmet, you should have your head examined. And if you're unlucky, that is exactly what you will have to do. Even a low-grade fastball can permanently damage or even kill you if it collides with your unprotected cranium. A solid batting helmet with double earflaps is the best insurance policy a hitter can buy. Rawlings and Wilson Team Sports both manufacture batting helmets of superior quality.

Light plastic batting helmets, such as the freebies that major-league teams give away on Helmet Day at the stadium, are too flimsy to protect your head from an errant fastball. Do not wear them to the plate. To offer effective protection, your helmet should

- ✔ Fit squarely on your head
- ✔ Feature ear holes that center over each of your ears
- ✔ Extend far enough to cover the delicate mastoid region (behind the ear)

Batting (and sliding) gloves

Batting gloves protect a hitter's most important tools — his hands — from painful blisters, cuts, and scrapes. Runners can wear them on the base paths to protect their hands while sliding; fielders can don them under their fielding gloves to reduce the sting of hard-hit balls. All Pro Sports (818-981-5264, www.allprosportshoes.com) carries batting gloves designed to withstand the rigors of a major-league season. For hitting, choose gloves that do not detract from your feel for the bat.

Pro-Hitter Corp. (845-634-1191, www.prohitter.com) has created Direct Protect, a doughnut-shaped rubber accessory that fits over and protects your thumb, the digit most susceptible to injury when you're working in the batter's box. It can be worn over your batting glove.

Sweatbands

When the temperature is scorching and perspiration soaks your body, sweatbands help keep your hands dry at the plate. Wilson Team Sports and Easton Sports (800-632-7866, www.eastonsports.com) produce the wristbands many major leaguers wear. *Remember:* Make sure you clean those sweatbands regularly, or the aroma they exude will clear out entire stadiums.

And if you'll permit us an indelicacy . . .

Male ballplayers should never take the field without wearing jock straps (athletic supporters) and protective cups. You don't really need to ask why, do you?

The way you wear your hat

We're not sure who wrote the major-league rule book, but it surely wasn't Ralph Lauren or Alan Flusser. The rule makers frown on any attempt at an on-field fashion statement that even hints at individuality. (As Jim Bouton, the irreverent pitcher for the New York Yankees and Seattle Pilots during the 1960s, once observed, "When baseball says it wants its players to show some flair, it means it wants us to wear our caps on a jaunty angle.") Baseball rules demand that teammates wear identical uniforms. Try to stand out by wearing different colored socks or donning a white fox cape, and the umpires won't permit you on the field (especially if they're part of the anti-fur movement). Home team uniforms must be white; visiting teams are required to wear a darker color. This requirement is meant to help fans, umpires, and especially players distinguish the teams from one another. If you have a base runner trapped in a rundown play and you slap the ball on a player whose uniform is the same hue as yours, you just tagged out your own third baseman.

Caps and Uniforms

Safety isn't the only consideration when dressing for the field — style and comfort matter, too. Want to dress your head like a major leaguer? New Era Cap Company (800-989-0445, www.neweracap.com) is an official manufacturer of major-league caps. Most major retail sporting goods chains, which include Foot Locker, Modells, Lids, Sports Authority, and Sears, carry baseball headwear. Your cap should fit snugly enough that the bill doesn't droop over your eyes to block your vision.

Russell Corporation (678-742-8000, www.russellcorp.com) has a major-league license to manufacture uniforms, batting practice jerseys, and baseball undershirts. However, Wilson and Rawlings also manufacture uniforms for several major-league teams. Uniform fit is a matter of personal comfort; your pants and jersey should permit unrestricted movement at the plate and in the field.

Preparing the Field for Practice and Play

After you've equipped the players for some baseball action, your team may want to better equip its field and practice facilities for serious training and playing. In that case, consider contacting some of the companies listed in Table 2-1 that equip the professionals.

Table 2-1	Training and Field Equipment		
Equipment	*Manufacturer*	*Web Address*	*Phone Number*
Backstops	L.A. Steelcraft Products	www.lasteelcraft.com	800-371-2438
Bases	C&H Baseball	www.chbaseball.com	941-727-1533
Batting cages	Lanier Rollaway Cages		800-716-9189
Field covers (tarpaulins)	Vantage Products International	www.vpisports.com	800-244-4457
General Field Equipment	Diamond Sports	www.diamond-sports.com	562-598-9717
Netting	C&H Baseball	www.chbaseball.com	941-727-1533
Pitching machines	American Iron Sports	www.americanironsports.net	866-709-4189
Portable Pitching Mounds	Horan Sports	www.horansports.com	484-919-8547
Radar guns	Applied Concepts	www.a-concepts.com	888-782-5537
Scoreboards	Barco Sports	www.barco.com/sports	435-753-2224
Seating	Southern Bleacher Company	www.southernbleacher.com	800-433-0912
Wall padding	Covermaster	www.covermaster.com	800-387-5808 or 416-745-1811
Wind screens	Adscreen Group	www.adscreengroup.com	877-393-5111

A reminder on equipment

Be sure to play baseball with the best equipment that you can obtain. Remember, you don't always have to spend a lot of money to equip yourself well and to have fun. The great Willie Mays used to play stickball, and he seems to have done pretty well for himself. Who knows?

In an attic or a garage somewhere, your family may have some good equipment just waiting to see daylight again. (And if you run across the old baseball spikes shown here, you've just found some shoes worn by Hall of Famer Ted Williams.)

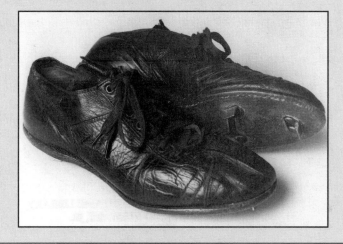

Chapter 3

The Rules of the Game

Major-league baseball has rules — lots and lots and lots of rules. We considered presenting all of them to you, but then we glanced through an abridged version of the official rule book. It was over 200 pages long. We could jam them into this chapter only if we switched to the following font size:

A batter is out when a third strike is legally caught by the catcher.

And, of course, the whole chapter would have to be single-spaced and would be three times as long. Not very practical, huh? You can just imagine the mountain of lawsuits our publisher would face from readers who suffered eyestrain while trying to discern the balk rule. So instead, we've opted to provide you with major-league baseball's most important rules: the regulations you have to know if you want to understand what is happening out there on the field.

Play Ball! Starting the Game

Actually, the umpire doesn't have to be that verbose when ordering a game to begin. He just has to call "Play" after first ensuring that each member of the defensive team (the hometown team in this case, because the visiting club always bats first in an inning) is in position and that the hitter is in the batter's box. What happens if the defensive team doesn't take the field? The umpire calls "Play," and the fielders have five minutes to assume their positions. Otherwise the ump, unless he deems their absence unavoidable, can forfeit the game to the visiting team.

When an umpire calls "Play," the ball is considered *alive*. No, it doesn't start tap dancing. The term just means that players can use the ball to make outs or get on base. Whenever the ball is alive, runners may advance on the base paths at their own peril; the team in the field can also tag them out. If the umpire calls "Time," the ball is *dead*. No action can take place on the field until the umpire again calls "Play." The ball is also rendered dead whenever a fielder falls into the dugout or the stands while making a catch. If the fielder steps into the dugout and makes the catch without falling, the ball is alive, and runners can proceed at their own peril.

Batting by the Book

Both team managers must present the home-plate umpire with their respective lineups before play begins. A hitter bats according to the order of that lineup throughout the entire game unless the manager removes him for a substitute.

After the pitcher comes to his set position or begins his windup, the hitter can't leave the batter's box unless the umpire grants his request for "Time." (See Chapter 6 for details on pitchers.) If the hitter leaves the box without the ump's permission, the pitcher can deliver a pitch, which may be called a strike. If a batter refuses to get into the batter's box, the umpire can order the pitcher to pitch. In that situation, the rules require the ump to call every pitch a strike regardless of whether it passes through the strike zone.

Making an out

If you're batting, you can be called out in the following situations:

- A fielder catches your fair or foul ball before it touches the ground. (The exception to this rule is a foul tip to the catcher with less than two strikes. See Appendix A for an explanation of the foul tip rule.)
- After you hit the ball, a fielder holding the ball tags either you or first base before you touch base.
- The catcher catches a third strike while you are at-bat.
- A ball that was initially hit or bunted fair hits your bat a second time while you are in fair territory.
- While running outside the foul lines, you obstruct a fielder's throw.
- You hit the ball with one or both feet outside the batter's box, or you step from one batter's box to the other while the pitcher winds up.
- You obstruct the catcher from fielding or throwing.

✔ You use a bat that has been tampered with in defiance of league specifications.

✔ You bat out of turn in the lineup. (***Note:*** The umpire calls this out only if the opposing team protests.)

✔ You hit a foul tip that the catcher catches for strike three.

A foul ball that isn't caught counts as a strike against the hitter. However, the umpire can't call a third strike on any *uncaught* foul. If a foul isn't caught, the hitter's at-bat continues.

Defining fair and foul

Right about now, you may be wondering which is fair territory and which is foul territory. Put simply, fair territory is that part of the playing field between and including the first- and third-base lines, from home base to the outfield fences. Foul territory is the section of the playing field outside the first- and third-base lines and behind home plate. (See Figure 3-1.)

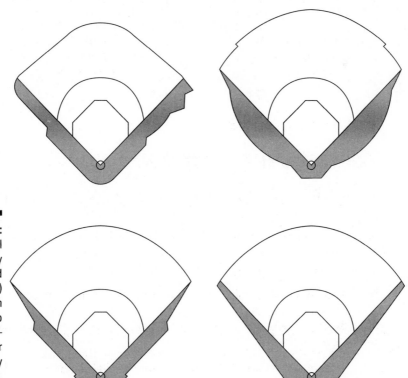

Figure 3-1: Foul territory (shaded here) varies from stadium to stadium — just like fair territory does.

Getting on base

Now that we've depressed all the hitters in the audience by revealing how many ways you can fail, it's time for a little positive feedback. You can get on base in the following situations:

- You hit a fair ball that is not caught by a fielder before it touches the ground.

- You hit a fair ball that touches the ground before a fielder catches it, and you reach base before the ball does (meaning the fielder's throw doesn't beat you to a base).

- You earn a walk when the umpire calls four pitches *balls* during your at-bat. (Balls are pitches thrown out of the strike zone that you do not swing at.)

- A pitch in the strike zone hits you without first touching your bat.

- The catcher obstructs your swing.

- You hit a fair ball beyond the playing field (a *home run*).

- You hit a fair, catchable ball, but the fielder makes an *error* (drops the ball or throws it past another fielder).

- The pitcher throws a third strike, but the catcher misses or drops the ball and you reach first base before the ball does.

- You hit a fair ball and a base runner is tagged out, or *forced out,* at another base, but you are safe at first base. (See Appendix A for the definition of a force-out.)

The Designated Hitter Rule

The designated hitter rule currently applies only to the American League. The *designated hitter* (DH) bats for the pitcher throughout the game without taking the field to play defense. Managers can let their pitchers hit, but if they do, they can't use a DH for the entire game. If a *pinch hitter* bats as a substitute for the DH, or if a *pinch runner* replaces the DH on base, the substitute becomes the DH. If a manager puts his DH in the field at some point in the game, the pitcher must bat in place of the substituted defensive player. After this move takes place, the DH role is terminated for that game.

The designated hitter is used during the World Series only when the American League representative is the home team.

What if you hit a ball that strikes a fielder?

It depends on how the ball reacts after it bangs into him. On April 5, 1998, Joe broadcast a game between the Arizona Diamondbacks and the San Francisco Giants that treated spectators to an unusual play. With his team down 3-1 in the fourth inning, Giants left fielder Barry Bonds led off the inning with a double off Arizona pitcher Andy Benes. Bonds advanced to third when teammate Jeff Kent grounded out.

Giants first baseman J. T. Snow followed with a line drive up the middle that appeared to ricochet off the pitcher's mound to Arizona shortstop Jay Bell, who promptly threw Snow out at first base while Bonds scored, or so Bonds thought. With Bonds sitting in the dugout, Diamondbacks skipper Buck Showalter signaled third baseman Matt Williams to retrieve the ball and tag third before another pitch was thrown. Williams complied, and umpire Randy Marsh ruled Bonds out. The inning was over, and the run didn't count.

Marsh ruled Bonds out because, unbeknownst to nearly everyone except the umpire and the Arizona manager, the ball never touched the mound or playing field. It had ricocheted from the pitcher's foot. Snow was out as soon as Bell snared his line drive. Bonds was out for leaving his base without tagging up (touching the base he occupied) after Bell's catch. (No one can blame Bonds, one of the smartest players in the game, for that. Like nearly everyone else, he was certain the ball had struck the mound before Bell caught it.) Had the ball dropped to the field after colliding with Benes's foot, Bonds would have been safe at home, and the inning would have continued. But because a fielder grabbed it before it touched the field, Snow and Bonds were both retired. A 1-6-6-3-5 double play if you were scoring at home — a combination that you probably won't witness twice in 10,000 games.

Baserunning Etiquette

Running the bases is much more dangerous than it may appear. Unfortunately, you can be *retired* (called out) on the base path in many, many ways. Chapter 8 offers more details about how to run bases effectively, but here are some basic rules to keep in mind:

✔ If a fielder tags you with a live ball while you're off the *bag* (or base), you're called out. However, no one can tag you out if you overrun or overslide first, provided you return immediately to that bag without making a turn toward second.

✔ If your teammate hits a ball that touches you in fair territory without first touching or passing any fielder except the pitcher, you're retired. When that happens, the ball is dead, and no other runners can advance or score on the play.

✔ If an umpire judges that you have hindered a fielder from making a play, you're called out.

Going into reverse gear

You can run the bases backwards, provided you circle them in the proper first-to-home order. New York Mets outfielder Jimmy Piersall did just that in 1963 to celebrate hitting his 100th career home run. However, his manager, Casey Stengel, released him shortly after the stunt, so maybe it's not such a good idea.

- If you run the bases in reverse order to confuse the defense (or if you are confused yourself!), you're retired.

- If a batted ball forces you to advance to another base, and the fielder possessing the ball tags that base before you reach it, you are called out. This occurs, for example, when you are on first base and the batter hits a ground ball to an infielder; you have no choice but to try to advance. (The following rule explains why.)

- Generosity is a virtue, but if you share a base with a teammate while the ball is alive, the defense can tag out the runner who should have advanced to the next base.

- If you pass another runner on the base path, you're called out.

- When advancing from base to base, you must tag each bag in its proper order, even when you hit a home run. If you miss a base and the defense notices it, they can get you out on an appeal play. (See Appendix A for an explanation of how an appeal play works.)

When you can't stray from the base line

The base line is a direct line running from home plate to first base, from first base to second base, from second base to third base, and from third base back to home plate. Between first and second, and between second and third, the base line isn't marked — but it still exists. Normally, you need not worry about staying near the base line when running the bases. In Chapter 8, you can find out the best way to round first base and go directly to second and how to lead off third base by moving into foul territory away from the base line. In these and other situations, you are allowed to wander from the base line because no opposing player is pursuing you with the ball. However, when someone is chasing after you with the ball trying to tag you out, you need to stay near the base line. You are not permitted to stray more than three feet (about a meter) outside the base line to avoid being tagged. If you do, you are called out. Do you think that this base line specification is unfair to runners? Just attend any Little League game, and you'll soon see baserunning chases that convince you of the wisdom of this ruling.

Rules Governing the Pitcher

Baseball mandates that the pitcher can throw from only two positions: the *set* and the *windup*. The set position is the stance a pitcher holds when he is turned sideways to home plate (facing either first or third base) and has the baseball tucked into his glove. The windup is the motion a pitcher goes into (such as lifting his front leg and pulling his throwing arm back) prior to releasing a pitch. (See Chapter 6 for more details on choreographing a pitch.)

After each pitch, the umpire insists that the catcher promptly throw the ball back to his pitcher. With no runners on base, the pitcher must throw the ball to home plate within 20 seconds of receiving it from either the umpire or the catcher. If the pitcher fails to do so, the umpire may (but seldom does) call a ball.

Avoiding the balk

With runners on base, after the pitcher goes into his windup or makes any movement associated with delivering the ball to home, the pitcher must not interrupt his motion or the umpire can call a balk. A *balk* occurs when a pitcher tries to catch a runner off base with a pickoff throw after he has started his delivery to the batter. To avoid balking, a pitcher standing on the rubber cannot raise either foot from the ground toward home plate unless he is starting his delivery. The umpire also calls a balk if the pitcher drops the ball while trying to deliver a pitch. A balk does not occur if the pitcher is in his set position when he throws to a base. (See Chapter 6 for more information on how to avoid a balk.)

Warming up

When the pitcher comes to the mound at the start of an inning or when he enters a game in relief, the umpire can allow him no more than one minute to throw eight warm-up pitches. Play is suspended during these warm-ups. An exception to this rule occurs when a pitcher relieves an injured teammate; then, he can take as long as he needs to finish his warm-ups.

The reasoning behind this rule is that unless a pitcher is taking over in an emergency situation, such as an injury to the previous pitcher, he should have been warming up in the *bullpen* (the practice area) prior to taking the field.

Visiting the mound

A manager or his coaches may visit the mound to consult with the pitcher only once each inning. If a manager or coach visits a second time during the inning, the pitcher must leave the game. However, if a manager, coach, or trainer goes to the mound because the pitcher has apparently suffered an injury, the umpire doesn't count it as an official visit. If a coach goes to the mound and removes a pitcher, and the manager then visits the mound to talk to the newly-arrived pitcher, those two visits count as one trip to the mound for that inning.

After a manager or coach leaves the 18-foot circle surrounding the pitcher's rubber, the umpire considers the mound visit officially concluded.

Catchers or fielders can visit the mound to discuss strategy with the pitcher at any point during an inning. Though the rules don't limit the number of these confabs, a good umpire will keep them to a reasonable minimum.

Throwing spitballs (and other pitches that go bump in the night)

Any wet or rough spot on a baseball can make that ball move more than usual — sometimes in unpredictable ways. At one time, a pitcher could touch his lips with his pitching hand while he was on the pitcher's mound. Heck, he could shove his whole hand and the ball into his mouth if they would fit. However, since the major-league spitball ban of 1920, a pitcher cannot touch his mouth as long as he is on the mound. He may not apply any foreign substance (such as mud or petroleum jelly) or spit to his hand, ball, or glove.

Regulations also forbid pitchers from defacing the ball in any way. For instance, some pitchers try to make their breaking balls drop or curve more sharply by nicking them with nails or scratching them with sandpaper. Some pitchers would bring a power saw out to the mound if they could figure out a way to hide it from the umpires.

If the ump catches you throwing a doctored pitch, he can automatically call the pitch a ball even if it passes through the heart of the strike zone. The rules then require him to warn you of the consequences if a second infraction occurs during that game. What happens if you throw another illegal pitch? The ump boots you from the field and the commissioner lightens your wallet with a large fine. You might even earn a suspension.

Immediate ejection is also the penalty if the umpire finds you in possession of a foreign substance on the mound, even if you don't apply it to a pitch (so leave those tubes of hair mousse in your lockers).

You may get away with throwing a pitch close to a batter to back him away from the plate, but deliberately hitting a player with a pitched ball is a no-no. If the umpire decides that a pitcher has intentionally thrown at a batter, he can expel the offender, as well as his manager, from the game even if the ball makes no contact with the batter. Or the umpire may warn the pitchers and the managers of both teams that another such pitch from either side will result in an immediate expulsion. As the major-league rules note, throwing at a batter's head is "unsportsmanlike and highly dangerous. It should be condemned by everybody."

An Umpire's Authority

You occasionally see two umpires reach conflicting decisions on the same play. When that happens, the umpire-in-chief (the fellow standing behind the catcher at home plate) gets the final say.

Any time anyone participating in the game — including the managers, coaches, and trainers — violates a rule, the umpire must report the infraction to the commissioner's office within 12 hours. The commissioner then decides what penalties, if any, to impose.

If a manager believes an umpire's decision violates the rules of baseball, he can protest the game to the league. He must declare his protest to the umpire immediately following the disputed decision and before the next play begins. Upon hearing the protest, the commissioner can order the game replayed if he believes the umpire was wrong and that his error adversely affected the protesting team's chances of winning the game.

The umpire can throw any player, manager, coach, or trainer out of a game if that person's voiced disapproval of a decision is, in the umpire's opinion, excessively violent or profane. Any voiced disapproval over a ball or strike call is grounds for automatic ejection. You can, however, dispute the umpire's "judgment" calls, such as whether a player is safe or out or whether a ball is hit fair or foul. Bumping or making any other violent contact with an umpire is a definite no-no. Most leagues levy severe penalties against players, coaches, or managers who assault any arbiter.

Baseball and steroids

In 2003, major-league baseball and the players' union negotiated a policy banning players from using steroids for performance enhancement. The new rules stipulate:

✔ From the start of spring training until the end of the regular season, players will be subject to one random drug test for steroids. There will be no testing during the off-season.

✔ If a player tests positive, he will undergo a follow-up test five to seven days later as insurance against a false positive (which can be triggered by a variety of legal nutritional supplements). If the player tests negative in the second round, the results are marked negative and no penalties are incurred.

✔ The commissioner's office will require any player who posts positive results during the first round of testing to undergo counseling and treatment. The player will then be subject to random testing throughout the season.

✔ After a second positive test, the commissioner can suspend a player for 15 days. The agreement calls for a 25-day suspension for a third offense, 50 days for a fourth, and a full-season ban for a fifth positive result.

The steroid ban does not yet apply to androstenedione or other over-the counter steroid precursors.

Reading Up on the Rules

You have enough information in this chapter to follow any big-league ballgame. However, if you want to study the rules in greater depth, pick up a copy of *Official Baseball Rules* published annually by *The Sporting News.* This book is a comprehensive work, complete with diagrams to help explain the most intricate calls and plays. Yet the publishers have produced a volume small enough to fit in your jacket pocket, so you'll have no trouble taking it to a game. You can also check out the sidebar "Baseball and its rules" for information about finding the rules online.

Baseball and its rules

Baseball has been governed by the same general rules for more than a century. If, by some miracle of science, you could traveled back in time to attend a game at Yankee Stadium in the late 1920s, you'd probably have a hard time noticing anything different from a modern game besides the designated-hitter rule. However, while the basics remain much the same, the details of many baseball rules have been modified over the years as the game has grown and evolved.

And while you can find lots of differences between the way your local Little League team plays and the way the New York Yankees play, quite often the same basic rules apply to both teams. Always check with local amateur leagues to find out their specific regulations.

The current code of rules governing the Major Leagues and most any other professional baseball teams can be found online at the official major-league Web site, www.mlb.com.

At this Web site, you can find the following information:

- Objectives of the game, the playing field, and equipment
- Definitions of terms
- Game preliminaries
- How to start and end the game
- How to call a dead ball versus a live ball (a ball in play)
- Rules governing the batter
- Rules governing the runner
- Rules governing the pitcher
- Rules governing the umpire
- Rules governing the official scorer

Part II
Taking Your Swings: How to Play the Game

The 5th Wave   By Rich Tennant

"Can I use it coach? My dad made it for me from an old telephone pole."

In this part . . .

*B*aseball may not appear to be as physically demanding as basketball, hockey, football, or soccer, but don't kid yourself — you need to be in top condition to play a full season. In this part, we start our training camp by getting your muscles stretched and pumped (and stretched again). Then we've invited nine major league superstars to give you advice on your hitting, pitching, throwing, running, and fielding.

Our guest coaches have a combined total of over 60 (and counting) All-Star Game appearances, 44 Gold Gloves, 9 Most Valuable Player Awards, and 2 Cy Young Awards. In this part, they reveal some secrets of their success and help you strengthen any weaknesses in your own game. Read this part even if you intend only to be a spectator because the information here gives you a deeper appreciation of what takes place on the field during a game. You'll quickly realize that something is always happening during a ball game, even when it looks like nothing is going on.

Chapter 4

Training: Getting into Baseball Shape

- -

In This Chapter

▶ Warming and stretching your muscles

▶ Developing abs fit for a slugger

▶ Using the medicine ball

▶ Sprinting

▶ Working with free weights

▶ Maintaining your rotator cuff

▶ Weighing in on the andro controversy

- -

*B*aseball players have to be in peak condition to survive the rigors of a long season. The game requires intense concentration and quick reactions; you can't let fatigue get in your way. A comprehensive training program can enhance your endurance, balance, coordination, speed and quickness (two different issues), flexibility, agility, and strength. The exercises described in this chapter are safe. However, you should have a complete physical before attempting any but the least stressful of them.

Trainers who transform 90-pound weaklings into Arnold Schwarzeneggers are of little value to you if they don't understand the demands of your sport. Ideally, you should work with people who have a background in baseball, either as trainers, coaches, or players. Stay away from drill sergeant types who demand one more rep even when the veins in your neck are pumped to bursting.

We've asked Gene Olivieri, who has trained pro athletes and helped get Richard Gere into buff shape for *An Officer and a Gentleman,* to oversee this chapter.

Warming Up

Your training program should start lightly and then gradually increase in intensity. A good warm-up raises your body temperature several degrees while rushing blood deep into the muscles and connective tissues you are about to challenge. A warm-up reduces the chance of ligament strains, muscle tears, and general soreness. You don't have to run a marathon to open up your capillaries; a continual 15-minute regimen should do the trick. Jumping jacks, bicycling, rowing on a machine, or bouncing on a trampoline can warm your muscle groups. Skipping rope is especially good because it also improves coordination.

Never start a workout cold. If you do, you risk an injury that could jeopardize your health and career.

A jogging circuit provides an ideal aerobic warm-up, and it requires no equipment except running shoes. Begin with a light 20-yard (18.3-meter) jog, going back and forth six times. Rest for a minute, and then repeat the exercise — only this time, swing your arms in circles on both sides. Rest for a minute, and then repeat the exercise while raising your arms over your head. Now that your heart is pumping a tad faster, use the exercises in the following sections to further raise the temperature of your muscles.

Jogging knee lifts

Start jogging again, but this time lift your knees toward your shoulders. Work your arms up and down in *opposite* step with your legs as you move. Repeat this three times over 20 yards (18.3 meters).

Skipping leg extensions

Extend both your arms in front of you to shoulder height. Skip forward slowly while extending your right leg toward your right hand, as shown in Figure 4-1. As you bring the right leg back down, extend the left leg in the same manner. Do this for 15 yards (13.7 meters). Do four repetitions.

Hamstring pulls are nagging injuries that too often sideline players whose legs are heavily muscled. Focus on your hamstrings during both of these exercises to ensure you are getting a full stretch.

Figure 4-1:
Skipping leg
extensions.

Stretching Out

Baseball is a game of sudden stops and starts, of instant acceleration. Tight muscles tear easily under such demands. Long, limber muscles increase your range of motion while decreasing the injury risks that accompany abrupt, jarring movements. Be sure to do the following stretches after your warm-up.

 It is important to take long, slow breaths while you stretch. If you hold your breath or breathe too quickly during these exercises, you won't get the full benefits (and you may hyperventilate!). Breathe into the stretch and visualize exhaling any muscle tension. Hold each stretch for at least 10 seconds and as long as 30 seconds. Perform three sets per stretch, increasing your range of motion (stretching a little further) with each succeeding set. Do not bounce.

Torso twist

Stand with your feet shoulder-width apart, your knees slightly bent, and your head erect. Using only your waist and thighs to provide torque, slowly twist your trunk and torso to the left, and then to the right. Your head should follow the torso, as shown in Figure 4-2. Rotate until you can see directly behind you. Let your arms flail out so that they gently slap against your upper chest with each rotation. Keep your elbows, wrists, and shoulders loose, and your arm muscles relaxed. Do 30 repetitions. This exercise limbers the muscles supporting the spinal column.

Figure 4-2:
The torso
twist.

Forward bend

Stand with your feet shoulder-width apart, your knees straight and locked.
Loosely fold your arms across your chest. Bend forward gently. Slowly drop
as low as you can with your folded arms hanging down, as shown in Figure 4-3.
Gradually lower your arms to a point a foot above your ankles. *Do not force
the stretch.*

Figure 4-3:
The
forward
bend.

After you've reached your lowest point, take a deep breath and start rocking gently up and down. Your head and neck should be loose and dangling. Rock up and down 12 times, shift to the left for 12 more repetitions, and then do a final 12 on the right. This exercise stretches your vertebrae.

Forward leg bend

Stand in front of some form of waist-level support, such as a short wall or a dance bar. Facing the support, raise up your right leg and place your heel on the support. Starting at your thigh, slowly pull your hands up the upraised leg until you can wrap your fingers around your toes.

Place your forehead on your knee (or as close to it as you can get) while gently pulling your toes back toward your head (see Figure 4-4). Take ten deep breaths, and then switch legs. Do two repetitions. This exercise stretches the tendons in the back of your legs.

Figure 4-4:
The forward
leg bend.

Shoulder roll

Stand with your feet shoulder-width apart and your knees slightly bent. Your arms should hang loosely at your sides. Roll your shoulders in a wide arc up toward your ears, circle toward the back, and then lower them (see Figure 4-5). Do 12 repetitions. Reverse the direction for a dozen more. Then simultaneously roll one shoulder forward and the other backward. (This one might take some concentration, and you'll look pretty funny trying to get it right!) Reverse those directions for the last 12 reps. This exercise stretches your shoulder muscles, tendons, and joints.

Figure 4-5:
The
shoulder
roll.

Triceps stretch

Stand with your feet shoulder-width apart and your knees slightly bent. Bending your elbow, bring your right hand behind your back and place the palm on the middle of your neck. Raise your left hand and place it on your right elbow. Gently pull the elbow to the left, as shown in Figure 4-6. Hold for 20 seconds, and then do the opposite arm. Do two reps for each arm. This exercise stretches your rear deltoids as well as your triceps. It limbers up your throwing arm.

Forearm and wrist stretch

Stand with your feet shoulder-width apart and your knees slightly bent. Extend your right arm in front of your torso with your palm parallel to the ground. Lift your right hand until its fingers point to the ceiling at a 90-degree angle.

Take the top of your right fingers in your left hand and gently pull the hand toward you, as shown in Figure 4-7. Hold the stretch for 15 seconds. Then point your right fingers to the ground and gently pull them toward you with your left. Hold for 15 seconds, and then repeat for the opposite hand. Do one rep for each hand. This exercise stretches your wrists and the muscles of your lower arms.

Figure 4-6:
The triceps stretch.

Figure 4-7:
The forearm and wrist stretch.

V-stretch

Sit on a flat surface with your legs straight and, without straining, spread your legs as far as they can go in a V-shape. Place your left hand on your right knee to keep your leg straightened. Lowering your chest to your right thigh, slowly reach out with your left hand and grab the toes of your right foot, as shown in Figure 4-8. Hold the stretch, and then do the opposite side. Do two reps for each side. This exercise stretches the glutes, lower back, and hamstrings.

Seated groin stretch

Sit with your heels drawn together and as close to the groin as possible. Gently push your knees to the floor with your elbows while keeping your back straight. Then hold your ankles and pull your upper body forward while maintaining your posture.

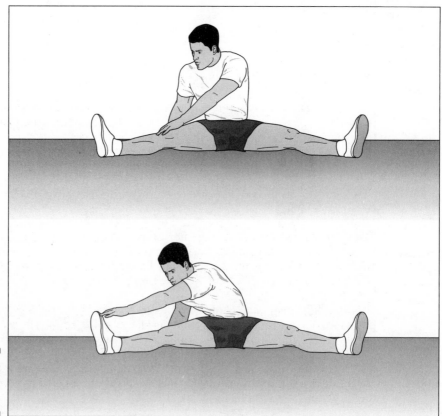

Figure 4-8:
The V-
stretch.

Knee pulls

Lie on your back with your knees up at a 90-degree angle. Place both hands around your right knee and gently pull it toward your chest, as shown in Figure 4-9. Hold for 15 seconds, and then do the left knee. Do four reps for each side. This exercise stretches your lower back.

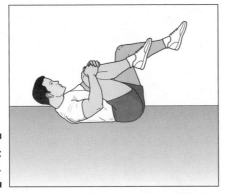

Figure 4-9:
Knee pulls.

Butterfly stretch

Sit on a flat surface with your legs in front of you in a V. Grab your ankles and pull them toward your groin. Let your knees rise off the ground. Then slowly lower your knees to the floor, as shown in Figure 4-10. Hold the stretch for 20 seconds. Do two reps. This exercise stretches the inner thighs and groin.

Dip splits

Stand upright with your feet together. Step forward with your left foot, as far as you can without straining. Balancing yourself on your left leg, slowly slide your right foot back while dipping your knee down. (You may want to brace yourself against a support the first few times you try this.)

Your left thigh should be parallel to the ground, and your right knee should be suspended just above the ground, as shown in Figure 4-11. If you don't use a support, extend your arms out to both sides for additional balance. While maintaining this position, gently rock up and down. Do six reps, and then repeat with the other leg. Do three sets for each side. This exercise stretches the hamstrings as well as the large muscles and tendons at the front of the thighs. It also strengthens your ankles.

Figure 4-10:
The butterfly
stretch.

Figure 4-11:
Dip splits.

Many ballplayers are employing nontraditional stretching methods to limber up for the field. Boston Red Sox ace Curt Schilling is among the many athletes who use Pilates to stay loose. New York Mets star Mike Piazza turned to yoga when he needed to become more nimble to transition from catcher to first baseman. You can study both these disciplines in *Pilates For Dummies* and *Yoga For Dummies,* both published by Wiley.

Pack That Trunk: Developing Slugger Abs

Most home-run hitters generate power up through their legs, hips, and abdomen. These three exercises will give you those six-pack abs that attract "oohs" and "aahs" on the baseball field as well as at the beach.

Captain crunch

Lie flat on your back with your knees bent at a 90-degree angle. Both feet should be on the ground, pointing forward, and parallel to each other. Lightly place your fingers on your temples while keeping your elbows in and pointed toward your knees. *Do not lock your hands behind your head.* Isolate your abdomen muscles by pushing the small of your back against the floor. Roll your shoulders up from the floor until you have raised them about five inches. Slowly lower yourself back to the start position. Do as many as you can. Repeat. Gradually increase the reps until you can do at least 50.

Locking your hands behind your head makes it easier to guide your head forward when you crunch up. Injury alert! Don't strain or tear your neck muscles by pulling your head forward during this exercise. Simply let your hands gently lift your head while simultaneously pulling up with your stomach muscles.

Reverse crunches

Lie flat on your back. Stretch your arms out to your sides (at a 45-degree angle) with your palms down on the floor. Keep your feet raised about 4 inches (10 centimeters) above the ground with your thighs parallel to the floor. While concentrating on your lower abs and pushing down with your pelvis, raise and bend your legs until your knees hover above your chest. Slowly return to the starting position. Repeat (if you can — these are tough!).

Do not let your legs or feet touch the ground during the crunches.

When you do crunches, those abs will soon start burning, but don't cheat. Maintaining a slow, controlled movement is the key to getting the most from these exercises.

Oblique twists

Lie flat on your back with your knees bent at a 90-degree angle. Both feet should be on the ground, pointing forward and parallel to each other. Place your right hand over your right ear. Roll your upper body up and to your left until your right elbow touches your left knee. Hold the contraction for a moment while tensing the left side of your waist. Slowly lower yourself back to the start position. Do as many reps as you can, then repeat the exercise for your right side.

Taking Your Medicine: Using the Medicine Ball

 Medicine balls may seem like relics from the 1890s, but they're making a comeback with baseball's strength trainers. When used properly, the balls can work a wide range of muscles; they target your abdominals, glutes, hip muscles, upper leg muscles, and back muscles, while also working the upper torso. These muscles provide balance as well as explosive rotational power (just what you need whether you're pitching or hitting). Medicine balls come in a variety of weights — generally 2 to 16 pounds (1 to 7.3 kilograms); if you've never used one before, start with nothing heavier than a 6-pound (2.7-kilogram) ball. Work slowly and concentrate on form. Rest one minute between sets. (You can slice that to 30 seconds as you build wind and endurance.) Do these exercises two or three times a week.

Basic rotation pass

Standing back-to-back with a partner, pass the ball back and forth in rapid rotation. You hand off the ball to your right and immediately accept the return on your left, as shown in Figure 4-12. Do this for 30 seconds for one set. Gradually work up to three sets and then start again with a heavier ball. This exercise builds your obliques and abdominals.

Figure 4-12:
The basic
rotation
pass.

Basic chest pass

You and your partner should stand approximately 10 feet (3 meters) apart. (If you don't have a partner, you can throw the ball against a wall.) Hold the ball at chest level. Using your wrists and fingertips, pass it to your partner as if you were passing a basketball. (See Figure 4-13.) Pass it rapidly back and forth for six repetitions. Work up to 12 reps. Do two to three sets.

Basic toss

With your partner standing at your feet, lie on a comfortable, flat surface with your knees bent at a 90-degree angle. Raise your shoulders by slightly contracting your abdominals. From this position, toss the ball to your partner. Catch his or her immediate return, lie back, raise and contract again, and repeat your toss. Start with 15 reps and work up to 25. Do one set. This exercise builds muscles in the chest, wrists, and fingers.

Hip toss

Stand laterally 10 feet (3 meters) from your partner. (You can also use a wall for this exercise.) Hold the ball with both hands at one hip. While keeping your lower body stationary, twist your torso and arms toward your partner while firing the ball. Try to use the same motion you employ while swinging a bat.

Figure 4-13:
The basic
chest pass.

Do a complete set, and then switch to work the opposite side. Start with 8 reps and work up to 12. Do two to three sets. This exercise works your obliques, hips, and lower back. It's another good drill for building torque.

Toe push

Lie on your back with the medicine ball on your chest. Bring your legs straight up to a 90-degree angle. Push the ball as close to the top of your toes as you can (as your shoulders lift from the ground). Hold this position for a moment, as shown in Figure 4-14, and then return to your starting position. Start with 15 reps and work up to 25. This exercise works the lower back, abdomen, chest, and shoulders.

Figure 4-14:
The toe
push.

Medicine ball jumps

Squat as close to the ground as your balance allows while holding the medicine ball in front of you at your knees. Jump up as high as you can while swinging the medicine ball upward. Land with your knees bent to absorb any shock. Return to your squat and repeat the exercise. Start with 6 reps and work up to 12. Do one set and then work up to three. This exercise works your quadriceps, hip flexors, and hamstrings. It gives you explosive drive for leaping.

Lunges

Do this drill slowly. Hold the ball above your head while standing with your feet shoulder-width apart. Lunge forward with your right leg until your chest is behind your knee. As you lunge, bring the ball forward until it is just above or parallel to your right ankle. Return to a standing position and repeat the drill using your left leg. Start with 6 reps and work up to 12. Do two to three sets. This exercise works your leg's entire muscle group while limbering your hamstrings and lower back.

You can also build upper body strength by cradling the ball in your arms and jogging short distances. Start at a weight and distance that are comfortable and then gradually increase both.

High-Intensity Leg Work: Sprinting

Jogging makes for a great warm-up and, when done over a long distance, builds wind and endurance. However, in baseball, running is done in short, sudden bursts, so sprints should be a regular part of your workout routine. The best place to sprint is on an actual baseball field. When you lack access to one, go to any field and set up your own "diamond" with markers 90 feet (27.4 meters) apart.

Make sure you warm up with a light jog and stretch (especially those hamstrings!) before attempting any sprints.

Hurdling sprints

After warming up, do this drill prior to sprinting. It teaches you the arm swing, stride, and leg lift that compose proper sprinting mechanics. Place 12 1-foot-high (30.5-centimeter) hurdles approximately 20 inches (50.8 centimeters) apart in a straight line. (You should be able to take two sprinting strides between each hurdle.) Start by running the circuit slowly while pulling your legs up high (or you'll trip), and swing your arms up at your side with each stride. After you are comfortable, sprint back and forth across the hurdle line, as shown in Figure 4-15. Start with two complete circuits per set and work up to four circuits. Start with two sets and then work up to four.

Figure 4-15:
Hurdling
sprints.

Sprinting for home

When you're ready, stand at home plate as if you're at-bat. (You can use a real bat or an imaginary one.) Swing, and then sprint to first as if you're trying to beat out a close play. Jog back to home plate, swing again, but this time sprint to second. Retrace your steps with another jog, swing, and sprint at top speed to third. Catch your breath, and then sprint for home as if a teammate has just hit a sacrifice fly and you're challenging outfielder Raul Mondesi, one of baseball's deadliest arms. Finish the rotation by hitting an inside-the-park homer and circling all the bases. (If you want to fantasize that the pitch was delivered by Greg Maddux with the score tied in the bottom of the ninth of a World Series seventh game, that's all right with us.) Do one complete circuit and then work up to two.

You can add variations to your sprinting drill. Stand at first and pretend to be stealing second or sprint to third on a ball hit into the gap. Start at second and try to score on a single to left-center. By recreating these game situations, you're building speed while practicing your game.

Playing Heavy Metal: Working with Free Weights

Baseball's approach to conditioning has changed radically over the last 20 years. Until the late 1970s, trainers frowned upon players lifting weights; they believed that weight training made you bulky and limited your range of motion. But in 1979, Brian Downing, a catcher with the California Angels, used a rigorous weightlifting regimen to transform himself into the Incredible Hulk. (Yes, that is what they called him.) In his new body, Brian added 70 points to his batting average and over 100 points to his slugging average. Those numbers caught everyone's attention. It wasn't long before clubs were opening weight-training rooms and actively encouraging their players to press the metal. Today, most players train with weights. It's one of the reasons (genetics is the other) why players are bigger and stronger than ever before.

However, before you even look at a dumbbell, a word or eight of caution. Start your weightlifting program with a certified trainer. A professional can teach proper form and devise a schedule that alternates body parts, allowing your muscles to heal. (Muscles do tear during lifting.) Proper form and a balanced schedule reduce risk of injury and help you get better, faster results. Use a spotter — someone who assists you if you slip or need help completing a rep — whenever you lift a heavy weight (especially when you're benching). Generally speaking, you should be able to lift a weight for at least eight reps. If you can't do eight, go lighter. After you can do 12 reps easily, go to the next higher weight and start at 8 reps again.

You'll be able to lift more if you work large muscle groups, such as the chest, before working smaller muscles like the biceps. To discover more about choosing trainers, proper form, weight-training equipment, vitamins, and nutrition, you may want to read *Fitness For Dummies* and *Weight Training For Dummies* by Susan Schlosberg and Liz Neporent (Wiley).

Whatever weight-training program you follow, combine it with a regular stretching regimen. You don't want to sacrifice flexibility in pursuit of bulk. And remember, you don't have to pump iron to excel in baseball. Texas Rangers slugger Juan Gonzalez returned to the ranks of elite sluggers and won the 1996 MVP award after he *curtailed* his weight-training program. During the two prior seasons, his megamuscles had hampered his swing. Hall of Famers Mickey Mantle, Ralph Kiner, and Jimmy Foxx hit the ball as far as anyone playing today, and they didn't touch free weights. However, weightlifting drills can strengthen your baseball muscles, provided you know which exercises to use.

We got some help on this section from performance specialist Jeff Sassone and the folks at the International Performance Institute, part of the Bollettieri Sports Academy in Bradenton, Florida (941-755-1000, www.bollettieri.com), a world-class sports facility devoted to improving all aspects of athletic performance. Jeff and company offer some weight-training exercises for any player who wants to pound some metal. Our experts are the same people who helped train 1997 Rookie of the Year Nomar Garciaparra, so listen closely to what they have to say.

Bench press

The bench press works your chest muscles. Lie with your back flat on a bench with your feet on the ground to either side. Grasp the barbell with an overhand grip at points that leave your hands a few inches wider than shoulder width. Tighten your abdominals and tuck your chin into your chest. The bar should be directly over your eyes. Lower the bar slowly to the middle of your chest, and then press it back up over your eyes.

Dumbbell bench press

This exercise also works the chest while emphasizing muscle balance. Lie flat on the bench with your feet on the floor. Grab the dumbbells in an overhand grip. Press them up directly over your shoulders with your palms facing forward. Lower them with control until your elbows are slightly below your shoulders. Push the weight back up while keeping your shoulder blades flat on the bench.

Flies

Lie flat on the bench with your feet on the floor and your arms to your sides. Grip a dumbbell in each hand. Hold the dumbbells parallel to your chest with your palms facing up. Extend your arms to push the dumbbells up from your chest. Keep your elbows slightly bent at the top of the motion. Lower the dumbbells in an arc. Complete the rep with your elbows on an even horizontal plane with the bench. Slowly bring the weights back over your chest while maintaining an arc. Keep your elbows slightly bent throughout the repetitions.

Close-grip bench press

Lie flat on the bench with your feet on the floor. Grip the barbell with both hands, about 6 inches (15 centimeters) apart. Lower the bar with control until it touches your chest. Then press back up to the starting position.

One-arm dumbbell row

Grab a dumbbell with your palm facing in. Keep your abdominals tight. Bend at the hips until your upper torso is parallel or nearly parallel to the floor. Keep your back slightly arched, and your knees slightly bent. Place your free hand on the bench for support. Allow the arm with the dumbbell to hang straight down from your shoulder. Pull the dumbbell up to your waist. At the top of this motion, your elbow should be tight to your side (keep it tight throughout) and pointing straight in back of you.

Squats

Place the barbell across your shoulders so that the weight feels evenly distributed. Your feet should be parallel to one another and spread slightly wider than shoulder width. Place your hands shoulder-width apart on the bar. Keep your head up and your shoulders back. Maintain a straight back with a slight arch at its base. Slowly bend your knees until your thighs are parallel to the floor. Rise back up. Do three sets. This is a power-hitter's exercise; it works all the large muscles, including the hips and glutes, which help you to drive a ball for distance.

Lunges

Set up as you did for the squat. However, instead of bending with both knees, step forward with your right leg. Slowly bend your right knee and lower your body while bending your left leg behind you. Keep your chest behind your right knee. Push back to your starting position and work the other leg. As an alternative to using the bar, you can also do this while holding a dumbbell in each hand at your side.

You must use a spotter for this exercise and wear a weight belt to protect your back. You may also want to lightly wrap your knees for additional support. And don't let your front knee extend past your foot.

Hammer curls

Grab a dumbbell in each hand. Hold them down at your sides with your palms facing each other. Raise the dumbbells simultaneously to the shoulders while keeping the palms facing each other and your thumbs up. Lower the weights with control and repeat.

Upright row

Grab a barbell with your hands about 6 inches (15 centimeters) apart in an overhand grip. Start with the bar resting on your thighs. With your elbows to the outside, pull the bar up to your chin. Keep your elbows above your wrist and straight. Lower the bar to your starting point with control and repeat.

Wrist curls

Kneel to the side of your bench. Place your forearms flat on the bench with your palms up. Let your hands dangle at your wrists over the edge of the bench. Grip a barbell (or a pair of dumbbells) between your fingers. Without moving your forearms, slowly lower the bar as far as possible, then slowly curl it back up as high as you can.

Curl to press

While standing, hold a dumbbell in each hand with your palms facing forward. Raise the dumbbells to your shoulders, keeping your elbows at your sides. Rotating your palms to face forward again, press the dumbbells overhead by extending your arms. Return the dumbbells to the starting position by lowering the weight with control.

Lying triceps extension

Lie on a bench while grasping your barbell in an overhand grip that is slightly less than shoulder-width apart. Without locking your elbows, straighten your arms until you raise the weight directly above midchest. Hold your elbows stationary as you bend your arms to *gently* lower the weight to your forehead. Raise the weight back above your chest and repeat. (See Figure 4-16.) Do three sets. This exercise builds up your triceps, the muscles that allow you to straighten your elbow. Strong triceps provide added insurance against elbow injuries and discomfort.

Figure 4-16:
Lying
triceps
extension.

When you are doing lying triceps extensions (a.k.a. brainbusters), one slip can cause serious injury. Start the exercise with a light weight; you may even use only the bar without any weights on it. And always use a spotter.

Keeping Your Rotator Well Oiled

Rotator cuff impingement has interrupted or terminated more pitching careers than any other baseball injury. It has also bedeviled position players. (All-star shortstop Rick Burleson's career ended shortly after he blew out his cuff making rifle throws to first base.)

Simply put, the rotator cuff keeps your arm in its socket. Strengthening the muscles around the cuff helps to prevent a devastating injury. Julian Fantechi, a trainer certified by the American Council on Exercise, recommends the following exercises to keep your throwing arm from breaking down. You should gradually increase the amount of weight you use in each of these exercises as you grow stronger.

Circles

This exercise helps to strengthen the scapular muscles. Spread your feet shoulder-width apart, and bend your torso slightly forward. Let your right arm hang directly in front of you while holding a five-pound weight. Keep your left arm at your side or bend it behind you. Circle your right arm in a tight clockwise motion while keeping it straight at the elbow. Do two sets of 15 circles, and then repeat with your left arm.

External shoulder rotations

This exercise also strengthens the scapular muscles. While holding a five-pound weight, kneel down and rest your right arm across the top of a weight bench so that the arm is parallel to the ground. Without moving your upper arm, slowly raise the weight until your upper arm and forearm form a 90-degree angle. Lower the weight until you resume the starting position. Do two sets of 15 repetitions, and then repeat with your left arm.

Side lateral raises

This exercise strengthens the supraspinatus, a key rotator-cuff muscle. While standing, hold five-pound dumbbells at your sides with an overhand grip. Laterally raise the weights to shoulder height with your palms facing down. Your arms should be parallel to the ground, and your elbows should be slightly bent at a 20-degree angle. Slowly return the weights to their original position and repeat. Maintain your elbow angle throughout. This exercise works the deltoids and strengthens the area around the rotator cuff. (You use the deltoids to swing your arms.) Do two sets of 12 reps.

Shoulder shrugs

This exercise strengthens the trapezius, rhomboids, and levator scapulae. Hold a pair of ten-pound dumbbells at your sides with your elbows locked. Slowly raise your shoulders up as if you were trying to touch your ears. Go as high as you can. Then slowly lower the weights back to the starting position. Don't roll your shoulders. (See Figure 4-17.) Do two sets of 12 reps.

Figure 4-17:
The
shoulder
shrug.

It Ain't Over 'til You Cool Down

Just as you have to warm up before working out, you have to cool down afterward. Do some light jogging or stretching. Then lie on the floor with your legs straight up and resting against a wall. Taking 10 or 15 minutes to gently come down from your workout limits your soreness while increasing your flexibility.

The andro controversy

Controversy broke out during the 1998 season when a reporter revealed that super-slugger Mark McGwire was taking *androstenedione*. The nutritional supplement, which supposedly helps weightlifters build muscle mass, is sold over the counter throughout the United States (though, as we write this, Senator Joseph Biden is introducing legislation that could ban or limit the supplement's sale).

The International Olympic Committee considers andro a performance-enhancing drug; athletes who compete in Olympic trials and competitions are banned from using it. If you compete in any league or sport that tests for performance enhancers, you should know that taking andro may very well trigger a false-positive result if you are tested for steroids. Major-league baseball's executive council commissioned a Harvard

(continued)

(continued)

University study to determine whether players should be barred from using andro, but the study's initial findings were inconclusive. Any ban of the drug would have to be ratified by the baseball player's union. Union chief Don Fehr and baseball commissioner Bud Selig have since started working together to draw up new ground rules regulating performance-enhancing supplements; they have already agreed to ban steroids and human growth hormone.

If you're considering taking androstenedione, you should weigh several issues. First, there is some question as to whether taking andro can actually bulk you up. Researchers at East Tennessee State University recently conducted a study that found andro lacked effectiveness as a muscle-mass enhancer or strength builder, though the supplement might speed your recovery time in between weightlifting reps. However, the amino acid *glutamine* will also help you bounce back quicker from a heavy workout. It has none of andro's side effects (mood changes and crawling acne among others), and glutamine has demonstrated some benefits for your heart and liver. It also costs much less.

No matter what supplement you ingest, you still have to invest long hours hitting the weight room if you want to build more mass. That means if you desire McGwirean results, you have to demonstrate the same discipline as the ultra-dedicated first baseman, who spent hours hefting heavy metal until the end of his career.

Second, andro alone can't make you a better hitter. Bulging biceps do not a slugger make. Ken Griffey, Jr., for example, has never lifted weights, yet he has led the American League in home runs four times. Barry Bonds's extraordinary vision, strike-zone discipline, and unsurpassed hand-eye coordination have more to do with his legendary longballs than his musculature.

Kansas City Royals outfielder Juan Gonzalez actually suffered a power outage when he bulked up too much in 1994. His homerun totals soared again only after he trained down. Ernie Banks, a member of baseball's 500 home-run club, and Henry Aaron, the Major League's career leader in four-baggers, were not especially large men. But they both had quick bats that enabled them to drive the ball great distances. When it comes to generating power, bat speed rather than body size is what matters. (That's why the 5'7", 160-pound Joe Morgan was able to lead the National League in slugging in 1976.)

Finally, andro is relatively new. None of the current studies doctors conduct with this supplement can predict its long-range impact on your health. Anyone interested in taking the supplement already has good reason to be wary. Manufacturers claim that andro works by triggering testosterone production. Many physicians believe excess testosterone may play a role in causing prostate cancer (though there are a number of doctors who believe the opposite is true).

If you're looking for a muscle builder, you're probably better off taking something with a lengthier track record. And you shouldn't consume any bulk-enhancing supplements or hormones without first speaking to your doctor.

(By the way, partway through the 1999 season, Big Mac publicly dropped andro from his training regimen. Forsaking the supplement didn't prevent him from hitting a major-league-high 65 home runs. Sammy Sosa, the only major-league player with three seasons of 60-plus home runs on his resume, has never taken andro. The muscular outfielder has, however, admitted a fondness for Flintstones vitamins; Dino is a particular favorite.)

Chapter 5

Swinging the Lumber: Hitting Like a Major Leaguer

. . . .

In This Chapter

▶ Preparing to hit

▶ Taking your stance and stride

▶ Making contact with the ball

▶ Hitting the ball where you want

▶ Bunting and moving runners

▶ Practicing and troubleshooting your swing

▶ Taking some advice from Rusty Staub

. . . .

*W*e could talk about hitting for five minutes or five hours without repeating ourselves. Advice on the subject can be as complex as an in-depth explanation of hip rotation or as simple as saying, "See the ball, hit the ball." Ted Williams once said, "Hitting big-league pitching is the most difficult thing to do in sports." Coming from the greatest hitter of the past 50 years, that statement may seem like bragging. However, most athletes who have taken their cuts on a baseball diamond would agree with Williams. Just ask Michael Jordan how hard it is to get good wood on the ball. The greatest basketball player of our time — perhaps of all time — struggled to hit .220 during his season in the minor leagues. Bo Jackson was a football superstar, and as a major-league baseball player, he was a fine outfielder with great speed, a prodigious arm, and awe-inspiring power. But Jackson's lifetime batting average was a modest .250. Jim Thorpe, undoubtedly the finest athlete in Olympic history, also hit little more than .250 during his six-year stint in the Major Leagues.

What makes hitting so difficult? Geometry, for one thing. As coaches have reminded hitters since baseball's earliest days, "The game is played with a round ball and a round bat, and you have to hit it square." Geography and physics complicate that challenge. Only 60 feet 6 inches (18.4 meters) separate the pitching mound from the batter's box. The average major-league pitcher throws his fastball 87 miles per hour, which means it takes the average fastball less than two-thirds of a second to travel from the pitcher's hand to your hitting zone. How quick is that? In the time it takes to think the phrase "two-thirds of a second," strike one is already past you.

So unless the hurler is soft-tossing a *knuckle ball,* a hitter has barely an instant to read the pitch. Is the pitcher throwing a *fastball,* a *slider,* a *change-up,* or a *curve?* If it's a fastball, is it a *four-seamer,* a *two-seamer,* or the dreaded split-fingered version? (Read all about these pitches in Chapter 6.) Where will it cross the plate — inside or out, up or down? Can you pull this pitch down the line or should you hit it to the opposite field? As you make these assessments, you must move your bat into the hitting zone. Of course, once you make contact, you have eight fielders in front of you (and one behind you) committed to transforming the ball you just hit into an out. No wonder the best hitters succeed only about three times out of ten.

A Hitter's Tools

If you're willing to put in the hours, you can overcome all these obstacles to make yourself a good hitter. How good depends on what you have to work with. To succeed, hitters need:

- ✔ **Excellent vision:** As the baseball adage declares, "You can't hit what you can't see." You need strong vision and depth perception to judge a ball's distance, speed, and spin. However, you don't have to have 20/20 vision in both eyes. Many major-league hitters have excelled while wearing corrective lenses. Michael Tucker, an outfielder for the 1997 Atlanta Braves, was not quite the nearsighted Mr. Magoo without his contacts, but he was close. Despite his poor uncorrected vision, Tucker hit .283 in 1997 while playing excellent defense. Frank Howard wore glasses as an outfielder/first baseman with the Washington Senators during the 1960s and '70s. He led the American League in home runs twice.

- ✔ **Quick reflexes:** After you recognize (or *read*) the pitch, your hand-eye coordination must be sharp enough to get your bat on the ball. The better your reflexes, the longer you can wait on a pitch.

- ✔ **Focus:** When you're up at the plate, fans, players, and coaches are yelling at you (and sometimes their words are not encouraging). Planes may be flying overhead, the wind may be swirling objects across your field of vision, the pitcher may have a funky motion, and you may be tempted to think about the error you made in the last inning. You must block out all these distractions and concentrate on the task at hand.

- ✔ **Upper body strength:** To swing a wooden bat (which often weighs two pounds or more) with controlled velocity, you must build up your arms, shoulders, chest, and wrists. You also need strong hands. If you have a weak grip, a pitcher can knock the bat right out of your hands.

✔ **Courage:** A fastball is a missile that can maim or even kill you. Hitters face that hard reality every time they step up to the plate, but you can't let it rattle you. If you're afraid of the ball, you're going to back off (or *bail out*) any time a pitch comes near you. You won't stay at the plate long enough to get a good look at the ball. You'll never be able to hit if you can't overcome your fear.

✔ **Sound strike zone judgment:** Hitters who come to the plate swinging at every pitch handicap themselves. You need to be able to recognize the strike zone while developing the patience and control not to swing at pitches outside it.

✔ **Adaptability:** You opened the season crushing inside fastballs. Now the pitchers around the league have gotten the message. (Trust me, they will. FedEx doesn't operate as quickly as the pitchers' grapevine.) So you're suddenly seeing a steady diet of outside breaking stuff. Adjust to the change — or your batting average will plummet.

✔ **Hitting hunger:** Some batters get two hits in their first two at-bats and think, at least subconsciously, that they're done for the day. Great hitters are never content. As Stan Musial, the former St. Louis Cardinals out-fielder and batting champion, has repeatedly said, "When I got two hits in a game, I came up wanting a third. If I got a third, I had to get a fourth. I never knew when I might go 0 for 4, so I was always *hungry* for more base hits."

That last item is something you either have or you don't, but you can develop the other attributes. We'll help you work on most of them throughout this chapter.

Picking Your Lumber

Before we write another word explaining how to hit, take a look at what you hit with. The bat you choose should feel comfortable. Big-league bats generally weigh between 32 and 36 ounces (around 1 kilogram). If you can snap a 36- to 38-ounce bat through the strike zone with control and velocity, go for it. When a pitched ball collides with a heavyweight bat, it travels farther.

However, don't choose a large, heavy bat thinking it will magically transform you into a power hitter. Big bats don't necessarily produce big hits. If you can't control your bat, your swing becomes awkward and long. You may have to start your swing early in the pitcher's delivery — and once you get it going, it's hard to stop. Pitchers, taking advantage of that swing, can continually fool you with breaking stuff. Pretty soon, you won't be hitting for power, you won't be hitting for singles, you won't be hitting *period*. You may as well use that big bat for kindling.

Bats come in various shapes. Find one that suits you. For instance, a bat with a medium handle and large barrel offers more hitting surface. However, you won't be able to snap it through the hitting zone as quickly as a bat with a very thin handle and a large barrel. Throughout most of my career, I swung an average-sized bat — it weighed 32 ounces (907 grams) and measured 34½ inches (87.6 centimeters) long — yet I still managed to lead the National League in slugging in 1976. It had a thin handle and a large barrel. Bat speed was the key to my power. With my light bat, I could wait longer on the ball, which allowed me more time to recognize the pitch. I could whip through the strike zone with a quick, compact swing. The large barrel added momentum and gave me all the hitting surface I wanted.

Some big-league hitters change bats depending on the pitcher. I would occasionally go to a heavier bat against soft-throwing left-handers. I knew I didn't have to be quite as quick against them, and the bat's additional mass helped me drive the ball. Other than those instances, however, I stayed with my regular bat. It gave me the bat speed, control, and balance I needed to cope with most situations.

If you're a younger player, you may want to think "light." If you're not sure what precise bat weight is right for you, simply choose a bat that's comfortable.

Holding the Bat

The first thing you should consider when gripping a bat is *to glove or not to glove.* Almost all big-leaguers wear batting gloves — some because it gives them a better hold on the bat, others because they have large endorsement contracts with glove companies. I *didn't* wear a glove when I hit because I liked the feel of the wood against my fingers. (I did, however, wear a golf glove when I was on base to protect my hands while sliding.) Whether you wear batting gloves is a matter of personal preference. If gloves improve your grip, wear them. (Some players prefer substances such as resin or pine tar to improve their grip.)

Get a grip

When you hold your bat, your hands should touch so they can work as a unit. Begin by placing your bat handle at the base of the fingers of both hands. Grip the bat with your fingers rather than in your palm; holding it with your palm deprives you of wrist action, flexibility, and bat speed. Align the middle knuckles of your top hand between the middle and lower knuckles of your bottom hand.

Choking up on the bat gave me better control. I would slide my hands an inch or two above the knob of the bat. Many people believe that choke hitters can't generate power, but Ted Williams choked up, and he has over 500 career home runs on his résumé. You *do* sacrifice some power with an extreme choke (five or more inches above the knob). See Figure 5-1 for an illustration of both grips.

If you're strong enough, you can slide your hands down to the knob without surrendering any control; this grip gives you a tad more plate coverage. Some sluggers bury their little fingers beneath the bat knob; they believe doing so helps their wrists and hands to work in better sync. You have to be extremely powerful to do this, though. Most hitters should stick with one of the more conventional grips.

When you're at-bat, hold the bat firmly but don't squeeze it; tension slows down your wrists and hands. Your grip automatically tightens as you swing. Hold the bat more firmly with your bottom hand than with your top one. Your bottom hand pulls your bat through the hitting zone.

As kids, we were told that our bats would break if we hit a ball on the bat label. That's an old wives' tale, but you should keep the label turned away from the pitcher anyway. The grain side of the bat gives you a harder hitting surface.

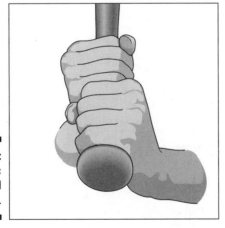
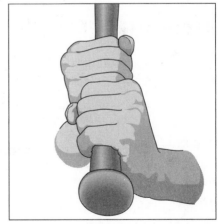

Figure 5-1:
The basic
bat grip and
choking up.

Bat and body position

Now that you have your bat in your hands, how close should you hold it to your body? Again, let comfort dictate your choice, but it should be no less than 5 inches and no more than 7 inches from your torso (about 13 to 18 centimeters). Holding your hands near your body keeps you on the inside of the ball. If you hold the bat out farther than that, your swing has too large an arc; you lose leverage and find it difficult to coordinate your hip and arm into your swing. If you bring the bat in too close, you restrict your movement and lose bat speed; your swing has a large loop, and it requires a long push to get your bat into the hitting zone. By the time you get the bat where you need it, that fastball is already past you (see Figure 5-2).

Figure 5-2:
Holding your
hands too
near or too
far from
your body
changes
your swing.

Hold your hands somewhere between the letters on your uniform front and your shoulders. Your elbows should be away from your body (as shown in Figure 5-3).

On chicken flaps and other eccentricities

Whenever I brought my arms too close to my body, I tended to upper-cut the ball. The result? Too many fly-ball outs. That habit was tough to break. The late Nellie Fox, a Hall of Fame second baseman and a player/coach when I played with the Houston Astros, suggested I flap my elbow whenever I was at the plate as a reminder to keep my arms away from my torso. I was only supposed to do this for a few days, but the "chicken flap" became part of my hitting routine. It kept my elbows out and also got me ready to hit.

Will flapping your elbows make you a better hitter? If you have the same problem I did, it may. However, rather than emulate my or some other player's quirk, you must develop your own method for getting comfortable at the plate.

My Cincinnati Reds teammate Tony Perez — one of the best clutch hitters I ever saw — used to continually regrip his bat. First, the fingers of one hand would open and close on the handle, and then the fingers of the other would do the same. It was as if he were playing a flute as he waited for the pitch. This method was nothing more than a rhythmic device that relaxed Tony while preparing him to hit.

Figure 5-3: The proper way to hold your bat.

Some players step out of the box after every pitch to windmill their bats. Next time you watch a game, pay attention to the hitters as they enter the batter's box. You'll probably detect a different idiosyncrasy with each player.

The point of all this is that you can do anything you want with the bat *before you start your swing.* However, as you attack the ball, your stride must carry you into your hitting zone. Stan Musial had a peek-a-boo crouch at the plate that made him look like a man peering around a corner (see Figure 5-4). Carl Yastrzemski, the great Boston Red Sox outfielder and batting champion, stood nearly upright at home — he only slightly flexed his knee and hip — while holding his bat high above his left ear. (Yaz was a left-handed hitter.) He looked like he was ringing a church bell. Musial and Yastrzemski had dissimilar stances, but their strides and hip rotations left them in the same position as they made contact with the ball.

So however you choose to carry your bat to the plate — on your shoulders, close to your body, parallel to the ground — is fine, as long as it allows you to quickly reach your ideal hitting position. And you can't know what impact your quirk has on your swing until you get into the batter's box to practice.

Figure 5-4:
Musial
demon-
strates
his unique
hitting style.

Stepping Up to the Plate

When you come up to hit, the first thing you must decide is where to stand in the batter's box. Placement in the box is a matter of personal preference. Edgar Martinez, an outstanding hitter for the Seattle Mariners, stands so far back in the box he's nearly out of it. This stance gives him more time to look over each pitch. Other batters stand in the rear of the box but far from the plate, up in the box and near the plate, or up in the box and far from the plate.

Any number of combinations is possible. I have short arms, so I stood close to the plate. This position gave me a better opportunity to reach strikes on the outside corner. (If your stance doesn't allow you access to those outside pitches, find another one.) Because I had a very quick bat, I felt comfortable standing far up in the batter's box. To discover what serves you best, hit from various positions in the box against live pitching.

The benefits of being up front

When you stand at the front of the box (see Figure 5-5), your stride brings you in front of home plate. Anything you hit in front of the plate has a better chance of staying fair. Standing in front also helps you against sinkerball and breaking ball pitchers; you're able to hit the ball before it drops below your swing. If you stand deep in the box against a good sinkerballer, you're giving him an advantage; his ball has more time to sink.

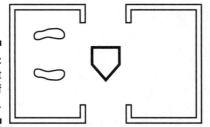

Figure 5-5:
Standing at
the front of
the box.

Standing at the front of the box also allows you to hit the curveball before it fully breaks. Even knuckle balls are easier to hit from this location; they have less time to dance. (I used to move as far up in the batter's box as I could against certain breaking ball pitchers; it took their best weapons away from them.)

Fastballs provide your up-front stance with its ultimate test. The closer you are to the pitching mound, the faster pitches reach you at the plate. If you can't handle fastballs from the front of the batter's box, you need to step back.

To develop bat speed and strength, I would swing a lead bat only with my front (right) arm. This exercise strengthens your front side, which pulls the bat through the hitting zone. I would do this 50 times a day during the off-season and 10 times before a game. Your daily regimen should also include 25 full swings with a bat that's heavier than the one you normally use in a game.

Stuck in the middle

Some batters take their swing from the middle of the box (see Figure 5-6). Hitting from the middle gives you a little more time to catch up with the fastball — but curveballs, sinkers, and knucklers also have more time to break. If you have only medium bat speed (something a coach can tell you), this is the place for you (at least until you develop a faster bat).

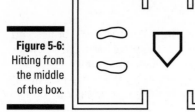

Figure 5-6:
Hitting from
the middle
of the box.

Tales from the deep

Obviously, standing deep in the box allows you the maximum time to cope with the fastball. But you have to be a great breaking ball hitter to consistently succeed in this location; you're giving the curve, sinker, and knuckler the best opportunity to work their magic. Because you'll be hitting balls on the plate and the angle of your bat is toward foul territory, their trajectory may carry more of them into foul territory. If you stand deep in the box and far from the plate, you may find it difficult to hit outside pitches (see Figure 5-7).

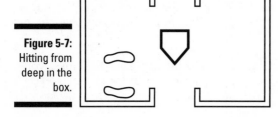

Figure 5-7:
Hitting from
deep in the
box.

Up close and personal

The toughest pitch to hit is the ball out and away from you. After getting in the batter's box, swing your bat to make sure you have full plate coverage. Stand close enough to home to reach pitches 4 inches (10 centimeters) off the outside corner. When you're close to the plate, the outside part of it becomes your middle, and you take away a strength from the pitcher. Sure, the pitcher can throw even farther outside, but if you're a disciplined batter you can take those pitches for balls. In the ninth inning of the 1975 World Series final game, I drove in the winning run when Red Sox left-hander Jim Burton threw me a slider that broke down and away. It would have been a perfect pitch *if I had been stand-ing farther off the plate.* Because I was close to the dish, I was able to reach over and hit it into left center field.

Tailoring Your Stance

Hitters can choose from three basic stances:

✔ **The open stance:** Your back foot is closer to the plate than your front foot.

✔ **The even or square stance:** Both feet are equidistant from the plate.

✔ **The closed stance:** Your front foot is closer to the plate than your back foot.

Figure 5-8 illustrates these stances for a right-handed hitter.

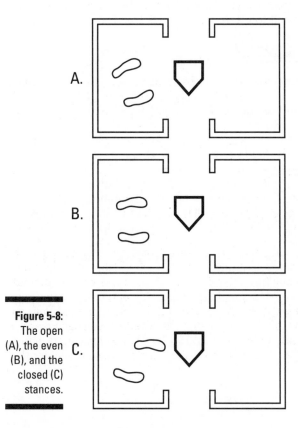

Figure 5-8:
The open (A), the even (B), and the closed (C) stances.

I always preferred the closed stance. Only hitters who can't rotate their hips out of the way properly need a somewhat open stance. (Your coach can tell you whether you have the right hip action.) The open stance frees your upper torso and automatically opens your hips, allowing you to drive your body and hands through the hitting zone while generating bat speed. The open stance also lets you turn your head so it faces the pitcher, which allows you to use both eyes simultaneously.

Everybody rotates away from the ball in order to hit. Open-stance hitters are already a half step away from the plate. They must, therefore, remind themselves not to pull off the pitch (move away from the plate a split second too soon) or they won't be able to hit the ball with any authority. For that reason, most major leaguers choose the closed stance or square stance.

Novice hitters should start with an even stance. It helps you keep your weight distributed evenly on the balls of both feet. (Now you know how the stance got its name.) As you gradually develop balance, reduce your stance an inch at a time until you find the closed stance that generates the most power.

Positioning Your Body

Your shoulders are slightly closed in a closed stance and more squared in the even or open versions. No matter which stance you choose, point your face toward the pitcher's mound so you can see the pitcher with both eyes.

Young hitters often make the mistake of looking out of only one eye. Sometimes they slightly cock their heads to the side so that one eye is closer to the pitcher than the other. This stance alters your depth perception. You need both eyes on a parallel plane if you are going to read the ball's spin and speed as quickly as possible. Tucking your chin behind your shoulder also limits your vision. Keep your head square and still throughout your stride and swing. You may hear broadcasters discuss how a hitter keeps his head down throughout his swing. That's always good policy. Keeping your head down keeps your eyes on the ball. Move your head, and your body follows — and your swing suffers.

When taking your stance, bend your knees slightly to allow greater freedom of movement. An erect stance restricts your lower body's maneuverability. How far you spread your legs apart is a matter of personal preference. I always felt more balanced with my feet spread slightly more than shoulder width (see Figure 5-9).

Figure 5-9:
A balanced batting stance.

Crouch for comfort

Some players, like the outfielder Rickey Henderson, go into an extremely wide crouch to shorten their strike zone. Rickey, the all-time stolen base king, will enter the Hall of Fame one day; he's proof that you can be productive hitting from a wide crouch. My former Cincinnati teammate Pete Rose hit out of a deep crouch with his bat on his shoulder. I don't think young players should copy that stance, but Pete used it to get more base hits than anyone in major-league history. It all comes down to comfort. I recommend a slight crouch with some flex in the knee and your upper body only slightly tilted toward the plate.

Bending too much from the top hinders your swing; as you straighten up during your stride, you lose sight of the pitch. Stay in your crouch as you stride. If the pitcher takes a long time between pitches, step out of the batter's box to stretch so you don't become rigid.

Can you dig it?

You hear a lot about *digging in* at the plate. All that term means is that the hitter is planting both feet firmly in the batter's box. Digging in gives you more traction and prevents you from slipping. Power hitters do it all the time because they want to rotate off a firm back foot as their hips open. This position helps them to explode into the hitting zone.

Striding for Power

Try hitting without taking a stride. If you stand still and swing, you can't generate any power. Your stride releases your energy and takes you into the pitch. It helps you pivot while bringing your hips, arms, and shoulders into action. You must hit from a strong front side; your stride ensures that you are successful by allowing you to firmly plant your front foot.

Looking before you stride

When I was first learning how to hit, someone gave me a poem that taught me a valuable lesson about strides. It went

> See the ball before your stride / Let it go if it's outside / If it's a curve and should break down / Jack up and hit it downtown.

This poem reminded me that I had to see the ball before starting my stride. If you move too soon, you're going to swing at the pitcher's arm motion instead of the ball. You won't get too many hits doing that. Always remember that you have more time to see and hit the ball than you think.

Some hitters watch the ball from the moment the pitcher puts it into his glove to start his windup. Don't bother with that because different motions may deceive you. Pitchers can rear back as if they are going to throw the ball through a wall, and then deliver a soft change-up. Or they can give you an easy, rocking-chair motion while throwing something hard and nasty.

Start looking for the ball when the pitcher drops his hand behind him to begin his throw to the plate. A pitcher's motion is like a batter's stance. A lot of idiosyncratic bells and whistles may be at the start of it, but eventually the pitcher has to come to a conventional release point. Concentrate on that point — say, the corner of a right-handed pitcher's right shoulder — because the ball comes out of that slot. As soon as you pick up the ball leaving his hand, react. Stride toward the pitch.

To make sure that you don't move too soon, try this exercise. Take batting practice and instruct the pitcher to occasionally complete his delivery *without throwing the ball.* If you find yourself moving into this phantom pitch, you need to discipline yourself at the plate.

Honing the length of your stride

Pitches lose speed from the moment they leave a pitcher's hand. When you stride toward the pitcher, you help the ball get to you quicker by shortening the distance it has to travel. So your stride should not be longer than your original batting stance. A long stride with a narrow stance also makes your head bob. The pitch seems as if it's jumping in and out of view. If your stance is 8 inches (20 centimeters) wide, make sure your stride is no wider than that.

When you over-stride, your upper body becomes unbalanced. Remember, the only purpose of a stride is to get your lower body into hitting position. Because your eyes are focused on the ball (at least they should be!), don't move your head or upper torso toward the pitch; you don't want to throw off your field of vision. Instead, stride into the ball with your lower body. After you stride, your head should still be in the middle of your body rather than leaning forward or backward. A hitter should glide and pop, not leap and sweep.

As you move toward the pitch, step away from your hands, or push your hands back, to let your body move forward (see Figure 5-10). If you take your hands with you as you stride, you lose bat speed and power. Keep your hands and shoulders in the same position they held in your stance. I started my stance with my hands at the end of my left armpit, just off my shoulder. They would still be in the same position after I took my stride.

Figure 5-10:
Beginning your stride.

Troubleshooting your stride

You know that your stride is too narrow and that you need to lengthen it when

- ✔ Your front side doesn't feel strong.
- ✔ Your legs collapse in mid-stride.

You know your stride is too wide when

- ✔ You can't generate any hip action.
- ✔ The ball seems as if it's jumping.

Players who over-stride can draw a line or lay a bat across the batter's box during practice to remind themselves not to stride beyond it. I always thought the best remedy for overstriding was concentration. If you focus, you can eliminate most mistakes from your game.

Slapping Down or Cutting Up: Two Approaches to Hitting

Almost everyone agrees that the ideal swing starts about armpit high and levels out as your bat comes to the ball. How much it levels out is a point of divergence.

Some instructors tell you to hit slightly down or even chop at the ball. (Ted Williams has told me that hitters can't hit down on the ball; they can only hit the ball's top half.) When I was playing, Matty Alou, a center fielder with the Pittsburgh Pirates, won a batting title (.342 in 1966) and posted a .307 lifetime batting average by slapping the ball on the ground. Matty had a slender, almost frail physique. Power was never going to be his game, so his hitting style suited him perfectly.

The King of Swing, Ted Williams, took the opposite approach from Alou. Ted's swing ended with a slight, upward arc. His swing permitted him to hit for power without hurting his batting average (.344 lifetime). Ted still preaches the slight uppercut swing to every hitter he meets. He persuaded Tony Gwynn, the San Diego Padres outfielder and eight-time National League batting champion, to try it in 1997. Gwynn had his best all-around season at the age of 37; he won another batting title and drove in more than 100 runs and slugged over .500 for the only time in his career. Yet he still managed to bat a league-leading .372, so he didn't sacrifice any base hits.

JOE SAYS

I'm in the Williams camp. Batters who hit the ball hard are going to put more runs on the board than those who don't. Runs, not hits or batting averages, win ballgames. If you hit down on the ball, it is difficult for you to drive it for doubles or home runs. Keep your swing level; and if you stay behind the ball, your swing will have a slight upward arc as your body rotates into the pitch.

Making Contact

Don't swing as soon as the pitcher releases the ball; wait until you recognize the pitch (its spin and speed) before attacking it. Cock your body with your stride and take that step away from your hands. As you go after the pitch, uncoil everything. Pivot forward, opening your hips as you transfer your weight from back foot to front. Brace your front leg. Bend your rear leg while pivoting your back foot. You know you have shifted your weight correctly if your rear toe ends up pointing directly downward (see Figure 5-11).

Figure 5-11:
The
anatomy
of making
contact.

During all this time, your hands and arms direct the bat's movement. Keep your elbows close to your body so that the bat travels in a tight circle. (Your hands and arms don't stay close to your body; good extension creates more bat speed.) Your bottom hand should pull the bat into the hitting zone while your top hand pushes and guides it (see Figure 5-12). The back surface of the bat should rest against your top hand's palm.

Figure 5-12:
Your hands
as you make
contact.

Your swing should bring your hands and arms in front of the plate with your bat trailing slightly behind for leverage — think of swinging an axe from the side. Make sure your wrists are firm as the bat moves into the hitting zone. Try to see the bat making contact with the ball. (You probably won't be able to, but just the attempt ensures that you're watching the ball throughout your swing.)

Remember that you want to hit the ball in front of the plate so it has a better chance of staying fair. As you finish your swing, the bat should make an almost complete circle around your upper body; most of your weight should be on your front foot.

Fine-Tuning Your Swing

Depending on a pitch's location, you can make small adjustments to your swing:

- ✔ **On pitches inside:** Rotate your hips out of the way quickly so that you can get the bat out in front faster. When you hit an inside pitch, the barrel of the bat should cover the inside of the plate.

- ✔ **On pitches outside:** Do the opposite of what you do with inside pitches. Keep your hips closed and go to the ball with your upper body. Try to drive the ball to the opposite field (to left field if you're left-handed, to right field if you're a righty).

✔ **On low pitches:** You shouldn't have to bend to hit a low strike. Give your swing slightly more arc as you go down to get the pitch.

✔ **On high pitches:** Many coaches tell you to get on top of the ball, but you can develop bad habits if you take that advice to an extreme. Because your hands should be at the top in your stride just before you start swinging, simply stay level (or high) a little longer and then hit through the ball.

✔ **When the pitcher has two strikes against you:** In this situation, you have to swing at anything near the plate. You can't count on the umpire calling a ball if the pitch is only an inch or so out of the strike zone. Shorten your stride and cut down on your swing by choking up another half-inch or so.

Following Through

Conventional baseball wisdom holds that the follow-through (shown in Figure 5-13), which occurs after the ball leaves your bat, is the last essential part of your swing. Some coaches tell you that if you don't have the proper follow-through, you can't hit the ball with power. It's true that concentrating on continuing your swing after the point of contact helps you to drive *through* the ball. But I think that people who emphasize the importance of follow-through have things backward. The reason you're not driving the ball with power is because you're not executing one or more of the other elements of your swing that produce a good follow-through. Following-through ensures that you hit *through* the ball, not *to* the ball.

Figure 5-13:
The classic follow-through.

By itself, a good follow-through doesn't help you hit. Why? Because the ball has left your bat! If you've done all the things we've talked about, your swing has already accomplished its purpose. A good follow-through results from properly executed mechanics; it is a finish, important only to the batter, not to the ball. A poorly balanced follow-through may tell you your swing is off, but the weak pop-up you just hit to the catcher already let you know that.

Dealing with the Strike Zone

The baseball rule book says the strike zone is a rectangle the width of home plate, extending from the top of the batter's knees to the letters across his uniform jersey. (See Chapter 1 for a diagram of the strike zone.) In practice, however, every player and umpire has his or her interpretation of the strike zone. Most umpires have a strike zone that starts at the bottom of the player's knee and finishes no higher than the top of his belt buckle. Rarely does an ump call a strike on a pitch at the letters.

Because the strike zone is supposed to have the same width as the plate, you wouldn't expect to see too much variance there. Yet some umpires call strikes on pitches 6 inches (15 centimeters) off the plate (mostly pitches on the outer edge, rarely inside). And some umps never call a strike on any ball that just nicks the plate's corners.

When you take batting practice, swing at pitches in your legally defined strike zone; you can adjust to an individual umpire's zone after you determine what it is. The best hitters take most of their swings at pitches in the strike zone. Some players are so strong that they can hit a pitch that is 1 or 2 inches off the plate. However, these so-called "bad-ball" hitters are rare. Discipline yourself to swing only at strikes.

To get a sense of your strike zone without swinging a bat, play catch with someone. Stand 60 feet (18.3 meters) apart (nearly the distance between home plate and the pitcher's mound), and keep your throws between each other's chest and knees. Move your tosses up and down within this area. Because you are facing the thrower dead-on, you can immediately detect from the ball's trajectory whether it's a strike or a ball.

After you know your strike zone, find out where your hot hitting spots are within it. In his book *The Science of Hitting* (a must-read for every ballplayer), Ted Williams broke down his strike zone in a diagram, which demonstrated that he batted .400 when he hit pitches down the heart of the plate but only .220 when he hit pitches that were low and outside. This diagram reminded Ted that he shouldn't swing at those low, outside pitches unless he already had two strikes and the ball was over the plate. All athletes must develop that same kind of self-awareness. You can never be a good hitter or player unless you know your strengths and weaknesses. If you aren't a good low ball hitter, lay off that pitch unless you have two strikes.

When the opposition gets shifty

Should you get a reputation as a pull hitter, opponents may try to stack their defenses against you. You could find yourself hitting against a *shift*. If you're a left-handed hitter, the shortstop moves toward the second-base side of the infield (for the hitter, the portion of the infield to the right of second base), the second baseman shifts towards first, the center fielder leans toward right, and the left fielder comes closer to center. If you're right-handed, the fielders move the other way. The most extreme shift in baseball history was the *Boudreau Shift*, which the Cleveland Indians employed against pull-hitter supreme Ted Williams. Whenever Williams came to bat, shortstop-manager Lou Boudreau would crowd the right side of the diamond with six fielders. (See the following figure.)

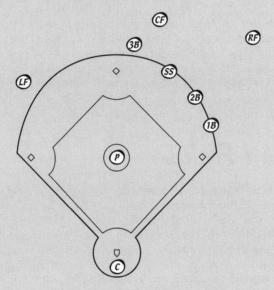

I hit against shifts during my career, though nothing as radical as the Boudreau version. The best thing you can do when confronted by one is forget it's there. A shift's biggest impact is psychological. If you look at it and think, "I'll never get a base hit against this," you may as well drop your bat and return to the dugout. I always believed that if I hit a solid line drive, it wouldn't be caught no matter how many fielders they stacked against me. Attack this stratagem with that same confidence. Of course, you can always destroy a shift by *dinking* (softly hitting) a single to the opposite field or bunting, but that's what the opposition wants you to do. They are trying to make you move away from your strength. Don't fall for it. Take your normal cuts at the plate (unless a single can drive in a run).

Judging the First Pitch

Should you swing or take the first pitch you see in an at-bat? It depends on the situation. I remember a minor-league game I played in Durham, North Carolina. My team was facing some rookie pitcher, and I opened the first inning by popping up on his first pitch. When I came back to the bench, my manager, Billy Goodman, a former American League batting champion, asked me, "What does that pitcher have?" Well, I didn't know what the pitcher had other than a fastball, and I couldn't even tell you how hard he threw that. I hadn't seen enough of his pitches. And that was Billy's point: The first time you face a pitcher you don't know, *take* as many pitches as you can. Find out how his curve ball breaks, which way his slider moves. Does he have a change-up? Does he throw every pitch from the same angle?

When you face pitchers you're familiar with, however, there are no hard rules about swinging or not swinging at the first pitch. In that situation, I always went to the plate looking to hit the first good pitch I saw. If it came on the pitcher's first offering, I swung. However, I invariably *took* (didn't swing at) a lot of first pitches simply because so many of them were thrown out of the strike zone.

Going to All Fields

Novice hitters should learn how to hit the ball to all fields. If a pitch is thrown away from you, hit it to the opposite field (right field if you're right-handed, left field if you're a lefty). If a pitch travels down the heart of the plate, smack it up the middle of the diamond. If the ball is thrown inside, jerk (or pull) it into left field if you're a right-hander or into right field if you're a lefty. As you gain experience, you may discover whether you are predominantly a *spray hitter* (a player who hits to all fields, such as Red Sox third baseman Bill Mueller, who won the American League batting title in 2003) or a *pull hitter* (a slugger like Jim Thome). See Figure 5-14.

I started my big-league career as a spray hitter but developed into a pull hitter as I got stronger. However, as a pull hitter, I could still slap a hit to the opposite field when the situation demanded it. A good spray hitter can pull the ball down the line when he needs an extra-base hit. The bottom line is you want to be as complete a hitter as possible.

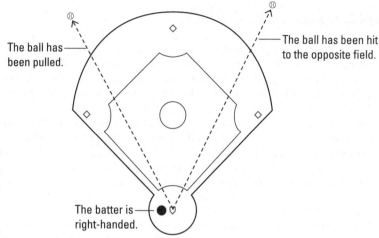

The ball has been pulled.

The ball has been hit to the opposite field.

The batter is right-handed.

Figure 5-14: Hitting the ball to all fields.

Hitting up the center or to the opposite field

You have to hit the ball a little later in order to hit to center *(straight-away)* or to the opposite field. To do this, take an even stance at the plate. Aim everything through the middle. This strategy causes you to hit the ball later.

Pulling the ball

Hit the ball early enough so that the bat meets the ball in front of you. Right-handed hitters pull the ball to the left side; left-handers pull to the right. If you're using a closed stance, you're going to naturally pull a lot of balls. (See the section "Tailoring Your Stance" earlier in this chapter.) The more closed your stance, the more you pull the ball. Crowd the plate as much as possible. This position expands the area from which you can pull. Make sure to plant your back foot firmly because you want something stationary to drive from. Planting your back foot also gives your swing more arc. Don't uppercut the ball; let your body, stride, and swing to give the ball power. As you start your swing, shift your weight to your front foot. This shifting keeps your bat level in the hitting zone for a longer period of time. Want to hit for more power? Keep your weight back a little longer.

Analyzing the Pitcher

Most hitters don't keep written notes on pitchers; they keep mental books documenting how pitchers have come at them in the past. If a pitcher has been unsuccessful trying to get you out with inside fastballs but has been burying you with outside breaking pitches, you can assume he's going to keep throwing those curves. However, you can't establish a pitching pattern off any one game. Maybe the pitcher's fastball was sluggish the night he never tried to bust it by you inside. He may have had an unusually wicked curve working that evening. The next time you face him, if his heater is hopping, he may get you out with fastballs inside all night. You may not even see his curveball. So you have to discover what a pitcher has working for him on game day.

I usually watched the opposing pitcher warm up in the bullpen to see what pitches he was throwing for strikes. Generally, if a pitcher can't control his slider or curve in the bullpen, he won't be able to control them in the game for at least an inning or two. Take those pitches for balls until he proves he can get them over the plate.

The Dying Art of Bunting

When you *bunt,* hold your bat in the hitting zone and let the ball make contact with it. The idea is to deaden the ball so that the base runners can advance (or you can get to first) while the opposing fielders run in to make a play. There comes a time in every baseball season when anyone — even hulking sluggers like Sammy Sosa or Carlos Delgado — should bunt. For example, say you're playing a game that decides whether you or your opponent clinches a championship. You come to bat with the winning run on first and nobody out in the bottom of the ninth inning. I don't care how many home runs you hit all season, your job is to bunt that runner to second base. Bunts can win ballgames, so everyone who swings a bat should know how to lay them down.

It's especially important for pitchers to learn how to bunt, even if they play in a league that allows designated-hitters. Depending on how many substitutions are made during a game, pitchers can be called on to hit even in designated hitter leagues. (For more on this rule, refer to Chapter 3.) Or you may play an interleague game in the home park of a team whose rules don't provide for a designated hitter. In the fourth inning of the second game of the 1997 World Series between the Cleveland Indians and Florida Marlins, Cleveland pitcher Chad Ojea — who had never batted in the Major Leagues because of the designated hitter rule — bunted two teammates to second and third. It was a crucial play. A two-run single then broke open the game, which the Indians eventually won. Had Ojea failed to get the bunt down — or, worse, bunted into a double play — the outcome may have been different.

Choosing your bunting stance

The most commonly used bunting stance is the *pivot.* Take your normal stance at the plate while waiting for the pitch. As the ball comes to the plate, pivot your upper body toward the pitch while keeping your feet in their stance position (see Figure 5-15).

Figure 5-15:
An ideal
bunting
stance.

The pivot has several advantages:

✔ You can flow into a pivot quickly, maintaining an element of surprise.

✔ In the event of a fake bunt — where you "show" bunt to pull in the infielders and then swing away to drive the ball past them — the pivot allows you to easily resume a standard batting stance.

✔ With a pivot stance, getting out of the path of errant pitches is easier.

The *squared-stance* is your other bunting option — and perhaps the best option for players just starting out. Bring your feet parallel to home plate and each other while keeping them shoulder-width apart (see Figure 5-16). This stance gives you better plate coverage and a longer look at the ball than the pivot, but it also has its drawbacks. You become more vulnerable to being hit by a pitch, you risk stepping out of the batter's box (in which case the umpire may call you out), and, because you have to get set in this position early, you decrease your chances of surprising the opposition. I prefer the pivot, but you should adopt whichever position is most comfortable for you.

Figure 5-16:
The squared-stance bunt.

Whether you pivot or square around to bunt, make sure you drop into a slight crouch and square your shoulders toward the pitcher. Shift your weight forward as you stand on the balls of your feet. Hold the bat handle firmly with your bottom hand so you can control it, but don't squeeze the handle or you may hit the ball too hard. Slide your top hand up near the bat label. Pinch the barrel with your fingers and thumb, your thumb on top. This action shapes the hand into a U that absorbs any impact when the ball strikes your bat. It also protects your fingers (see Figure 5-17).

Many bunters hold their bats parallel to the ground while waiting for the pitch. I think it is better to hold the top of the bat barrel slightly higher than the handle. This strategy keeps you on top of the ball, which is where the bunter has to be. If you come up underneath the pitch, you pop it up. If you hit the ball dead center, you produce a soft line drive that can be converted into a double play.

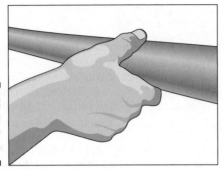

Figure 5-17:
Holding the
bat for the
bunt.

Hold the bat near the top of your strike zone so you know that any pitch over your bat is a ball. This prevents you from offering at high pitches, which are the hardest to bunt. Try to bunt a low pitch. Watch the ball make contact with the bat in front of you and the plate. Give with the ball, don't push it. You should experience the sensation of "catching" the ball with your bat and guiding it to its destination. Let your bottom hand direct the bat's angle.

Bunting into a sacrifice

With the *sacrifice bunt,* the bunter advances the base runners while giving up a chance for a base hit. With a runner on first, bunt toward the area between the mound and the first baseman. With a runner on second or runners on first and second, bunt toward the third baseman to bring him off the bag (see Figure 5-18).

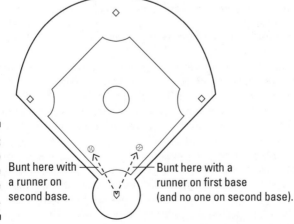

Figure 5-18:
Where to
place the
sacrifice
bunt.

Bunt here with
a runner on
second base.

Bunt here with a
runner on first base
(and no one on second base).

Running the squeeze play

The *squeeze play* is a sacrifice bunt with a runner on third base. If a manager calls for a squeeze play, it's usually during the later innings of a close game with less than two outs. On a *safety squeeze,* the runner breaks for home only after you drop your bunt on the infield. If the bunt isn't good, the runner stays at third. As the bunter, your job is to push the ball away from the pitcher and toward first or third base.

The *suicide squeeze* is a riskier play. It requires the runner to dash toward home plate as the ball leaves the pitcher's hand. *He is coming home no matter what kind of bunt you drop.* You can't take the pitch even if it's out of the strike zone. You must bunt the ball somewhere.

Don't be too finicky about placement. With the runner bearing down on home, just bunt the ball to the ground in fair territory, and you drive in a run. Even if you bunt it foul with less than two strikes on you, the worst that can happen is the runner gets sent back to third. If you don't make contact with the ball, the catcher has the runner dead at the plate (which is why it's called the *suicide* squeeze).

Bunting for hits

To successfully bunt for a hit, you must catch the opposition unaware. This is where the pivot gives you an advantage: It allows you to deceive the infielders longer than the squared-around stance. To bunt for a hit, you should be in motion as the bat makes contact with the ball. You should also grip the bat a little more firmly than you did for the sacrifice.

Left-handed hitters use *drag bunts,* so named because the bunter appears to drag the ball along the first base line as he runs toward first (see Figure 5-19). I beat out a drag bunt to get a hit in the seventh game of the 1975 World Series.

To execute the drag bunt, shift your weight onto your right foot as you pivot and step toward first base. Hold the bat solidly with its head pointed toward third. Don't pull back the bat or the ball will go foul. You should be moving into your second stride as you make contact with the ball. With your running start, you should beat out the bunt, if it stays fair (see Figure 5-20).

Right-handers and left-handers can execute *push* or *dump* bunts for base hits. If you bat right-handed, start with your weight on your right (the rear) foot. As you move to bunt the ball, quickly shift your weight forward into your left foot. Push the ball past the pitcher toward the hole between first and second. Run immediately after making contact. If you're a lefty hitter, reverse your weight shift and tap the ball down the third base line. Run immediately after making contact.

Figure 5-19:
Brett Butler
executes
the drag
bunt.

Figure 5-20:
The drag
bunt.

Faking the bunt

You can fake a bunt when a teammate is trying to steal a base. A successful decoy may get the infielders moving in the wrong direction. When you pull back the bat, you force the catcher to stay back so it takes him longer to get to the ball. You can also fake a bunt, pivot back to your hitting stance, and take a short, easy swing (a *swinging bunt*) to slash or chop the ball past the infielders as they mistakenly charge toward home. Square around when you're attempting to help the base stealer; use the pivot stance if you're using the ruse to get a base hit.

Executing the Hit-and-Run

As the batter on a hit-and-run play, your primary responsibilities are to protect the runner and to hit the ball on the ground. Swing and make contact with the pitch, no matter where it's thrown. If the pitch is out of the strike zone, lunge at it and try to get a piece of the ball. The runner takes off without a base-stealing lead, so if you miss that pitch, the catcher will have little difficulty throwing him out. If you hit a line drive at a fielder with the runner moving, it's virtually an automatic double play.

Take your usual swing, but hit slightly down on the ball. You may hit the ball through an area vacated by an infielder who moves to cover second base against the runner breaking from first. The manager usually initiates the play with one or no outs. However, a veteran hitter, suspecting the opposition is going to pitch him a certain way, can call the play with a sign to his base runner.

Turning the Run-and-Hit

The run-and-hit is generally called with a fast runner at first. The play is similar to the hit-and-run, but the hitter's task is less specific. The runner breaks for second after the pitcher commits to throwing the ball toward home. The runner should approach this like a straight steal. You're not obligated to swing at the pitch unless it's a strike (which is why the runner should be fast — if you take the pitch, he has to steal second). You can also put the ball in play anywhere rather than having to hit through the right side of the infield. With his running start, the base runner should be able to get to third on any ball hit out of the infield. An *extra-base hit* (anything more than a single) should score him from first.

Walking Aggressively

You can help your team by getting a base on balls, but you shouldn't go to the plate looking to draw a walk; you may lose your aggressiveness. Instead, work the count against the pitcher by expanding and contracting the strike zone according to the count.

For example, I was a pull-hitter, so I preferred to hit the ball inside. If the first pitch to me was a ball, I shaved 2 inches (5 centimeters) off the outside portion of my strike zone. The next pitch could be a strike, but I wouldn't swing at it if it was on the outer edge of the plate. If it *was* a strike, I'd expand my zone by 2 inches (but I'd never let it become larger than the umpire's strike zone). However, if the ump called it ball two, I'd cut another 2 inches from the outside of my strike zone. On a three-ball and one-strike count, my strike zone would be about half its normal width: from the middle of the plate in. To get me out, the pitcher now had to throw two straight strikes rather than one. That 3–1 pitch was exactly where I wanted it, or I wasn't swinging. If the pitcher came inside where I was looking, I could drive that ball a long way. If he threw a strike on the outside corner, I still had another crack at him. Ball four would put me on first base. All the percentages were working in my favor. On a 3–2 count, I'd expand the strike zone out again and protect more of the plate. By altering my strike zone on each pitch, I increased my chances of drawing walks while remaining aggressive at the same time.

Getting the Most Out of Batting Practice

Batting practice is usually divided into rounds. On most of the teams I played for, we would take ten swings in the first round, seven in the second, five in the third, four in the fourth, three in the fifth, and one in the last. Use your first round of batting practice to get loose. Start by laying down two bunts, one as a sacrifice, the other for a base hit. Then work on your swing.

This first round is essentially a warm-up. You're getting comfortable with your timing, stance, and stride while working on your batting eye. Don't try to kill the ball. A lot of hitters are playing *long ball* (trying to hit a home run) when they take batting practice. They're not working on anything in particular; they're just trying to see who can hit the ball farthest. That's a waste of time, especially if you aren't a home-run hitter. Just make contact and aim to hit the ball through the middle.

Starting with the second round, you should be simulating game conditions. Work on every aspect of your hitting. Try to pull the ball on one pitch and hit it up the middle on another. Poke one to the opposite field. Then let a swing rip without caring where the ball goes. Do this on every round.

If you want to play some long ball, do it on your last swing. After taking your last practice swing, trot around the bases to keep loose while practicing your left turns.

Working with Your Batting Practice Pitcher

During batting practice, have the pitcher throw you nothing but fastballs in the first round so that you can get your timing. Then have the pitcher work in some curves, sliders, and change-ups. If you take 30 swings, 8 of them should be against breaking balls. Facing a knuckle baller in tonight's game? If your pitcher can throw a knuckler, ask to see some of those, too.

You may discover that pitches in a certain location are giving you trouble. Ask the batting practice pitcher to throw to that spot so you can work on them. Usually you know what the pitcher is going to throw. However, every so often you should take a round in which the pitcher can throw any pitch to any spot at any time without telling you in advance. This element of surprise helps hone your concentration and prepares you for actual game conditions.

Other Practice Tips

Besides facing live pitching during batting practice, you can do a number of things away from the ballpark to improve your hitting. Here are some of my favorites.

Hit from a batting tee

I used one throughout my career. Adjust the tee's height (see Figure 5-21) and set its position so that you are hitting the ball inside, outside, or down the middle of your strike zone. No matter which side you choose, always set the tee up in front of the plate.

Hitting off the tee forces you to concentrate on hitting a particular spot on the ball. It helps to prevent you from *bailing out* (pulling away from the pitch) while quickening your bat.

Figure 5-21:
The batting tee is a great way to practice.

Swing in front of a full-length mirror

I'm not advocating narcissism here. Swinging in front of a mirror lets you check your entire stance and stride.

Play pepper

In *pepper,* the batter stands no more than 10 feet (3 meters) opposite several fielders who are lined up side by side. One fielder throws the ball; the batter taps it back. (Don't take a full swing or you may decapitate someone.) The fielder who fields that ball quickly tosses it back toward the hitter, who taps it again. And so on. This game teaches you to keep your eye on the ball and make contact.

Work with grips and rollers

You need strong hands and wrists to hit. Use hand grips and wrist rolls to strengthen them. You can also squeeze a ball of putty to develop your grip.

Develop your hand-eye coordination

I used to punch a speed bag to develop my hand-eye coordination. Playing catch is also great practice. (Playing catch improves your fielding, but learning how to gauge the speed of the ball also helps you at the plate.) Play paddle ball, tennis, racquetball, or any sport that demands quick reactions and excellent hand-eye coordination. Table tennis is an excellent choice because the ball moves so quickly toward you and you have to hit it out front, which is precisely what you have to do with a baseball.

Troubleshooting Your Batting

You can work on specific problems during batting practice. Here are some common hitting flaws that often lead to slumps and some suggestions for correcting them.

Hitting off your heels

If you have your weight back on your heels, your body and bat move away from the plate as you swing. Outside pitches and off-speed stuff may give you trouble. You won't be able to hit with any power. **Remedy:** Concentrate on keeping your weight on the balls of your feet while you stride toward the pitcher.

Chopping

Slumping, novice hitters often chop down at the ball just to make contact. Swinging in this manner decreases your hitting area. Also, you can't drive the ball with this swing; you simply hit a lot of grounders (mostly for outs). **Remedy:** Make sure that you transfer your weight properly. When you transfer your weight to your front foot, your bat remains level. Keep your weight on your back foot, drop your rear shoulder (you can't chop with your shoulder down), and take your usual swing.

Uppercutting

When you *uppercut* the ball, you raise your front shoulder while dropping your rear shoulder and dipping your back knee. Batters who uppercut tend to strike out a lot. You can also forget about hitting high pitches with any authority. Raising your front shoulder moves your head out of its level plane, which prevents you from seeing the ball well. **Remedy:** Uppercutters keep their weight on their back foot too long, so level your shoulder and make sure you transfer your weight from front to back. Finish your swing with a slightly upward arc, but avoid any exaggerated uppercutting.

Hitching

If you have a *hitch,* you're dropping your hands just before you swing. A hitch is okay, as long as you can get your hands in good hitting position before the ball arrives. Frank Robinson had a hitch; he dropped his hands below his belt, but he always got them back in time to hit. The last time I checked, his plaque was in the Hall of Fame. Unfortunately, too many hitters compensate for their hitches with rushed, upward swings. This hitch produces the same poor results as an extreme uppercut. **Remedy:** Keep your hands level and still.

Locking the front hip

Locking your front hip makes it impossible to transfer the weight from your rear foot to your front foot during your swing. You can't pivot properly. This fault significantly decreases your power. **Remedy:** Open your stance and concentrate on stepping toward the pitcher.

Lunging

Batters who *lunge* at the ball step into the pitch too early. This misstep throws off your timing, power, and bat control. Hank Aaron would occasionally lunge with his upper body, but he could drive the ball because he always kept his hands back. **Remedy:** Be patient. Wait until you read the pitch before you swing. Make sure your stride is no longer than your original stance. *Keep your hands back.*

Bobbing your head

If you bob or turn your head, you lose sight of the ball for a second. When you pick the ball up again (*if* you pick it up again), it is either almost past you or appears to be jumping at you. **Remedy:** Keep your head level and still throughout your stance, stride, and swing. If your stride is making your head bob, shorten it. Remember, your stride should be no longer than your stance.

JOE SAYS

Some thoughts on slumps

If you go into a slump, take extra batting practice and focus on the hitting fundamentals that I describe in this chapter. Make sure your hands are properly positioned. Are they working together as a unit? Have a coach or teammate observe whether you're over-striding. Practice hitting the ball back through the middle of the diamond. Hitting the ball up the middle prevents you from uppercutting, pulling off the pitch, or hitting it too soon.

If practice doesn't seem to help, take a few days off. You may simply be fatigued. Remember that slumps are inevitable; there isn't a single Hall of Famer who didn't experience them. Babe Ruth was one of the greatest offensive forces baseball has ever produced; he hit .118 in the 1922 World Series. Try to remain confident and optimistic. If you've hit before, you will hit again, so don't lose your aggressiveness. In 1976, I batted .000 in the National League Championship Series against the Philadelphia Phillies. I didn't get a hit or a run batted in (RBI). However, in the World Series that immediately followed, I hit .333 with one home run, three runs scored, and two RBIs in four games. (See photo below.)

Stepping in the bucket

Stepping in the bucket is another way of saying you're striding away from the pitch. The uneven weight distribution results in a loss of power. Because you're moving away from the plate, you can't hit the outside pitch. **Remedy:** Close your stance and concentrate on striding toward the pitcher.

Overcoming the Fear of Getting Hit

Some batters stride away from the pitch because they're afraid of being hit by the ball. To be successful, batters must be aggressive. If you can't overcome your fear, you won't be able to hit. I can't tell you how not to be afraid, but perhaps I can calm your concerns with a few facts:

- ✔ **It hurts only for a little while.** Many young players are afraid of getting hit by the ball because it has never happened to them before. They imagine the experience to be much more painful than it actually is. When batters do get hit, it's usually in a fleshy spot. Unless you've broken something (which rarely happens), the pain subsides quickly.

- ✔ **Pitchers don't often hit batters.** Rarely does a pitched ball seriously injure a hitter at any level — from Little League to the pros. I averaged around 600 plate appearances a season and stood way up front in the batter's box and close to the plate. Yet I rarely got hit by a pitch more than twice a year. Many of those pitches just grazed my uniform. I have been struck solidly by pitches, but I was never injured so badly that I had to leave a ballgame or miss any playing time. Ground balls have hit me in the face during fielding practice (is that embarrassing!), but I've never been hit in the face by a pitch.

- ✔ **If your mechanics are sound, you can get out of the way.** Muhammad Ali, the great former heavyweight boxing champion, once said, "The punch that knocks you out is the one you don't see." Batters should remember that. If you keep your eyes (both of them!) on the ball, it's hard to get hit by a pitch, especially in the head. Your head is the easiest part of your body to move out of harm's way.

- ✔ **Batting helmets work.** Ron Cey, the former third baseman of the Los Angeles Dodgers, got hit in the head by a Goose Gossage fastball during the 1981 World Series. That's like taking a bazooka shell off the old noggin. However, Cey's batting helmet absorbed nearly the entire impact. He not only played the next game, he hit a home run. The moral: Never step up to the plate without wearing your helmet.

However, don't let the helmet give you a sense of false confidence. Getting hit in the head is dangerous and painful. It shouldn't happen to you as long as you stay alert at the plate.

Postscript: Some Advice for Pinch Hitters from Rusty Staub

When your manager asks you to come off the bench cold and go to the plate in a critical situation, he's handing you one of the most difficult assignments in baseball. Pinch-hitting is a specialized skill. I rarely pinch-hit more than ten times in any one season, so I've enlisted an expert to give us some advice on the subject. My good friend and former Houston Astros teammate Rusty Staub wasn't just a great pinch hitter; he was a great hitter, period. He had a disciplined eye, superb bat speed, and excellent balance at the plate. During his career, Rusty amassed 2,716 base hits, 292 home runs, and 1,486 runs batted in while compiling a .279 lifetime batting average. He drove in 100 or more runs three times.

As a pinch hitter for the New York Mets during his final three seasons, Rusty was the top of the line. He led the National League in pinch hits in 1983 and 1984. During the 1983 season, he tied a major-league record with eight consecutive pinch hits; his 24 pinch hits that year also drove in 25 runs. That's delivering in the clutch. So when Staub talks about pinch hitting, he's like Smith-Barney on investing; we all have to listen.

"More than anything else, a pinch hitter has to be emotionally strong. That season I tied the major-league record for consecutive pinch hits, people forget that I was 0-for-April. I did walk a few times, but that didn't ease my frustration. It hurt because there were a couple of games we could have won if I had come through. And it's not as though you know you're coming back at the pitchers the following day like you do when you play regularly. A pinch hitter might go four or five games before he gets another at-bat. So you can't let your failures eat at you.

"When you are primarily a pinch hitter, you don't get to take as many batting practice swings as the regulars. Come to the park a little earlier and take extra b.p. (batting practice) as often as you can. Once the game starts, study that opposing starting pitcher intensely because you may be facing him in a later inning. What is working for him today? What is the catcher calling, and what does the pitcher seem to be shaking off? What sort of strike zone is the umpire giving him? If the umpire is giving him the outside of the plate, you have to adjust, not the ump. Just look at what happened during the (1997 National League) playoffs between Atlanta and Florida. You had that game where Eric Gregg was calling strikes on pitches way outside all day. What do you do as a hitter? Complain throughout the game while you go 0-for-4? If you're smart, you move up on the plate and make the pitcher try to get you out inside.

"You should also talk to your teammates after they take their swings against a pitcher. Find out what kind of stuff he has. Then see if you can pick up some nuance that tells you what the pitcher is throwing.

"I picked up enough pitches in my career to know what was coming about 40 percent of the time. It wasn't difficult if you observed closely. For example, Rick Wise (a pitcher with the Philadelphia Phillies and other teams) used to hold the ball with his hand in the glove. Then he put the glove right in front of his chest. If he dropped the glove all the way during the windup, almost to touch his body, he was throwing a fastball. But when he gripped the curveball or his change-up, he would drop the glove only 6 inches. That was blatant. When Tony Cloninger pitched for the Braves, he wore a long sweatshirt, even if it was 110 degrees. When he was at the top of his stretch, that sweatshirt would recede from his wrist. If you saw a lot of wrist, Tony was throwing a fastball. If you saw a little bit of wrist, it would be the curve or slider. No wrist? He was throwing the change. At one time, when Nolan Ryan had to pitch out of a windup, he would look down at the ground before delivering the fastball; if he looked at the catcher, he was bringing the curve. With the stuff he had, that didn't always help, but at least you got a little better shot at him.

"Besides studying the pitcher, you should also examine the park conditions. Is the wind blowing in or out? Is it blowing in different directions in different parts of the park? Is there a sun field (an outfield position that exposes a fielder's eyes to the glare of the sun)? If you hit the ball down the line, is it likely to stay fair or foul? Is the grass slowing down the ball? In Dodger Stadium, when I played, if you bunted the ball off the grass and it hit the mud, it stayed fair. In the old Astrodome, Joe and I knew that if you bunted the ball down the line, the turf moved the ball towards foul territory. Recognizing these idiosyncrasies helps you to bring as many plusses to the plate as you can. Every hitter should know these things, but it is especially important for pinch hitters. You only have that one chance per game; you have to make the most of it."

Chapter 6

Winning the Arms Race: Pitching Like a Major Leaguer

*P*itching is the most valuable commodity in baseball. Teams don't reach the postseason without possessing solid *starting rotations* (pitching lineups) backed by deep *bullpens* (relief pitchers). Any manager will tell you that strong pitching is the best insurance against long losing streaks. When your club surrenders only three or four runs every game, you can find a way to win even with the weakest offense. A gifted hitter can galvanize an entire lineup, but a dominant pitcher can do more to elevate a team than any position player can. Even a last-place club can compete like a world champion if it has a top gun on the mound.

Find that opinion hard to believe? Open up a baseball encyclopedia and look up the 1972 Philadelphia Phillies. You'll see a team whose .358 won-lost percentage was the worst in the National League that season. Yet when Steve Carlton pitched for the Phillies, they played .730 ball. No team came within 110 points of that mark. If Philadelphia could have cloned Carlton, the club would have won its division by 22 games.

And Carlton is only one of the many examples we could have presented to support our point. Tom Seaver, Walter Johnson, Bob Gibson, Ferguson Jenkins, Gaylord Perry, Grover Alexander — the record books are filled with the names of men who transformed their clubs from victims to predators every time they strode to the center of the diamond. Each of these pitchers had powerful arms, sound mechanics, a genius for pitch selection, and an unquenchable competitive spirit. Now, we can't give you Kerry Wood's arm, Jason Schmidt's drive, or Greg Maddux's head. But in this chapter we show you the proper way to throw the various pitches you need to get hitters out. The rest you have to develop between the lines.

We've enlisted help from both sides of the mound for this section. Bob Gibson is our right-hander. During his 17-year career with the St. Louis Cardinals, Bob won 251 games, struck out 3,117 batters, posted five 20-win seasons, won two Cy Young Awards, and was named a National League Most Valuable Player — an award few pitchers have on their résumés. And he's also a Hall of Famer.

Bob was a power pitcher, so for help with *off-speed* (non-fastball) stuff, we have Bill Lee. As a member of the Boston Red Sox and Montreal Expos, Bill was one of the leading left-handers of the 1970s. He wasn't overpowering; Bill got hitters out with movement and great control.

Note: For information on special rules for pitchers, see Chapter 3. And be sure to check out the defensive strategies, including the pickoff move, for pitchers in Chapter 7.

It All Starts with Your Stance

Stances are as individual as the pitchers who assume them. Find a stance on the mound that leaves you balanced and comfortable. Your weight should be evenly distributed and your hands relaxed. Keep your glove hand and ball hand together so you don't let the hitter see your grip on the ball (it may tip him off to which pitch you intend to throw). As you take the sign from your catcher, your *pivot foot* (right foot for right-handers, left foot for left-handers) must touch the pitching rubber.

If you're left-handed, place your pivot foot on the left end of the rubber. If you're right-handed, do the reverse. Face the plate squarely.

Your Windup, Thrust, and Release

Your windup should get the full force of your body behind the pitch.

1. **From your stance, start releasing the momentum by taking a short step back behind the rubber with your striding foot (left foot for right-handers, right foot for lefties).**

   Avoid taking a large step or you will throw off your balance. You should be gripping the ball in the glove at some point between the top of your shoulder and high above your head. (See Figure 6-1.)

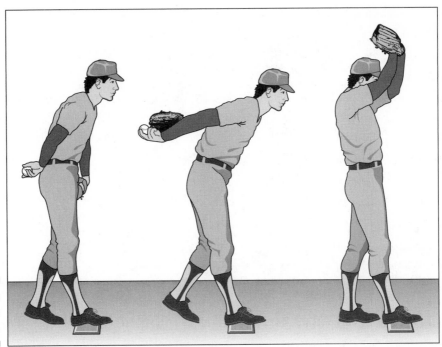

Figure 6-1:
Starting the
windup.

2. **Pivot as you lift your striding foot to bring it back over the rubber. Lift your striding knee to your chest.**

   This is your leg kick, but if you actually do kick out, you may disturb your balance. Keep your head steady and over your rear foot. (See Figure 6-2.)

3. **Bring your hands down (somewhere between your belt and chest) and separate them. Nearly all your weight should be on your pivot leg.**

   That leg should be slightly bent. As you pivot back, turn your striding foot until it is perpendicular to the rubber. Your hips and shoulders should be closed to the batter.

"Don't try to copy your windup from some other pitcher. Find out what is comfortable for you. If someone were to give you a ball and tell you to go into your windup, 99 percent of the time that basic motion is what will serve you best because it's what's most natural for you. We may have to alter your mechanics — the positioning of your arm or something like that — but not your natural motion. If you're a coach and you have a youngster who isn't comfortable winding up, don't make him do it. Let him pitch without a windup." — Bob Gibson

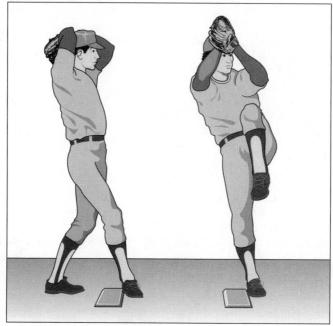

Figure 6-2:
Beginning
your leg
kick.

4. **Maintain the weight on your back foot until your leg kick is at its high-est point. Then start shifting your weight forward toward home plate. (See Figure 6-3.)**

5. **Bring your striding leg down and plant it with your foot pointed toward home.**

   As the striding foot hits the ground, your hips should open (but keep your front shoulder closed). Your throwing arm should be raised behind your head to its highest point with your wrist cocked back. Your striding leg should be slightly bent. Lower your body and thrust from the pitching rubber.

   "You have to get your hips into this. It's very much like playing golf or hit-ting. To play golf, you have to turn your hips away from the ball and then bring them back with your swing. To hit, you turn your hips away from the plate, and then come back. Same thing as a pitcher, you bring your hips to the side and then come back forward." — Bob Gibson

6. **As you bring your throwing arm around, bring your glove hand for-ward just above your elbow with the palm up.**

   Keep your elbow high so you can trace a wide arc with your throwing arm. Do not, however, trace so wide an arc that it throws off your balance. To get the most movement on the ball, deliver your pitch with a three-quarters motion.

Figure 6-3:
Starting to
come home.

"If you were to stand erect while facing home plate and point your arm out straight from your shoulder and then put your elbow and hand up at a 90-degree angle, you'd see and feel the proper angle (for delivering a pitch). You'll see pitchers who go higher or lower, but the 90-degree angle is the easiest on your arm. Most pitchers — and a lot of them don't even know they're doing this — will have their arm in this spot just as they begin their thrust." — Bob Gibson

7. **Release the ball with your head over your striding leg and your arm fully extended.**

   Your elbow should be at or above shoulder level, your forearm parallel to the ground. Your pivot foot should come forward with its heel up as your hip (throwing-hand side) drives toward home plate. (See Figure 6-4.)

"Don't try to muscle the pitch to get greater velocity. When you tighten the arm to throw, it's like a hitter trying to hit a home run and swinging too hard. His bat gets very slow. The same thing will happen with your arm. Keep your hand, wrist, and arm relaxed so you can pop the ball at the very last second. You get your velocity in front of the rubber, not behind the rubber. The ideal thing would be for you to use your arm like a whip, but not everyone is capable of doing that." — Bob Gibson

Figure 6-4:
Releasing
the ball.

The Follow-Through

"Follow-through is very important for a pitcher. If you cut off your follow-through, you won't be able to pop the ball for velocity." — Bob Gibson

After you release the pitch, your pivot foot should continue to move forward until it is parallel or slightly in front of your striding foot. Bring the elbow of your glove hand back toward your hip (as if you were elbowing someone behind you). Your throwing arm should sweep across your body on a diagonal and end on the first-base side (if you are right-handed) or third-base side (if you are left-handed) of your knee. (See Figure 6-5.) Ideally, this follow-through should leave you in perfect fielding position: weight balanced evenly on the balls of your feet, knees bent, and your glove ready to field anything hit your way.

"If your follow-through ends with you in perfect fielding position, fine. But don't let it get in the way of your main objective, getting the ball to the plate with location and something on it. If I had tried to come out in perfect fielding position all the time, I probably wouldn't have gotten anybody out because I would have had to cut my follow-through off. I wasn't willing to do that. So I just made sure I recovered quickly enough after my follow-through to field the ball." — Bob Gibson

Authors' note: Gibson's follow-through often ended with him facing first base, but he recovered quickly enough to earn nine consecutive Gold Glove awards.

Figure 6-5:
Following-
through with
the pitch.

Pitching from the Stretch

With runners on, you have to discard your full windup; it leaves your leg in the air so long that opponents are able to steal bases easily. Instead, pitch from the set or stretch position. Stand sideways with your rear foot against the front edge of the rubber and your front shoulder aligned with home. Your feet should be a little less than shoulder width apart with your front foot's heel even with the rear of your back foot's arch. (See Figure 6-6.)

Figure 6-6:
Getting into
the stretch
position.

Instead of winding up to deliver the ball, simply stretch your arms above your head and bring your ball and glove hands to a complete stop somewhere between your chest and belt. The rest of the delivery is similar to the one you use out of your windup, except you need less kick and pivot and more push from the pitching rubber.

"Pitching from the stretch is no different from pitching with a windup. You're simply cutting off the windup, but at the point where you rotate your hips you should be in the same position as when you take your full windup." — Bob Gibson

Heat and Other Weapons in Your Pitching Arsenal

Ninety-two mph, 94 mph, 100 mph — the numbers reported by the speed-obsessed media may lead you to believe that a fastball's velocity is its most important attribute. It isn't. More critical to a pitcher's success is the fastball's movement and location. Pitchers should also be able to change speeds to throw off the batter's timing. If a fastball doesn't move much, a competent major-league hitter can time it after a few viewings no matter how many speed records it shatters. Case in point: When Hideki Irabu, the Japanese League pitching star, made his American major-league debut with the New York Yankees, his best fastball clocked in at 98 mph. Few pitchers can match his speed. However, during his first season with New York, Irabu's pitches were straight as a string. After opponents got their swings grooved, they were hitting long shots off of him. After Yankee pitching coach Mel Stottlemyre taught Irabu how to make his ball move more (Stottlemyre altered Irabu's grip), the pitcher enjoyed greater success.

"You can teach a pitcher to increase his movement on the ball. It's all a matter of how you hold and release the ball. If you release the ball with your fingers pointed straight up, there's a good chance the ball won't move. But if you just cock the ball to one side or the other, it will move if you work at it." — Bob Gibson

Four-time Cy Young Award winner Greg Maddux, on the other hand, rarely throws harder than 88 mph. That's only a little above average for a major leaguer. However, Maddux has been successful because he can put the ball wherever he wants it. His pitches not only move, but they move late. A batter may think that he has honed in on a Maddux pitch, only to find that the ball has darted in on his hands at the very last second. The right-hander rarely throws two consecutive pitches at the same speed. Like most great pitchers, Maddux throws a variety of pitches, including a slider, curve, and change-up.

Every pitcher, no matter how hard he throws, should have at least three strong pitches — something hard, something that breaks, and something off-speed — in his arsenal. With that advice in mind, take a look at your options in the following sections.

The four-seam fastball

The *four-seamer* is considered the basic fastball. Grip it with your top two fingers across the seams at their widest point. Nestle your thumb under the ball across the bottom seam. Curl your ring and little fingers along one side. Your middle and index fingers should be about a half-inch apart. If they touch, the ball can slide, making it difficult to control. If you spread them too far, you can limit the wrist action you need to pitch. Hold the ball away from your palm with your fingertips. (See Figure 6-7.)

Figure 6-7:
The four-seam fastball.

Keeping your fingers in the center of the ball limits its movement. However, if you bring your digits a bit closer together and move them off-center to the left, the ball runs (moves to either side) or sinks. Placing your fingers off-center to the right causes the ball to break in on a left-handed batter and break away from a righty.

The two-seam fastball

The *two-seam fastball* moves more than the four-seamer. To throw it, grip the ball along its two seams with your middle and index fingers. Position your thumb under the ball. Your ring and little fingers are off to the side of the ball, slightly behind your gripping fingers. Exert pressure with your middle finger and thumb. To throw a sinking fastball, move your top fingers so that they hook a seam. Throw the ball like a fastball and let your grip do the rest.

For a variation on this theme, you can grip the ball with your middle and index fingers across the two seams at their narrowest point (the portion of an official major-league baseball that bears the league president's signature). Maintain pressure with your thumb and middle finger. With this two-seam grip, the ball should move more to the side.

Some pitchers turn their hands down and in when they release the two-seamer. This action slows the ball's break, which can throw off a hitter's timing; however, if it doesn't, that pitch is an excellent candidate for a home run.

"As a right-handed pitcher, if I threw the two-seamer to a right-handed hitter, the ball would usually sink or curve into him. If I threw that same pitch to the left-hander, it would sink and move away from him. Most left-handed hitters are low-ball hitters, which means that a two-seamer would be right in their wheelhouse. So I'm going to throw the four-seamer to him; that pitch will ride in on his hands." — Bob Gibson

The slider

A hybrid, the *slider* is part fastball, part breaking ball. We list it with the other fastballs because it's more effective the harder it's thrown. The key to an effective slider is its late break. The pitch should resemble a fastball until it approaches the hitter. Then it should veer sharply to the side.

Grip the slider with the index and middle fingers across the two widest seams. Keep your fingers slightly off-center, toward the outside of the ball. Your thumb should be tucked under the ball, and your ring and little fingers should be off to its side. Exert pressure with your thumb and middle finger. (See Figure 6-8.)

Figure 6-8:
The slider.

When you throw the ball, *keep your wrist loose!* Throwing this pitch with a stiff wrist can strain and damage your elbow.

You also shouldn't twist your wrist as you release the slider (a mistake commonly made by pitchers who think twisting imparts greater spin on the pitch — it does, but it also increases the chances of injury). Instead, throw it like a fastball, but imagine cutting through the ball with your middle finger as you deliver the pitch. Keep your fingers on top of the ball until the moment of release.

"If you twist your wrist like you're throwing a curve, you won't get that extra bite on the pitch. That ball will have a big, slow break. Instead, turn the ball with your first two fingers and your thumb as if you were turning a doorknob." — Bob Gibson

The split-fingered fastball

The *split-fingered fastball* is the child of the *forkball,* a pitch that was thrown with great effectiveness by such relief-pitching stars as Elroy Face and Lindy McDaniel during the 1960s. Pitchers held the forkball between the first two joints of their middle and index fingers. When thrown by a good fastball pitcher, it was more like a good change-up than a power pitch. You don't hold today's split-finger (or *splitter*) as high between your fingers as the forkball, which means you can throw it with greater velocity. Split your middle and index fingers and grip the ball along its seams. Do not jam it past the midway point of your fingers. (See Figure 6-9.)

Figure 6-9:
The split-fingered fastball.

"Throw the pitch with a fastball motion and plenty of wrist. When properly delivered, the splitter should look like a fastball until it reaches the plate. Then the pitch should dive down as if the bottom has dropped out from under it." — Bill Lee

The curveball

Good *curveballs* (also known as *deuces, hooks,* and *Uncle Charlies*) have put more hitters out of work than all the baseball strikes combined. If you have a hook that you can throw for strikes, batters can't *sit back on* (wait for) the fastball even when the count is in their favor. Hitters never look worse than when they swing at a curve after guessing a fastball.

To throw the curve, grip the ball with your middle and index fingers across the seams at their widest part. Hold it farther back in your hand than the fastball, but don't let it touch your palm or you won't get enough spin. Your object here is to get more of your finger surface in contact with the ball. Curl your ring and little fingers into your palm. Exert pressure with your middle finger and thumb; keep the index finger loose against the ball. (See Figure 6-10.)

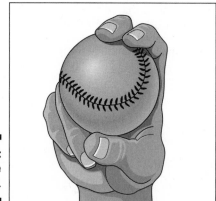

Figure 6-10: The curveball.

"As you bring your arm forward in your motion, your wrist should be cocked and rotating inward. Your palm and ball should face you as your hand passes your head. While keeping your elbow high, turn your wrist and snap down as you release the ball over your index finger. The back of your hand should be facing the batter as the pitch leaves your fingers." — Bill Lee

Make sure you follow through with your motion, or your curve ball will hang (stay up in the strike zone where a hitter likes it). Pitchers who throw a lot of hanging curves often want to hang themselves because batters tend to smack those pitches a long, long way.

The three-fingered change-up

Change-ups make your fastballs more effective by making them seem faster by comparison. You can use a variety of change-up grips, but the *three-fingered change-up* is the easiest to master. Hold the ball back against your palm with your index finger, middle finger, and ring finger spread across the seams at their widest point. Nestle the thumb and pinky against each other under the ball. (See Figure 6-11.)

Figure 6-11:
The three-fingered change-up.

"Exert equal pressure with all five fingers. Keep your wrist stiff. Bring it straight down as if you were lowering a window shade. Don't pick a corner with this pitch; throw it down the middle of the plate." — Bill Lee

The circle change-up

Hold the *circle change-up* like the three-finger change-up — only join the index finger and thumb in a circle on the side of the ball. (See Figure 6-12.) The best change-ups look like fastballs out of the pitcher's hand. However, they take more time to reach home plate and can upset the timing of any hitter looking for something hard and fast.

The palmball

The *palmball* is an off-speed pitch, a change of pace designed to mess with the hitter's rhythm. Unlike all other pitches, the ball is held tight against the palm. Your middle and index fingers rest across the top of the two widest seams. Your ring and little fingers rest against one side; your thumb is slightly raised along the other. Exert pressure on the ball with your ring finger and thumb. (See Figure 6-13.) Throw this pitch with your usual fastball motion. As you release the pitch, straighten out your fingers and make sure your hand is behind the ball rather than on top of it. You want the ball to slip from between your thumb and fingers.

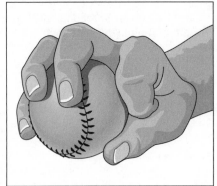

Figure 6-12:
The circle change-up.

Figure 6-13:
The palmball.

"Pitchers make the mistake of trying to underthrow their change-ups, reducing their arm's speed to slow the pitch. Throw the ball as if it were a fastball and let your grip and motion do the work." — Bill Lee

The screwball

Throw the *screwball* pitch only at your own peril; this pitch is murder on the arm. A reverse curveball, the *scroogie* is held like a four-seam fastball (see Figure 6-7). The index finger and thumb provide all the pressure, but you release the ball off your middle finger.

Come over the top with this pitch as if it were a fastball. However, just before you release the ball, turn your wrist, forearm, and elbow inward in a corkscrew motion. The rotation should be the opposite of your curveball. When thrown by a left-hander (which most screwballers are), the ball breaks down and away from right-handed hitters. However, it breaks down and in on left-handed hitters, which they like a lot; that's why left-handed hitters usually hit left-handed scroogie artists so well.

The knuckle ball

The *knuckle ball* is the one pitch that is more effective the slower you throw it. Knuckle balls are difficult to control because their movement is so erratic. Often, the pitcher who throws one has no idea how it will move or where. Knucklers dart, dance, jump, break, swerve, and rise. Sometimes these pitches perform two or three of these motions in the same flight. Most batters hate to hit against the knuckler; a good one can throw off their swings for weeks.

The trick to throwing the pitch is to eliminate as much of the ball rotation as you can. Despite its name, the ball is rarely thrown off the knuckles. Instead, dig the tips of your index, middle, and ring fingers (make sure your nails are always trimmed if you are going to throw this pitch) into just below the seams of the ball. Keep your thumb and little finger on the side. (See Figure 6-14.)

"Don't throw the knuckle ball; push it towards home plate with a stiff wrist out of your usual motion. Imagine you're tossing a pair of socks into the hamper. As you release the ball, extend your fingers straight out towards home plate." — Bill Lee

Figure 6-14:
The knuckle ball.

Before You Take the Mound

You can increase the effectiveness of all your pitches if you throw them with the same motion. Have your coaches and teammates watch you on the mound to see if you make any subtle gestures that may reveal which pitch you are about to deliver. Never throw a half-hearted pitch. If you don't agree with the sign from your catcher, shake him off (shake your head "no"). Wait until he calls for something that inspires more enthusiasm or comes out to the mound to discuss the options.

Don't let a hitter beat you on your second-best pitch. With the game on the line, go with your best stuff, even if that means matching your strength against the hitter's.

A word from Bob Gibson on throwing hard

"One of the lost arts in pitching is being able to throw the ball hard. Too many pitchers are throwing trick pitches at a very young age. Being able to throw the fastball with as much velocity as you can is more important. But the number one thing for any pitcher is control — being able to throw the ball where you want when you want to. Try using the same release point every time.

If you don't know where your release point is, your ball is going to be everywhere. You also have to know yourself. For instance, if my ball was high, I knew there were two things I could be doing wrong. One was I had screwed up my release point, the other was I had taken too long a stride. When you understand your error, you can make adjustments on the mound."

Chapter 7

The Third Dimension: Defense

*W*inning teams play good defense. We tend to think of power pitchers and sluggers as the dominant forces on a baseball diamond, but a great defensive player can be just as intimidating. When New York Mets center fielder Mike Cameron defies the earth's pull to make yet another leaping, rally-crippling snatch of what appears to be a sure double, watch how many shoulders sag in the opposing dugout. Plays like that can slaughter hope before it gains full maturity, deflating the victimized hitter and his club while elevating the team on the other side of the field.

Cameron, third baseman Eric Chavez, and second baseman Pokey Reese are among the premier fielders playing today. These Gold Glovers have sure hands, fast reactions, and strong, accurate arms. They get to balls that other fielders merely wave at. However, you wouldn't call any one of them a "natural" fielder — someone who was born to steal base hits — because there is no such thing. The only way to become a great defender is to work at it.

This chapter begins with some general fielding tips. Then we turn the floor over to an all-star team of consultants for advice on how to play each of the nine positions. (That's right, pitchers are part of the defensive mix, too.)

The Good Hands People

No matter which position you play, you need to have what ball players call *good hands.* However, *quick hands* and *soft hands* would be more accurate terms. If you have them, your hands adjust swiftly to bad hops, erratic bounces, or wild throws. Some people are born with quick hands, but most of us must develop them.

One way to develop quick hands is to play the game *short hop.* Stand 4 to 5 feet (1.2 to 1.5 meters) apart from a partner. Throw the ball to each other so that the ball bounces on a short hop, forcing the fielder receiving the throw to reach and adjust on every toss. Keep score to make the drill interesting. The first player to miss three short hops loses the round. Start again until you complete a five-round game. While practicing this drill, concentrate on using both hands for every catch. Training your hands to work in unison makes you a more coordinated fielder.

Picking a Position

Want to know which position is right for you? This section examines the particular qualities that each position requires so that you can see how you measure up.

Catcher

You must have a high threshold of pain to play catcher. Foul balls are going to ricochet off your fingers and feet, you may take an occasional fastball or bat on the mask, and you can count on at least one home plate collision every week. Catchers must have strong legs — you spend half the game squatting while wearing heavy equipment. If you're going to play the position properly, you must possess a powerful, accurate arm, although you can compensate for an average throwing arm with a quick release.

If you want an example of how a strong arm can completely neutralize base stealers, just watch Charles Johnson or Ivan Rodriguez intimidate a team from behind the plate. They both throw out a high percentage of potential base thieves, but more impressive is how few runners attempt to steal against them.

Besides having physical stamina, catchers must be mentally tough. Catching is draining work; you are in on every pitch of the game. If your pitcher takes the mound without his best stuff, you're the one who has to improvise a strategy to retire batters with his secondary pitches. With every hitter, that computer between your ears is working in overdrive, trying to recollect or decipher the hitter's weaknesses and strengths.

Are you immersed in a batting slump? No matter how many oh-fers you've taken, you need to put your hitting woes out of your mind the moment you squat behind home plate. You must place your entire focus on aiding your pitcher in the battle against the hitter.

Finally, you have to be a practical psychologist — if your pitcher is getting battered, you have to know whether he needs a pat on the back or a good swift kick in the rear.

What's glove got to do with it? (With apologies to Tina Turner)

Your glove (or mitt) is your most important fielding tool. It should fit snugly enough that it won't come off when you catch a ball in its tip. However, your glove should not be so tight that it restricts wrist flexibility or movement. How big should your glove be? That depends on what position you play.

✔ Catcher's mitts are always large, but yours shouldn't be so big that you cannot control it. Choose a mitt that you can open and close in a split second. (See Chapter 2 for some preliminary details on gloves and how to select them.)

✔ At first base, catching the ball is your primary concern. Digging the ball out of the mitt to get off your own throw is a secondary issue. Your first baseman's mitt should be as long as you can comfortably manage so that you can snag wide, errant tosses in the glove's webbing.

✔ Third basemen should also opt for large gloves. Balls are hit so quickly to third that you often only have time to block the ball or knock it down. You also have to field many

balls hit wide to your left and right. A big glove helps you cover more territory.

✔ Second base is the position of quick throws; use the smallest glove possible here so that the ball won't stick deep in its pocket. Choosing a small glove to play second is also a matter of self-preservation — at times you may have 220 solid pounds of seething base runner bearing down on you to break up the double play (as well as any part of your anatomy he can reach). In these cases, you don't want to spend a split second more time than necessary searching for the ball before unleashing your throw.

✔ Shortstops must get the ball out of their gloves quickly, too. But they must also be able to catch grounders cleanly when they range wide in the hole. A medium-sized glove is in order for this position.

✔ Outfielders are primarily interested in catching the ball. They have little need for a quick release. If you're playing the outfield, use the longest glove that the rules permit. (See Chapter 2 for rules about gloves.)

Ideally, catchers should have a low center of gravity, like the 5-foot-8-inch Ivan Rodriguez. This body type gives the pitcher a better target and also offers the umpire a clearer perspective of each pitch. For example, seeing over a tall catcher like 6-foot-2-inch Charles Johnson can be difficult for an umpire; that size may occasionally cost his pitcher a low strike. (And that about sums up the only weakness — if you can call it that — in Charles's game. He is one of the best defensive catchers to ever pull on a pair of shin guards.)

First base

Left-handed throwers have an advantage playing first base. As a first baseman, all your throws to the infield go to your right; if you throw left-handed, the play is always in front of you. Right-handed throwers often have to whirl completely around before they can toss the ball to another base. First basemen don't need particularly strong arms; they rarely throw more than 60 feet (18.3 meters). But your arm must be accurate, particularly on the 3-6-3 (first-to-short-to-first) double play when you're throwing into the runner.

First basemen should have enough range to cover their half of the hole between first and second. You need quick reactions and agility to cope with the opposition's bunting game. (Watch how Derek Lee of the Chicago Cubs pounces on bunts with the nimbleness of a middle infielder.) First basemen catch more throws than any other fielders, with the exception of the catcher. Depending on how the thrower grips the ball prior to release, those throws can sink, rise, or dart to either side of you. You have to be prepared to gather in tosses from every angle. If catching the ball is a liability for you, move to another position.

Second base

Second base is a paradox. I've played enough of it to know that this can be the easiest infield position for catching the ball — you don't have to cleanly catch a ground ball to record an out. Your proximity to first base allows you plenty of time to simply knock the ball down and make the short toss to the bag.

However, second base is also the most difficult position because you're a sitting duck on the double play. You often wait for a throw with your back to some runner who is eager to tear you in half with his slide. (Think football and hockey players are the only athletes who relish a little hard contact? George "Boomer" Scott — a hulking bruiser of a base runner when he played with the Boston Red Sox and Milwaukee Brewers during the 1970s — often wore a necklace, which he gleefully claimed was constructed from retired second basemen's teeth. And George was one of the more genteel of baseball's crash artists.) Your attitude has to be, "The double play takes priority over my physical well-being. I'm going to turn the play first and *then* look for the runner."

Too many otherwise-skilled second basemen hurt their teams by letting their fear of injury prevent them from turning two (getting both outs on a double play). The key to not getting creamed is to catch your shortstop's ball cleanly so you have time to plant your left foot on the bag. When you throw toward first base, you gain the momentum to leap out of the way of the base runner. Second basemen who bobble that toss from the shortstop tend to freeze for a split second before they recover. This hesitation leaves them prone to collision.

In addition, a second baseman needs to be a take-charge type, an infield captain who can direct where a play should go. (Between pitches, the second baseman can indicate where the ball should be thrown if hit by the batter.) Because you move around so much — for example, when you have to cover first base on a bunt — you must concentrate on positioning a little more than the other infielders. Luis Castillo, a member of the 2003 National League Gold Glove team, is an excellent example of a second baseman who positions himself well on every hitter.

Because most of your throws are short, you don't need a powerful arm to play second base. However, your throws must be precise and quick (particularly when you are relaying an outfield throw to another base) and you must be able to throw under pressure (being exerted by that base runner bearing down on you).

Shortstop

Shortstop is the most difficult infield position to play. Shortstops must be able to field grounders cleanly because they rarely have time to knock a ball down and throw out the runner. Because you have more territory to cover than any other infielder, you have to be far-ranging.

Tall, lean players, like Derek Jeter (6 feet 3 inches) and Edgar Renteria (6 feet 1 inch), are ideally built to play shortstop; they can stretch out over more ground and reach out farther than smaller infielders. However, a relatively short player like 5-foot-9-inch Rey Ordonez can outplay almost anyone at this position because he is so quick. This position demands a powerful throwing arm to make the throw from the hole (near the third-base side of the infield) or from deep behind second base.

Third base

Like the catcher, a third baseman must be willing to absorb a few body blows. You play close to home plate; if a right-handed hitter pulls the ball sharply, you often won't have time to get your glove into fielding position. That's when you have to throw your body in front of the ball, block it, get to your feet, and throw out the runner. That's why third basemen like Adrian Beltre are studies in black and blue by midseason. You take a lot of punishment at third base.

Great third basemen usually have powerful arms; they need them to make long throws across the diamond. If you can throw with velocity, you can make up some of the time you lose blocking the ball and picking it up. However, Brooks Robinson, who won more Gold Gloves than any other third baseman, had an average arm at best. He compensated with a quick release and by positioning himself so that he seldom had to make the long throws required of most third basemen.

Third base is a reflex position; you must be able to react quickly to balls hit sharply to either side of you. A great third baseman, such as Ken Caminiti, could go to the line to his right as well as to the hole on his left. Ken's agility was one of the reasons he has several Gold Gloves sitting on his mantel. (A little later in this chapter, Ken tells you why he was so good at going to either side.)

Left field

Left field is the easiest position to play. Of the three outfielders, the left fielder makes the shortest throws, so he can get by with a below-average arm. Fly balls hit to left don't curve as much as fly balls hit to right. When batters hit the ball to the opposite field, it tends to *slice*. Because so many more hitters bat right-handed than left-handed, the left fielder doesn't have to handle many sliced balls (those fly balls that seem to keep moving farther away from the pursuing outfielder no matter how hard he runs).

Left fielders must be able to *charge the ball* (catch it while running toward it) properly; their close proximity and direct angle to home offer them numerous opportunities to throw out runners at the plate. Charging the ball gives them the momentum to unleash strong throws. Tampa Bay's Carl Crawford demonstrates the gifts a left fielder must have to excel. He's fast, goes back well on balls hit over his head, expertly plays balls hit down the line, and has a powerful arm that rarely misses its target. Watch how he lines up his entire body behind a throw. He's a walking — make that running — clinic on left-field play.

Center field

Center fielders should have accurate, strong arms; they're going to run down more balls than the other two outfielders and consequently have to make more throws. (***Note:*** If you charge the ball quickly and have a quick release, you can get by without having a strong arm.)

Speed and quickness are two more requisites for center field. (A relatively slow player who positions himself well, on the other hand, can play either left or right field.) You cannot play center unless you can run; you have too much territory to cover. In addition to chasing after fly balls, you back up your fellow outfielders on any fly balls or grounders hit your way.

Center fielders must be able to get a good jump on the ball; they need to react and accelerate quickly. Players like Jim Edmonds and Andruw Jones move at the crack of the bat. Excellent lateral movement is another must. Edmonds and Torri Hunter are among the best at going to either side to make a catch.

As a center fielder, you also have to understand your limitations. If you don't go back on the ball well, don't play too shallow. If you have trouble coming in, don't play too deep. A great center fielder like Andruw Jones has no difficulty coming in or going out, so he plays deep to steal extra base hits from the opposition.

Finally, the center fielder must be assertive — the entire outfield is your domain. If you call for a catch, the other outfielders must give way. On balls hit to the left or right fielders, you direct the play. (For more on where to go on a particular play, see Chapter 9.)

Right field

The first thing that managers look for in a right fielder is a strong arm. Right fielders have to make longer throws than anyone else on the diamond, sometimes throwing from deep in the right-field corner to third or home. (Vladimir Guerrero does that as well as anyone; he has a howitzer of an arm.) Because hits to right tend to curve or fade away from the fielder, you must be proficient at reading the ball's angle.

Pitcher

For this chapter, we're looking at the pitcher solely as a defensive player. You are 60 feet 6 inches (18.4 meters) away from the hitter, so you must have quicker reactions than anyone else in the infield. For your own safety, you should be able to catch the ball cleanly, but this skill is not a requirement. If you can simply knock the ball down in front of you, you usually have plenty of time to throw out even the fastest runners. Young pitchers often ignore fielding fundamentals; they seem to think all they need to win ballgames is a lively arm. However, most of baseball's elite pitchers — players such as Gold Glovers Greg Maddux and Mike Mussina — are excellent fielders. They know how to execute — to do those little things that help them win close ballgames. That's one of the reasons they're among their league's pitching leaders year after year.

Loading the Cannon: Getting Your Arm Ready for the Field

A poor throw can undermine the best glove work. Before exploring any other aspect of fielding, in this section we review the mechanics of throwing. To start, you need to warm up your arm. You and your throwing partner should stand 10 feet (3 meters) apart and gently lob the ball to each other. As your arm starts to feel loose and warm, gradually increase the velocity of your throws. If you're a young adult, toss the ball from four throwing angles:

- ✔ Over the top
- ✔ Three-quarters
- ✔ Sidearm
- ✔ Underhand

After you feel completely loose, stretch and strengthen your arm by gradually increasing the distance between you and your throwing partner.

Players under the age of 16 should throw only overhand or three-quarters to develop arm strength. Resist any temptation to throw sidearm or underhand.

Getting a grip

When you grip the ball, your middle and index fingers should be approximately 1 inch (2.54 centimeters) apart, *across* the seams. Place your thumb on the ball's underside, directly below your middle finger. Press the ball with your thumb and middle finger. Because you want your throws to travel straight and true, always throw with your fingers across the seams (see Figure 7-1). Placing your fingers *with* the seams causes the ball to sink or sail (a no-no unless you're a pitcher throwing to a hitter).

Make sure that you hold the ball out in your fingers because, if you hold the ball back in your palm as you throw, you won't generate enough velocity. Don't squeeze the ball; hold it just firmly enough to maintain control. Practice grabbing the ball and finding your across-the-seams grip without peeking.

Figure 7-1:
How to grip
the ball
before
throwing.

Delivering the throw

How you throw the ball depends on the position you play. Most outfielders throw the ball overhand for maximum power. The exception occurs on a *shoestring catch* (a ball caught, usually on the run, near your feet). If a runner is trying to advance on that play, the outfielder has to throw underhand or sidearm, or he won't get rid of the ball quickly enough.

Infielders rarely have time to straighten up and throw over the top; whenever you rear back to throw, you concede about 12 feet (3.6 meters) to the base runner. So you should throw three-quarters, sidearm, or underhand depending on the situation. On the double play, a second baseman or shortstop must throw from wherever he catches the ball. If you catch it high, throw overhand; if you catch it low, throw underhand.

To make an accurate, powerful overhand throw:

1. **Start the throw by squaring yourself toward your target and swinging your throwing arm back to your side in an arc.**

   Tilt your upper torso back on your throwing side, while keeping your other shoulder (and your eyes) pointed toward your target. Your wrist should be cocked and ready to throw.

2. **Step and thrust forward as you swing your arm directly over your shoulder and toward your target.**

   Make sure you extend your arm fully. Keep your elbow higher than your throwing shoulder (see Figure 7-2).

Figure 7-2:
Making the
overhand
throw.

3. **Plant your front (striding) foot while pushing off your rear (pivot) foot. To get maximum velocity on your throw, snap your wrist downward as you release the ball.**

   Your arm should continue to sweep in front of you and down to your side. As you follow through, your glove hand should come up behind you for balance. Allow your lower body to follow your upper body's momentum toward the target.

4. **Bring your pivot foot forward until it is parallel to your striding foot.**

   Use this same motion for the three-quarter throw from the outfield, but bring your elbow around on a 45-degree angle.

Infielders often throw sidearm and don't have time for a lot of motion when they throw. To throw sidearm, bring your throwing arm back in a short arc. Step toward your target and thrust forward as you swing your arm back in an arc that is parallel to the ground. You often cannot get your whole body behind this throw, so put as much shoulder and wrist into it as you can. Aim your throw for the middle of your target's torso.

You usually must throw underhand when you're close to your target or have to quickly toss a ball you have caught below your knees and to the side. Using a bowling motion, flip the ball toward your target's chest. Because you cannot get anything behind this throw, give it a good wrist snap as you release the ball.

Determining how hard is too hard

You don't have to air everything out on every throw you make. I don't believe throwing consistently hard is likely to hurt or tire your arm. However, if you are trying to throw the ball through a wall on every play, you can strain your muscles over the course of a season. Rick Burleson, a first-rate shortstop for the Red Sox and Angels from the mid-'70s to early-'80s, had a cannon arm whose power he demonstrated on nearly every throw. By age 30, a torn rotator cuff (an arm injury more common to pitchers than fielders) finished his career as a starting shortstop.

A Word about Errors

The first thing you have to remember is that every player makes errors. Don't let it get you down, though. In 1976, for example, I made 13 errors (nearly one every two weeks) while still winning a Gold Glove at second base. In 1980, when I was with Houston, our left fielder Jose Cruz led the National League with 11 errors, and he still managed to catch nearly 97 percent of the balls hit his way. (By the way, Jose was a fine outfielder; he just had one of those years.)

On the upside, if you have good range and play aggressively, you're going to commit fumbles on balls that other fielders don't even reach. Most errors come on grounders that are hit directly at you. (If you have any talent for catching a baseball, you rarely muff a fly ball.)

Fielders who fumble grounders tend to freeze for an instant instead of being aggressive. This lack of aggressiveness is what broadcasters mean when they say that the fielder *let the ball play him.* Whenever a ground ball is hit toward you, charge it immediately so you can gauge its hop; if you fail to charge right away, you can misperceive the ball's bounce.

When you do commit an error, don't let it discourage you. Dwell on it and you'll probably boot another ball because you're not concentrating on the play at hand. As former National League Gold Glove third baseman Ken Caminiti says, "If you know in your heart that you gave a ball your best effort, you just shrug the error off as part of the game. Keep your focus on the game and get ready for the next play. Don't spend any time thinking negatively. Be aggressive. You should want that next ball hit to you because you *know* — not just *think* — you're going to make the play." That's the kind of confidence every fielder must have.

Don't short-leg

Fear of fumbles can sap you of aggressiveness. Some players, rather than charging a ball full-out, time their approaches so they and the ball arrive at a spot simultaneously. If they catch the ball, it looks like a dazzling play. If they miss it, the official scorer usually deems it a hit instead of an error. It's called *short-legging* the ball, and it is a capital crime. You aren't on the field to look pretty or compile a gaudy fielding percentage. You're there to help your team win. Short-leggers invariably cost their clubs victories. When you're on the diamond, give everything you have to every play.

Avoid those hidden errors

Mental errors don't appear in anyone's box score, but they are often more costly than physical mistakes. When you commit a *rock* (make a boneheaded play) like throwing to the wrong base, it's usually because you did not anticipate the situation. As each hitter steps up to the plate, review all your options.

For example, you're the second baseman with a man on first and one out. Right away you should not only be thinking double play, but how to execute it. If the ball is hit to the shortstop or third baseman, you have to cover second. Hit to the pitcher? You're backing up the shortstop's play at second base. And so on. Cover all the possibilities so that when the ball hits the bat, you are ready to execute. You don't have to waste a second wondering what to do — you can simply react.

Six Tips for Fielding Grounders

Fielding a ground ball is easy if you have sound fundamentals. To put yourself in position to make a play, you should do the following:

- **Charge the ball whenever you can.** If you hang back, the ball has more time to take a bad hop. Maintain a short, quick stride rather than one that is long and uncontrollable. You should be able to stop abruptly.

- **Stay down on the ball.** Keep your body, including your buttocks, low to the ground. Standing straight up makes it difficult to gauge the ball's hop. You want your eyes down low for a good look at the ball. Keep your eyes on the ball; watch it go into your glove. After you catch it, look where you're going to throw it.

- **Keep your weight balanced evenly on the balls of both feet when you take your fielding stance (unless you're anticipating a specific play).** Having your knees slightly bent allows the freedom of movement you need to burst out of your stance in pursuit of the ball.

✔ **Use both hands to field whenever possible.** Catch the ball with your glove near the ground facing up and your bare palm above it facing down. If a ball takes a bad hop, using two hands gives you a better chance to corral it. The ball may drop into your glove after hitting the palm of your hand, or it may drop in front of you. Then you can pick it up in time to throw out the runner. If you use only one hand and the grounder takes a bad hop, the ball will get by you. Using both hands also allows you to get your throws off quickly.

✔ **Let your hands "give" a bit when the ball makes contact with your glove.** Cradle the ball in your glove as if you were catching a raw egg.

✔ **Keep your arms extended so that you catch the ball in front of you.** Try to field the ball in the middle of your body so that if the ball hits you on the bad hop, it drops in front of you. If it hits off to your side, the ball can bounce away from you.

Practice your throws so that you can take the ball out of your glove without looking at it. Remember, you want to grab the ball across the seams to ensure an accurate throw. You must be able to get your preferred grip on the ball while looking at your target, *not the ball.*

There will be times when you shouldn't even attempt a throw. For example, suppose that Alfonso Soriano is speeding toward first on a slow grounder. If you realize that you have no chance to make an accurate throw, hold the ball. Yes, you just put a runner on first, but that decision is better than letting Soriano take second or third (and he will) if you throw the ball wildly.

Positioning Yourself for a Strong Defense

No matter where you play on the field, knowledge and anticipation are the keys to positioning. Prior to the game, your pitcher should have told you and your teammates how he plans to throw to the opposing batters. You need to combine that information with all the data you have on those hitters. For example, when I was with the Reds, Jack Billingham may have tried to catch Billy Williams (a terrifying left-handed hitter with the Chicago Cubs) off-balance with a slow curve. I knew Billy would probably pull that pitch toward right field. If Jack threw his fastball away, Billy would probably shoot it to the opposite field. However, if Reggie Jackson — a slugger who hit over 500 home runs in the American League — was the hitter, Jack may have thrown a fastball away. Most left-handed hitters would hit that pitch to the opposite field in left. But Reggie was strong enough to pull the fastball away into right field with authority. I had to know all these tendencies so I could position myself accordingly.

After your mental data file on the opposing players is complete, you can reposition yourself for each hitter that comes to the plate; you may even change your position from pitch to pitch. Say that your catcher calls for the fastball inside, you're going to lean to the left or right depending on the hitter's tendencies. Because smart hitters adapt to situations, you must do the same. For example, with the first baseman holding a runner on first, a left-handed hitting genius like Ichiro Suzuki can shoot balls through that big hole on the right side of the infield. If you were playing second in that circumstance, you would lean more toward first to get a better jump on balls hit toward the hole. If no one was on base, you would play closer to second. However, if the pitcher was going inside on Ichiro, you would cheat toward first.

Fielding Line Drives

Catching a line drive is a reaction play — you either catch it or you don't. However, if you can't catch a line drive cleanly, you must knock it down so you have some opportunity to pick it up and throw. Whenever you have to leap for a line drive, watch the ball until it enters your glove (professional players call this "looking the ball into your glove").

Fielding Fly Balls

Later in this chapter, some fine major-league outfielders give you tips on the proper way to catch a fly ball. For the moment, I want to talk about *pop flies,* those weakly hit fly balls that don't make it out of the infield. On pop flies, you should run to wherever you expect the ball to drop. Catch the ball in front of you on your forehand side. Don't play the ball so that you have to run to catch it at the last moment. If you have to go back on a pop fly, run sideways rather than backpedaling (though you can backpedal if you're only going a few steps). You don't want to risk tangling your feet. Get stationary so the ball comes straight down into your glove. Position yourself so that if you fail to catch the ball, it hits you in the chest rather than the head or shoulders. Keep your arms extended but loose: That way, if you bobble the ball, you have a second chance to catch it before it hits the ground.

Whenever you see infielders or outfielders collide on a pop fly, you know that someone wasn't paying attention. I always told our outfielders to yell so I could get out of the way if they were going to catch a pop-up. If you both yell for the catch, you won't hear each other. When I was with the Astros, our left fielder, Jesus Alou, and our shortstop, Hector Torres, were both yelling as they went after a pop fly. They collided and Hector nearly choked to death on his tongue. Make sure that you have your signals straight before each game so you can avoid that kind of catastrophe.

The infield fly rule

Umpires may invoke the *infield fly rule* only when all three of the following conditions are met:

☞ There are less than two outs.

☞ Base runners occupy first and second base; or first, second, and third.

☞ The batter hits a fair fly ball to the infield, which the umpire believes can be caught by an infielder making "an ordinary effort."

By yelling "infield fly!" (usually while waving his arms), the umpire automatically rules the hitter out, even if the ball is not caught. The runners may advance only at their own peril.

Why have such a rule? When a pop fly is hit to the infield, the runners assume the ball will be caught, so they stay anchored at the bases. If there were no infield fly rule and the fielder deliberately dropped the ball, the runners would be forced to advance (to make room on the bases for the hitter). Because they could not begin running until the ball came down, the runners' late starts could make them easy victims of a double or even a triple play. Baseball's rule makers saw this as "stealing outs through deception," so they enacted the infield fly rule in 1895.

With a fast runner on first base, I've seen infielders deliberately drop pop flies so they could get the force-out at second. The idea is to erase a base-stealing threat or replace a speedy runner with a slower one. I don't believe that is ever good policy. Baseballs can take funny hops; if a pop fly hits the ground and bounces away from you, you may not get anybody out.

Playing the Field: Position by Position

I played second base my entire career. (Well, almost my entire career. I did play 16 games in left field while I was with the Astros and three games at third base for the San Francisco Giants.) So I've enlisted some of the best fielders of the last 30 years to share the nuances of the other positions. You can find examples of their expertise sprinkled throughout the rest of this chapter.

From Behind the Plate: Catcher

Good catchers are field generals. Because they call the pitches from behind the plate, they dictate a team's defensive strategy. The better receivers (catchers) can also set a tone for an entire ball club. For example, when Johnny Bench joined the Reds, he brought an intimidating presence to the field that immediately transformed Cincinnati into a cockier, more aggressive team. Joe Girardi, a receiver on three New York Yankee world champion

Conferring on the mound

Managers, coaches, catchers, or infielders sometimes initiate *mound conferences* when a pitcher is in a jam (the opposition is smacking his best stuff all over the lot). Mound conferences are sometimes used to stall for extra time while a reliever warms up. The pitcher and his teammates discuss his mechanics (if anyone detects a flaw in his delivery), his emotional well-being (they want to calm and encourage him), the situation (as if he doesn't know that already), or even the weather (to take his mind off his troubles).

Participate in these meetings only when you have something specific to accomplish. I would go to the mound when I thought our pitcher was throwing a certain pitch too often or to give him a breather in a tight spot. If he had just thrown a long series of bad pitches, I may tell him to approach the next pitch as if it were the first one of the ballgame, just to get him out of the rut. If you don't have anything constructive to add to these conferences, stay put — small talk slaughters genuine communication. The player who keeps running to the mound when he has nothing to say risks not being heard when he finally does have something to contribute.

teams, was an intense individual who raised his pitchers' concentration level the moment he squatted behind the plate. Charles Johnson represents the epitome of cool. When he caught for the Florida Marlins, he could even compose the emotional volcano that is Kevin Brown when that talented but temperamental right-hander got into one of his rare jams.

A catcher must be able to recognize the strengths and limitations of his pitchers and the opposing hitters. His arm must be powerful enough to provide base thieves with some incentive not to run. Receivers are often thought of as slow, blocky types. Most of them aren't speedy, but they need to be quick enough to scurry from behind the plate on bunts.

All of a game's action flows from the catcher's *signs.* (See the upcoming section "Flashing signs: The secret language of catchers.") Because everything starts with this position, it's an appropriate place to begin our defensive tour. Throughout this section, you get tips from the player who redefined the position — Johnny Bench. Johnny came to the Major Leagues with the Cincinnati Reds in 1968 and promptly won the first of his ten consecutive Gold Gloves — a record for major-league catchers.

I could go on for pages about this Hall of Famer's accomplishments, among them two Most Valuable Player Awards and 12 All-Star Game starts. However, no roll of honors or litany of dry statistics could summarize the Bench career better than the words of his former Reds manager, Sparky Anderson, who proclaimed, "Johnny Bench is the standard against which all other catchers must be compared. As the total package, no one who has ever played the position can touch him."

Setting up

Catchers are the only players in baseball who set up defensively in foul territory. How deeply you position yourself behind the plate depends on the hitter: You should get as close to home as you can without getting struck by the bat. Hitters who stand back deep in the box force you to stay back. If a hitter moves up in the box, you should also move forward. The closer you come to home plate, the better positioned you'll be to handle bunts, foul tips, wild pitches, and would-be base thieves.

Though each player brings a different wrinkle to his job, all catchers assume two basic stances behind home plate. The first is a set-up that puts you in position to deliver signs to your pitcher. Drop into a squat; keep your knees parallel with your weight evenly distributed on the balls of your feet. (See Figure 7-3.) To assume the second stance, put one foot slightly behind the other to help maintain balance. Spread your knees so that they provide a strong but comfortable base. Drop your rump until it is below your knees but slightly above your heels. Your upper body should be straight but never stiff.

Figure 7-3: A basic catching stance.

"You don't have to follow any 'Spalding Guide' model when you get behind the plate. People have different physical makeups, so they are going to squat differently. If you try to assume a position that doesn't fit your body, it will not work. Do whatever feels comfortable and balanced so that you can move either way on a pitch or block a ball in the dirt. Don't restrict yourself by holding your elbows too far in so that you're blocked from reaching across." — Johnny Bench

Flashing signs: The secret language of catchers

To flash signs, extend your right hand between your thighs. Point your right knee at the pitcher; this position shields your signals from the opposition's first-base coach. You can prevent the third-base coach from stealing your signs by holding your glove in front of your left knee. Most catchers give signs by extending one or more fingers. To avoid confusion, keep your signals basic: one finger for the fastball, two for the curve, three for a change-up, four for any other pitch your pitcher throws, such as a slider or screwball. Spread your fingers as wide as you can when you give signs. You want to make sure your pitchers can see each digit clearly. (See Figure 7-4.)

Figure 7-4:
Giving clear
signs to
your pitcher.

"Depending on the shadows and your pitcher's vision, you might want to tape your fingers to give him a better look at what you're flashing. Sometimes you have to improvise. When I was with the Reds, one of our pitchers, Wayne Simpson, had a corneal abrasion on the day he was scheduled to pitch. He couldn't wear his contacts on the mound. I could have painted my fingers in neon and he wouldn't have seen them. So I set the glove on the side of my knee for a fastball, on top of my knee for a breaking ball. Wayne pitched a two-hit shutout." — Johnny Bench

You can also transmit signs through the *pump system.* Using this method, you indicate which pitch you want by the number of times you flash the sign. (Pump one fist for a fastball, two for a curve, and so on.) Call for pitch location by holding your palms up (for high pitches) or down (for low). Pointing away from or toward a batter tells your pitchers whether the next pitch should be inside or out.

"You might go to the pump if you have an indication that the other team has stolen your signs, or with a runner on second. Whatever method you use, always make sure you and your pitcher are on the same page. The worst nightmare is to be giving signs during a game and suddenly realize that you have no communication whatsoever with the pitcher." — Johnny Bench

After a runner gets to second, where he has almost as good a view of the catcher's signs as the pitcher, things get more complicated. You must alter your signs so the runner cannot decipher them. One way to confuse him is to give several different signs in sequence after first deciding with your pitcher which of these is the genuine article. Or you can prearrange with your pitcher to combine two signs to get the appropriate signal. For example, you can flash one finger (fastball) as your first sign, three fingers (change-up) as a second, and two fingers (curve) as a third. If you and your pitcher have agreed to combine sign one (one finger) and sign three (two fingers) when a runner is on second, the addition produces the three-fingered signal for the change-up. (It's important that your infielders are also privy to your signs in all their various guises so they can set up properly on each pitch.)

"You can use physical signs to indicate an addition. For example, I might go to my mask to add one, or touch my chest protector to add two. Hitters will try to peek at your signs to gain an edge. If you catch them doing it, you can set it up with your pitcher to throw an inside pitch after you call for something outside. And I mean way inside — like around the hitter's neck. That will give him some incentive to stop peeking. If you think he's checking out your location behind the plate, to see if you're setting up inside or out, set up inside — but call for something away. Or stay centered and don't move in or out until your pitcher starts to unwind with his pitch." — Johnny Bench

When you give signs, make sure that neither your fingers nor hands extend below your thighs (where an alert opponent can observe them). Keep your elbow as still as possible; if the opposition detects you wiggling your elbow when you call for a breaking pitch, they can feast on your pitcher's fastballs.

When you're ready to catch

After you've given your sign, you can hop from your set-up position into your receiving (or *ready*) stance. Bring your rump up to just below knee level while keeping your thighs parallel to the ground. Stay low to give your pitcher a good target. This alteration shouldn't raise you as much as it makes you more compact. Shift your weight forward onto the balls of your feet until your heels are lightly touching the ground. Your feet should be shoulder width, with your right foot a few inches in front of your left. Turn your knees and feet slightly out. (See Figure 7-5.)

Figure 7-5:
Getting
ready to
receive
the pitch.

In front of your knee, bend the forearm of your catching hand at a 45-degree angle from your body. Don't lock your elbows or place them inside your knees — if you do, catching pitches far out of the strike zone is nearly impossible. When nobody is on base, protect your bare hand by tucking it behind you. With runners on, keep your bare hand in a relaxed fist behind the webbing of your glove. Grab the pitch with your throwing hand as soon as it is delivered.

Your pitcher should be able to look directly into your mitt after you set up a target. Centering your glove to your body gives the pitcher a clearer view. If you call an inside pitch, you have to shift your target inside; do the reverse for outside pitches. Don't shift your body until the last possible moment or you'll tip off the opposition. Always keep your target within the strike zone. After you set up your target, maintain the target until the ball has left the pitcher's hand.

"You have to know what your pitcher wants to use as a target. For instance, Tom Seaver may have thrown to my shinguards — right shinguard, left shinguard — depending on which side the batter swung from and whether we wanted to go in or out. Or he would pitch to one of my shoulders. Other guys looked to my glove. When you set a target with your glove, do not hold it straight up so your wrist is cocked into a L-shape. Angle the glove so you can stay flexible enough to rotate to the left or right." — Johnny Bench

Receiving the pitch

Catch the ball in the strike zone. If you receive it on the edge of the zone, the pitch's force can move your glove enough to transform a strike into a ball.

Don't stab at the pitch; let it come to you. If you must, sway with the pitches on the borders of (or just outside) the strike zone. However, avoid any extreme movements: Any radical body shift may persuade the umpire that the pitch is a ball even if it is in the strike zone.

When a pitch is legitimately outside the strike zone, don't try to steal a call by pulling it back into the zone with your glove. Umpires resent this trick, and they can punish you by refusing to call borderline pitches in your favor for the rest of the game. You can, however, *frame* a pitch by subtly rolling your wrists to rotate the glove up or down. To do this, keep your arm and torso stationary. Rotate the glove down on high pitches, up on low pitches.

"On an outside pitch to a right-handed hitter, keep the largest portion of your glove over the plate while catching the ball in your web. Do just the opposite against a left-hander. Always try to catch the ball in the web." — Johnny Bench

Tracking errant pitches

With runners on base, your pitcher must know he can throw a low pitch without having to worry that you'll let it skip by you. He'll have that confidence after you demonstrate your ability to dig those babies out of the dirt. To do that, you must forget about catching when runners are on base. Instead, concentrate on blocking the ball while anticipating that every pitch will be a bad one.

If the ball in the dirt comes directly to you, drop to your knees and face the ball squarely. Get your hands low and centered. Drop your chin onto your chest to protect your throat. With your shoulders hunched, push forward to smother the ball. Should the pitch look as if it will veer to your right, step toward the ball with your right foot while dropping to your knee with your other leg. Move your glove and bare hand to the space between your foot and knee. Keep both hands between your legs but close to your body. (See Figure 7-6.)

On high pitches, raise your glove slightly higher than the ball. Angle your glove downward so that if you miss the catch, the ball drops in front of you. If you keep your glove too low or angled upward, the ball can glance off it and skip in back of you. The runners will like that; it means extra bases for sure.

Figure 7-6:
Blocking
balls in the
dirt.

To catch a thief

Though it's not fair, catchers usually establish their defensive reputations with their throwing arms. (Though a receiver's game-calling ability provides a better measure of his value to a team.) Most teams prize those catchers who can curtail the opposition's running game. Like the other fielders, you must practice gripping the ball and removing it from the glove without looking. Your speed with this maneuver improves with repetition.

"You have to be quick. The good base stealers get down to second in about 3.1 seconds. It takes the average pitcher about 1.5 seconds to get the ball to home plate (from the start of his windup). That leaves you 1.5 seconds to throw the ball 127 feet, 3 inches to a target 6 inches above the bag on the first base side so the infielder has 1/10 of a second to make the tag. And then you have to hope the umpire is in position to make the call." — Johnny Bench

As a catcher, your throws must be straight and true. A proper grip ensures that they are. Grab the ball across the seams where they are widest apart. If your grip is off on your first try, rotate the ball as you cock your arm to throw.

Your grip, cock, and release should constitute one continuous motion. As you grip the ball, bring your glove hand back to your right shoulder while closing your left one. With the ball in hand, bring your right arm slightly above and past your ear. As your right arm comes forward to throw, aim your left shoulder at the target. Keep your glove arm parallel to the ground. Throw overhand; sidearm deliveries tend to tail away from their targets. As you release the ball, snap your wrist downward.

"You can't practice enough the transfer of the ball from glove to hand. You have to keep doing it until reaching in and grabbing that ball across the seams becomes second nature. Practice this even when you are having a simple catch. When you're behind the plate and you make the transfer with your shoulder closed, step straight with your toes pointed towards your target so that your arm follows your body line." — Johnny Bench

To catch today's speediest runners, you have to get the ball off to your fielders quickly. Therefore, you must try to throw while still coming out of your crouch. Major-league catchers generally choose from among three throwing styles:

✔ **The step and throw:** Recommended for catchers with average arms, it allows you to put more of your body behind each throw. Just before you catch the ball, step forward about 6 inches (15.2 centimeters) with your right foot while pointing it toward second base. After you possess the ball, turn your hips as you draw back your arm, stride forward with your left foot, and throw.

✔ **The jump pivot:** The moment the ball hits your glove, jump to your feet and plant your left foot below the spot where you just gave your target while making a 90-degree turn to plant your right foot. Take a short stride toward second and throw.

✔ **The rock and throw:** This throw requires a powerful throwing arm because it entails little body movement. As you receive the ball, rock back on your right foot. Rise from your crouch with your arm cocked. Shift your weight forward to your left foot and throw.

"When people talk about throwing out base runners, they are almost always thinking about arms, but they should be thinking about feet. A catcher has to have quick feet so he can 'get under himself' and move fluidly from a receiving position to a throwing position. Your feet will get your shoulders turned and in position to throw." — Johnny Bench

Derailing the double steal

With base runners on first and third, the catcher must be alert for the *double steal*. On this play, the runner on first breaks for second hoping to draw a throw while the runner on third scores. Before stepping toward second to throw (if that is your choice), check the runner at third. If he has just broken for the plate, throw to third or hold the ball and get him in a rundown. You are virtually conceding second base to the runner on first, so failing to get the man at third leaves you with two runners in scoring position. If the runner on third breaks for home as your throw heads for second, be prepared for your second baseman or shortstop to cut off your throw and return the ball to you at the plate.

Blocking the plate

Throughout the season, the catcher is involved in numerous collisions at home. How well you block the plate determines if you get the out while staying off the disabled list. As the runner steams toward home, spread your legs a little wider than shoulder width and anchor your left foot about 18 inches (45.7 centimeters) in front of the plate. (See Figure 7-7.)

Figure 7-7:
Blocking the
runner from
scoring.

"When you block the plate, remember it is better to be a live coward than a dead hero. I always let the runner see at least half the plate, so he has the option of going around me. If he can't see the plate, he has no alternative but to try to go through you or over you. If you persuade him to slide, you have him on the ground, where you can control what he is trying to do. As you block the plate, keep your toes pointed up the third base line and aimed directly at the runner. Should you angle the leg, the impact of the collision could permanently damage your knee." — Johnny Bench

After you have the ball and the runner has committed to sliding away from you, move your left leg until you block the plate entirely. Grip the ball in your bare hand while turning the back of your glove toward the runner to protect your inner wrist. As the runner slides in, drive down on top of him with your shin guards to prevent him from reaching the plate. With the ball held firmly in the glove, you can tag him with the back of your mitt. If other runners are on base, see if any other plays are developing as soon as you make the tag at home.

These instructions assume that you're handling an accurate throw. If the throw is slightly off to either side, you can pull it in by shifting your right foot without leaving your position. However, if the throw is far off-line, abandon the tagging position and do what you must to get a glove on the ball. If the runner decides to come in standing up, roll away from him as you apply the tag. Avoid head-on collisions.

A catcher cannot block the plate unless he is receiving a throw or is already in possession of the ball — otherwise it's obstruction.

Getting help

Catchers should have no difficulty seeing runners break from first when a right-handed hitter is at the plate. However, a left-handed hitter may block his view. Your first baseman has to let you know when the runner is taking off. (You should anticipate the steal on every pitch.)

Neither lefties nor righties can obstruct your view when a runner tries to heist third. However, with a righty at the plate, the angle of the pitch determines the launching point of your throw. On outside pitches, step forward with your right foot and then step toward third with your left so you can throw in front of the hitter. If the pitch arrives inside, throw from behind the hitter. Step to the side with your left foot, shift your weight to your right, step toward third with your left, and throw.

Pickoffs and pitchouts

Pitchers aren't the only players who can pick a runner off base. The catcher can also initiate a pickoff play whenever a runner strays too far from a bag. If the count is favorable (one ball or less), you can begin the pickoff play with a *pitchout*. After first signaling your pitcher, step into the opposite batter's box just as he starts to the plate; jump in earlier and you risk committing a balk. Ideally, the pitchout should come to you at your letters, but be prepared for a throw that is either too low or too high. As soon as you get the ball, throw to the fielder covering the targeted base.

When the count is not in your favor, call for a strike on the outside corner to set up the *pickoff*. As your pitcher delivers the ball, step back into throwing position with your right foot. Close your body by bringing both hands to the top of the letters. Pivot off your right foot, step in the direction of your target with your left foot, and throw.

You want the umpire to call a strike, so don't pop up too soon or you may obstruct his view of the pitch.

Fielding pop-ups

The best way to field pop-ups is to do it by the numbers:

1. **As the ball goes up, turn your back to the field and scan the sky for the ball.**
2. **Move toward the ball with your catcher's mask in your bare hand. (If you throw it too early, you risk tripping over it.)**
3. **After the ball reaches its apex and you sense where it will descend, toss your mask away and move in for the catch.**
4. **Catch the ball over your head with both hands.**

   The fingers of your glove should be slanted upward. Don't stab. Allow the ball to come to you.

After judging where a pop is going to come down, it's usually wise to back up one more step so that the ball doesn't wind up behind you — fouls usually drift back a little more than one expects.

Right-handed hitters usually pop up inside pitches to the right and outside pitches to the left. Left-handed batters do the reverse.

"The pop-up behind home plate reacts like a banana. The ball will drift towards the stands as it goes up and curve back towards the field when it descends. So when the ball is popped up in back of you, turn around quickly, stop, and slowly move towards the ball while remembering it will come back to you a few feet." — Johnny Bench

Thwarting the bunt

The catcher is in the best position to field and throw balls bunted directly in front of the plate. When the ball is bunted in your territory, stay low as you pounce in front of the plate, scoop the ball up with both hands, and then make your throw. (See Figure 7-8.) Your attention should be on the bunt, so call for the ball loudly to avoid a collision with any incoming fielders. When the bunt is beyond your reach, become a traffic cop. Call out which fielder should handle the ball and tell him where to throw it.

Let the force be with you

When the bases are *loaded* (a runner on every base) and a ground ball is hit, anticipate that the infielder will throw home for the force-out. You do not have to tag the runner to get the out. You simply must touch home plate while possessing the ball. When a force at home is in order, toss your mask away. Plant your right foot in the middle of home plate so you can move in either direction on a bad throw. Put your left foot in front of the plate. Be pre-pared to stretch like a first baseman to snare a short throw. With less than two outs, forget about the base runner as soon as you catch the ball. He's out! (Remember, your foot was on the plate.) Immediately pivot to your right, face first, and throw to complete the double play.

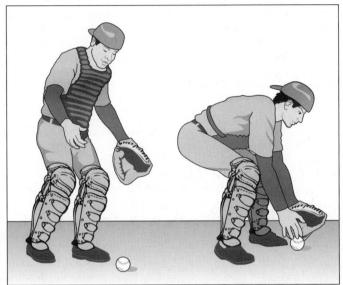

Figure 7-8:
Scooping
up a bunt.

You Can't Hide at First Base

Keith Hernandez and Willie McCovey will act as our guides at first base. I've never seen a better first baseman than Keith; no one could match him cover-ing the hole between first and second or charging bunts. Mr. Hernandez won more Gold Gloves (11) than any other first baseman, and in 1979, he shared a National League MVP award with Willie Stargell.

Hall of Famer Willie McCovey played first base for 22 seasons, most of them with the San Francisco Giants and San Diego Padres. Willie won the Rookie of the Year Award in 1959 and was named MVP in 1969. His work at first base earned him the name "Stretch" — an homage to his ability to keep one foot on the bag while reaching wild throws.

"We have to dispel the myth that first base is an old man's position, and that you can put just anybody at the bag and expect them to play it well. The first base-man handles the ball more than anyone on the field except the pitcher or catcher. So you must have good hands. You have to have a little quarterback in you to lead the pitcher with your throws when he goes for the putout at first. A first baseman has to save wild throws from his infielders. Quick reactions are a

must. If you charge in on a bunt, and the ball goes to the third-base side, you must immediately retract to get back to cover first. First basemen have so many responsibilities. You cannot hide a defensively weak player eak at this position."
— *Willie McCovey*

"You have time to make a methodical decision on what the ball will do: Will it sink, will it run, will it be a short hop in the dirt, will it be over my head, or will it be a long pop? About the only play where you don't have much time is the little chopper to your second baseman. He has to come in running, bare-hand the ball, and throw it to you underhand. That's the toughest throw from the infield. A boom-boom play, he's throwing on the run and he's putting everything on it because it's going to be close. You have to commit before the throw is there and hope he makes the throw somewhere close to you.

"When you're holding a runner on first base, that's when it becomes a hot corner, a little bit like third base. You have to react quickly. My father was a good fielding first baseman and the greatest drill he ever taught me was when I was learning to scoop, which requires good reflexes. He used a tennis ball so that if I got hit in the face I didn't get hurt. Even if you're a major leaguer switching to first base and you've never played there before, it's a good way to get over any initial fear. Go to first and have someone throw you short hops, in-between hops, bad throws. You know that tennis ball isn't going to hurt you, so you can concentrate and develop the skills to read the ball and react. As a kid, I also used to throw the ball for hours off the garage door. I'd get closer and closer to the door and throw as hard as I could. That's certainly working your reflexes."
— *Keith Hernandez*

Developing footwork and balance

"You have to be graceful; a first baseman should have loose muscles so he can move easily. Rudolf Nureyev, the ballet star, once came to me after a game and said I moved like a ballet dancer in the field. That was the greatest compliment I ever received for my fielding. If you're awkward, take a ballet class or study tai chi or some other discipline to improve your balance. If you weight train, make sure you stretch those muscles to stay loose." — *Willie McCovey*

Taking target practice

First basemen should generally play as deep as they can in the field. However, they must be able to get to the bag and set a target in time for the other fielders to make their throws. Taking those throws while putting your foot on first for the out has to become second nature. Your foot should hit the front inside corner of the bag. (See Figure 7-9.)

"Learning footwork is the most difficult transition for anyone just starting to learn how to play first base. You can't master that overnight. First base has to become second nature, an extension of your body. I remember the first drills I had with my father. When you take throws, you're straddling the bag and then you just kind of skip, back left, back right. A little curl-hop back and forth. So one time your right foot is on the corner of the bag on the side facing the catcher, and then you come back and your left foot is on the outfield side of the bag. Back and forth, back and forth. Then do it from two or three steps away. Then you expand it. After a while, I got within five feet of the bag and that would be my last look at it. I knew where it was. You do this drill relaxed. Loose arms, loose legs, like you're dancing. Don't look down. If you have to look down for the bag in the beginning, fine. When you can do it without looking down, you're gaining familiarity with the bag." — Keith Hernandez

You should have your target at first set when the infielder looks up to throw. Keep your weight evenly balanced on the balls of your feet so you can immediately shift to your left or right. Willie says, "A good first baseman will anticipate a bad throw on every play. That way he can easily adjust." Make sure your body is facing the fielder. Don't stretch for a ball until it's in the air and you are sure of its direction.

Figure 7-9:
Taking
the throw
at first.

Handling bad throws

Low throws are usually the toughest to handle. Try to take the low throw before it bounces. If you can't do that, get to it as soon as it hops so it won't bounce away from you. On high throws, you can stay on the bag while stretching for the ball, make a leaping grab off the bag, or move back into foul territory.

"Any time you get a bad throw, your first objective is to catch the ball. Don't worry about keeping your feet on the bag or getting the base runner out. If you catch the ball but it's too late to get the runner, you have a man on first. However, if the ball gets past you because you were stuck on the bag, the runners can advance an extra base." — Willie McCovey

On plays where the pitcher or second baseman is too close to you to make a hard overhand throw, he will probably try to feed you an underhanded toss. Help him by setting a big target with your glove.

"You would be surprised by the number of pitchers who cannot properly throw to first base after making a play. On those soft toss plays, you have to anticipate that the pitcher will throw it over your head." — Willie McCovey

Holding on

When you *hold a runner on,* you shorten his lead off first to deny him a head start to second. Place the back of your right foot against the front inside corner of first while keeping your left foot along the base line. Your feet should be no more than shoulder length apart. Give your pitcher a good waist-high target with your glove.

As the ball is delivered to the plate, cross over with your left foot and bounce as quickly as you can toward second base. Get in a position to cover as much fair territory as possible. As the pitch approaches the plate, you should be in your crouch, facing the batter.

When runners are on first or second, or the man on first is slow, the first baseman can play *behind the runner* rather than hold him on. To play behind the runner, position yourself just inside the runner's left shoulder.

When second base is not occupied, make sure that the pitcher knows when you play behind a runner. Pitchers need to be reminded not to make a pickoff throw. Never assume that the pitcher knows instinctively that you've chosen to play behind a slow runner.

Covering bunts

Play bunts aggressively or you won't play them at all. Charge the plate as your pitcher delivers the ball home. Countless baseball instructional guides advise first basemen to listen for their catchers to tell them where their throws are going (first, second, or third). This advice is fine if you're not playing in a packed stadium where the roar of the crowd makes it impossible to hear yourself think. Under those conditions, you must be able to immediately recognize where the play is developing and throw accordingly.

"Stay aggressive. When someone bunted, I always felt that if I didn't get the lead runner, I failed. I also realized that if a player got down a great bunt, there was only so much you could do. Or if a speed burner was on first like they had on the Cardinals — say Vince Coleman or Ozzie Smith or Tommie Herr — you weren't going to throw one of those guys out unless it was a horrible bunt.

"You come up with the ball ready to throw to second and then you make your decision. If you see there is no play, you have plenty of time to throw to first base. I see so many guys come in on the bunt as if they've already made up their minds to get the easy out (at first base), even when the pitcher's running. Even if a pitcher's running hard, most of them aren't fast. You have time to field that bunt aggressively and in the same motion make as if you are going to throw to second. And if you make your read and there's no out at second, just reset and throw to first." — Keith Hernandez

"Usually everyone in the stadium knows when a bunt is in order. However, there are some players and managers who will try to surprise you with a bunt. (Note: This usually occurs when the batter is trying to bunt for a base hit rather than a sacrifice.) If you study hitters closely, you can pick up some signs that telegraph a bunt is coming. For instance, some batters will look down towards you for an extra moment or two before bunting the ball your way. Other guys might choke up on the bat a little bit more. Watch what each hitter does when he bunts, and remember any quirks you can detect." — Willie McCovey

Fielding cutoff throws

If runners are in scoring position, the first baseman is responsible for cutting off the throw on balls hit to right or center. The third baseman takes most cut-offs from left, but if he can't get into position, you have to cover for him. Give your outfielder a good target by holding your hand and glove chest high. (All infielders should do this.) Where should you stand to receive the cutoff? Some coaches advise that you take it at a midpoint between second base and the pitcher's mound. Others want you to cut the ball off from behind the mound.

"There is an advantage to cutting the ball off between second base and the pitcher's mound. If you are behind the mound, on the home plate side of the diamond, you risk having the ball hit the mound or pitching rubber and bouncing away from you." — Willie McCovey

"You have to read whether the throw is going to clear the mound, or hit the mound and kick up into the air. And you have plenty of time to read it; it's a long throw in. There's no rush to make a judgment. You even have time to check where the runners are." — Keith Hernandez

As you accept the relay from the outfield, wave your arms so the outfielder doesn't waste time trying to find you. Listen for a teammate (usually your catcher) to tell you where your throw is going (or if you should let the ball go through). The instructions should be this simple:

✔ "Cut, Cut!" — Cut off the ball and hold it.

✔ "Cut and Relay!" — Cut off the ball and throw to a specific base.

If the fielder thinks you should let the ball go through, he shouldn't yell anything. When you are setting up for a relay, line up your body in the same direction as your target. For example, if you are throwing to third, your body should be facing left center.

"Catch the ball on your glove side so you don't have to turn all the way around to throw. Practice catching the ball, taking it out of your mitt, and delivering the throw all in one graceful motion. Too many first basemen break this down into two parts. That extra motion is often the difference between a runner being safe or out." — Willie McCovey

"Once you make up your mind that you are going to cut off the throw, don't wait for the ball to come to you. Commit. Rush to the ball so you cut a second off the throw." — Keith Hernandez

When the pitcher must cover first

If you play deep, the pitcher is going to cover many grounders hit to the right side. He heads to first base in case you can't get there in time to make the tag on your own. If you can get to the ball and field it near first base, make the tag (tag the base) yourself. Make sure you wave off the pitcher so he is out of harm's way.

When fielding the ball takes you too far from first to make an unassisted putout, you must get the ball to your pitcher. If the distance is short enough, lead the pitcher to first with a firm underhanded toss that hits him chest-high. Balls fielded on their way to the second-base hole may require you to throw overhand. Again, you should lead the pitcher to the bag with a chest-high toss.

"A lot of first basemen will catch the ball, stay where they caught it, and then underhand it to the pitcher. Catch the ball and run towards the bag! Give the pitcher a big shovel pass, as if you're throwing a bowling ball. You're shortening the distance between the throw, making it easier for the pitcher. Try to hit him with the throw waist- to letter-high." — Keith Hernandez

Doing the 3-6-3 (first-to-short-to-first double play)

Many first basemen will tell you this play is the most difficult play they make. To initiate this double play if you're left-handed (as most first basemen should be), pivot clockwise — to your glove-hand side — to unleash a throw.

If you're right-handed and the ball is hit directly at you, turn clockwise to throw. However, if the ball is hit to your left, you probably have to pivot counter-clockwise before throwing.

Your first throw is the key to making this double play. Nine out of ten times, you field the ball in the same line as the runner going to second. You must be able to throw the ball to your shortstop without hitting that runner. Then you have to get back to bag for the return throw. Because this play is always going to be close, you need to stretch before catching the ball on the return. (Sometimes this play goes 3-4-3, first-to-second-to-first. If he must throw to the second baseman, the first baseman's responsibilities remain the same.)

"Make sure you get that lead runner. Too many first basemen are so concerned with getting back to the bag to get that second out, they end up throwing the ball away and fail to get anyone. If you don't have a clear shot, take an extra side-step to create a throwing lane to the shortstop. Try to get the throw to your short-stop in a spot to his liking. (Note: Many favor receiving the ball chest high.) But if you can't do that, make the best throw you can and depend on the shortstop's athleticism to complete the play." — Willie McCovey

"I just realized one day while I was taking ground balls, that I was always look-ing at my throw to make sure it was perfect. I said to myself, 'Once it's out of my hand, even if it's a bad throw, I can't do anything about it. So why waste my time looking at it.' I wanted to make sure the throw was good so I'd watch it fifteen, twenty feet out of my hand, and that wasted two seconds getting back to the bag. Now the key, obviously, is not to break back to first base too soon, before you get rid of the ball. So I just started working on it. Once that ball was out of my hand, I might have looked at it for a split second but then I got back to the bag." — Keith Hernandez

Second (Base) to None

Joe couldn't find a second baseman for this team, so he's doing the honors himself. His collaborator, editor, and publishers couldn't be more pleased. From 1973 to 1977, Joe's play at second won him five consecutive National League Gold Glove awards. He was tutored in the field by two of the greatest second basemen in baseball history — Nellie Fox and the Grand Master of the Keystone, Bill Mazeroski.

Setting up

A second baseman's stance in the field should distribute his weight evenly on the balls of both feet. This position allows you to move easily to one side or another. As the pitcher goes into his windup, look directly at the batter. But don't look at his body. Instead, imagine he is swinging through a rectangular box that is as wide as home plate and extends from his shoulders to the tops of his toes. Watch that box. The ball will come to you from some spot within it. Make sure you're on the balls of your feet and ready to move when you see the bat and ball collide. (See Figure 7-10.)

"Be relaxed but alert at all times in the field. If you stay in one position too long, your body will tense; this will slow your reactions when the ball is hit. To alleviate tension, move your hands while you are in your stance. I often rested my hands on my knees as the pitcher wound up. An infielder has to do that to ensure that he is bending forward far enough. But as soon as the pitcher released the ball, I would raise my hands about 5 inches to give myself greater freedom of movement." — Joe Morgan

Your skills and the situation determine how deeply you play your position. However, if you're fielding on artificial turf, the ball will shoot to you much quicker than it will on grass. Play two to five steps deeper. You should also remember that you can't slide to a ball hit to either side of you on the turf. You have to field the ball and continue moving.

Whose ball is it, anyway?

On balls stroked up the middle of the diamond, who has first call: the shortstop or the second baseman? That's the shortstop's ball. Because he is moving toward first base on the play, he can make a stronger, more accurate throw than the second baseman (who is moving away from first).

"Just because it's the shortstop's play doesn't mean you don't have any responsibility. Get behind your shortstop and be ready to catch the ball in case it gets by him." — Joe Morgan

Blocking the ball

Nellie Fox was a three-time Gold Glove winner who led American League second basemen in putouts nine times. He taught me the best way to stop a ball you cannot catch cleanly from entering the outfield: Get down on one knee and block it with your body.

If this posture is not comfortable, find another way to get down on the ball. With a runner on second, do everything possible — dive in front of it if you have to — to prevent the ball from rolling into the outfield. Your methods may lack grace, but they get the job done.

"Because the second baseman rarely makes a long throw, he doesn't always have to catch a ball cleanly. Always remember that if you simply knock a ball down, you will usually have plenty of time to toss out the runner." — Joe Morgan

Figure 7-10:
Getting
ready for
the play.

Getting the ball to first

When you have to throw the ball to someone like our friend Willie McCovey at first base, aim for an area between his belt buckle and his chest. This strategy allows you some margin of error if your throw is too high or low. Your throws should be on the money as often as possible. If you have to take a throw from a teammate, give him a chest-high target.

In most situations, you can wait until the first baseman reaches his bag before throwing to him. However, if the runner is some flash like Carlos Beltran or Marlon Byrd, you may not have time to see if the first baseman is in place. Your job in that instance is to throw the ball to the bag; it's the first sacker's responsibility to somehow get to it.

"Make sure any player you are throwing to gets a good look at the ball. Take it out of your glove as quickly as possible so he can see it in your hand. This will help him to better gauge your throw's velocity and trajectory. When you bring back your arm to throw, make sure your glove doesn't block your target's view of the ball." — Joe Morgan

Preventing grand larceny: Defending against the steal

One of the oldest maxims in baseball dictates who covers second — the shortstop or second baseman — on an attempted steal. The shortstop covers if the batter is left-handed. When the batter is right-handed, the second baseman has to make the play. However, like all good rules, this one does have its exception. If the batter is a good hit-and-run man or opposite field hitter like Placido Polanco, the second baseman and shortstop can switch assignments. Placido is a right-handed batter who excels at hitting behind the runner. Any second baseman who covers the bag on every steal attempt is inviting Placido to slap the ball through the vacated hole and into right field. So you have to play the major-league version of cat-and-mouse with him. Your shortstop may cover for a pitch or even two. Then you may cover for the next couple of pitches. Keep switching so he doesn't know whether to pull the ball or go the other way.

"You and your shortstop must communicate to each other who will cover on the attempted steal. Before the game, decide between yourselves who will make the call. Keep the signals simple. Shield the front of your face with your glove. When you want your shortstop to cover second, open your mouth and purse your lips as if you were saying, 'You!' If you are going to take the catcher's throw, keep your mouth closed with your lips tightened to indicate, 'Me!'" — Joe Morgan

Picking runners off

In a *pickoff play,* the pitcher tries to catch a runner off base with an unexpected throw. You're not merely jockeying for an out with this play; you're also attempting to reduce the runner's lead. Just the threat of a pickoff can appreciably change the game. With the runner anchored at the base, your outfielders have a better opportunity to throw him out on a base hit; you have more time to execute plays in the infield.

"If the second baseman is covering the bag on the pickoff play, the shortstop must get behind him to back up any errant throws. If the shortstop is covering, the second baseman must reciprocate." — Joe Morgan

Pickoff plays come in two basic varieties.

- ✔ In the **time play,** the pitcher signals to the infielder covering second by glancing at him before looking toward the catcher. As the pitcher faces home, he and the infielder start counting, "One second, two seconds, three seconds." On three, the pitcher spins and throws; the infielder breaks for the bag. If everything is in sync, the infielder and the throw should arrive at second base simultaneously.
- ✔ **Daylight pickoff** plays don't require a count. The pitcher whirls and throws to second as soon as he sees a large enough space or "daylight" between the infielder and the runner.

"I dislike daylight plays because they can so easily backfire. Suppose you're trying to fake a runner back to the bag. The pitcher might mistakenly think you're breaking for second. If he attempts a pickoff, you have to scramble back to make the play. Often, you can't. The ball flies untouched into center field, the runner races to second or even home. Stick to the time play; there's less opportunity for error." — Joe Morgan

Executing the rundown

Rundowns occur (among other times) when a pickoff traps a runner between two bases. While tossing the ball to each other, you and your teammates chase the runner back and forth until he can be tagged. Making as few throws as possible is the key to an effective rundown. The more throws you make, the greater the chance one of you will toss the ball away.

After the rundown begins, you should try to force the runner back to the base he just left. The fielder with the ball should hold it high and away from his glove so the other fielders can see it. Whoever is waiting to receive the throw must give the player with the ball a target. For example, say a right-handed throwing teammate is chasing the runner back to you at second. You should stand to the left of the incoming runner. This position affords the thrower a clear view of your glove. If the thrower is left-handed, take a step to the other side. By using your glove as a target, your teammate is less likely to hit the runner with the throw.

During rundowns, fielders must stay out of the base line while they await the ball. If you stand in line with the runner, his body may prevent you from seeing your teammate's throw. If the runner crashes into you on the base line when you don't have the ball, the umpire can award him the bag on fielders' interference, also called *obstruction*.

"Never fake a throw during a rundown; you might fake out your teammates as well as the runner. Always hold the ball high so your teammate can see it. Cock your arm back only when you intend to release the ball. When you're not involved in a rundown, choose an unoccupied base to back up. Stay out of the action unless the ball gets by someone and comes in your direction." — Joe Morgan

Tagging the big-league way

When a runner slides into a base you're defending, tag him on his foot, toe, or whatever other part of his anatomy is closest to the bag. Try to tag his hand if he attempts a head-first slide. Tag a runner who arrives at the base standing up anywhere you can reach him.

Don't attempt a tag with the pocket of your glove facing the runner or he may kick the ball away from you. (And yes, that's a legal play. New York Giants second basemen Eddie Stanky pulled it on New York Yankees shortstop Phil Rizzuto during the 1951 World Series. The ball went trickling into center field. Instead of being called out, Stanky was safe. The Giants went on to score five runs that inning.) Instead, hold the ball firmly as you swipe the runner with the back of your glove.

Covering first

Both your pitcher and first baseman usually try to field any slow-hit balls between first and the pitcher's mound. With first base unattended, the second baseman must cover. You must become a first baseman. Go to the inside of the bag with your rear foot. Lean into the diamond to give the thrower a proper chest-high target with your glove. Maintain your balance so you can spring to either side on a bad throw.

Handling relays and cutoffs at second

You're playing second base. With a man on first, the batter smacks the ball down the right field line. Cinch double. What do you do? Don't stand at second waiting for a throw. Instead, turn to face the right fielder from a point midway between first and second base. If the runner on first tries to score, your job is to relay the right fielder's throw to the catcher at home plate. If the runner is heading toward third when you get the ball, try to nip him at that base. (Check out Joe's Baseball Playbook in Chapter 9 to study your assignments on all of baseball's basic plays.)

Any time the batter drives a ball into the gap (between the outfielders), there's going to be a relay. Make sure the outfielder makes the longest throw; between the two of you, he should have the stronger arm. Go out just far enough for the outfielder to reach you with a throw. After you get the ball, your job is to deliver a short, accurate throw to the appropriate base.

On balls hit to the left or left center field gaps, the shortstop accepts the relay. The second baseman must back up any balls that get by him. You must also let the shortstop know where to throw the ball. If he has to turn and look, he surrenders about 12 feet (3.6 meters) to the runner. While the outfielder's throw is in flight, observe the runners so you can tell the shortstop which base offers the best opportunity for a play. Identify the bag by yelling to the shortstop, "Second base!" or "Third base!" or "Home plate!"

Turning two

Ask any infielder: The *double play* (DP) is the greatest play in baseball (other than the triple play, which is so rare you can't even think about it). When you turn a double play in a crucial situation, you immediately become the most popular guy on your club. Teammates shower you with high fives, pitchers want to buy you dinner, and managers name their firstborn after you. Nothing short of a win is more pleasing to a fielder than getting two outs with one ball.

Carly Simon knew the secret to executing the double play: Anticipation. (Great, now we're going to have *that* song humming in our heads for the rest of the month!) Whenever the opportunity for the double play presents itself — runners on first, first and second, or first, second, and third with less than two out — the second baseman must automatically think about turning two. Move a couple of steps closer to second and in toward the plate. You sacrifice a little range with this positioning, but it enables you to get to the bag quickly.

Charge for the base as soon as the ball is hit to the left side of the diamond. When you get within three steps of second base — and with practice, you instinctively know when you are — shorten your stride. Take choppier, quicker steps to ensure that you don't overrun the bag. You must maintain body control as you reach second, or you'll have trouble adjusting to a poor throw.

If you're a novice at second, look for the bag when you first run toward it. After you know where it is, put your focus on the fielder. Give him the best chest-high target you can. However, stay alert in case the ball veers off on an angle. As the fielder cocks to throw, your attention should go to the ball.

"The double play transpires so quickly, you must eventually learn to locate the bag without looking. When I first came up to the Major Leagues, I would work on starting the double play with our first baseman and shortstop for an hour and a half a day before practice. We did this until I was able to get to the bag without even glancing at it." — Joe Morgan

To complete the double play, you must catch the ball, force-out the runner from first by tagging second base, pivot, and relay the ball to your first baseman. It sounds like several parts, but they're all parts of the same motion held together by your pivot. (See Figure 7-11.) You have different ways to pivot on the double play:

✔ Many second basemen straddle the bag. As they catch the ball, second base is between their feet. They touch the bag with their left foot while throwing to first.

✔ Second basemen with unusually strong arms sometimes use the push-off method. They catch the ball behind the bag, tag the front of the base with their rear foot, and then push off it as if it were a pitching rubber for their throws to first.

"I learned the quickest and, in my opinion, best way to pivot by studying Bill Mazeroski. As a Gold Glove second baseman with the Pittsburgh Pirates, Maz led National League second basemen in double plays a record eight consecutive seasons (1960 to 1967). He was, and remains, the unchallenged king of the DP. Like Maz, I would catch my shortstop's throw out in front of my body. While crossing second, I would step on the center of the bag with my left foot. Then I would pivot and throw from wherever I caught the ball. If I gloved the ball high, my throw would be overhand or three-quarters. Feed the ball to me at my waist, and I relayed it sidearm. Any ball caught below my waist was delivered to first with an underhand toss. Your primary concern is to get rid of the ball as quickly and accurately as you can. Some players drag their foot across the bag when making the force-out at second. I think that practice upsets a fielder's rhythm on the double play. If you instead step on the center of the bag, your motion continues uninterrupted. This also helps build some momentum behind your throw to first." — Joe Morgan

Figure 7-11:
The pivot for
the double
play.

The care and feeding of your shortstop

Some double plays require a role reversal: Your shortstop makes the pivot.
You have to field the ball and then feed it to him for the relay to first. It is
important to know where your double-play partner prefers to catch the ball.

Note: Many second basemen throw to the shortstop backhand in a double
play — a backhand throw is less likely to sail high than an underhand toss. If
you're close enough to the bag to do so, a backhand throw is preferred.

*"For example, when I was with the Reds, our shortstop Davey Concepcion liked
to take the throw on the outfield side of second. So I would give it to him chest-
high (the easiest ball to handle and throw while on the move) on the bag's outside edge. I've also played with some shortstops who wanted my toss on the
inside of the bag. However, no matter what your shortstop prefers, you shouldn't
wait to make the ideal throw. If you're off balance, get the ball to your partner
any way you can and let him make the adjustment. If your double-play partner
hasn't reached the bag, feed the ball to him wherever he is. Never make him
wait for the ball or you can disrupt his timing." — Joe Morgan*

Dealing with the runner

As I've said, the second baseman's job is to make the double play before looking for the incoming runner. If you're continually concerned about getting hit
at second, you can't play the position. One way to defend yourself against a

collision is to get the ball to first as soon as you can. Don't worry about hitting the runner. Your quick throw will compel him to slide that much sooner. The sooner he slides, the longer it takes him to reach you at the base.

A last word on second

None of the suggestions I've just passed on to you are absolutes. Eighty percent of the time, you execute a play at second in the manner I've described in this chapter. However, some situations — such as when a throw is off line or the runner arrives at second faster than you anticipated — demand improvisation. When these situations occur, remember that your bottom line is to make the play any way you can. Get the out!

Cookin' at the Hot Corner

Third base is called the *hot corner* because the third baseman is so close to home plate he tends to field a lot of hot smashes. The position demands a strong arm, hair-trigger reflexes, and a ton of heart. All three attributes come to mind when we think about our third base "coach," the 1996 National League Most Valuable Player Ken Caminiti of the San Diego Padres.

The basic stance

Plays develop so quickly at the hot corner that third basemen must be able to shift out of position in an instant. Many third basemen set up in the lowest crouch on the field so they can spring up to the left or right. Ken won three consecutive Gold Gloves without the benefit of an exaggerated crouch.

"For my basic stance — we're talking about when I don't smell bunt or some other play — I put my left foot slightly behind my right foot and bounce back on it. Now my focus is on the hitter, but I watch the pitcher with my peripheral vision. As he brings his leg down and arm through in his windup, I bring my left foot parallel with my right while transferring my weight evenly to the balls of both feet. As the ball crosses the plate, I bend forward a bit but not in a full squat. This leaves me balanced and open to move freely to either side." — Ken Caminiti

That word again: Anticipation

Ken didn't rely solely on his reflexes and proper weight distribution to glove the bazooka shots aimed his way. Like all great third basemen, he combined a sixth sense with concrete data to anticipate where the batter was likely to hit the ball.

"Most of the time, I like to know what the pitcher is throwing to a batter, so I can prepare myself accordingly. So I will peek through the batter's legs to pick up a catcher's signs to the pitcher. Or I might have the shortstop relay the sign. I prefer to take them directly from the catcher, so there's no chance of miscommunication. Let's say the catcher calls for something off-speed. If the batter begins to swing before that pitch reaches the plate, you know he has to hit that ball down the line or into foul territory. You're going to lean towards the line. The trick is to focus not on contact but before the ball meets the bat." — Ken Caminiti

Checking the real estate

Before the first game of every away series, the third baseman (as well as the other fielders) should examine how a ballpark's topography may affect play. Never take anything for granted; groundskeepers or the elements may have altered a park since you last played there.

"I'll spend some time seeing just how far it is from my position to the stands; that tells me how far I can run without banging into a railing. I'm going to roll the ball down the line to see if it tends to stay fair or roll foul. That helps me decide if I'm going to pick up that bunt down the line or let it go." — Ken Caminiti

Fast hands for slow rollers

The grab and throw on bunts or slow rollers tapped to third is among the most difficult of all infield plays. Ken fielded those balls as well as anyone who has ever played the position.

"To make those plays, you have to first get a good jump on the ball. On the bunt, try to key off the hitter to see if he gives it away (before trying to lay it down). His back foot can tell you a lot. For instance, a lot of right-handed hitters will drop that back foot before attempting a drag bunt. Left-handed hitters can be more difficult to spot. Kenny Lofton — who's probably the best I've seen at this — waits to the last moment and then just drops the bat on the ball. Brett Butler (one of the great bunters of the past 20 years) did the same thing. I try to take the bunt away from guys like him by playing all the way in and daring him to hit it by me. On those slow rollers, you have to bust it as hard as you can the moment you see the play. But you also have to maintain your timing. Get to the ball with stutter steps so that your left foot is even with the ball when you drop down to scoop it. Depending on how quickly you get there and the runner's speed, you glove the ball, take a step towards the base you're throwing to, and let it rip. On some plays, though, you just have to bare-hand the ball and throw in one continuous motion. That's a do-or-die play; you don't think, just react." — Ken Caminiti

Figure 7-12 shows you how to bare-hand the slow roller.

Figure 7-12:
Fielding and
throwing the
slow roller
in one
motion.

Playing mind games

Persuade a runner to hang close to third base, and you decrease his chances of scoring on a short fly ball or hard-hit grounder. How do you get a runner to anchor near third? Ken employed numerous fakes and moves to keep the runner honest.

"I'll make a move towards third or fake one to get the runner back, to keep him thinking. If you suspect a squeeze play is on (when the batter tries to bunt the runner on third base home), you can stand right next to the runner so he can't get too big a lead. When the pitcher starts up, I'll dart back to the bag just to cross the runner up." — Ken Caminiti

A basic rule to get two

Middle infielders usually attempt to get the ball to each other in a particular spot — at the letters, to the inside of the bag — on the double play. Their proximity to each other allows them this luxury. As Ken points out, third basemen don't need to be quite as specific.

"Things happen so quickly at third, many times the shortstop or second baseman hasn't reached the bag by the time you're ready to throw. So I just try to throw the ball directly over the base and let the fielders get to it. If a fielder is already at the base, I try to deliver it to his glove side." — Ken Caminiti

Some last words from third

"You can't play this position scared. If you're just starting out, it may seem as if things happen too quickly at third, but your body will react in time if you let it. Take the field with the attitude that you want every ball hit to you and that you are going to make the play. Third base calls for a lot of long throws, so you must be able to throw overhand. However, there will be some plays where you don't have time for anything but a sidearm throw; you've got to know how much time you have to make the play. Who the runner is, how the ball is hit, and the angle from which you are throwing all factor into that decision. You have to know all these things if you're going to do your job. The key to having good range and quick reactions at third is concentration. Lay back and you are going to miss some plays you could have made. You should be focused on every pitch of the game so that you can anticipate your next move. By the end of the game, the third baseman should feel drained." — Ken Caminiti

Ranging Wide: Playing Shortstop

All the infield fundamentals reviewed in this chapter — throwing, fielding grounders, positioning, and so on — can be applied to this position. Shortstops should also read our section on second base. The shortstop is nearly a mirror of the second baseman except he has more ground to cover and must make longer throws. A second baseman's longest throw to first is barely more than 90 feet. The average throw for a shortstop to the same base is 110 feet. Because of the greater distance, you must be able to catch grounders cleanly or you won't survive at this position. If you knock balls down as a second baseman sometimes does, you may not have time to throw out the runner. Because you're responsible for so much territory, you must study the hitters throughout your league so you can position yourself properly in every situation.

Our coaches for this position are two shortstops who have proven they know how to handle big plays. New York Yankees captain Derek Jeter has been a human highlight film in nearly every postseason since he entered the majors in 1996. A six-time member of the American League All-Star team, Derek has played a pivotal defensive position on Yankee teams that have won seven divisional titles, six American League championships, and four World Series crowns. In 2004, he played the best defense of his career and earned a place on Rawlings' American League Gold Glove team.

In 1995, Barry Larkin of the Cincinnati Reds became only the fourth shortstop to win the National League's Most Valuable Player award. Barry has also won three Gold Gloves (1994–96) and helped lead the Reds to a World Series championship in 1990. In his prime, he earned a reputation as one of baseball's great double-play artists, as well as being one of the best throwing shortstops ever.

Setting up

Because you must roam to either side at short, keep your weight balanced. Your feet should be a little more than shoulder width apart with your legs bent slightly in a semi-crouch. You often have less time than any other infielder to make a play, so you must be continually thinking about how to react if the ball is hit a certain way. It's hard to turn on the jet packs from a stationary position, so put your body in motion by taking two steps forward as the pitch approaches the plate. You have a direct view to home plate. Watching the catcher's signs lets you know what the pitcher is going to throw. If you feel the hitter is going to hit a certain pitch to your left or right, cheat a step in that direction.

"The most important thing is to field the ball cleanly, and — for the advanced player — catch it with your momentum carrying you towards wherever you are going to throw, second or first. You always hear that you should look the ball into the glove, but you should also look at the ball as you remove it from the glove. A lot of times, guys catch the ball and immediately look for their target instead of at the ball — as if someone was going to move first base. Then they have to double-clutch or regrip the ball before throwing, and that can cost outs."
— Barry Larkin

"Probably the biggest key for me, because I'm tall, is to stay down. If the ball bounces up, you want to come up with the ball as opposed to going down and stabbing at it. So stay low. Once I have the ball, I try to pick up my target and make sure my momentum is going in his direction. The weight shift when you throw is very similar to when you're hitting. You plant your foot. As you bring back you arm, your weight goes into that back leg. Then you move your weight forward as you bring your arm around to throw." — *Derek Jeter*

Getting the ball to first

Shortstops often run full-out, so you must avoid tangling your legs. When you dart to your right, pivot on your right leg and cross over with your left. On balls hit to your left, do the reverse.

"When I throw to first, the first baseman's chest is the target. And I think the key is to throw through the target, not to it. That way I make sure I get something on the throw. You need a strong arm to play short. The best thing to build arm strength is playing long toss. I started doing that when I was younger and I still do it now before games. Just play catch at long distances, as far as you can throw it and as you get stronger, move back a little bit more." — *Derek Jeter*

"When you're in the hole and can't get on top of your throw, you might have to sidearm the ball to first base. You see a lot of inexperienced shortstops wasting a lot of motion trying to get something on that throw. If you're going toward first, get your wrist into the ball and snap off that throw. Your momentum will help

put something on the ball. If I'm moving toward third when I catch the ball, I contort my body to get off a throw. I try to keep my front (left) foot closed, so my toe is pointed toward the left field stands. Then I throw against my body and use torque to propel a snap throw. On a play like that, you don't have to throw the ball all the way to first. (Former Reds Gold Glove shortstop) Davey Concepcion taught me how to bounce the ball on one hop to the first baseman. Shortstops should work on that play in practice." — Barry Larkin

If you dive for a ball — something shortstops do frequently — you must get to your feet immediately. However, don't rush the play.

"Too often, young shortstops who dive start trying to throw the ball before they really catch it. Catch the ball, hit the ground, pop up, and make the throw. When a guy tries to throw the ball before he catches it, he stands a good chance of dropping it. With practice, you'll learn to pop up quickly after a dive with the ball securely in your possession. This should leave you plenty of time to get off a good throw. Studying martial arts helped me with this. One of the first things I learned was how to roll with a fall so I wouldn't be rigid when I hit the ground. If you can learn how to roll with your dive, your momentum will help get you to your feet." — Barry Larkin

Backhanded compliments

After ranging far to your right, you may still be unable to get in front of the ball. You have to make a backhand play in those situations.

"This should always be a play of last resort. You should be trying to increase your range daily so that you don't have to backhand too many plays. If you're not rangy, play a little deeper to compensate. When you do have to backhand the ball as you go towards the hole, try to catch it just beyond your left foot. Stop your momentum, plant on your right foot, step to your left and throw." — Barry Larkin

"When I backhand, I prefer to take it off the middle of my right feet. Then I can bring my left foot over and get momentum going towards first base. You can increase your range at shortstop by doing lateral movement drills, anything that gets you moving or shuffling side to side. Have someone roll a ball to your left, then your right, then have them mix it up. As you go along, (your partner) can roll the ball wider and wider until you're covering more ground." — Derek Jeter

Figure 7-13 shows you the position for a backhand play.

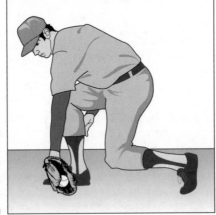

Figure 7-13:
The
backhand
play.

The wisdom of an open-glove policy

This advice should be common sense: It is much easier to catch a ball with a glove that is fully open than with one that is half or completely closed. All infielders should know this (although you would be surprised at how many major-league infielders approach grounders with half-opened mitts), but it is especially important for the shortstop, who has little time to bobble the ball.

As you reach the ball, slow down and bend with your legs rather than your back. Lower your glove on an angle to the ground and open the glove wide. The fingers should be touching the field and your palm should be lifted up slightly toward you. (See Figure 7-14.)

Figure 7-14:
The
shortstop's
glove has to
be ready.

Doubling up

Like the second baseman, the shortstop can start double plays (his usual function) or act as the pivot man. If the ball is hit within three or four steps of second base, you usually don't need to involve your second baseman. Simply step on the bag with your left foot, push off, and throw off your right foot. Do this in one fluid motion. In other double-play situations, the shortstop's role changes:

- ✔ On balls hit near second, but not close enough to permit an unassisted play, give your second baseman a chest-high, underhanded toss. Throw sidearm to your second baseman on balls hit directly to you or just to your right.

- ✔ You must turn the pivot on the double play on balls hit to the right side of the infield. Get to the bag immediately.

- ✔ When the ball is hit so far to your right that you have to extend, take the time to plant your right foot and make a strong throw to second. You usually get only the lead runner on this play (which, by the way, should always be your priority), though the second baseman may be able to turn two if your throw is strong and accurate (and the runner heading toward first isn't very fast).

- ✔ On slowly hit grounders, forget about the double play. The shortstop must know the speed of each base runner so he can decide whether to attempt the force at second or get the out at first.

"When I'm the pivot man on the double play, I prefer to receive the ball on the left field side of second. As I get to the bag, I slow my momentum so that I can adjust if the throw to me isn't where I expect it. On the pivot, if the ball is to my right, I step to it with my right foot and drag my left foot over the bag. If the throw is on my left, I step to it with my left foot and drag my right." — Barry Larkin

"The biggest key to remember is you can't get the double play unless you get that first out. Make sure you catch the ball and tag second. Then you turn your body towards first base, get that momentum going towards first for the throw, and remember to avoid the runner coming in." — Derek Jeter

A last word on playing shortstop

"The great plays — the diving catches, the behind-the-back flips — are made because your fundamentals are sound. You've studied your positioning; you're aware of the situation and all the things that can happen. When you catch the ball, you look it into your glove and watch as you take it out. You do all the basics. Then when the ball is hit, your athletic ability and reactions take over. The great plays will come naturally because you will be in position to make them." — Barry Larkin

"If you're not hitting (well) the biggest thing you must realize is that you have to separate the two (defense and offense). When you're playing shortstop, defense is more important than offense. You can always help your team win by making the plays in the field. Consistency is everything. Making the routine play, game after game, that's your job. You should always be thinking about what you're going to do before it happens. Depending on the situation, think about the different scenarios, so that when you get the ball, you're not surprised. You don't waste time thinking about what you're going to do. You already know."
— *Derek Jeter*

That Extra Infielder: The Pitcher

Retiring batters isn't the only responsibility pitchers have. When you're on the mound, you must cover a base or back up a fielder on nearly every play. (Refer to Chapter 9, the playbook, to learn your various assignments.) You have to be quick enough to flag down hot smashes up the middle (or at least get out of their way so one of your infielders can catch them) and pounce on bunts. When runners stray far from the bag, you have to drive them back with a look or a pickoff move. On many infield plays, you're the traffic cop directing your teammates, so you must stay cool and alert.

For advice on how pitchers can field their position properly, we turn to one of Joe's opponents from the 1975 World Series, Bill Lee. The Red Sox left-hander was one of the smoothest fielders in the game, quick on bunts, fundamentally sound on grounders, and capable of the amazing play. (The behind-the-back catch of line drives hit up the middle was a Lee specialty.)

Getting into fielding position: The follow-through

Pitching mechanics are covered in some depth in Chapter 6. Ideally, when you emerge from your follow-through, you should be in a position to field anything hit toward you. Your body should be squared toward home plate, your feet should be parallel and shoulder-width apart, and your weight should be evenly distributed over the balls of your feet. Few pitchers on any level come out of their follow-through perfectly positioned to field. However, you should strive to come as close to the ideal as you can.

"Never forget that your number-one concern is getting the hitter out. If you can't come out of your follow-through in the ideal fielding position, you can compensate by keeping your eyes peeled on home plate and watching for the ball off the bat. Then let your reactions take over if the ball is hit towards you."
— *Bill Lee*

Fielding aggressively

Try to field as many balls hit between you and first as you can. Anytime you can keep that first baseman near the bag, you're helping your team's defensive alignment.

- ✔ On bunt plays, charge balls that are hit directly toward you.
- ✔ On balls to the extreme side of you, field only those that look as if they will stop rolling before one of your infielders reaches it.

"As you go after the ball, don't focus on the runner. Instead, watch the ball into your glove. Don't rush your throw after fielding it. Get a good grip on the ball. Keep moving towards your target as you step and throw. If you have to spin and throw, keep a low center of gravity; it will make you quicker. If you're close to the base and the fielder isn't there, lead him to the bag with an underhand toss. However, if your fielder is on or near the bag and you aren't too close, hit the target he gives you with a strong overhand throw. Aim for his chest." — Bill Lee

On plays that require you to cover first base, go to a spot approximately 6 feet (1.8 meters) from first on the base line. Run parallel to the base line as you cut toward first. As you reach the bag, shorten your strides so you can adjust to any bad throws.

"Touch the inside of the base on the home plate side with your right foot. This will prevent your momentum from carrying you into the runner (a must to avoid) or into foul territory." — Bill Lee

Keeping runners close

Anytime you keep a base runner anchored near a base, you not only reduce his chances to steal, you also make it more difficult to take an extra base or score on a long hit. Making numerous pickoff throws will chase a runner back to a base. Bill recommends three other things you can do to hold a runner on without making a throw:

- ✔ Use the same motion to first as you do to home. Don't give the runner any extra movement to pick up on. Be especially careful that you don't reveal your intentions with slight head or eye movements. Good base runners are studying you constantly and pick up on the tiniest quirks.
- ✔ Disrupt the runner's timing by altering your rhythm as you move into your set position and go into your windup. Remember you're not changing movement here, just the timing of your movement. Don't fall into any consistent rhythms. Hold the ball during your set position for varying time periods.

✔ If you're left-handed, just watch the runner. If you don't move to throw, he can't go anywhere. (Well, technically he can, but the odds are you'll throw him out.)

"Always try to be quick to home plate. If the runner does take off, you will save your catcher a stride when he tries to throw the runner out. If you're slow to the plate, your catcher doesn't have a chance against the faster base stealers. He won't be able to get them unless he's Dirty Harry Callahan and he's toting his .44 Magnum." — Bill Lee

Catching the runner off base

You can attempt to pick off a runner anytime your foot is off the pitching rubber (that's to say when you are in the set position or going into your stretch). If you're a right-hander trying to pick off a runner at first, push off your right foot while pivoting toward the bag with your left foot. Keep your upper torso open so you throw overhand rather than across your body. (See Figure 7-15.)

Figure 7-15:
The right-hander's pickoff move.

Avoiding balks

Deceptiveness is one of the keys to an effective pickoff throw. However, you can't be so deceptive that the umpire calls you for a *balk* (see Appendix A for a definition). You can avoid balking while attempting a pickoff at first by doing the following:

✔ When you're in the set position, take the sign from your catcher with your foot on the rubber and your hands visibly separated.

✔ After you have your sign, bring your hands together and pause one full second before going into your delivery.

✔ If you swing your striding foot past the rear portion of the pitching rubber, you must deliver a pitch.

✔ Move only your head while in the set position. If you shrug your shoulders or move your legs or hands, the umpire can nail you for a balk.

✔ If you make any motion toward a base, throw to it. You must complete any movement you start without interruption until you are in the set position.

✔ Always step directly toward the bag you are throwing to. You may step and fake a throw to second or third, but you cannot fake a throw to first without first stepping off the rubber.

✔ If you want to move out of the set position without incurring a balk, step off the rubber.

✔ Never make a pitching motion unless you have the ball.

✔ Don't drop the ball during your delivery.

"It may sound funny, but don't even scratch your nose or wipe your mouth when you're on the rubber with a runner on first. I've seen guys called for balks for doing just those things. You're concentrating so hard on the hitter, something itches, and you just do the natural thing. Just make sure you step off the rubber first." — Bill Lee

If you're a left-hander, you don't need to pivot because you are already facing first. All you have to do is snap off a sidearm throw while stepping toward first. When you raise your striding leg out of the set position, there will be a moment when it points toward first. Unlike the right-hander, you now have the option of throwing to the bag or continuing your motion toward home plate. (See Figure 7-16.)

Pickoffs at second are more complicated. As Joe points out earlier (see "Picking runners off"), you can employ a time play by signaling your second baseman or shortstop as you check the runner at second. On a 1-2-3 time play, the count begins when you turn back to face the hitter. On two, you should turn back toward second as the fielder breaks for the bag. On three, throw the ball at the fielder's knees and over the base. On the daylight play, the fielder sneaks up near the bag. You throw as soon as you see daylight between the fielder (usually the shortstop) and the runner.

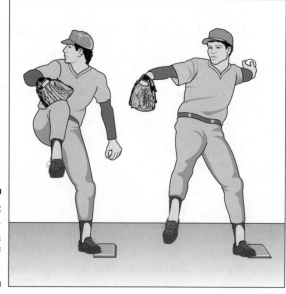

Figure 7-16:
The left-hander's pickoff move.

"I know Joe prefers the time play, but, as a pitcher, I have to go the other way. I like the daylight play's spontaneity and the fact that you are reacting to your shortstop's movements. Time plays can go awry if you and your fielder aren't synchronized. That was always a problem for me. My middle infielders were usually on Greenwich time and I was on Somalian time." — Bill Lee

You shouldn't attempt many pickoffs at third because it's a bad percentage play. Few runners steal home, and if you throw the ball away, you've just given the opposition a run. To pick the runner off at third, the right-hander and left-hander reverse the mechanics they use when throwing to first.

"Don't even think about this play with two outs. The runner cannot score on an out and no one wants to face his manager after making the inning-ending out on an attempted steal of home. Concentrate on the hitter; he's the one who can hurt you." — Bill Lee

Where Fly Balls Go to Die: Playing the Outfield

Oh boy, do outfielders have the life. They don't have to worry about kamikaze base runners bearing down on them during the double play, hot line drives sizzling toward their craniums, or which base to cover on any given play. All they have to do is saunter after the occasional fly ball, throw it back toward the infield, and work on their suntans.

Yeah, right.

Playing the outfield is like playing any other position. It demands discipline, hard work, and knowledge. You must be able to gauge fly balls that come at you from diverse angles, understand the mechanics behind a good throw, and know what to do with the ball after you catch it. On balls hit into the gap, you must sprint full out, time your extension and catch, and then throw to the right base in one fluid move.

Infielders can afford to take their time on many plays. Outfielders are so far from the action, they don't have a half-moment to spare on any ball that sets runners in motion. Infielders can bobble or even drop a ball and still record an out. If an outfielder drops a ball, the hitter is not only on first base, he probably takes an extra base. Outfielders don't collide with base runners, but they can run into the occasional wall. (And unlike human beings, those structures have no "give" to them.) So you have to know what you're doing out there to avoid hurting yourself and your team.

Our chief outfield coach is Mr. Center Field, the incomparable Willie Mays. We believe that Carly Simon, a die-hard baseball fan so we're quoting her twice, was thinking of Mays corralling a fly ball when she sang, "Nobody Does It Better." Willie holds the major-league record with 12 consecutive Gold Gloves for outfield play. He's also the all-time major-league leader in total outfield chances accepted. Runners rarely took liberties with Mays's powerful throwing arm. He once hit a long drive that fell just beyond the reach of a diving outfielder for extra bases. The broadcaster covering the game summed up Willie's fielding prowess by saying, "The only man who could have caught that ball just hit it."

Ken Griffey, Sr., the 1980 All-Star Most Valuable Player, also shares his thoughts on outfield play in this section. Griffey patrolled all three outfield positions during a 19-year major-league career spent largely with the Cincinnati Reds and New York Yankees. Sparky Anderson said, "Kenny is an example of how a person can make himself into an outstanding fielder through hard work. He was a defensive weapon wherever he played, and he charged the ball as well as any outfielder of his day." We also bring in Rusty Staub, a smart outfielder whose powerful throwing arm was feared throughout baseball, for a word or two of expertise.

Setting up

Because they have more real estate to cover, outfielders have more positioning options than infielders. Where you play depends on the hitter, the pitcher, the situation, and the count. For example, John Olerud is a left-handed hitter with good power to all fields. He can hit the ball with authority anywhere. However, against a hard-throwing right-hander like Pedro Martinez, John is more likely to pull the ball when the count is in his favor. Conversely, if a hitter is behind in the count (he has more strikes on him than balls), he tends to protect the plate and hit the ball to the opposite field. So if Martinez has a 3-ball 1-strike count on Olerud, Pedro's outfielders should shade closer toward right field.

However, if you're playing the outfield behind left-handed pitcher Randy Johnson, you may not move toward right if you don't believe Olerud can pull Johnson's fastball. And even that is not an absolute. Suppose it's a close game in the late innings and Johnson has lost some of the hop from his fastball. You may think that Olerud, who is looking to drive the ball for extra bases, may now indeed be able to pull on the tiring Johnson.

When setting up in the outfield, you must also consider your limitations and those of your teammates. Do you go back on balls well but have more difficulty on balls that pull you in? Play shallow. Do you move to your left better than your right? You have to compensate when a right-handed pull hitter is at the plate. Does your center fielder have a weak throwing arm? With the winning run on third and less than two out, you may have to take a ball that he would normally catch, so you can attempt the throw home. All of these factors — plus the field conditions for that day — determine where you play on each pitch.

Taking your basic stance

You should set up in the outfield with a square stance:

- ✔ Keep your feet parallel, shoulder-width apart, and pointed toward home plate.
- ✔ Get into a semi-crouch with your weight evenly distributed over the balls of both feet.
- ✔ Rest your hands on your knees but drop them as the ball approaches the plate.

This stance gives you momentum to chase the ball if it is hit beyond the infield. (See Figure 7-17.) Because your weight is evenly balanced over both feet, you can move to either side quickly. If it looks as if the ball will be hit over your head, put the toes of whatever foot is on the ball side behind the heel of your other foot. (This is called a *drop step.*)

"Get as loose as possible before the game starts. Give yourself 15 minutes to stretch, do calisthenics, and some light running. Don't bring any tension to the outfield; it will rob you of quickness." — Ken Griffey, Sr.

Figure 7-17:
The basic
outfield
stance.

Taking off from jump street

What is the one thing you hear said about any great outfielder? He gets a
good jump on the ball. Your eyes, ears, and head determine how quickly you
break for a fly ball. If you've done your homework, you should already know
where the batter most often hits the ball.

*"Getting a good jump on the ball starts at home plate. You have to know who is
hitting. If you don't know where the hitter tends to hit the ball, how can you get a
good jump on it? If you start moving as you see the ball coming over the infield,
you're too late. Study the hitters so you can anticipate what will happen before a
certain pitch is thrown. For example, Billy Williams (a Hall of Fame outfielder
with the Chicago Cubs) was a left-handed pull-hitter. But he would take the
breaking ball to left-center (the opposite field). So I had to make sure our pitchers worked him inside, but way inside or he would hit the ball out of the park.
I'd play him straightaway in that spot. If I knew we were going to throw him off-
speed stuff away in San Francisco, I'd anticipate going towards left. Now, if you
don't know the hitter, talk to the pitcher. Find out how he's going to work him.
Tell him you're going to play straightaway until you see the batter over a few
games."* — Willie Mays

Concentrate on the pitcher-batter confrontation. You may not be able to tell
what kind of pitch has been thrown, but you can at least observe its location.
Notice if the batter is getting a late hack (swing) or is in front of the ball. Your
knowledge of the hitter and pitcher should then give you some idea of where
the ball is likely to land.

"Depending on who was on the mound, I would key off of the pitcher's fastball and how the hitter was reacting to it. That would tell me if the hitter could pull the ball, or, if he was a little late, hit it the other way. Or just hit it back up the middle." — Ken Griffey, Sr.

Another indicator of how far a ball will travel is the sound made when the bat hits the ball.

"Here's a little game my teammates and I used to play during batting practice to sharpen our ears. We would stand with our backs to home plate and try to identify where a ball would be hit without peeking. All we had to guide us was the sound of the ball against the wood. Practice that day after day and, after a while, you can take off at the crack of the bat. It becomes instinctive." — Rusty Staub

Outfielders usually move laterally on fly balls. To achieve maximum acceleration, pivot and push off the foot nearest the ball as you rise out of your semi-crouch. Cross over with your outside foot. If you must angle your run, stride first with the foot nearest the ball. Pivot on both feet whenever the batter hits the ball over your head.

"When you are going into the gap, don't keep your eyes on the ball. Train yourself to recognize where the ball will probably land and run to that area. After four or five steps, you can glance up to check the flight of the ball." — Ken Griffey, Sr.

You don't have to move much on balls hit right at you, but you do have to determine whether the ball will rise or sink. Don't take a step until you can read the ball's trajectory.

Making the catch

Pursue fly balls aggressively. If you drift over to time the catch of a ball, you aren't in position to throw. You may also be unable to adjust if you misjudge a ball's flight or a sudden gust carries it farther than you anticipated. Hustle on every play.

"The wind can be a factor when you go for a catch. You might run to the spot where you think the ball is coming down only to find out the wind has carried it another six feet or held it up so that it drops in front of you. Check which way the wind is blowing before the game starts. Then keep checking it every inning after that because the direction can change. I always looked at the flags to see where the wind was blowing. Some games would start with the wind blowing in, and then it would start blowing out after only a few innings." — Willie Mays

Using both hands, catch the ball out in front of your body and over your throwing shoulder. (See Figure 7-18.) If you're left-handed, your right foot should be forward; if you throw from the right side, your left foot is out in front. This position leaves you in the correct position to get off a good throw. Take a short hop to close the shoulders and hips on your glove side, and then move through the ball as you throw overhand with a cross-seam grip.

You will instill sound habits if you catch every ball as if you have to throw it to a base, even when there aren't any runners on the base paths.

"Before a ball is hit, you have to be thinking baseball. What is the situation? How many are out? Are you behind or ahead and by how many runs? Who comes up next? When a ball gets by you in the gap with one out, you don't want that batter to get more than two bases. He can score from third without a base hit with less than two out. So your throw is going to third." — Willie Mays

"Practice taking the ball out of your glove in a cross-seam grip until you can do it blindfolded. Do it every time you grab a baseball. For maximum power, throw the ball over the top whenever you can and have your momentum pointed towards your target. The best way to build your arm strength for these throws is to play catch as often as possible. And I don't mean just randomly tossing the ball back and forth. Play catch with a purpose. Make a game of hitting a target every time you throw. If you deliver the ball up near your catching partner's face, you get two points; at his chest, one. Low point man buys the soft drinks. Try to hit a specific target even when you're just loosening up." — Rusty Staub

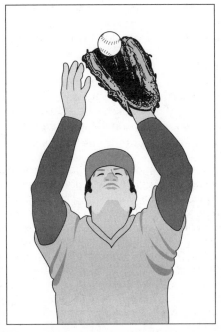

Figure 7-18:
Catching
the fly ball.

"I tried to make my throws so that my teammates didn't get hurt. What I mean is that I would give them a ball high that they could handle. I didn't want them to have to reach down as the runner was sliding in because that's where the fielder can get injured. But on a throw to the catcher, I would throw low, even bounce the throw, because he has all that protection and if he stays low he can block the plate better. Now, when you make a throw, you're not always trying to get the base runner, you're trying to get the guy who hit the ball. If that hitter is slow, you might get him if he tries to take the extra base. So I would hit my cutoff man on purpose, try to catch that hitter running to second. I always tried to keep my throws to the cutoff man chest-high where he could handle them." — *Willie Mays*

Don't fall into the gap

Any time a ball is hit into the gap or power alley, one outfielder should try to cut off the ball, while another should run at a deeper angle to back up the play. Usually the fielder closest to the ball goes for it. On plays where the ball is equidistant from both fielders, the center fielder has priority. However, to avoid mix-ups, especially on balls hit between two players, you and your fellow outfielders should call loudly for any ball you pursue.

Coming in on a ball

During practice, learn how to read the trajectory of balls far in front of you so you can instantly decide if you should make the putout or catch it on a bounce. If you have to play the bounce, slow down while keeping your body and glove in front of the ball. That way, if you don't catch it cleanly, you can knock it down.

"Make sure you catch this ball belt-high or chest-high so that you keep your eyes on the ball. It will be easier to handle." — *Ken Griffey, Sr.*

"Again, you have to know your hitter. A strong hitter might hit a line drive that will hang up a little longer; someone not as strong, the ball might just die. And the wind might blow the ball up, down, or even to the side. Which is why you have to know what's happening in the ballpark at all times." — *Willie Mays*

Going out on a ball

Most major leaguers will tell you the most difficult fly ball to catch is the one smacked over your head. Inexperienced outfielders often start back pedaling on that ball, which is the worst thing they can do. If you back pedal, you don't see the ball clearly because your head is bobbing up and down, you can't generate any speed (which is why marathoners do not run backward), and you can't jump if you need to.

"I would try to catch the ball like a wide receiver in football, over my left shoulder or right shoulder depending on where the ball is hit. And I'm getting in position to throw that ball while I'm making the catch. If you see a picture of my catch against Vic Wertz in the 1954 World Series, I caught the ball over my shoulder because I could see the ball better. I looked directly over my shoulder. And the left side of my body was ready to throw before I even caught the ball." (Note: Mays is referring to perhaps the most famous catch ever made. With his back to the plate, Mays galloped full speed into deepest center to catch Wertz's booming line drive some 450 feet from home plate. He then uncorked a perfect throw.) — Willie Mays

"Outfielders tangle themselves on that play when they start off on the wrong foot. If a ball is hit over your right shoulder, drop step back with your right foot. Cross over with your left foot and stay angled sideways as you go back. If it is hit over your left shoulder, do the reverse." (See Figure 7-19.) — Ken Griffey, Sr.

Figure 7-19: Going back on the fly ball.

You have to catch grounders, too

With runners on, outfielders should charge ground balls as aggressively as infielders. They must catch the ball in a position that allows them to unleash a good throw. Field the ball on your glove side with your glove-side foot down. Close off your upper body with a short hop, stride with your left foot, and throw over the top with a cross-seam grip.

"When no one is on base, all you want to do is keep the ground ball in front of you. If it gets by, the runner is taking extra bases. Get in front of it, get down on one knee, and block the ball." (See Figure 7-20.) — Ken Griffey, Sr.

"You have to charge that ball and keep it in front of you like an infielder. I didn't practice doing that in the outfield. Instead, I took grounders at second or short-stop during practice. So when I went to the outfield, grounders were a piece of cake." — Willie Mays

Figure 7-20:
Keeping
the ground
ball in front
of you.

Chapter 8

The Science of Baserunning

. . . .

In This Chapter

▶ Running to first

▶ Leading off any base

▶ Navigating the base paths

▶ Sliding like a pro

▶ Breaking up the double play

▶ Stealing (without getting caught)

. . . .

*B*aserunning has always been the most underrated aspect of baseball offense. Teams win or lose more games on the base paths than most fans realize. Clubs that consistently win close games are the ones whose players can go from first to third on singles, break up double plays, score on short fly balls or ground-ball outs, and take the extra base whenever it is offered.

Anyone can become a proficient base runner. You don't need speed; you simply need to be alert, aggressive, and smart. Pete Rose was one of the best base runners I ever played with or against. From the stands, Pete appeared fast because he hustled all the time, but he had only average speed. In a game I played against him in the Houston Astrodome, Pete went from first to third on a sharp single to right. You don't see that happen often on AstroTurf — singles bounce to the outfielders so quickly that base runners usually advance only one base. But Pete executed plays like that all the time because he was hustling from his very first step toward second. He also made it his business to know where the ball was hit and the strength of the outfielder's arm.

Pete went from first to third as well as any player in the majors because of his head, not his legs. In this chapter, we show you how to take a page from his book by developing your baserunning savvy.

Accelerating Out of the Box

When you get a hit, you should be hustling toward first base the moment the ball leaves your bat. It doesn't matter which foot you lead with as long as you maintain balance and your initial move propels you toward first. Always run in a straight line as close to the foul line as possible so that if a fielder's throw hits you, the umpire won't call you out for obstruction (see Figure 8-1). Don't overstride. Stay low for your first few steps to build acceleration and then explode into your normal running form.

Figure 8-1:
The quickest way to first base is a straight line.

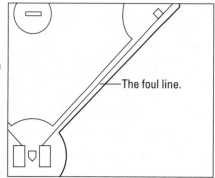

—The foul line.

If a fielder is going to try to throw you out at first base, don't just run to first base, run *through* it. Always touch the front of the bag as you cross over it. Continue running several steps down the right field line before making your right turn into foul territory. If you do this after touching first, you can't be tagged out for leaving the bag. However, if you turn left toward second base, the fielder can tag you out before you get back to first. (See Figure 8-2.) As you run through first, glance over your right shoulder to see if you can advance to second on an error. (For instance, the fielder has thrown the ball past the first baseman and into the dugout, so you have enough time to get to second base safely.)

Most of the time, you shouldn't bother to watch the ball as you dash toward first. Watching the ball slows you down. The only time you should watch the ball is if it's going toward one of the outfield gaps or over an outfielder's head. You can pick up most of those balls with a quick glance. If you can't, tilt your head slightly (and don't break stride) for a better view. Still can't pick it up? Then rely on your first-base coach to tell you whether you should run through first or turn toward second.

Stay alert after singling to right field. If you make a wide turn at first, a charging right fielder may still get you out by throwing behind you to the first baseman.

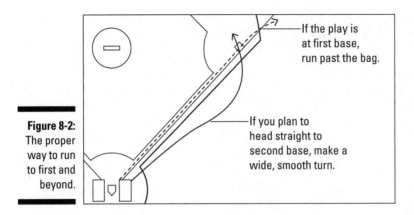

Figure 8-2:
The proper way to run to first and beyond.

If the play is at first base, run past the bag.

If you plan to head straight to second base, make a wide, smooth turn.

There may be times when you should slide into first base — for example, if a high throw draws the first baseman off the bag and he has to tag you for the out. If you slide while he's leaping for the ball, it is nearly impossible for him to get the ball down in time to nail you. Some players slide into first on force-outs, but I think this is bad policy. It may feel as if sliding or jumping into first on your final step gets you to the bag quicker, but it actually slows you down.

Taking Your Lead

Baseball is, as they say, a game of inches; you're often safe or out by the barest of margins. Any time you can use your lead to shorten the distance from one base to another, you gain an advantage for your team — you're inching that much closer to your ultimate objective: home plate.

Leading off first

After you're on first, keep your left foot against the bag while you check the alignment of the fielders and pick up any signs from the third-base coach. Remind yourself of the number of outs. Don't move off first until you know the pitcher has the ball. While closely watching the pitcher receive his signs, take several shuffle steps from the bag (do not cross your left foot over your right; you can get tangled if you have to dive back to first on a pickoff). This position is your *primary lead.* (See Figure 8-3.)

Your goal is to gradually get as far from first base as you can without getting *picked off* (thrown out). How far a lead you take depends on a number of factors: whether the pitcher is a righty or lefty, how good his move is, your size, and your reflexes. Tall players can take long leads — but so can short, quick players. Finding your ideal lead length is a matter of trial and error. However, most major-league runners prefer to be a step or two and a dive away from first.

Figure 8-3:
Taking a
primary
lead.

When taking your lead, balance your weight evenly on the balls of both feet. Do not lean toward first or second. Drop into a slight crouch and flex your knees so that you can move quickly in either direction. This stance is known as a *two-way lead*. Your feet should be parallel to each other, shoulder width apart, and pointed toward the pitcher. (Maury Wills, who ran the bases well enough to steal 104 bases for the Dodgers in 1962, used to turn his right foot a little toward second base so he could pivot quicker.)

Let your arms hang loosely in front of you. Keep your eyes on the pitcher the moment you step from the bag. Watch for the pickoff play! Imagine a straight line leading from the outer edge of first base to the outer edge of second. Stand even with that line or a little bit in front of it. Leading off the bag from behind that line costs you extra steps. (See Figure 8-4.) It also makes it appear to the pitcher that there is a wider distance between you and first base than there actually is. You invite additional pickoff throws when you stand too far back.

As the pitcher throws toward home, you should assume your *secondary lead*. Take a crossover step and a hop toward second while watching the action at the plate. In a perfectly-timed crossover, your right foot hits the ground a split second before the ball reaches home. When the ball passes the hitter or if the hitter hits the ball in the air directly at an infielder, stop on your right foot, turn, and get back to first. If the ball gets past the catcher or if the batter hits a grounder or a longer fly ball, push off your right foot and run toward second.

Remember: Don't leave the base until you know the location of the ball. Base runners must stay constantly alert for pickoff plays and hidden ball tricks.

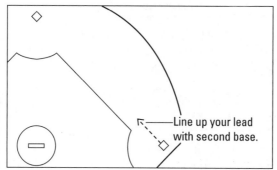

Figure 8-4:
Leading off
first base.

—Line up your lead
with second base.

Fly balls are tricky; if a fielder catches one, you must get back to first before you get thrown out. If the batter hits a fly ball that looks catchable, you should move far enough off first base that you can make it safely to second (or beyond) if the ball is dropped, but not so far that you can't get back to first safely if the ball is caught. If the batter hits a medium fly ball, run no farther than halfway to second base until you see how the play evolves. You can run farther toward second on a deep fly.

Always remember that if the outfielder catches the ball before it touches the ground, you must get back to first. If the outfielder's throw reaches that bag before you do, you've just run into a double play. As you trot toward your dugout, you will notice a livid fellow with smoke coming out of his ears and veins in his head threatening to explode. That's your manager. The doghouse you just slid into belongs to him.

Leading off second

You can take a longer lead off second than off first. Generally, no one holds you close to the bag because the pitcher can't look directly at you; he has to wheel and turn to pick you off; you rarely see anyone pull off that play.

If you're going to steal, set up in a straight line to third. Otherwise, stay a few feet behind the base line. Take your primary lead. Advance as the pitcher delivers to the plate. You should be 15 to 18 feet (4.6 to 5.5 meters) from second as the ball crosses home plate.

If your team already has two outs, extend your primary lead off second to about 20 feet (6 meters), but set up about 3 to 5 feet (.9 to 1.5 meters) behind second base. This lead puts you in a better position to round third and head for home on a base hit. You don't have to worry about being part of a double play, so you can take off at the crack of the bat. (See Figure 8-5.)

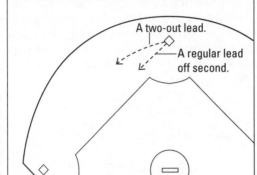

Figure 8-5:
Two ways to
lead off
second.

Leading off third

Managers have exiled base runners to Devil's Island for getting picked off at third base. Therefore, your primary lead off third should put you no farther from the bag than the opposing third baseman. Take this lead in foul territory so you won't be called out if a batted ball hits you. (See Figure 8-6.)

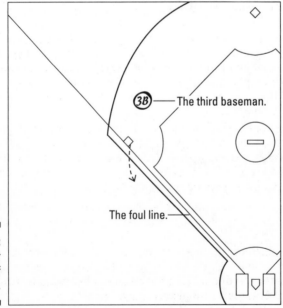

Figure 8-6:
Taking your
lead off
third.

As the pitcher delivers the pitch to his catcher, take a two- or three-step walking lead toward home. You should land on your right foot, ready to break for the plate or return to third, just as the pitch approaches the batter. This movement leaves you in position to score easily on a wild pitch, passed ball, or ground out. It also allows you to pivot back toward third if the catcher handles the pitch cleanly.

Disguising the hit-and-run play

As the base runner on a hit-and-run play, don't depart from your normal lead or you may signal your intentions to the opposition. Timing matters more to the successful execution of this play than the size of your lead does. You must make sure the pitcher delivers the ball before you break from the base. (You can review how to execute the hit-and-run in Chapter 5.)

Reading Your Opposition

Great base runners take the extra base *before* the ball is hit. Prior to your game, watch the opposing fielders during practice to see the strength and accuracy of their arms. When you reach first base during the game, observe how deeply the outfielders are playing the hitter. If the left fielder is playing deep, and your teammate hits a shallow fly in his direction, you can take off without holding up to see if the ball is caught. Notice if the outfielders are leaning in any particular direction. If the outfield is *shaded* (leaning) toward left, and the hitter smacks the ball down the right field line, you can go for at least two bases.

Also observe if any of the outfielders are left-handed throwers. If a left-handed center fielder has to go to his right in pursuit of a hit, he must turn and make an off-balance throw to nail you at third. On a single to right center field, a right-handed center fielder cannot throw to third until he turns completely around. That gives you an extra moment to slide in safely.

Rounding the Bag

All right, you've just pounded a ball into the outfield and you're thinking double all the way. You're not running through first and up the right field foul line on this play. Instead, head straight for first as you normally would. When you're about 15 feet (4.6 meters) from the bag, veer slightly toward foul territory, and then cut in toward the infield. As you pass first base on a nearly straight line toward second, touch the bag with your foot. It doesn't matter which one you use. However, you have a shorter turn to make by touching the inside part of the bag with your left foot. (See Figure 8-7.) Make sure that you touch enough of first base for the umpire to witness the contact. Scamper to second base.

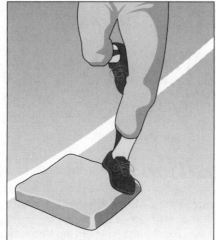

Figure 8-7:
How to
round first.

Tagging Up

After a fly ball is caught, base runners must touch the base they occupy before advancing to the next bag. This action is known as *tagging up*. If you are halfway between first and second when a deep fly is hit, you must return to first to touch the bag. Take off for second only *after* the ball and fielder make contact. You can advance in this manner from any base.

When you tag up from first, your right foot should be on the inside edge of the bag. This position leaves your right side open so you can follow the ball's flight more easily. If you're tagging up from third, your left foot should be on the bag. Tagging from second? The situation determines which foot you should place on the bag. On a ball hit to left or left center, it's your right foot. When the ball is hit to right field or right center, switch to your left foot.

As you tag up, drop into a crouch. Extend your front foot 18 to 24 inches (46 to 61 centimeters), depending on your leg length, from the base. Shift your weight forward. Watch the ball! The moment it touches the outfielder's glove, push into your stride toward the next base. You don't have to wait for the outfielder to catch it cleanly.

The force-out

Force-out is a term that you need to be familiar with because it occurs frequently in baseball — and it's often misunderstood by the novice player and viewer alike. (A trip to your local Little League game should convince you of that!) A force-out (or *force play*) takes place when a batted ground ball forces a runner to advance to the next base, but that base or the runner is tagged by a fielder holding the ball before the runner reaches the base.

Under what circumstances does a batted ground ball force a base runner to advance?

✔ A runner on first must *always* try to advance to second base.

✔ A runner on second base must try to advance to third base if another runner is on first base.

✔ A runner on third base must try to advance home if runners are on first and second base (in this case, the bases are *loaded,* and a force-out is possible at any base, including home).

Of course, if you're the defensive player, it is easier to tag the base in a force play situation (or throw to another fielder who may step on the base) rather than tag the runner — because tagging a runner may knock the ball out of your hand. You don't need to do both. And don't think that you must literally tag the base. Simply step on the base while holding the ball in either your bare or your gloved hand.

Under what circumstances does a base runner not need to advance when the batter hits a ground ball? (If this information seems like overkill, don't forget your visit to the Little League game.)

✔ A runner on second base need not run if no one is on first base.

✔ A runner on third base need not run if either first base or second base is empty.

✔ Runners on both third base and second base need not run if first base is empty.

In the preceding situations, go to the next base only if you can make it safely — and remember that the defensive player must tag you with the ball instead of simply touching the base that you are running to. If you don't think that you can make it to the next base safely, simply stay put!

With two out, don't wait for a fly ball to be touched before you run. If the ball is caught, the inning is over, anyway. Be prepared to run on any fly ball — and hope that the fielder misses or drops it.

Using Your Coaches

You may feel as if you're alone on those base paths; you're not. Think of the base coaches as part of your running team. Use them. When you get to first base, the coach there can be a fount of valuable knowledge. He can remind you how many outs have been recorded (if he doesn't and you're not sure, ask him), reveal a quirk he has detected in the pitcher's motion (so you can get a better lead or steal a base), or tell you something about the outfielders (such as which one seems hobbled or isn't throwing particularly well that day). This is just the kind of information you need to make appropriate decisions on the base paths.

The third-base coach is your beacon. If you've lost sight of the ball or are unsure whether you should advance to the next base, watch his signs. No matter how much experience you have, heed the third-base coach in most situations. He has a better view of the entire field than you do. You may think you're running faster than you are, or you may not realize how quickly an outfielder has gotten to the ball. A good third-base coach can gauge all that for you.

Sliding Safely

"Slide, Kelly, Slide" — the popular saloon song from the 1890s — was written in honor of Boston Red Stocking superstar Mike "King" Kelly. While the lone umpire was looking elsewhere, Kelly would often help his team to an extra base by cutting across the infield from first and sliding into third without touching second. (Kelly wasn't the only guy to try this stunt back then, by the way.) You can't pull that play today (too many umps and TV cameras to catch you), but you can grab runs and wins for your team if you know how to slide properly. Often, the only difference between the umpire calling you safe or out on the bases is the quality of your slide.

Practice sliding as diligently as you work on the other aspects of your game. You don't need to do this on a baseball diamond. My brothers and I used to practice in our backyard. Get into a pair of tennis shoes and sliding pads, wet some grass, put down a base, and practice all your slides. It's important to be able to slide on both sides. George Foster, one of my teammates on the Reds, could slide only on one side no matter how a play developed. Many times he could have been safe but was tagged out simply because he couldn't elude the tag. As you practice, you develop a feel for when you should start your slide.

The straight-leg slide

The *straight-leg slide* is my favorite. It gets you to the bag as quickly as possible while leaving you in position to bounce up and advance to another base if a misplay occurs. Because your top leg is straight and aimed at the bag, you have less chance of catching your spikes in the dirt (a leading cause of ankle injuries).

Start this slide about 10 feet (3 meters) from the bag. Push off your rear foot and lift both legs up. Your body should glide forward feet first. Slide straight in (you can do this on either side) with the toe and foot of your top leg pointed in a straight line toward the middle of the bag. Your bottom leg is bent under you. (See Figure 8-8.)

Figure 8-8:
The straight-leg slide.

The bent-leg slide

The *bent-leg slide* is a variation of the straight-leg slide. To launch the slide, push off your rear foot and lift up both legs. Then tuck your rear leg under your slightly flexed top leg at a 90-degree angle (this pairing should resemble a figure 4). Maintain a semi-sitting position with your torso arched back and hands held high as you slide. Hold your chin close to your chest so you can see the base and the ball. Aim for the middle of the bag with your top leg. Touch the base with your heel (which prevents your cleats from catching on the bag).

The *pop-up slide* is the bent-leg slide with a wrinkle. You start this slide about 8 feet (2.4 meters) from the bag. Don't lean back. As your top leg hits the base, push up with your bottom foot. The momentum brings you to your feet, ready to advance if a misplay occurs.

Lou Brock, the all-time National League leader in stolen bases, used the pop-up slide to great effect (see Figure 8-9). It left him in position to take an extra base on a misplay. However, I don't like to see it used unless someone has already overthrown the ball when you start your slide. Too many runners have been called out when they were safe simply because their pop-up slides didn't afford the umpires a long-enough look to make the correct calls.

Figure 8-9:
Lou Brock is
ready to pop
up and run
some more
in a misplay.

The headfirst slide

This slide is nothing more than a dive into a swimming pool — without any water. You're hurtling yourself at great speed onto a hard surface that has little or no give. Pete Rose slid headfirst for more than 20 years and never even cracked a fingernail (see Figure 8-10). Don't let that fool you. The headfirst slide can be dangerous. A descending fielder can spike your hands, the ball can hit you in the head, or you can jam your fingers and hands against the base if you hold them too low. In the 1997 National League Championship Series, Florida Marlin shortstop Edgar Renteria knee-blocked a headfirst sliding Kenny Lofton from reaching second base. If Kenny had slid straight in, Renteria couldn't have blocked him.

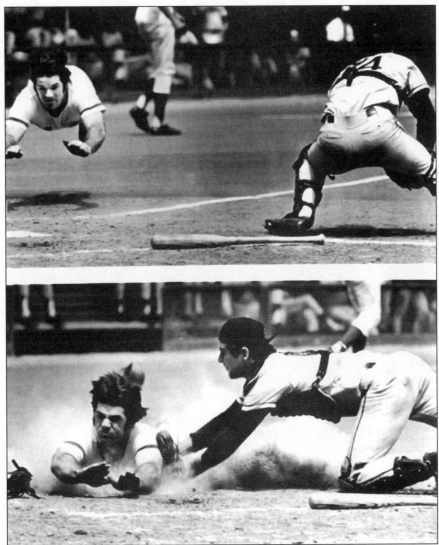

Figure 8-10:
Pete Rose
was known
for his
headfirst
slides.

If you're still not dissuaded from going in head first, at least minimize your risk by executing the slide properly. Start the headfirst slide by gradually lowering your body until you are about 8 feet (2.4 meters) from the bag. Extend your arms while you launch yourself off your rear leg. Keep your body straight, but relaxed, so that your forearms, chest, and thighs hit the ground simultaneously (this absorbs the shock). Stay alert and hold up your hands and head while sliding! (See Figure 8-11.) Should you attempt to execute a literal headfirst slide, you risk a sprained neck, concussion, or worse. I especially don't like to see young players, from high school on down, sliding headfirst. Too much can go wrong.

Figure 8-11:
The headfirst slide.

You may find it difficult to keep your hands up when attempting any type of slide. Wearing sliding gloves offers you some protection from injury.

The hook slide

The *hook slide* was supposedly the brainchild of Mike Kelly. It may have helped inspire that song they wrote about him, but it's basically a desperation play that you should use only when trying to evade a probable tag.

Let me set it up. You're on first. The batter hits the ball to right field. You cruise around second and burst toward third. The right fielder, however, has gotten a perfect bounce and has already fired the ball to the third baseman. As the ball beats you to the bag it pulls the third baseman toward his right. A hook slide to your right (the third baseman's left) is your only hope of avoiding an out.

Always execute the hook slide to the opposite side of wherever the tag will originate. If the throw comes in from the outfield side, slide to your left. Should it come from the infield side, slide to your right.

To hook slide to your left, push off on your right foot and drop to your left side. Your outer calf and thigh absorb the slide's impact. Keep your right leg relatively straight with a slight knee flex (your right leg slides to the right of the bag). Scissor your left leg out toward the base. While sliding past the base, reach out with the toes of your left foot or either hand. Touch the bag at its nearest corner. (See Figure 8-12.)

Figure 8-12: The hook slide.

If the fielder is about to tag your hand as you try to touch the base, you can pull your hand back. As the fielder's momentum carries him to one side, reach out to grab the bag with your other hand.

Remember to stay in contact with the bag until the fielder returns the ball to the pitcher or the umpire calls time.

To hook slide to your right (say, on a throw from the catcher), do everything I just described — only in reverse. Practice the hook slide from both sides. Don't use this slide on force plays; it slows you down when you need to get to the bag as quickly as possible.

Maury Wills was the greatest hook slider I ever saw. He could reach either corner of the base with the tip of his toe. This presented the fielder attempting a tag with the smallest target possible. With most runners, I only had to put the ball in the middle of the base to get them. They would slide right into it. I couldn't do that with Maury. You had to look for him, which is why he was so elusive.

You should also be aware of the risks involved with the hook. Your body's momentum can easily pull you too far past the base or make you miss it completely. Catching your spikes on the bag is another danger. Do this, and you can tear or break something. Keeping your knees slightly bent and both feet sideways offers you some protection. (See the hook slide in action in Figure 8-13.)

Figure 8-13:
Joe Morgan demon-
strates a
hook slide
against the
master hook
slider Maury
Wills.

Safety tips

To avoid injury while sliding, regardless of which type of slide you use, try to hold both hands in the air. Many major-league ballplayers hold a clump of dirt in each hand to remind them to hold their hands high on the base paths. (Don't ask me how *that* custom started.) Wearing sliding gloves is a further precaution. And always remember the four cardinal rules of sliding:

- When in doubt, slide.
- Never be tentative (half-hearted slides are the most dangerous).
- It is always better to slide early rather than late.
- Never slide head first into home or when breaking up the double play (you don't want to expose your head and neck on contact plays).

Breaking Up Is Hard to Do: Preventing the Double Play

In the final game of the 1975 World Series, the Cincinnati Reds and I were losing 3–0 to the Boston Red Sox in the top of the sixth. Pete Rose led off that inning with a single against Red Sox left-hander Bill Lee. With one out, our catcher Johnny Bench hit a sure double-play ball to Boston shortstop Rick Burleson. Burleson shoveled the ball to his second baseman Denny Doyle to start the double play. Doyle attempted to get a throw off to first, but Pete barreled into him just as the ball was leaving his hand. Though Pete was out, his hard (but perfectly legal) slide forced Doyle to throw wildly into the Boston dugout. Bench was safe; the inning, which should have been over, continued. The next batter, Tony Perez, hit a two-run homer that propelled us toward a 4–3 win and a world championship. Our comeback in that game started with Pete's slide.

Anytime you break up a double play, you snatch an out from the box score; you give your team an extra opportunity to score and win. To execute this maneuver, you must know how to slide properly. You should also know the rules governing the play:

 ✔ You must be on the ground when you make contact with the fielder.

 ✔ You must be able to reach the bag with some part of your body during your slide.

As the runner trying to break up the double play, your assignment is to get to second base as quickly as you can while making a good, hard slide. You're not looking to hurt anyone, so forget about any rolling blocks. (I had one thrown at me in 1968. It crumpled my knee and put me on the disabled list for the entire season. Inflicting that sort of injury is not your objective.) The idea is either to knock the pivot man (the second baseman or shortstop) off-balance or to disrupt his timing by making him leap or hurry his throw.

Start your takeout with your normal straight-leg slide. However, try to hook your top leg's foot under the pivot man's striding foot to knock it out from under him. Keep your weight on your bottom leg. When you take your usual slide, you aim for the base. Your objective here is to reach the fielder. Slide on whatever side of the bag he pivots from.

Though you don't have to hit the pivot man to break up the double play, you should try to do exactly that. This potential collision forces him to jump out of the way. Minimize the chance of injury by sliding with your spikes held below the pivot man's knee. Should you make contact, you will hit his shins or lower, where you won't break anything. Avoid hitting any fielder from the knee up.

Colliding with the Catcher at Home Plate

Catchers have this thing about base runners; they don't like to see them sliding across home plate. So good catchers do everything they can to stop you. Catchers are usually built like small condominiums. They wear heavy protective gear, and many of them enjoy a good crunch at the plate. Getting through them can be a daunting task, but you have to do it whenever you have the chance to score a run, particularly in a close game. Take the easy route whenever possible — if you can see the plate and know you can touch it, launch into your slide.

However, if the catcher has the plate completely blocked, you must barrel through him. There is no elegant way to do this. Just get low so you have your center of gravity working with you and keep your head away from the point of contact.

The catcher can block the plate only if he possesses the ball. If he blocks it without having the ball, he is guilty of obstruction, and the umpire will declare you safe at home after the collision.

Profile of a Base Thief

All great base stealers have a love of larceny. They derive joy from picking the opposing team's pockets, especially in pressure situations. To excel as a base thief, you have to be cocky. When you get to first base, your body language and demeanor should announce, "I'm stealing and there's nothing anyone can do to stop me!" You have to embrace the role of intimidator.

Base stealers make things happen. During the 1975 World Series, Boston pitcher Reggie Cleveland walked me to open the sixth inning of the fifth game. He threw over to first base seven times before throwing a strike to the batter Johnny Bench. Then he made four more throws to first. When he delivered another pitch, I took off for second but Bench fouled off the ball. What did Cleveland do then? He made five more tosses to first. This didn't bother me a bit. Cleveland was concentrating more on me than the batter, which is precisely what I wanted. On Cleveland's next pitch, Bench singled, and then Tony Perez came up to hit a three-run homer. The lesson here is that you don't need to steal a base to help your team; just the threat of a theft can rattle a pitcher into making a critical mistake. If the pitcher is playing cat-and-mouse with you, he can't focus fully on the hitter.

Stealing a lot of bases with your team far ahead or behind doesn't mark you as a great thief — many runners can steal in those situations because the opposing pitcher is paying little attention to them. He's either cruising to a win or concentrating solely on getting the batter out. Far more valuable are the runners like Juan Pierre, who ignite their offenses by stealing in the early innings or during the late portions of a close game.

A good base thief should be successful on at least 75 percent of his stolen base attempts. If your percentage is below that, your attempts are hurting your team.

What every base thief should know: Reading the pitcher

Ninety percent of all stolen bases come off the pitcher rather than the catcher. If you waited until the pitch reached home plate before you tried to steal, you would be thrown out 95 percent of the time. However, if you get a good jump as the pitcher delivers the ball, a catcher can do little to get you out, even if you aren't blessed with exceptional speed. In the fifth game of the 1997 World Series, Marlins first baseman Darren Daulton caught the Cleveland pitcher napping and stole second base. Darren has undergone nine knee operations, which have left him nearly immobile. Yet he got such a good lead that he was able to steal second against Sandy Alomar, one of the best throwing catchers in the business. Had the Indians' pitcher been paying more attention to first base, Darren never would have attempted a steal.

Base runners should study the opposing pitcher the moment he takes the mound. See if he has two distinct motions: one when he throws home and another when he tosses the ball to first to hold a runner on. Watch the pitcher throw to the plate from the stretch; note what body parts he moves first. Then see whether he does anything different when he throws to first base. See if he sets his feet differently on his pickoff move. Try to detect any quirk that can reveal the pitcher's intentions. In his final major-league season, Yankee outfielder Paul O'Neill stole 22 bases in 25 tries, a fabulous percentage. No one would describe Paul as a speed merchant back then, but he was one of the headiest players around and taught himself to read the pitchers' moves.

Ironically, good pitchers are often the easiest to steal on. Erratic pitchers typically use different release points from pitch to pitch (which is what makes them erratic). You never know when they are going to let go of the ball. The better pitchers have purer mechanics. They establish a rhythm and stick to it. Pedro Martinez, a three-time Cy Young Award winner, does the same thing to hit his release point on nearly every pitch. So a runner may be able to spot some clue in his motion when he plans to throw to first base (of course, when Pedro is working the mound, getting a runner to first base to begin with is the first challenge).

After you have a pitcher's pattern down, take off for second the moment he moves toward his release point. He might indicate this move with a hand gesture or some slight leg motion. Even a pitcher's eyes can fall into a pattern. Many pitchers take a quick glance toward first before throwing home; when they don't sneak a look toward you, they're throwing to your base.

You can also figure out pitchers by observing their body language. Watch the pitcher's rear leg. If it moves off the rubber, the throw is coming toward you. To throw to the plate, every pitcher must close either his hip or his front shoulder. He also must bend his rear knee while rocking onto his back foot. After the pitcher does any of these things, the rules state he can no longer throw to your base. You should immediately break for the next bag. If the pitcher breaks his motion to throw toward any base, the umpire should call a balk, which allows you and any other base runners to advance.

If you're on first base, left-handed pitchers are traditionally harder to steal on than right-handers because the lefty looks directly at you when he assumes the set position. However, this also means you are looking directly at him so he is easier to read — if you know what to look for. Scrutinize his glove, the ball, and his motion. If a *southpaw* (a left-hander) tilts back his upper body, he is probably throwing to first; a turning of the shoulder to the right usually precedes a pitch to the plate. When he bends his rear leg, he is most likely preparing to push off toward home.

When a righty is on the mound, observe his right heel and shoulder. He cannot pitch unless his right foot touches the pitching rubber. Throwing to first requires him to pivot on that foot. If he lifts his right heel, get back to the bag. An open right shoulder also indicates a throw to first.

Lead — and runs will follow

Base thieves can choose between a *walking lead* and a *stationary lead.* Lou Brock, the former Cardinal outfielder, used a walking lead. Brock was faster than most players, but he wasn't especially quick out of his first few steps (most taller players find it difficult to accelerate from a dead stop). He would walk two or three small steps to gain momentum before taking off toward second base. If you require a few steps to accelerate, this is the lead for you. A walking lead does, however, have one disadvantage: A good pitcher can stop you from moving by simply holding the ball. If you continue to stroll, the pitcher can pick you off.

For that reason, I prefer the stationary lead, when a batter takes a few strides off first base then stands still while the pitcher prepares to throw. The pitcher can still hold the ball, but the batter is not budging until the pitcher makes his first move to the plate.

Remember: Whichever baserunning lead you choose, use the same one whether you're stealing a base or not. Set up the same way on every lead. You don't want to telegraph your intentions to the pitcher. He's watching you for clues as closely as you're watching him.

The key to stealing third

Stealing third is generally easier than stealing second. You can take a bigger lead at second than at first without drawing many throws. If your timing is good, you can also take off from second before the pitcher actually releases the ball.

Pitchers generally find it more difficult to pick runners off at second than at first; the timing between the pitcher and his fielder must be precise. To catch you at second, either the second baseman or the shortstop has to cover or *cheat* (lean) toward the bag; this leaning opens up a hole for the batter. Alert coaches let you know when the fielders are sneaking in on you.

The potential to steal third depends on the batter at the plate. If a right-handed hitter is at-bat, you have an advantage because the catcher must throw over or around him to get the ball to third. But never try to steal third with a lefty at the plate, unless you get such a good jump that even a perfect throw cannot beat you.

Stealing third isn't a good gamble unless your success rate is 90 percent or better. Because you're already in scoring position at second, getting picked off can devastate your offense. Stealing third when your team is more than two runs behind is foolish. And making the first or last out of an inning at third, whether through an attempted steal or simply by running the bases, is considered a big mistake.

The only reason to steal third with fewer than two outs in a close ballgame is so you can score on a fly ball or ground out. However, if you're a proficient base thief, it does makes sense to steal third with two outs; being on third rather than second in that situation offers you nine more opportunities to score. Memorize the following list and dazzle your friends with your baseball erudition.

If you are on third, you can score on

- A balk
- An infield hit
- A wild pitch
- A passed ball
- A one-base infield error
- A fielder's choice (where the hitter and any other base runners are safe)
- Baserunning interference
- Catcher's interference
- A steal of home

Home, stolen home

Speaking of stealing home (how's that for a segue?), think long and hard about it — the odds are against you. If you must, only attempt a steal of home during the late innings of a close, low-scoring ballgame with two men out and a weak hitter at the plate. Obviously, home plate is the one base you steal entirely on the pitcher, because the catcher makes no throw on this play. Your best victims are pitchers with unusually slow deliveries or long windups.

Stealing: Know when to say "No"

The 1975 World Series serves as a great setting for a base-stealing lesson. In the bottom of the ninth inning of the fourth game, I was batting while our center fielder, Cesar Geronimo, was on second and Pete Rose was on first. We were trailing 5–4. Right-hander Luis Tiant was pitching for Boston. I was trying to concentrate on Tiant, always a difficult task because he had a thousand different herky-jerky moves and hesitations with which he distracted hitters.

Geronimo suddenly raced toward third just as Tiant went into his delivery. His unexpected movement pulled my attention away from the pitcher for a split second. By the time I looked back toward Tiant, the ball was nearly down the heart of the plate. A perfect pitch to drive for extra bases. However, that momentary lapse of concentration left me with little time to swing. My weak, late swing produced an inning-ending, rally-killing pop-up. That was the best pitch I'd seen all night. I blew it.

Cesar should not have been running at that point. He was already in scoring position, we were trailing by a run, and Tiant was tiring (he threw an arm-wringing 163 pitches in that game). Given those circumstances, a base runner has to give his team's number three hitter — usually an RBI man — a chance to drive him in. To be a great base stealer, you must be aggressive, but you also have to know when to throw on the brakes for the good of the team.

Having a right-handed batter at the plate when you attempt to steal home provides you with two advantages. First, the hitter obstructs the catcher's view of you at third. Second, if the batter remains in the box until just before you arrive at home, he can prevent the catcher from getting in position for the tag.

Delayed, double, and fake steals

With the *delayed steal,* slide-step into your regular lead when the pitcher releases the ball and then count 1-2-3. This should slow your takeoff just long enough to persuade the catcher and infielders that you aren't stealing. Race for second after you finish counting. (You may also first break out of your lead and return to first to camouflage your intentions.) Catchers have no way of knowing who will cover second base on a delayed steal until either the second baseman or shortstop moves toward the bag. If you've caught those two infielders napping and no one covers second, the catcher has to hold onto the ball or risk throwing it into the outfield.

Double steals are possible whenever two bases are occupied. With runners on first and second, this play is nothing more than two straight steals occurring simultaneously. With only one out, the catcher will probably try to erase the lead runner heading to third. With two out, he may go after the slower of the two base stealers.

With runners on first and third, double steals become more complex. Imagine you're the runner on third. Your teammate on first should break full-out for second as the pitcher delivers the ball. You move down the line toward home. Halt as the catcher receives the pitch. Don't move until the catcher commits to throwing the runner out at second. Be alert in case he fakes a toss to the bag and instead throws to his pitcher, who fires back the ball for a play at the plate. The throw's *trajectory* should tell you if it's going to second base or to the pitcher — the throw will be higher if it is going all the way to second base, so hesitate long enough to see this. Dash home as soon as the throw bound for second base leaves the catcher's hand.

If you're the runner on first for this play, your primary goal is helping your teammate at third score. You may break for second while the pitcher is in his set position. Should your movement distract the pitcher, he may balk (see Chapter 3 for details on the balk). In that case, both runners advance one base. Attract a throw to first, and you can force a rundown. While you jockey to elude the tag, the runner on third can score.

Fake steals open the infield for the batter at the plate. You can bluff the opposition by taking two and a half quick strides out of your primary lead before coming to a halt. Your movement should draw the infielders out of position, because one of them must cover second base.

Chapter 9

Joe's Baseball Playbook

• •

In This Chapter

▶ Handling singles

▶ Fielding doubles or triples

▶ Covering bunts

▶ Setting up for pop flies

• •

*W*e could write an entire book devoted to defensive situations and strategies. These 26 plays are the ones you encounter in almost every game. It doesn't matter whether you coach or play in Little League, high school, college, a professional league, or your company's softball team; make sure you have a handle on these plays.

If you want to know more about the defensive role of each player on the field as well as some of the vocabulary used to describe these plays, be sure to check out Chapter 7. To read the diagrams that follow, here is all that you need to know:

Symbol	Meaning
ⓟ	Pitcher
ⓒ	Catcher
①Ⓑ	First baseman
②Ⓑ	Second baseman
ⓢⓢ	Shortstop
③Ⓑ	Third baseman
ⓇⒻ	Right fielder
ⒸⒻ	Center fielder
ⓁⒻ	Left fielder
⟶	Path of a player
- - - ->	Path of the ball

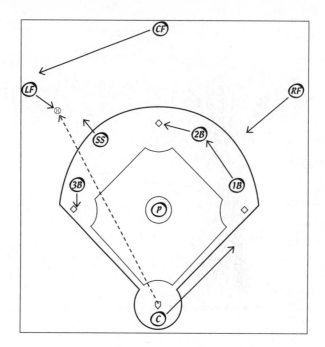

Single to left: Bases empty

Catcher: Cover first base in case the runner takes a too-wide turn.

Pitcher: Back up any throw to second base.

First baseman: Check that the batter touches first base and then back up the incoming throw to second base.

Second baseman: Cover second base.

Shortstop: Pursue the ball; then line up between the left fielder and second base to take the cutoff throw.

Third baseman: Cover third base.

Left fielder: Field the ball and throw it to the cutoff man (the shortstop). If the shortstop is out of position, throw to second base.

Center fielder: Run to back up the left fielder.

Right fielder: Move toward the infield to cover a poor throw from the left fielder to the second baseman.

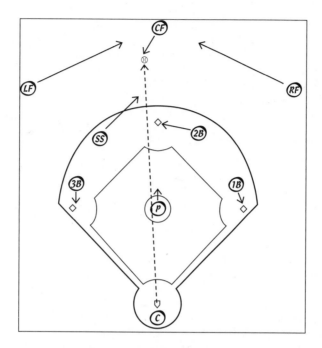

Single to center: Bases empty

Catcher: Cover home plate.

Pitcher: Stay near the mound and back up any throw to second base.

First baseman: Make sure the batter touches first base, and then cover the base inside.

Second baseman: Go to second base to take the throw.

Shortstop: Go out to be the cutoff man for second base.

Third baseman: Cover third base.

Left fielder: Back up the center fielder.

Center fielder: Field the ball and throw it to second base or the cutoff man (shortstop).

Right fielder: Back up the center fielder.

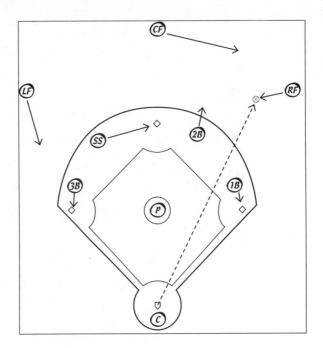

Single to right: Bases empty

Catcher: Cover home plate.

Pitcher: Follow the flight of the ball and then decide where to back up (usually second base).

First baseman: Check that the batter touches first base; then cover the base inside.

Second baseman: Pursue the ball; then take the cutoff position between the right fielder and second base.

Shortstop: Cover second base.

Third baseman: Cover third base.

Left fielder: Move toward the infield in case the right fielder makes a bad throw to second base.

Center fielder: Back up the right fielder.

Right fielder: Field the hit and make the cutoff throw to the second baseman. If the second baseman is out of position, throw it to second base.

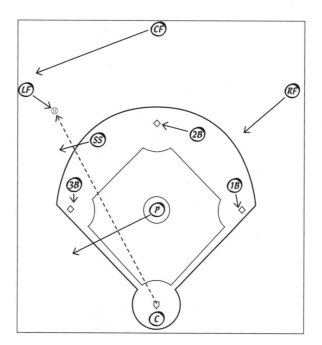

Single to left: Runner on first, or runners on first and third

Catcher: Cover home plate.

Pitcher: Follow the flight of the ball and then decide where to back up (usually third base).

First baseman: Make sure the batter touches first base, and then cover the base inside.

Second baseman: Cover second base.

Shortstop: Line up between the left fielder and third base for the cutoff throw.

Third baseman: Back up the shortstop (then cover third once the ball is caught).

Left fielder: Field the ball and throw it to the cutoff man (the shortstop). If the shortstop is out of position, throw it to third base.

Center fielder: Back up the left fielder.

Right fielder: Move toward the infield to field any bad throws.

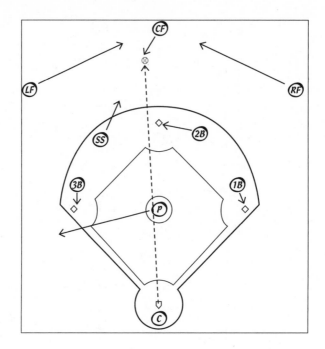

Single to center: Runner on first, or runners on first and third

Catcher: Cover home plate.

Pitcher: Back up the throw to third base.

First baseman: Check that the batter touches first base; then cover the base inside.

Second baseman: Cover second base.

Shortstop: Line up for the cutoff throw between the center fielder and third base.

Third baseman: Cover third base.

Left fielder: Back up the center fielder.

Center fielder: Field the hit and throw it to the cutoff man (the shortstop). If the shortstop is out of position, throw it to third base.

Right fielder: Back up the center fielder.

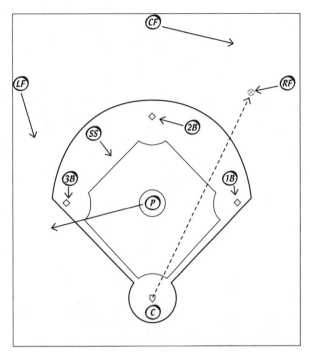

Single to right: Runner on first, or runners on first and third

Catcher: Cover home plate.

Pitcher: Back up third base.

First baseman: Make sure that the batter touches first base, and then cover the base inside.

Second baseman: Cover second base.

Shortstop: Line up for the cutoff throw between the right fielder and third base.

Third baseman: Cover third base.

Left fielder: Back up the throw to third base.

Center fielder: Back up the right fielder.

Right fielder: Field the hit and throw it to the cutoff man (the shortstop).

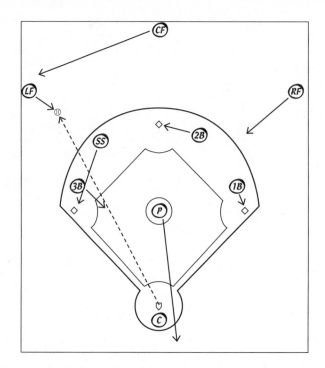

Single to left: Runner on second, runners on first and second, or bases loaded

Catcher: Cover home plate.

Pitcher: Back up the throw at home plate.

First baseman: Cover first base.

Second baseman: Cover second base.

Shortstop: Cover third base.

Third baseman: Take the cutoff position for a throw to home plate.

Left fielder: Field the hit and throw it to the cutoff man (the third baseman).

Center fielder: Back up the left fielder.

Right fielder: Back up any throw to second.

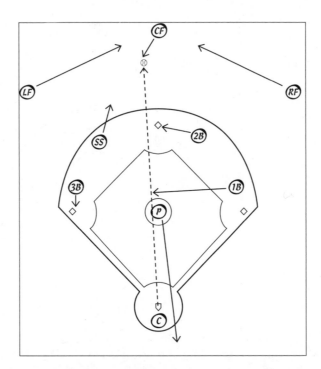

Single to center: Runner on second, runners on first and second, or bases loaded

Catcher: Cover home plate.

Pitcher: Back up the catcher at home plate.

First baseman: Take the cutoff position near the mound for a throw to home plate.

Second baseman: Cover second base.

Shortstop: Take the cutoff position for a throw to third base.

Third baseman: Cover third base.

Left fielder: Back up the center fielder and then become a quarterback. Tell the center fielder where the throw should be going.

Center fielder: Field the hit, listen for the left or right fielder's instructions, throw to one of the two cutoff men: the shortstop (if the play is at third base) or the first baseman (if the play is at home plate).

Right fielder: Back up the center fielder and then become a quarterback. Tell the center fielder where the throw should be going.

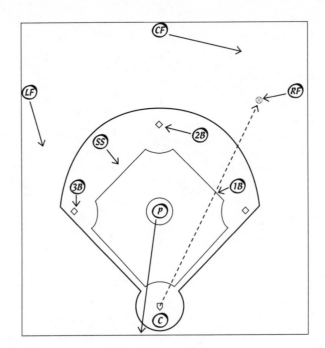

Single to right: Runner on second, runners on first and second, or bases loaded

Catcher: Cover home plate.

Pitcher: Stand outside the base paths between third base and home plate, watch the play evolve, and back up the throw (usually at home plate).

First baseman: Take the cutoff position for the throw to home plate.

Second baseman: Cover second base.

Shortstop: Take the cutoff position for the throw to third base.

Third baseman: Cover third base.

Left fielder: Come toward third base in order to be able to back up at third or second base, depending on where the play is evolving.

Center fielder: Back up the right fielder and tell him where to throw.

Right fielder: Field the ball, listen for the center fielder's instructions, and throw to the appropriate cutoff man: the shortstop (on a play at third base) or the first baseman (on a play at home plate).

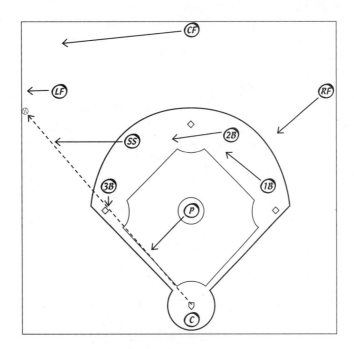

Double, possible triple down the left field line: Bases empty

Catcher: Cover home plate.

Pitcher: Back up third base.

First baseman: Make sure the batter touches first base; then trail the runner to second base.

Second baseman: Go to the trail position behind the shortstop. Stay near second base.

Shortstop: Take the cutoff position down the left field line.

Third baseman: Cover third base.

Left fielder: Field the hit and make the cutoff throw to the shortstop.

Center fielder: Back up the left fielder.

Right fielder: Back up any throw to second base.

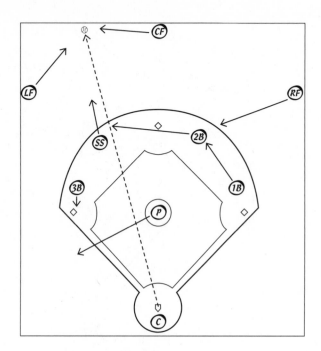

Double, possible triple to the left center field gap: Bases empty

Catcher: Cover home plate.

Pitcher: Back up third base.

First baseman: Make sure the batter touches first base and then trail him to second.

Second baseman: Go to the trail position behind the shortstop.

Third baseman: Cover third base.

Shortstop: Line up with third base and the fielder for the cutoff throw.

Left fielder: Back up the center fielder.

Center fielder: Field the hit and then make the cutoff throw to the shortstop.

Right fielder: Back up any throw to second base.

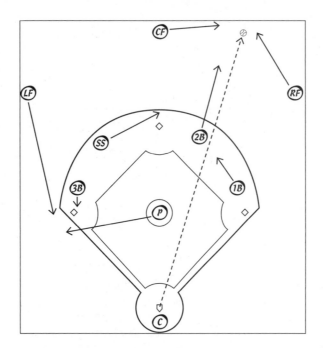

Double, possible triple to the right center field gap: Bases empty

Catcher: Cover home plate.

Pitcher: Back up third base.

First baseman: Check that the batter touches first base, and then trail him to second base.

Second baseman: Line up with third base and the center fielder for the cutoff throw.

Shortstop: Get to the trail position behind the second baseman.

Third baseman: Cover third base.

Left fielder: Back up any throw to third base.

Center fielder: Field the hit and make the cutoff throw to the second baseman.

Right fielder: Back up the center fielder.

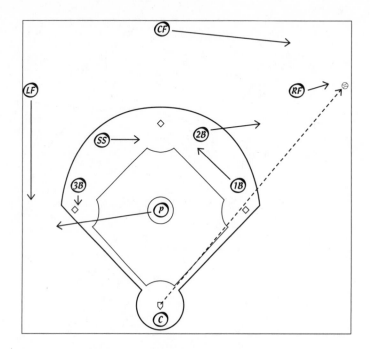

Double, possible triple down the right field line: Bases empty

Catcher: Cover home plate.

Pitcher: Back up third base.

First baseman: Check that the batter touches first base, and then trail him to second base.

Second baseman: Line up with third base and the right fielder for the cutoff throw.

Shortstop: Get to the trail position behind the second baseman.

Third baseman: Cover third base.

Left fielder: Back up any throw to third base.

Center fielder: Back up the right fielder.

Right fielder: Field the hit and then make the cutoff throw to the second baseman.

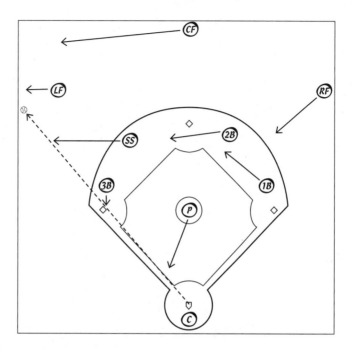

Double, possible triple down the left field line: Runners on base

Catcher: Cover home plate.

Pitcher: Stand between home plate and third base (closer to home), watch the play evolve, and back up the throw.

First baseman: Check that the batter touches first base, and then trail the runner to second base.

Second baseman: Get to the trail position behind the shortstop. Let the shortstop know where to throw.

Shortstop: Line up between home plate and the left fielder for the cutoff throw.

Third baseman: Cover third base.

Left fielder: Field the hit and make the cutoff throw to the shortstop.

Center fielder: Back up the left fielder.

Right fielder: Back up any throw to second base.

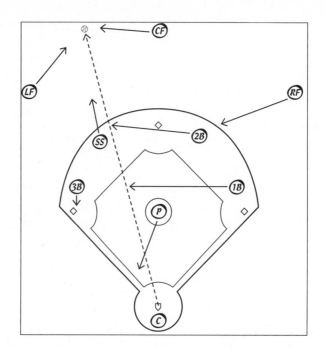

Double, possible triple to the left center field gap: Runners on base

Catcher: Cover home plate.

Pitcher: Stand between home plate and third base (closer to home), watch the play evolve, and back up the throw.

First baseman: Take the cutoff position for a throw to the plate.

Second baseman: Get to the trail position behind the shortstop. Let the shortstop know where to throw.

Shortstop: Line up with home plate and the fielder for the cutoff throw.

Third baseman: Cover third base.

Left fielder: Back up the center fielder.

Center fielder: Field the hit and make the cutoff throw to the shortstop.

Right fielder: Back up any throw to second base.

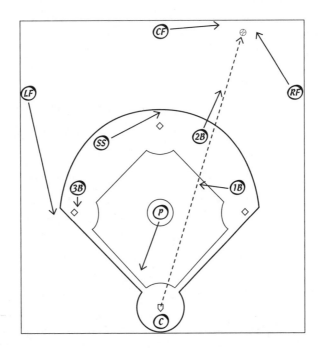

Double, possible triple to the right center field gap: Runners on base

Catcher: Cover home plate.

Pitcher: Stand between home plate and third base (closer to home), watch the play evolve, and back up the throw.

First baseman: Take the cutoff position for a throw to the plate.

Second baseman: Line up with home plate and the fielder for the cutoff throw.

Shortstop: Get to the trail position behind the second baseman. Tell the second baseman where to make the throw.

Third baseman: Cover third base.

Left fielder: Back up any throw to third base.

Center fielder: Field the hit and make the cutoff throw to the second baseman.

Right fielder: Back up the center fielder.

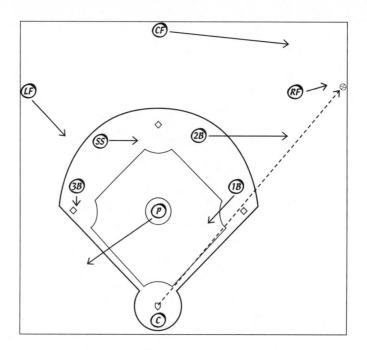

Double, possible triple down the right field line: Runners on base

Catcher: Cover home plate.

Pitcher: Stand outside the base paths halfway between home plate and third base, watch the play evolve, and back up the throw.

First baseman: Take the cutoff position for a throw to the plate.

Second baseman: Line up with home plate and the fielder for the cutoff throw.

Shortstop: Get behind the second baseman. Tell the second baseman where to make the throw. Be the cutoff man for a play at third base.

Left fielder: Back up any throw to second base or third base.

Center fielder: Back up the right fielder.

Right fielder: Field the hit and make the cutoff throw to the second baseman.

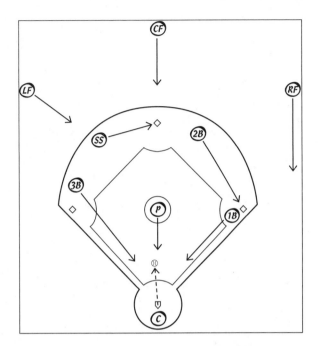

Sacrifice bunt: Runner on first

Catcher: Tell the infielders where to throw.

Pitcher: Cover the middle of the infield. If you field the ball, listen to the catcher's instructions, and then throw to the appropriate base.

First baseman: After holding the runner on first base, charge and cover the right side of the infield. If you field the ball, listen for the catcher's instructions, and then throw to the appropriate base.

Second baseman: Cover first base.

Shortstop: Cover second base.

Third baseman: Charge toward home plate and cover the left side of the infield. (Be prepared to retreat quickly to third base to prevent the runner from advancing there.) If you field the ball, listen to the catcher's instructions, and then throw to the appropriate base.

Left fielder: Come toward the infield in order to back up poor throws.

Center fielder: Back up any throw to second base.

Right fielder: Back up any throw to first base.

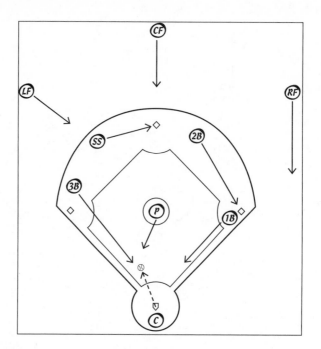

Sacrifice bunt: Runners on first and second, the infield goes for the out at first

Catcher: Tell the infielders where the throw is going.

Pitcher: Cover the third base line. If you field the ball, listen to the catcher's instructions and then throw to the first base.

First baseman: Cover the right side of the infield. If you field the ball, listen for the catcher's instructions, and then throw to first base.

Second baseman: Cover first base.

Shortstop: Cover second base.

Third baseman: Charge and cover the left side of the infield. If you field the ball, listen to the catcher's instructions, and then throw to the first base.

Left fielder: Back up any throw to second base or third base.

Center fielder: Back up any throw to second base.

Right fielder: Back up any throw to first base.

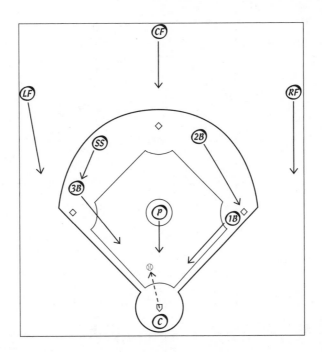

Wheel play: Batter puts down a sacrifice bunt with runners on first and second, the defense goes for the force-out at third

Catcher: Tell the infielders where the throw is going. (Remember that the center fielder is covering second on this play.)

Pitcher: The shortstop should break for third base before you deliver the pitch. Cover the middle of the infield. If you field the ball, listen to the catcher's instructions, and then throw to the appropriate base.

First baseman: Cover the right side of the infield. If you field the ball, listen for the catcher's instructions, and then throw to the appropriate base.

Second baseman: Cover first base.

Shortstop: Get behind the lead runner's right shoulder and break for third base as the pitcher sets.

Third baseman: Charge and cover the left side of the infield. If you field the ball, listen to the catcher's instructions, and then throw to the appropriate base.

Left fielder: Back up any throw to third base.

Center fielder: Come toward the infield to cover second base.

Right fielder: Back up any throw to first base.

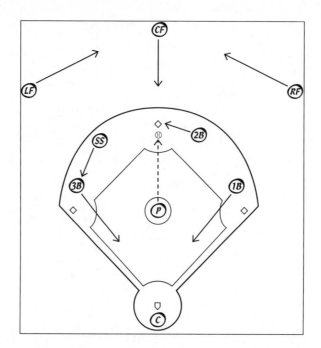

Wheel play fake: Runners on first and second with a pickoff play going to second

Catcher: Cover home plate.

Pitcher: As the shortstop breaks for third base, make your pickoff throw to second base.

First baseman: Cover the right side of the infield as if the wheel play were on.

Second baseman: Fake a step toward first base, and then break for second base for the pickoff throw.

Shortstop: Position yourself behind the runner's right shoulder. Break for third base as if the wheel play were on.

Third baseman: Charge and cover the left side of the infield.

Left fielder: Back up the center fielder.

Center fielder: Back up the throw to second base.

Right fielder: Back up the center fielder.

For the wheel play fake to work, everyone must go about his initial assignment as if the play is actually on.

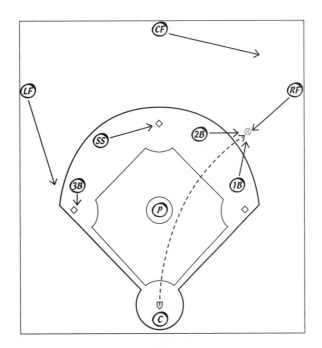

Pop fly to shallow right field

Catcher: If the bases are empty, back up a possible throw to first base; otherwise, cover home plate.

Pitcher: Call for a fielder if the ball is in the infield proper; if not, cover first.

First baseman: Call for a catch if you feel that you can make the play; however, you must back off if the right fielder or the second baseman calls for the ball.

Second baseman: Call for a catch, but back off if the right fielder calls you off.

Shortstop: Cover second base.

Third baseman: Cover third base.

Left fielder: Back up any throw to third base.

Center fielder: Back up the right fielder.

Right fielder: Call for the catch if you feel you can make the play. All other fielders must yield to you.

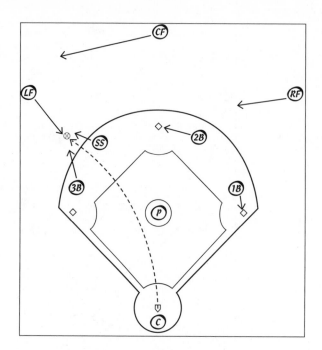

Pop fly to shallow left field

Catcher: If the bases are empty, back up a possible throw to third base; otherwise, cover home plate.

Pitcher: Call a fielder if the ball is close to the infield; if not, cover third base.

First baseman: Cover first base.

Second baseman: Cover second base.

Shortstop: Call for the ball if you think you can make the play. Give way if the left fielder calls for it.

Third baseman: Call for the catch if you think you can make the play. However, you must back off if the shortstop or left fielder calls you off.

Left fielder: Call for the ball if you think you can make the play. All other fielders must yield to you.

Center fielder: Back up the left fielder.

Right fielder: Back up any throw to second base.

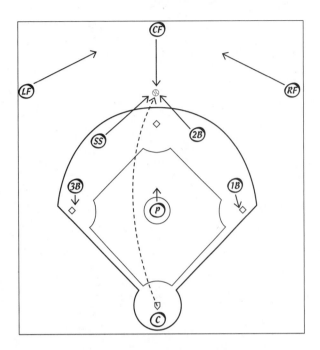

Pop fly to shallow center field

Catcher: Cover home plate.

Pitcher: Direct the infielders. If the shortstop and second baseman both go for the ball, cover second base if the first baseman is unable to do so.

First baseman: Cover first base unless the shortstop and second baseman both go for the ball. Then you must cover second.

Second baseman: Call for the ball if you think you can make the play. Back off if either the center fielder calls for it or if the shortstop calls for it before you do. Either you or the shortstop must retreat to cover second base.

Shortstop: Call for the ball if you think you can make the play. Give way if the center fielder calls for it or if the second baseman calls for it before you do. Either you or the second baseman must retreat to cover second base.

Third baseman: Cover third base.

Left fielder: Back up the center fielder.

Center fielder: Call for the ball if you think you can make the play. All other fielders must yield to you.

Right fielder: Back up the center fielder.

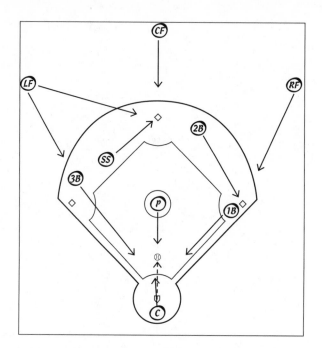

Basic bunt defense drill: With or without runners on

Catcher: Step in front of home plate.

Pitcher: Charge in from the mound, toward home plate.

First baseman: Charge toward home plate.

Second baseman: Cover first base.

Shortstop: Cover second base.

Third baseman: Charge toward home plate.

Right fielder: Back up the throw to first base.

Center fielder: Back up the throw to second base.

Left fielder: With a runner on second, back up the throw to third base. With a runner only on first, back up the throw to the left of second base.

Note: If the throw goes home or to either first or second base, the third baseman retreats back to third after the throw is executed.

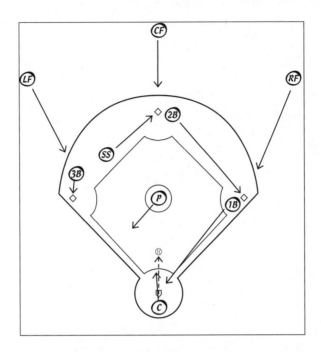

Basic bunt defense drill: Runner on second

Catcher: Step in front of home plate.

Pitcher: Charge in on a right angle to cover the third base side.

First baseman: Charge toward home plate.

Second baseman: Cover first base.

Shortstop: Cover second base.

Third baseman: Cover third base.

Right fielder: Back up a throw to first base.

Center fielder: Back up a throw to second base.

Left fielder: Back up a throw to third base.

Note: If the hitter bunts the ball hard and cleanly to a fielder, the defensive team should go after the lead out at second. If the hitter bunts the ball softly, the fielder should look for the play at third, but if the runner is bearing down on the bag, the fielder should throw to first for the "easy" out. If the fielder bobbles the ball, go for the out at first, but don't rush your throw to compensate for the bobble. Rushed throws often sail past their targets.

Part III

From Little League to the Major Leagues: Organized Baseball

In this part . . .

*B*aseball is everywhere — you just have to know where to find it. In this part, we introduce you to the wide variety of organized baseball leagues. Weighing and comparing player performances is one of the great pleasures of baseball, so we also show you how to understand the measurements that do so — baseball statistics. Also in this part, Sparky Anderson joins us to show you how a major league manager's thought processes work. Veteran umpire Harry Wendelstedt, Jr. reveals how baseball's arbiters should conduct themselves on the field. You find out about baseball jobs that don't require you to swing a bat or throw a pitch. And finally, we explain major league baseball's playoff system and the World Series.

Chapter 10

T-Ball to College Baseball and Everything in Between

*W*hether you're 5 or 55, male or female, you don't have to regard baseball merely as a spectator sport. If you want to compete in an informal atmosphere, your local parks department can make a baseball diamond available for pickup games. (You should always reserve field time in advance, especially if you have a number of leagues competing in your town.) Throughout the United States and Canada, thousands of baseball leagues and associations also offer nonprofessional players of all ages and genders an opportunity for organized competition.

The league that you or your child joins does not have to be affiliated with **USA Baseball** (919-474-8721, www.usabaseball.com), but if it is, be assured that the organization conforms to a rigorous standard. USA Baseball is the national governing body of amateur baseball. Members include the Little League, the Amateur Athletic Union, the National High School Coaches Association, PONY Baseball, the Police Athletic League, the YMCA, and the NCAA. USA Baseball is also responsible for picking (with the help of a national network of college coaches) and training the U.S. Olympic baseball team. At the start of the 2004 season, 135 USA Baseball alumni were playing in the Major Leagues. Their ranks included such stars as Barry Bonds, Nomar Garciaparra, Shawn Green, Todd Helton, and Jason Giambi. In the land of Blue Jays, **Baseball Canada** (613-748-5606, www.baseball.ca) is the prominent amateur organization.

T-Ball: A Good Place to Start

T-ball is baseball's version of miniature golf. The baseball is served on a batting tee, bases are never more than 60 feet apart, and everything else is scaled down so that children (usually 8 years old and under) can experience the joys of the national pastime without risking physical harm. The **T-Ball USA Association** (203-381-1440, www.teeballusa.org), based in Stratford, Connecticut, does not run any leagues or teams of its own, but it does assist many leading amateur organizations with their T-ball programs.

This nonprofit association also runs clinics to teach coaches and parents the rudiments of baseball. For more information about the program, pick up a copy of *The Official T-Ball USA Family Guide to Tee Ball* by Bing Broido (Masters Press).

Amateur Leagues for All Ages

Little League Baseball (570-326-1921, www.littleleague.org) is played in every state in the U.S. and in over 100 countries. With more than two and a half million participants (including over 300,000 female players), 100,000 volunteers, and 7,000 leagues, Little League is the world's largest organized youth sports program. Leagues are required to play an annual schedule of at least 12 games. A recently developed program, Little League Child Protection, requires member leagues to conduct background checks on certain volunteers. The organization also maintains a museum and conducts instructional clinics for umpires and managers. It annually sponsors an international World Series in seven divisions.

Does Little League baseball provide a first step to the big leagues? An estimated 80 percent of all major-league players participated in Little League baseball. Current major leaguers who played in the Little League World Series, held each year in Williamsport, Pennsylvania, include Gary Sheffield, Dan Wilson, and Wilson Alvarez.

You can keep up with the latest Little League events by visiting the Little League Web site (www.littleleague.org) and ordering its ASAP newsletters, which offer advice on safety and instruction, or the e-zine, *Little League News.* Subscriptions are free. You should also contact the Little League for a complete list of its instructional manuals and magazines.

The **Babe Ruth League** (609-695-1434, www.baberuthleague.org) operates in 48 states in the U.S. (Hawaii and Alaska are the exceptions). Founded in 1951, the organization is currently composed of over 900,000 players on

44,000 teams in 6,200 leagues. Five- and 6-year-olds in this league play T-ball; 7- and 8-year-olds play with bases 60 feet (18.2 meters) apart and hit against a slow pitching machine or a coach. At ages 9 and 10, players face some live pitching. Babe Ruth League players do not, however, compete on fields with major-league dimensions until they are 13, when they enter a prep program. Age classifications top out at 18.

This league stresses player participation over winning and is famous for teaching the proper way to play the game. And Joe Morgan can tell you that reputation is well-deserved. He participated in the Oakland chapter of the Babe Ruth League as a member of the Qwik Way Drive-In team.

Over 400,000 players on 24,000 teams in 11 states participate in **Dixie Youth Baseball** (903-927-2255, www.dixie.org), the leading youth baseball program in the southern United States. Five divisions compose the association's baseball programs. The Youth T-Ball division caters to children ages 8 and under. The oldest division, Dixie Majors Baseball, is for players ages 15 to 18. Championship tournaments are held for the four oldest divisions during the first week of August. Dixie also sponsors softball leagues.

Competition is probably fiercest in leagues sponsored by the **Amateur Athletic Union** (407-934-7200, www.aausports.org), which boasts associations in all 50 states in the U.S. Like professional clubs, many member teams travel out of their locales to play games. Players participate in 12 divisions with age limits ranging from 9 to 20. Amateur Athletic Union championships are decided in tournaments featuring double-pool play. Teams are seeded before the first round. Winners go on to play in the National Championship Tournament, and losers participate in a consolation bracket.

Other youth baseball organizations include:

- **All American Amateur Baseball Association** in Zanesville, Ohio (614-453-8531, www.johnstownpa.com/aaaba)
- **American Legion Baseball** in Indianapolis, Indiana (317-630-1213, www.baseball.legion.org)
- **Continental Amateur Baseball Association** in Westerville, Ohio (740-382-4620, www.cababaseball.com)
- **Dizzy Dean Baseball** in Hernando, Missouri (662-429-4365, www.dizzy deanbbinc.org)
- **George Kelly Amateur Baseball Federation** in Altoona, Pennsylvania (814-941-9293)
- **Hap Dumont Baseball** in Wichita, Kansas (316-721-1779, www.hapdumont baseball.com)

✔ **National Association of Police Athletic Leagues** in Palm Beach, Florida (561-844-1823, www.nationalpal.org)

✔ **PONY Baseball** in Washington, Pennsylvania (412-225-1060, www.pony.org)

✔ **U.S. Amateur Baseball Association** in Edmonds, Washington (425-776-7130, www.usaba.com)

✔ **U.S. Amateur Baseball Federation** in Chula Vista, California (619-934-2551, www.usabf.com)

Your child and the child within you can compete in the **National Amateur Baseball Federation** (301-464-5400, www.nabf.com), which has 350,000 participants in 85 franchises across the U.S. Founded in 1914, this is the only all-volunteer amateur baseball organization in the country. For younger players, classifications advance from Rookie (ages 10 and under) to Senior level (ages 18 and under). Players between the ages of 19 and 22 compete in the college classification. If you're over 22, you can recapture your youth at the Majors level, an unlimited classification. Many former college players and professionals who have reacquired their amateur status compete in this division. Member teams play anywhere from 30 to 100 games per year in local competition. The best of these teams participate in round-robin championship tournaments scheduled between mid-July and late August.

Two other organizations have unlimited classifications. The **American Amateur Baseball Congress** (269-781-2002, www.aabc.us) holds August tournaments in seven divisions named for Hall of Famers: Roberto Clemente (ages 8 and under), Willie Mays (10 and under), Pee Wee Reese (12 and under), Sandy Koufax (14 and under), Mickey Mantle (16 and under), Connie Mack (18 and under), and Stan Musial (unlimited). The **Continental Amateur Baseball Association** (740-382-4620, www.cababaseball.com) maintains competitive balance by spreading players out among 12 classifications (ages 9 and under to unlimited). You can find out everything you need to know about this organization from its Web site.

Founded by former Detroit Tiger minor leaguer John Young in 1988, **Restore Baseball in the Inner Cities** (RBI) annually brings the national pastime to over 100,000 urban youths across the U.S. RBI teams compete to participate in an annual World Series, which is held in a major-league park. Girls' softball has been part of the program since 1994. Major League Baseball contributes a portion of the RBI budget, and big-league players such as pitching ace Kevin Brown have also pledged their financial support. To find out how you, your community, or your company can get behind this laudable organization, call 212-931-7897.

The Collegiate Talent Pool

The first baseball game played between two colleges took place on July 1, 1859, when Amherst beat Pittsfield 73–32. (Evidently, they thought they were playing football.) Only 35 feet (10.6 meters) separated the pitcher from the batter, and the bases were a mere 60 feet (18.2 meters) apart. Few of the great college players of the late 1800s ever donned a major-league uniform; most college men didn't consider baseball to be a respectable profession. However, the ascent of Christy Mathewson of Bucknell University, the elegant and erudite Hall of Fame pitcher for the New York Giants, considerably altered that attitude. Matty had been president of his class and a member of a literary society, and he could beat ten opponents at chess simultaneously. He demonstrated that one could play professional baseball without surrendering the title "gentleman." Largely due to his influence — as well as that of other turn-of-the-century college stars who turned pro (such as Hall of Famers Eddie Collins and Harry Hooper), American campuses became incubators for major-league talent.

Today, over two-thirds of all major-league players have a college education. Collegiate baseball — which is intensely scrutinized by major-league scouts — provides the perfect stage for aspiring major leaguers to showcase their talents. The National Collegiate Athletic Association (NCAA) is, of course, the big kahuna of the college game. Over 250 colleges — among them Mathewson's beloved Bucknell — compete in its 29 Division I conferences. Other NCAA college baseball squads play in either Division II or III. The NCAA Division I College World Series takes place during the first week of June. Both championship series for the other two divisions take place during the final week of May.

Major-league baseball chooses its fledgling pros from among high school and college players in the annual Rule IV draft. Each team gets one pick per round until the talent pool is exhausted. Players picked in the first few rounds are considered the best prospects; however, getting picked in a high round is no guarantee of success. One-third of first-round picks never play a single inning of major-league baseball. And many late-round picks have gone on to all-star careers. For example, Mike Piazza, perhaps the greatest hitting catcher of all time, was the Los Angeles Dodgers' 62nd-round pick in 1988. That means clubs preferred more than 1,600 players — enough bodies to stock the rosters for the entire major leagues and then some — to this almost certain future Hall of Famer.

The following list is just a sampling of some recent major-league players who were passed over until the late rounds of the annual draft:

- Mike Piazza (Dodgers, 1988, 62nd round)
- Mark Grace (Cubs, 1985, 24th round)
- Jeff Kent (Blue Jays, 1989, 20th round)
- Mike Bordick (Athletics, 1986, signed as undrafted free agent)
- Scott Brosius (Athletics, 1987, 20th round)
- Richie Sexson (Indians, 1993, 24th round)
- Marvin Bernard (Giants, 1992, 50th round)
- Bernard Gilkey (Cardinals, 1984, undrafted free agent)
- John Smoltz (Tigers, 1985, 22nd round)
- Andy Pettite (Yankees, 1990, 22nd round)
- Robb Nen (Rangers, 1987, 32nd round)
- Jeff Zimmerman (Rangers, 1998, unsigned free agent)

Chapter 11

The Minors and Other Leagues

In This Chapter

▶ Following American minor-league action

▶ Recognizing Japanese leagues and players

▶ Vacationing with tropical teams and winter leagues

▶ Playing béisbol, Cuban-style

▶ Reading up on the minor leagues

Major-league baseball isn't the only game in town (especially if you live in Helena, Montana, or Rome, Italy). Thousands of amateur and professional baseball leagues offer games to fans all over the globe. Japan, Mexico, Holland, Cuba, Venezuela, Italy, Korea, and China are just some of the countries that have embraced our national pastime. And who knows how many amateur leagues are flourishing throughout the world — the number must easily reach five figures. Baseball fever . . . it's catching and spreading everywhere!

The American Minor Leagues

Major-league organizations often send their young players to the minor leagues to hone their talents before joining the big club. Veteran ballplayers sometimes visit the minors, too. A major-league player usually rehabs his injuries in the minors before returning to the big leagues, and if his performance has slipped and he is trying to recapture the magic, he may step down to the minors for a while. Most minor-league players have something to prove. And while the youngsters want to show their organizations that they're ready to step up to the big leagues, declining veteran players are eager to convince a team that they can still compete in the majors.

Because nearly everyone on the field is highly motivated, you often see a hustling, rollicking brand of baseball in the minors. The level of skills on display varies from league to league, team to team, and player to player, but the level of thrills is consistently high from Triple-A ball down to the Rookie Leagues. Most minor leaguers have large dreams but small salaries. They play a game they love not for dollars but for glory. Their innocent, fervent aspirations will fail to touch your heart only if you don't have one.

Minor-league franchises — where are they?

Nineteen minor leagues were operating under one umbrella organization — the National Association — in 1999. For most of the twentieth century, a second umbrella organization — the American Association — had also overseen minor-league play. But at the end of the 1998 season, the American Association folded. Its member teams were dispersed among the remaining minor leagues.

The number of teams in each minor league may vary from year to year. Most minor-league clubs are owned by major-league organizations that absorb all the operating costs. A few are independent entities, though even they have working agreements with clubs that underwrite much (if not all) of their overhead costs. When the working agreement expires, a minor-league club can switch its major-league affiliation (which it might do if it has greater proximity to another big-league team).

At the end of the 2004 season, the National Association leagues and franchises were competing under the following alignments (2004 major-league affiliations are listed in parentheses):

Class AAA (Triple A)

- **The International League:** Charlotte (White Sox), Columbus (Yankees), Norfolk (Mets), Ottawa (Orioles), Pawtucket (Red Sox), Richmond (Braves), Rochester (Twins), Scranton/Wilkes-Barre (Phillies), Syracuse (Blue Jays), Toledo (Tigers), *Buffalo (Indians), *Indianapolis (Brewers), Durham (Devil Rays), and *Louisville (Reds)

- **Pacific Coast League:** Edmonton (Washington), Salt Lake (Angels), Las Vegas (Dodgers), Portland (Padres), Sacramento (Athletics), Tucson (Diamondbacks), Tacoma (Mariners), Fresno (Giants), Albuquerque (Marlins), Colorado Springs (Rockies), *Oklahoma (Rangers), *Nashville (Pirates), Memphis (Cardinals), *New Orleans (Astros), *Iowa (Cubs), and *Omaha (Royals)

✔ **The Mexican League (ML)** is also a Triple A member of the National Association. All its teams are independent entities with no major-league affiliations. The ML consists of 16 franchises playing in two divisions:

- **Northern Division:** Monterrey Sultanes, Monclova Acereros, Saltillo Saraperos, Vaqueros Alguna, San Luis Potosi Tuneros, Tiajuana Toros, Aguascalientes Rieleros, and Puebla Pericos

- **Southern Division:** Yucatan Leones, Campeche Piratas, Tabasco Olmecas, Mexico Diablos Rojos, Veracruz Rojos, Tigres de Angelopolis, Oaxaca Guerreros, and Cancun Langosteros

Mexican League teams play a 122-game schedule that begins in March and ends in early August. The top two teams in each zone and the third-place clubs with the best records compete in a three-tiered playoff. The two finalists decide the Mexican League champion in a best-of-seven series.

*Indicates a former American Association franchise.

The lower minors

We could present all the minor-league teams and their affiliations, but then this would turn into a book of lists. Instead, in Table 11-1, we present one last list of the other National Association leagues.

Table 11-1	National Association Leagues	
Class AA (Double A)	*Class A (Advanced)*	*Class A*
Eastern League	California League	Midwest League
Southern League	Carolina League	
South Atlantic League	Florida State League	
Texas League		
Short-Season Class A	*Rookie (Advanced)*	*Rookie*
New York-Penn League	Appalachian League	Arizona League
Northwest League	Pioneer League	Dominican Summer League
		Gulf Coast League

Five independent minor leagues operated in 2003 (down from ten in 1997): the Atlantic League, the Frontier League, the Northern League, the Northeast League, and the Central League. The Southwestern League is due to commence play in 2005. Most of these clubs operate without any major-league affiliation.

Not just another minor-league team

Bill Murray, actor-comedian-*Saturday Night Live* alumnus, is one of the principle owners of Minnesota's St. Paul Saints, a Northern League entry. Under club president Mike Veeck, the Saints have proven to be as entertaining as the brilliant Murray himself. Chia Pet Night, MASH Night (featuring a give-away of balls bearing camouflage patterns), Ron Popeil Vegamatic Day, Whoopee Cushion Night . . . no promotion pushes the envelope too far as long as it pulls fans into the Saints' home park. St. Paul has also become a proving ground for former major leaguers eager to return from injury, retirement, or some other career detour. Slugger Darryl Strawberry launched his successful major-league comeback with the Saints. Veeck's commitment to goofiness, if not downright lunacy (he once tried introducing Vasectomy Night — don't ask!), pays off at the box office. St. Paul is one of the few professional baseball franchises that sells out every game before opening day. The team's official motto: "Fun is good!"

By the end of the 2003 season, major-league teams had signed over 30 players from the Atlantic League alone, proof that the independent leagues have become a formidable incubator for professional talent. Kevin Millar, J.D. Drew, and Ben Weber are some of the major leaguers who spent time perfecting their trade in an independent league. Los Angeles Dodgers pitcher Hideo Nomo is one of the owners of the Elmira Pioneers in the Northeast League.

You will see some strange transactions in these maverick circuits. The Minneapolis Loons once sold reliever Kerry Lightenberg to the National League's Atlanta Braves for six dozen bats and two dozen baseballs. And the Pacific Suns of the now defunct Western League traded pitcher Ken Krahenbuhl to the Greensville Bluesmen for a player to be named later . . . and 10 pounds of catfish.

If you want to follow the progress of your favorite club's top farm-team prospects, the bi-weekly publication *Baseball America* provides stats for every player as well as scouting reports on many top prospects at every minor-league level. If you want to know which teams are associated with any of the minor or independent leagues, refer to Appendix B for a league's address or phone number, or obtain the information from the most current copy of *The Baseball America Directory*.

Experience not always necessary

Few players make it to the majors without first playing in the minor leagues. However, a fair number of those who made their professional debuts in the Major Leagues and were never sent down to the minors would eventually win

Minor-league stars

Minor-league audiences have witnessed some phenomenal performances over the years. In 1954, Joe Bauman, a first baseman with Roswell, hit 72 home runs to establish a minor-league baseball record that still stands. Tony Lazzeri, who would eventually star at second base for the New York Yankees, drove in 222 runs for San Francisco of the Pacific Coast League in 1925 (his team played 197 games that year). In 1922, pitcher Joe Boehler won 38 games for Tulsa of the Western League. In 1951, Willie Mays compiled an astounding .477 batting average over 35 games for the Minneapolis Millers. Mays was promptly summoned by his parent club, the New York Giants, and never spent another day in the minors.

Some players' lifetime totals are equally staggering. Hector Espino, a slugging first baseman, hit a minor-league career record 484 home runs, primarily for teams in the Mexican League. Bill Thomas won 383 games while pitching for various teams and leagues. Right-hander Frank Shellenback holds the Pacific Coast League career wins record with 295. Because he relied primarily on a spitball, Shellenback's major-league prospects were shattered when the major-league owners banned that slippery pitch. Ox Eckhardt spent parts of 13 seasons with various minor-league clubs; he retired with the highest career batting average in minor-league history — a dazzling .367.

Buzz Arlett won 108 games in his first six minor-league seasons (1918–23). He won 29 games while pitching for Oakland in the Pacific Coast League in 1920. He also enjoyed two 25-win seasons. However, after hurting his arm, he switched to the outfield and hit 432 career homers. In 1931, the 32-year-old Arlett earned a spot on the Philadelphia Phillies of the National League. In his only major-league season, he hit .313 with 18 home runs and 72 runs batted in. Despite this fine showing, the Phillies released him after the season and no other major-league team picked him up. (Apparently, Arlett was considered a dreadful fielder, though many minor-league historians claim he was an adequate glove man.) And special note should be taken of left-hander George Brunet. Between the majors and minors, he pitched in professional ball for 33 years (1953–1985). In his final season, Brunet compiled a minuscule 1.94 earned run average in the heavy-hitting Mexican League; he was 48 years old.

The minors have also showcased their share of legendary teams. The best of these may be the 1937 Newark Bears, a New York Yankee affiliate that featured such future major-league stars as second baseman Joe Gordon (an eventual American League MVP), outfielder Charlie "King Kong" Keller, first baseman George McQuinn, and pitcher Atley Donald. This group won the International League pennant by 25½ games with a 109–41 record.

baseball's highest honor — induction into the Baseball Hall of Fame in Cooperstown. Their ranks include

- Pitcher Walter Johnson (417 wins)
- Pitcher Catfish Hunter (224 wins)
- Pitcher Chief Bender (212 wins)
- Pitcher Ted Lyons (260 wins)

- ✔ Pitcher Sandy Koufax (165 wins, 3 Cy Young Awards)
- ✔ Pitcher Bob Feller (266 wins)
- ✔ Pitcher Eddie Plank (326 wins)
- ✔ Pitcher Eppa Rixey (266 wins)
- ✔ Shortstop Ernie Banks (512 home runs)

   Banks, who played his entire career with the Chicago Cubs, spent half of it at first base. He won two consecutive MVP awards (1958–59) while playing shortstop.

- ✔ Shortstop Bobby Wallace (the greatest fielding shortstop of his era)

   Wallace's glove work was so spectacular, he is one of the handful of men who played 25 years or more in the majors. In 1902, he was baseball's highest-paid player.

- ✔ Second baseman Frank Frisch (.316 lifetime batting average)
- ✔ First baseman George Sisler (.340 lifetime batting average)
- ✔ Outfielder Mel Ott (511 homers)
- ✔ Outfielder Al Kaline (3,007 career hits)
- ✔ Outfielder Dave Winfield (3,110 hits, 1,833 RBI)

Baseball in Japan

Historians credit Horace Wilson, an American professor based in Tokyo during the 1870s, as the founder of Japanese baseball. Wilson's students called the game *yakyu* (field ball) or *beisu boru*. Amateur baseball flourished in Japan during the early part of the twentieth century. American teams regularly toured the country, and many top U.S. stars — including Frankie Frisch, Babe Ruth, and Casey Stengel — helped teach the nuances of the game to an enthusiastic Japanese audience. Ty Cobb, baseball's career hit king at the time, held baseball clinics in Japan in 1928. Masanori Murakami, a left-handed reliever with the San Francisco Giants from 1964–65, was the first native-born Japanese player to play major-league baseball in the United States.

Japan's major leagues

Japan's first professional team, Nihon Undo Kyokai, was formed in 1920. Two more professional teams appeared in 1921, but all three disbanded by 1923 due to a lack of competition. Matsutaro Shoriki, a newspaper magnate, re-introduced professional baseball to his country when he formed the all-pro team Dai Nippon (the forerunner of the current Tokyo Giants) in 1934. Two years later, Shoriki and a group of businesspeople formed Japan's first professional league. In 1950, that league split into the Central and Pacific Leagues. Today, six teams operate in each of the two leagues (see Table 11-2).

Table 11-2	Japanese Baseball
Central League	*Pacific League*
Chunichi Dragons	Chiba Lotte Marines
Hanshin Tigers	Fukuoka Daiei Hawks
Hiroshima Toyo Carp	Kintetsu Buffaloes
Yakult Swallows	Nippon Ham Fighters
Yokohama Bay Stars	Orix Blue Wave
Tokyo Yomiuri Giants	Seibu Lions

Both leagues include tie games in their standings. Japanese teams carry 28 players on their major-league rosters, though only 25 are eligible to play in any one game. Each organization has a 70-man roster, including minor leaguers. Foreign (non-Japanese) players may hold four of these roster spots. Teams play a 135-game schedule (home and away game breakdowns vary each season) with no playoffs. Regular season games begin during the first week of April and end by the final week of September. The top teams in each league compete in the best-of-seven Japan Series — their version of America's World Series — in mid-October.

The quality of Japanese baseball has improved dramatically during the last two decades, though it is still not on par with the American game. American scouts also have enormous regard for Japanese infield play, which generally equals, if not surpasses, U.S. major-league standards. However, Japanese outfielders and catchers lack the throwing strength of American major leaguers. Japanese pitching is impressive, but power hitters are scarce. Whereas the league used to be dominated by control artists, fireballers such as Hideo Nomo and Kazuhisa Ishii have emerged to successfully compete in the United States. Elite hitters Ichiro Suzuki and Hideki "Godzilla" Matsui have also won fame while playing in the North American major leagues.

The stars

Like the United States, Japan boasts its share of legendary baseball heroes, all of whom would have been stars no matter where they played. Their numbers include

- Sadaharu Oh: He's the winner of 15 home-run titles, 9 MVP awards, 5 batting championships, and 13 RBI crowns while hitting — are you seated? — 868 career home runs.

- Tetsuharu Kawahami: Japan's "God of Batting" hit .377 in 1951 and managed the Tokyo Giants to 11 pennants in 14 years, including 9 straight Japan Series victories.

- Katsuya Nomura: The "Johnny Bench of Japan" hit 657 home runs from 1954 to 1980 while catching 2,918 games.

- Masaichi Kaneda: This left-hander posted 400 career wins and 4,900 strikeouts from 1950 to 1964 while playing with a club that finished in the upper half of the league standings only once.

- Yutaka Enatsu: He struck out 401 batters in 329 innings in 1968.

- Kazuhisa Inao: This pitcher won 42 games as the Nishitetsu Lions' ace in 1961.

Nothing lost in translation: A Japanese baseball mini-glossary

Japanese announcers have their own versions of many common American baseball terms. These are some of the words you will frequently hear when you tune into Japanese baseball broadcasts on your cable or satellite TV:

- Anda (ahn-dah): A single
- Daseki (dah-sek-ee): An at-bat or plate appearance
- Dasha (da-shaw): The hitter at the plate
- Fohku (fo-koo): Forkball
- Gida (gee-dah): A sacrifice bunt
- Honrui (hahn-roo-ee): Home plate
- Honruida (hahn-roo-ee-dah): A home run
- Ichirui (eechie-roo-ee): First base
- Kaabu (kah-boo): Curveball
- Naiya Anda (ny-ah-ahn-dah): Infield hit
- Nirui (nee-roo-ee): Second base
- Niruida (nee-roo-ee-dah): A double
- Raito-mae (rye-toe-mah-ee): Base hit to right field
- Refuto-mae (rah-fu-toh-mah-ee): Base hit to left
- Sanrui (sahn-roo-ee): Third base
- Sanruida (sahn-roo-ee-dah): A triple
- Senshu (sen-shoe): A player (preceded by the individual's name, such as Matsui-senshu)
- Senta backscreen (sentah-baku-skreen): A home run over the center field fence
- Senta-mae (sentah-mah-ee): Base hit to center field
- Streto (streh-to): Fastball
- Suraida (soo-rye-dah): Slider
- Toshu (toe-shoe): Pitcher

New Asian Frontiers

Over the past 15 years, professional baseball has become wildly popular in two of Japan's neighboring countries. Taiwan is home to the Chinese Professional Baseball League. Founded in 1990, the league's six teams play a 110-game schedule. Four teams compose the Taiwan Major League, which offers fans a 96-game schedule.

The Korean Baseball Organization has been operating since 1982. Its eight clubs compete in a 132-game season. Chan Ho Park, who made his major-league debut with the L.A. Dodgers in 1994, is the first native-born Korean player to achieve stardom in the United States.

Tropical Leagues

In Mexico, Central America, and the Caribbean, baseball is nothing so sedate as a pastime; it's a passion. U.S. sailors and students introduced the game to Cuba around 1866. (See "The Cuban Juggernaut" later in this chapter.) The Cubans, in turn, brought baseball to Puerto Rico, the Dominican Republic, Panama, Mexico, Nicaragua, Venezuela, and Colombia.

The Caribbean Baseball Confederation

With the exception of the Mexican League, which is part of the American minor leagues, most other teams south of the equator play in one of the leagues that compose the Caribbean Baseball Confederation (CBC). These associations are referred to as Winter Leagues because their seasons begin in late October or November. There is no regular-season interleague play, but the league champions do compete against each other in the Caribbean World Series held each year in early February.

The following leagues make up the CBC:

- **The Dominican League:** Founded in 1951, its six teams play a 60-game schedule that begins in late October and usually ends just before the start of the new year. Each organization has a 30-man roster. At the end of the season, the four teams with the best winning percentages meet in a round-robin tournament. The two survivors play a best-of-seven series to determine the league champion. Dominican League franchises include Aguilas, Azucareros, Escogido, Estrellas, Licey, and the Northern Giants (located in San Francisco de Macoris).

✔ **The Mexican-Pacific League:** Not to be confused with the Triple A Mexican League, the MPL was founded in 1958. Its eight teams play a 68-game schedule. The season opens around mid-October and ends in late December. Rosters are limited to 27 players. At the end of the season, the six clubs with the best winning percentages meet in the best-of-seven quarterfinals. The three winners of those series join the loser of the best-of-seven semifinals with the best regular season record. Two finalists emerge from those series to play a best-of-seven league championship. Mexican-Pacific League franchises include Culiacan, Guasave, Hermosillo, Mochis, Mazatlan, Mexicali, Navojoa, and Obregon.

✔ **The Puerto Rican League:** Founded in 1938, the oldest Caribbean league features six teams and a 48-game schedule. Clubs begin regular season play in early November and finish in early January. Twenty-six players compose each roster. At season's end, the league's top four teams meet in the best-of-seven semifinals. A best-of-nine final determines the league champion. Puerto Rican League teams include Caguas Carolina, Criollos, Mayaguez, Ponce, San Juan, and Santurce.

✔ **The Venezuelan League:** Founded in 1946, the league has eight teams in two divisions. The teams play a 62-game schedule that starts in late October and usually ends by New Year's Eve. Rosters are limited to 27 players. Each division's top two teams join a wild-card entry (whichever third-place club has the better regular-season record) in a 16-game round-robin series. The two teams that win that series meet in a best-of-seven playoff for the league championship. Venezuelan League teams include Caracas, La Guaira, Magallanes, and Oriente in the East Division, and Aragua, Lara, Occidente, and Zulia in the West.

Other winter leagues

Two other leagues also supply U.S. fans with baseball entertainment during the fall and winter months. The Arizona Fall League, which begins its 50-game season in early October, is a terrific place to watch the top prospects of some of your favorite major-league teams improve their games. All of the league's six teams have multiple working agreements with various major-league clubs.

The Maryland Fall League, a four-team confederation that features a 42-game schedule, debuted in 1998. Each club carries 28 players on its roster, many of them Class AA and A prospects putting in a little overtime to hone their skills.

Check out Appendix B for more information on these leagues.

The Cuban Juggernaut

Emilio Sabourin founded *Liga de Beisbol Profesional,* Cuba's first organized league, in 1878. Cuba later had a minor-league entry, the Havana Sugar Kings, in the International League (AAA). Players from the island who went on to star in the American major leagues included Tony Oliva, Minnie Minoso, Camilo Pascual, Dolf Lucque, Zoilo Versalles, Luis Tiant, Tony Perez, Rey Ordonez, and Orlando "El Duque" Hernandez.

However, shortly after Fidel Castro took power in 1959, the International League transferred the Havana franchise to Jersey City, New Jersey. Castro reacted by banning professional baseball throughout the country. He disbanded all pro teams and forbade Cuba's players from signing major-league contracts. The flow of Cuban talent to the United States was stemmed at the source.

Castro, a rabid baseball fan who had once been a middling pitching prospect, sought to fill the void by establishing the amateurs-only Cuban League. Its 16 franchises (representing 14 cities) start by playing a 65-game schedule. Eight of these teams go on to participate in a 63-game second season called the Selected Series. Four clubs from that competition continue playing during a February postseason that culminates with the *Series Nacional,* Cuba's version of the World Series.

Most observers agree that Cuba is the world's epicenter for amateur baseball. From 1987 to 1996, the island's national team posted an 80–1 record in international competition. It has not lost a Pan American Games baseball tournament since 1963.

I covered the historic game between the Baltimore Orioles and Cuban All-Stars in Havana on March 28, 1999. Five Cuban players made a lasting impression on me. Third baseman Omar Linares, long touted as the island's top baseball star, is an exceptional athlete with a good idea at the plate and obvious power. He's something on the order of the Phillies' Scott Rolen. Given some seasoning in the high minors, German Mesa and Marty Paret, both wide-ranging shortstops, could play in the big leagues. Pitcher Jose Ibar possesses pinpoint control although he's not overpowering. He'd probably make it as a long reliever in the majors. Another pitcher, Jose Contrares, looked like the real deal, gifted with a lively fastball, devastating splitter, sharp control, and genuine mound smarts. He pitched impressively as a spot-starter and reliever for the New York Yankees in 2003 and had earned a place in that club's starting rotation as we go to press in 2004.

Required Reading for Minor-League Fans

Your local library or bookstore is loaded with many fine books about minor-league and international baseball. Here's a sampling:

- *Stolen Season: A Journey through America and Baseball's Minor Leagues* (Random House) by David Lamb. In this remarkable book, the author — a foreign correspondent — rediscovers America by traveling the minor-league circuit.

- *The Society of American Baseball Research's Minor League Baseball Stars* and *Minor League Baseball Stars.* Both of these books offer complete surveys of minor-league records. The two volumes include stats for 300 minor-league stars as well as profiles of the most successful minor-league managers. Both volumes are available through SABR, whose contact information is listed in Appendix B.

- *The Story of Minor League Baseball: A History of the Game of Professional Baseball in the United States with Particular Reference to Its Growth and Development in the Smaller Cities and Towns of the Nation* edited by Robert Finch, Ben Morgan, and Henry Addington. Its title is the length of some books, but this volume delivers what it promises. Packed with records and stats, it is the most comprehensive book ever written on minor-league baseball as it was played during the first half of the twentieth century. You might have to tap a Web site featuring backlisted sports titles to find it, but this book is well worth the search.

- *Sadaharu Oh!: The Zen Way of Baseball* (New York Times Books) by Sadaharu Oh and David Falkner. No book offers more insight into the life of a Japanese baseball player.

- *Foul Ball: My Life and Hard Times Trying to Save an Old Ballpark* (Midpoint Trade Books) by Jim Bouton. A baseball love story. Bouton, a former 20-game winner with the New York Yankees and author of the baseball classic *Ball Four,* recounts how he and a few dedicated townspeople tried to save the oldest minor-league ballpark in America from the wrecking ball.

Chapter 12

There Are Tricks to This Game: Coaching

*B*aseball managers are responsible for all on-field decisions affecting their teams. Professional baseball managers (usually with the help of an array of coaches) decide what to emphasize in training camp, which players make up the team's roster (though contract considerations determine much of that), who bats where in the starting lineup, and who sits on the bench.

Below the professional level, baseball managers — often called *coaches* — face even more responsibilities. In addition to making decisions about what happens on the field, managers must decide how to effectively encourage younger players while still offering them sound advice and constructive criticism. In this chapter, we explore how to do all these things and still find time to enjoy the game.

A Manager's Role

BASEBALL SPEAK

During games, managers decide which strategy to employ from inning to inning (though many professional managers trust their veteran players to make those decisions for themselves). Managers call for, among other things, sacrifice bunts, hit-and-run plays, and stolen base attempts. They occasionally flash the *take sign* when they don't want a hitter to swing at a particular pitch.

Managers impact a game most dramatically with their choices of substitutions. Picking the right pinch hitter or relief pitcher often spells the difference between victory and defeat. Some people say that a great major-league manager can add six victories to a team's total during a 162-game season. That may not sound like much, but because every game you don't win is a loss, five additional wins translate into a ten-game spread in the standings. (For example, a team with a mediocre manager may go 81–81 during a 162-game season. If a great manager milks five more wins out of that team, it finishes 86–76.) That spread can mean the difference between having a disastrous season or a respectable one, between being an also-ran or a pennant contender.

It's difficult to calculate how many games incompetent managers cost their teams. If a manager's strategy is unsound or the lineup selections fail to maximize a club's offensive potential, you may be looking at another ten-game spread in the other direction. However, much depends on the makeup of the club; a well-schooled, veteran team can band together to overcome a poor skipper (manager). But if the manager is also a divisive presence in the clubhouse, an entire season may be undermined.

Managerial responsibilities deepen and broaden below the pro and college levels. If you're coaching a high school or youth team, you must spend more time teaching fundamentals to your inexperienced charges. That task requires patience. Besides being a manager, you sometimes have to assume the role of psychologist and parent figure, especially if your players are preteens. Many of your young players may be going nose-to-nose with loss, failure, and rejection for the first time in their lives. If you guide them with compassion, each defeat becomes an opportunity for growth and insight. If you ignore their pain, or worse, exacerbate it with ridicule or cold silence, you may scar them for life. Your responsibility is nothing less than that.

Sparky Anderson's Winning Advice

Coaches and managers can find hitting, pitching, training, and defensive tips to pass along to their players throughout Part II of this book. You can also find 26 defensive strategies in Chapter 9. However, nothing written on any of those pages can illustrate how a manager thinks. To do that, we have brought in the most successful baseball manager of the last 40 years. In 26 seasons as manager of the Cincinnati Reds and Detroit Tigers, Sparky Anderson won 2,194 games (only two managers in baseball history have won more), three world championships, five league championships, and seven division titles. He's the only skipper to guide teams to World Series championships in both leagues. So sit back and discover how a master manager approaches the game.

Note: Although Sparky Anderson's advice stems from his experience as a manager in the Major Leagues, what he says can be applied to coaching baseball at almost any level.

Know your players

"You should develop enough of a feel for your players that you can sense if something is off just by walking through the clubhouse. This means you have to be able to read a player's face and body language, his whole demeanor, so that you can head off a problem before it threatens the team. This also means you have to talk to your players constantly to get some insight into how they think. And that doesn't just mean talking baseball. Find out about their hobbies, their families, the movie they watched the night before. Anything. Listen closely and you'll find out what your players are all about — that will help you deal with them.

"Don't think the players have to adjust to your personality. It's the other way around. You have to find out what inspires your players and what turns them off. Some managers say they treat all their players the same, but that's impossible. Everyone on your team is different, and they must be treated as individuals.

"Knowing your players also means understanding their strengths and limitations. If a left-handed junkballer is on the mound, and you send up a pinch hitter who has difficulty with slow stuff, whose fault is it when he makes an out? That's your out because you asked him to do something he couldn't do."

Avoid having a happy bench

"You hear about those utility players who play very little but are content with their role on the club. I love those guys — as long as they're on someone else's club. I never wanted anyone on my roster who was happy about not playing. You want guys who want to be out on the field, so that when you give them a chance, they're going to bring some fire to the lineup."

But don't let them get too unhappy

"Keep your bench and your regular starters fresh by weaving players in and out of the lineup all season. In 1976, the Reds had a tremendous starting lineup; we won the division by ten games and were 7–0 in the playoffs and World Series. Our eight regulars each had over 500 plate appearances, but we played them as a unit only 57 times during the season. We gave everyone a chance to contribute."

Know the elements of a winning team

"Pitching, defense, speed, and power, in that order. Power is marvelous, but when you put up eight runs and the other team puts up nine, it can be draining. When you have great pitching, you stop the other team from moving. You can create enough runs to win without using the long ball. On defense, if you give the other team only 27 outs, you have a chance. Give them 28 or 30 outs (by making errors or making mental mistakes), and you're handing their big sluggers extra at-bats to beat you.

The purpose of major-league spring training

"Number one, your team should leave camp in top physical condition. If a player is not in condition when the season starts, you're dead with him because he'll be out of shape all season. Number two, drill those fundamentals constantly. For example, in spring training games, any time a runner was on first and a ground ball was hit through to center or right, I wanted him to go to third. I didn't care if we were down by ten runs. If they got thrown out, fine, it was part of the learning process. That's how they found out when they could take that extra base and when they couldn't. I never cared if we won a single game during spring training. My whole focus was on preparation for the regular season."

"When you have speed, you can drive the other team crazy. I'm not just talking about stolen bases here. I mean going from first to third, pulling the hit-and-run, faking steals, doing anything that injects movement into the game. When you do that, it's hard for the opposition to get set defensively. I always liked playing against teams that could only slug; if you took away their long balls, you had them. But teams that are always on the go can beat you so many different ways."

Use those first five innings

"Don't get the idea I don't like power. During innings one through five, I always wanted to destroy the other team, beat them up so badly that they went home crying to Mama that they didn't want to play anymore. So we'd play for the big inning and try to blow the opposition out of the park. One of the reasons you do that is that almost every club today has a big closer. A Mariano Rivera. You don't want to get into a war with those guys because nine times out of ten, you'll lose. If you bury the other team early, the closer never even gets up. However, come the sixth inning, if you don't have a lead, you have only 12 outs left to get something going. Now you have to grind it out, steal more, sacrifice runners, do all the little things to create some runs. If your team can't do that, you're stuck."

Criticize in private

"If you want players to be loyal, don't show them up. We had a game in Houston where a player on second was thrown out on an attempted steal of third for the final out of the inning. Now, you should never make the last out of an inning at third, and when a player does it, everyone knows he pulled a rock. When the reporters asked me about it after the game, I said, 'I had a hunch and I sent him.' Well, of course I hadn't, but I was deflecting the blame away from him. Why humiliate him when he already feels bad? You can bet he and I are going to have a long discussion about the mistake, but we'll do that in private. Once a player knows you're going to protect him that way, he'll be receptive to anything you tell him; he'll give you the best effort he's got.

"When some move you make doesn't pay off, never pass the buck. I was managing the Tigers in the ninth inning of a 2–2 tie. We put men on first and second with nobody out. Nine times out of ten, your next hitter is bunting, giving himself up to move those runners into scoring position. But if Cecil Fielder was coming up, there's no way I was asking him to bunt. Cecil was a slugger; bunting wasn't something he did well. So I would just let him do his thing, swing away, to drive in that winning run. If he hits into a double-play, I'm going to take the heat. After the game, I'm going to let everyone know it was my call."

Exercise tough love

"The hardest part of managing is letting a star player know he can't do it anymore. Stars don't want to believe that. Before breaking the news, you must evaluate if the player can still contribute in a different role. For instance, maybe this person can still be effective playing in fewer games against certain types of pitchers. Perhaps he can contribute in a platoon role. Do whatever you can to get the maximum out of whatever talent remains. Then you have to discover if the player will accept this limited role. If you decide he can't perform in any role on your club, give it to him straight. Some may want you to break the news gently, others may want it without any sugar coating. That's where your knowledge of the player comes into use. I would start by asking the player, 'Have I ever lied to you?' After he said no, I would continue, 'Then I'm not going to start now,' and I would give him my honest evaluation. Of course, this only works if you already built a foundation of trust with the player. That is one reason why you should never lie to your players."

Work with your coaches

"Grant them full authority in their area of expertise. Trust that they will get everything done exactly as you discussed it. Don't be checking up on them in the field. Never second-guess anyone. If your third-base coach sends in a runner and the player is thrown out by 20 feet, don't say a word. In 26 years, I never questioned any of my third-base coaches' decisions. Once when a coach tried to apologize for sending a runner who was thrown out, I said, 'Hey, I'm glad you're out there and not me.' That should be your attitude. You also shouldn't think that just because you're the manager, you're superior to your coaches. Each of them will have an area of the game where they know much more than you ever will. Use that knowledge. Go to them for advice.

"You must also back up your coaches. My pitching coach with the Cincinnati Reds, Larry Shepard, used to lace into our pitchers so badly, you could hear

Choosing a pinch hitter

"I rarely picked pinch hitters on a strict platoon basis (lefty hitters versus right-handed pitchers, right-handed hitters versus lefties). Instead, I looked at how you matched up against the pitcher's stuff. If there was a hard-throwing right-hander on the mound, and I had a lefty whose bat wasn't that quick and a right-hander who loved to hit the fastball, the right-hander is going up to the plate. I was more interested in what kind of pitches you could handle than what side of the batter's box you stood in. When I brought in relievers, I applied the same thinking, only in reverse. If I knew a hitter hated the breaking ball, I was bringing in a curveballer even if it meant bringing in a left-hander to face a righty. Now this means you not only have to know what your team can do, you have to know the opposition's personnel as well. I also always tried to save my best pinch hitter for the late innings when he could come up with the game on the line."

him from down the hall. More than once I was tempted to go down to prevent what sounded like murder. I never left my chair. Larry knew his pitchers and understood what it took to motivate them. I had to put my faith in that. And it worked. Our pitchers respected him because he got the most out of their abilities."

Fear nothing

"You know what made Billy Martin (the late skipper of the New York Yankees and other clubs) one of the all-time great managers? Billy was absolutely fearless. He would make moves that he knew would bring him a lot of heat from the press and fans if they backfired, but he didn't care what they said. If he thought a play would win him a ballgame, he put it on no matter how crazy it looked to everyone else. Managers can't be afraid of criticism. No one ever wins anything by playing it safe."

Keep it all in perspective

"I never knew any manager who put together a great record without great players. They are what it is all about. Once you think you're the most important part of the team, it's time to look for another line of work. If you're coaching Little League, baseball is supposed to be fun for these kids, so don't overemphasize winning or losing. The best part of your game should be the hot dogs and soft drinks afterwards. And parents shouldn't take things too seriously, either. How can any parent get upset when their child goes 0 for 4 when I can take them to Children's Hospital and introduce them to kids who have only six months to live? Wipe your little ones' tears, give them a big hug, and let them know you'll love them even if they never get another hit."

Chapter 13

Men in Blue: Umpiring Like a Professional

*U*mpiring is a demanding job. While a hitter must concentrate on maybe 15 or 20 pitches per game, a home-plate umpire must maintain his focus for 260 to 300 pitches per game. On the bases, umpires must be as precise as microsurgeons. That's because baseball is not, as some claim, a game of inches; most of the time a tenth of an inch is the difference between a call of out or safe. So even though they never appear in a lineup, umpires make a critical difference in the outcome of a game.

If you choose to umpire, you assume a great responsibility. The job is demanding and difficult. For more than 33 years, one of the best in the business was National League umpire Harry Wendelstedt, Jr. A consummate professional respected for his fairness and integrity, Wendelstedt also served four terms as President of the Major League Umpires Association. The Harry Wendelstedt School for Umpires (see the end of the chapter for contact information) has sent more umpires to the Major Leagues than any other school.

In this chapter, we invited Wendelstedt to share his thoughts on umpiring. Listen closely to what he has to say; this is one umpire you don't want to argue with.

The Intangibles

"We can teach an umpire the rules and positions, but we can't teach judgment. You're born with that or develop it by the time you're ready to umpire. You have to be able to make the correct decision in stressful situations. You must be able to think on your feet. And you have to be physically fit so you can get into position in time to make the call.

"Good vision is another requirement. You can wear glasses or contacts to bring your vision up to speed, but you have to be able to see well enough to do your job. I was lucky. I had 20/10 vision for the first 25 years of my career, and then it went to 20/20. That's very helpful.

"You also have to possess the desire to do what is right. Sometimes it's easy to take the easy path. For example, if it's a tie score, two men out in the bottom of the ninth, bases loaded, the count is three balls, two strikes, and the pitcher throws a pitch that's just on the corner, you'd better be prepared to call that strike three and head into the tenth inning. If the pitch is just off the plate, again, you call it ball four, ballgame over."

Going by the Book

"If you don't have a firm knowledge of the rule book and all its nuances, you will never be able to umpire on any level and do it well. I'm not just talking about memorization, either. I've had people come to my school who can quote you every rule in the book verbatim, tell you what page it's on and even the paragraph. But they wouldn't recognize that play if it happened right in front of them. You must be able to translate those words into practical application. The rule book must be firmly entrenched in your being as well as your mind."

Calling Balls and Strikes

"Behind the plate, you must assume a stance that allows you to watch the entire flight of the pitch without moving. A good plate umpire stays still throughout the pitch. If you have to move, it can distort your perception and cause you to miss some pitches. You sometimes hear umpires criticized for taking their time making a call. They are just doing their jobs. Good timing is a key element to good umpiring. By that I mean you have to let happen everything that can happen. When people talk about a delayed call, the umpire is just exercising good timing. There is nothing worse than a bang-bang play in which the umpire yells, 'He's out,' only to discover the ball has trickled from the fielder's glove before he made the tag."

On the Base Paths: Positioning Yourself to Make the Call

"Establish a 90-degree angle on each play on the bases as the ball is batted. If a play is going to be made at your bag, you watch the fielder make his throw to ensure it's true. Then your eyes go directly to the bag. You're looking for the runner's foot. You should be able to pick up the flight of the throw with your peripheral vision. Then you listen for the sound of the ball striking the glove and you make your call.

"You are using your ears as well as your eyes on that call, especially on a close play.

"An umpire in the field also has to be aware of where the ball is hit. You don't want to be in the path of a ball so that it strikes your body and interferes with a play. There is one secret for making sure this doesn't happen: Get out of the way! Ballplayers are taught to move instinctively towards the ball. As an umpire, you have to give up that instinct. Learn to pivot so you can get out of the ball's path."

Fair or Foul?

"On a fly ball hit down or near either of the foul lines (which, by the way are really fair lines since any ball that stays on the line is in fair territory), you must straddle the line. Follow the flight of the ball in conjunction with the foul pole. If you are off that line, it can change your perception and you could very well call a fair ball foul or vice versa.

"Any time you're not in the proper position to make a call, you're cheating yourself as an umpire. Below the major-league level, there will be times when you're the only umpire or one of only two umpires on the field. If you're working behind the plate and another umpire is at first, it may be impossible for you to assume the correct position when a drive is smashed over third. The ball just moves too quickly. But you have to get as close to the right position as possible."

Umpiring Diplomacy

"When you find yourself in a heated dispute with a player, manager, or coach, you must try to defuse the situation. In order to control both sides, you must exert control over yourself. Don't allow yourself to be pulled into a screaming match. Keeping a level tone, calm the person down by saying something like,

'I want to hear what you have to say, but I can't do that if you're screaming. Just tell me what you have on your mind.' Get them talking in a conversational tone. Let them have their say, then move on. Don't tolerate any excessive abuse.

"With me, a person ran into trouble whenever they put the word 'you' in front of whatever they were yelling. There is profanity on the ball field; you have to tolerate some of that. But when they put a 'you' in front of an expletive, they're making things personal. That's when they're in trouble. You allow someone to heap personal abuse on you, and you will get buried, not just by other players and managers but by your own umpiring partners who won't take that abuse. It's important to maintain the dignity of the position.

"I've met a lot of people who think umpires enjoy throwing people out of games. We don't. The art of arguing in baseball, for an umpire, is to let someone say their piece, to let off some steam, but keep them in the game. I also found that if people know you're fair and reasonable, that you give 100 percent to your job, they give you a certain amount of respect on the field. So it doesn't become necessary to toss them."

Asking for Help

"There will be times when your vision is blocked on a play. For instance, a coach comes over and says, 'Harry, you blew that call — the ball popped out of his glove before he made the play.' If I suspect the fielder or runner's body blocked my view of the entire play, I have an obligation to talk to my partners, who saw the play from another angle, and ask if they saw anything happen. If my partner says, 'The ball popped out, Harry, the runner was safe,' I'm going to change the call."

Dispelling a Baseball Myth

"You often hear that established veterans like Tony Gwynn and Greg Maddux get more than their fair share of calls in their favor. Not true. Umpires don't favor anyone. The reason Greg Maddux has more strikes called for him by the umpire is because Greg Maddux throws more strikes than any pitcher in baseball. He can paint that corner all day long, which is why he is probably the best control pitcher of this decade. And you don't have to worry about the great hitters getting any calls, because if the pitch is close, they're swinging. You're not going to have to make too many calls on Tony Gwynn with a 3–2 count and a pitch on the corner because he's going to be hacking. You'll rarely see him take a good pitch in that situation."

Surviving the Pressure Cooker

"I have felt butterflies fluttering in my stomach before every game I ever umpired, particularly before a World Series or playoff game. That's part of the job. If you don't feel butterflies, then you don't care enough. I wanted to do my very best every time I walked on the field, and that creates pressure. But you learn to love the excitement. I worked five World Series, and, as with any game, you have to bear down on every pitch. That high level of concentration you take to the field will help you overcome any nervousness you might feel. After you call a pitch or two, the butterflies disappear and you settle into what you normally do. All distractions phase out. When I worked World Series games, there were as many as 50,000 or more screaming fans in the stadium. I wouldn't hear them. I was too focused on the pitch and the play. You go into a zone of total concentration, just like a player."

Contact Wendelstedt's umpiring school at 88 St. Andrews Drive, Ormond Beach, Florida 32174; phone 386-672-4879; Web site www.umpireschool.com.

Chapter 14

Major-League Baseball

*Y*ou can follow 30 teams — 16 in the National League and 14 in the American League — under the current major-league alignment. Spring training starts in late February (when pitchers and catchers report) and continues through March. Each team plays 162 regular season games (81 games at home, 81 in opponents' parks) that begin around April 1. Interleague play (which started in 1997) between National and American League clubs takes place during June, August, and September. The regular season ends during the final week of September, and postseason play starts in the first week of October with the two-round League Championship Series. These series produce a champion for each league (to find out how, see Chapter 17). The two league champions battle each other for the major-league championship in the World Series in late October.

Major-League Baseball Administration

The Office of Major League Baseball is in New York City (see Appendix B for full contact information). Major-league team owners officially elected Allan "Bud" Selig, the former owner of the Milwaukee Brewers, as commissioner of baseball in 1999. His office enforces rules and policies among the owners for both leagues. Robert Dupoy and Sandy Alderson run baseball's day-to-day business operations. Robert Manfred of the Major League Baseball Player Relations Committee represents the owners' interests in labor negotiations, and Rich Levin serves as major-league baseball's executive director of public relations.

The American and National leagues also maintain offices in New York City (and you can also find their addresses in Appendix B). The leagues no longer have individual presidents. The baseball commissioner and his executive staff implement policy, issue directives, approve contracts, and have jurisdiction over all league matters — including player fines, protests, and other disputes.

Donald Fehr doesn't own a club, swat home runs, or throw any high fastballs, yet he may very well be the most powerful man in baseball. Fehr is the executive director of the Major League Players Association, the baseball players' union. (The address for its offices is also in Appendix B.)

Think you have the stuff to play in the Show? The Major League Scouting Bureau holds tryouts around the United States every June. To participate in a tryout camp, you must be at least 16 years old. You must bring your own equipment and sign a liability waiver before taking the field. If you're under 21, a parent or guardian must also sign the waiver. There's no fee to try out, and you can register 30 minutes before camp opens. To discover the location of the tryout camp nearest you, go online to www.mlb.com.

The Major-League Franchises

William Hulbert founded the National League (NL) in 1876. Chicago, New York, Philadelphia, Cincinnati, Louisville, Hartford, St. Louis, and Boston provided homes for the original eight franchises. The NL expanded to 10 teams in 1962, 12 (in two divisions) in 1969, and 14 in 1993.

In October of 1997, Commissioner Selig announced that the Milwaukee Brewers of the American League Central Division would be the first major-league baseball team in this century to switch leagues. The Brewers began play in the National League in 1998. Milwaukee's switch and the addition of the Arizona Diamondbacks expansion team currently give the National League 16 teams competing under the three-division alignment shown in Table 14-1. (See Appendix B for contact information on all the major-league clubs.)

Table 14-1	The National League	
NL East	*NL Central*	*NL West*
Atlanta Braves	Chicago Cubs	Arizona Diamondbacks
Florida Marlins	Cincinnati Reds	Colorado Rockies
New York Mets	Houston Astros	Los Angeles Dodgers
Philadelphia Phillies	Milwaukee Brewers	San Francisco Giants
Washington (Expos)	Pittsburgh Pirates	San Diego Padres
	St. Louis Cardinals	

Ban Johnson founded the American League (AL) in 1900 and declared it a major league the following season. However, it was not officially recognized as a major league until 1903. The original eight franchises included Chicago, Boston, Detroit, Philadelphia, Baltimore, Washington, Cleveland, and Milwaukee. The league expanded to 10 teams in 1961, 12 (in two divisions) in 1969, and 14 in 1977.

The AL adopted three-division play in 1998, when the Detroit Tigers moved from the American League East to replace the Brewers in the newly formed Central division. The Tampa Bay Devil Rays, another expansion team, took Detroit's slot in the East (see Table 14-2).

Table 14-2	The American League	
AL East	*AL Central*	*AL West*
Baltimore Orioles	Chicago White Sox	Anaheim Angels
Boston Red Sox	Cleveland Indians	Oakland Athletics
New York Yankees	Detroit Tigers	Seattle Mariners
Tampa Bay Devil Rays	Kansas City Royals	Texas Rangers
Toronto Blue Jays	Minnesota Twins	

Each club carries 25 players on its regular-season roster (15 to 16 position players and 10 to 11 pitchers). Rosters expand from 25 up to 40 players on September 1, when many teams give their better minor-league prospects a taste of the Major Leagues. However, only those players who are on the roster before that time are eligible for postseason play.

A club captures first place in its division by compiling the best won-lost percentage. (You can discover how to calculate that percentage by consulting Chapter 16.)

One for the Major-League History Books

Both leagues have rich histories that have been vividly captured in countless books. The best of these include

✔ Harold Seymour's *Baseball — The Early Years* and *Baseball — The Golden Age* (Oxford University Press). Critics have hailed Seymour as baseball's greatest historian. *The Early Years* covers the game from the pre–Civil War years to 1903. *The Golden Age* follows the game until 1930. Seymour presents baseball against a historical backdrop that provides the reader with a sociological context for changes within the sport.

✔ The recently published eighth edition of *Total Baseball* (Sport Classic Books) is the game's ultimate reference work. Esteemed baseball historian John Thorn and co-editors Phil Birnbaum and Bill Deane have loaded their encyclopedia with statistics on every major-league player who ever pulled on a pair of spikes. This 2,600-page-plus volume contains league, team, and ballpark histories, all-time leader lists in every major category, a ranking of baseball's 100 most influential figures, and illuminating essays on such topics as the origins of baseball, the historical impact of Barry Bonds, Jackie Robinson and the breaking of baseball's color line, and the fact and fiction behind the "Moneyball" phenomenon. The new edition also includes over 200 photos and illustrations. You can order copies through www.sportclassicbooks.com.

✔ In *Rob Neyer's Big Book of Baseball Lineups* (Fireside), the crack ESPN baseball analyst answers many long-standing baseball arguments (Mantle or DiMaggio, Maddux or Spahn). He starts a few new debates by presenting a series of lineups (including All-Time, All-Rookie, and All-Bust) for each major-league franchise with thought-provoking tidbits and essays on every player picked.

Many of the best baseball books, such as Leonard Koppett's *Thinking Man's Guide To Baseball* and *Nice Guys Finish Last* by Leo Durocher (with Ed Linn), are currently out of print. You may be able to track them down at the Alibris Web site (www.alibris.com). Alibris couldn't be simpler to use — key in the book title, press Go, and within seconds you have a list of hard-to-find books available at various prices based on condition.

HEADS UP

Society for American Baseball Research

Is Mike Piazza the best hitting catcher of all time? Did Babe Ruth really call his home run against the Cubs in the 1932 World Series? What team originally drafted Tom Seaver out of college and how did they lose him?

You can find out the answers to these and many more questions by joining the Society for American Baseball Research (SABR). Founded in 1971, SABR is a nonprofit organization dedicated to the preservation of baseball history. Its two annual publications, *The National Pastime* and *The Research Journal,* are, by themselves, worth the $35 yearly membership dues ($20 for students or seniors; $45 for fans living in Canada or Mexico; $50 if you live overseas). However, members also have access to the SABR Lending Library, whose comprehensive inventory includes microfilm reproductions of *Sporting Life* (1883–1917) and *The Sporting News* (1886–1957). Besides the two annual publications, SABR annually sends its members nine newsletters and a special magazine dedicated to a specific topic, such as the Negro Leagues, minor-league baseball stars, or nineteenth-century baseball stars. You can also participate in various research committees with top baseball historians.

For membership information — and this is one organization every baseball fan should join — call SABR at 216-575-0500. (You can also find their address and Web site address in Appendix B.)

Chapter 15

Off-the-Field Baseball Jobs and How to Snag Them

Alright, so you don't have Barry Bonds's awesome power, Greg Maddux's pinpoint control, or Cesar Izturis's astonishing reflexes. You can still get a position in baseball and even one day find yourself in the Hall of Fame. (Twenty former team executives are currently honored in that noble shrine.) So don't abandon your Field of Dreams if you can't make the cut as a player. This chapter describes various positions you can pursue even if your batting average has never broken .100.

Bat and Ball Handlers

No, Bat Boys and Bat Girls are not denizens of Gotham City. They're the ballplayers' on-field valets, in charge of keeping their equipment — particularly their bludgeons of choice — ready at all times. Bat Boys and Bat Girls sit in the dugouts and clear the field of any bats that players toss aside. They then store the bats in their proper slots in the bat rack.

Ball Boys and Ball Girls usually sit on the field in foul territory. They're always gloved because their chief job is to retrieve foul grounders. They never retrieve fly balls because those remain in the province of the fielders. Ball Boys and Ball Girls must be able to defend themselves against the occasional searing line drive, which means good reflexes and manual dexterity are a must.

You can apply for bat- and ball-handling jobs by sending a letter to your local team's head of stadium operations. In filling these positions, clubs look for teenagers with solid academic records. High marks in conduct carry a lot of weight, so include some glowing letters of reference from your principal and/or teachers with your application.

Ticket Takers and Ushers

Ticket takers dispense tickets at the ballpark. Ushers must correctly read those ducats and then direct their holders to the appropriate seats. Ushers are also walking information centers. Throughout the game, patrons ask ushers a bevy of questions including where the restrooms are, how to get to the parking lot, and where to go for first aid.

A good usher is familiar with the entire workings of the ballpark and its surroundings. Ushers are also the first line of defense against rowdy customers. However, that doesn't make them members of ballpark security. If a fan gets out of line, an usher calls the head usher or security personnel for assistance. Write your local team for an application for these positions.

Vendors

Vendors sell a variety of foods, beverages, and souvenirs throughout the ballpark. Most vendors work strictly on commission. Which products you sell on a particular night depends on seniority or a random number drawing. How much money you make is often simply a matter of what product you draw. If you're selling beer or hot dogs, you'll probably have a healthy bottom line for the evening. But if you're stuck hawking ice cream sundaes on a frigid night in September, the only compensation you're taking home is the memory of the game. Seniority also determines which part of the ballpark you work in, another important consideration.

Vendors should be physically fit. Those trays strapped around your neck can be heavy, and you're on your feet for most of the game. You can, of course, take the occasional rest, but when you're sitting, you aren't earning.

Teams or the companies that run their concessions advertise for vendors just before the start of the season. However, referrals are key to getting these jobs. If someone who is already vending in a ballpark recommends you for a position, you have a much better chance of getting it. If your application for a vending job is turned down, don't be discouraged. Keep checking back to see whether a position has opened up. Vendors have grueling jobs, and the turnover rate is high.

Groundskeepers

Groundskeepers maintain the diamond's sparkle. They keep the playing field smooth and dry and the grass trimmed (unless management wants it otherwise). Groundskeepers also smooth out the infield dirt in between innings. In more sophisticated parks, groundskeepers oversee a system of underground pumps and drainage devices.

Rain delays are the true test of a groundskeeping crew's mettle. They must cover the field with a tarpaulin quickly before that downpour renders the diamond unplayable.

Maintaining healthy sod is also one of the groundskeeper's primary responsibilities. For that reason, many groundskeepers study their craft in school. Many universities feature agriculture programs that offer majors in soil science with specialties in grounds management. If you want to be a groundskeeper for a team (or for your local golf course, park, or anywhere else the green stuff grows), earning a sheepskin from one of these institutions gives you a powerful advantage. Most groundskeepers start off as interns through their university programs and then go on to regular positions.

If you want to apply for a job with a club, call to find out the name of its grounds crew chief and then direct your resume to him or her.

Trainers

Trainers supervise a team's conditioning, strengthening, and injury rehabilitation programs. They also administer sophisticated first aid whenever someone is injured on the field. (And it isn't unusual for them to assist someone injured in the stands.) Teams look for trainers who are college-educated and board certified in sports medicine. You can send your resume to a team's head trainer for consideration, but many of these jobs are snagged through referrals.

Public Address Announcers

"Now batting for the New York Yankees. . . ." If your baseball dream is to follow in the footsteps of the legendary, sonorous Yankee Stadium p.a. announcer Bob Sheppard, you need more than just a good set of pipes. Teams aren't necessarily looking for James Earl Jones to announce the lineups at their games (though they wouldn't turn down the voice of Darth Vader if he applied for the job). Teams do want announcers with clear enunciation.

Anyone who sounds like Elmer Fudd with his voice box stuck in a blender probably shouldn't apply. You have to audition to win this spot, and some teams may want to first hear you on tape as part of a screening process.

Broadcasters

In the Major Leagues, at least two broadcasters work in both the TV and radio booths. One is a *play-by-play announcer* who describes the action of the game. His or her partner is the *analyst,* usually a former major-league player or manager, who explains why something happened, speculates on what is about to happen, and shares some insight on baseball nuances. Below the majors, most broadcasters work solo. If you haven't played or managed, a degree in broadcasting is almost a must here. Teams looking for broadcasters require an audition tape, so it would be worthwhile for you to get a job calling games for your campus radio station.

Front Office Jobs

If you have ambitions of being a *general manager* — the executive honcho who wheels and deals while guiding a baseball franchise's fortunes — you must be willing to start at the bottom. Front office interns and administrative assistants often work long hours for little money. Each team offers a variety of entry-level executive positions. Clubs prefer to fill these slots with applicants who possess degrees in sports administration. If at all possible, choose a university whose sports administration program provides interns for local teams. Internships give you the hands-on experience that stands out on your resume. They also offer you an opportunity to network with the people who make the hiring decisions.

Note: Anyone seeking a front office or broadcast position should attend professional baseball's *Winter Meetings.* Usually held in December, this annual gathering is where you find everyone who is anyone from the executive ranks of the major and minor leagues. As soon as you discover where the meetings are being held (the office of Major League Baseball can give you that information), book your flight and hotel reservations. It's best to stay at the same hotel as the executives so you can do some schmoozing. Send your resume to the team you're targeting well in advance of the meetings. You should also enroll in the employment opportunities seminar conducted annually at this gathering by The National Association of Professional Baseball Leagues (201 Bayshore Drive, St. Petersburg, Florida 33731). During the meetings, you will find any available front office or broadcasting jobs listed in the NAPBL office, usually located in the hotel where the executives stay.

Major-League Team Owners

Playing hardball with the big boys doesn't require much. All you need to start is about half a billion dollars in discretionary income.

Baseball job seekers should subscribe to *The Sports Market Place Directory,* published by Grey House Publishing (800-562-2139). This 1,800-page directory — which you can also order on CD-ROM — carries a comprehensive listing of teams and other companies involved in the sports industry. You'll find listings for key contacts in each organization with their mailing, e-mail, and Web site addresses as well as fax and phone numbers. If you want to contact a major- or minor-league team to inquire about a position or send off a resume, you can also grab the latest copy of the *Baseball America Directory* (800-845-2726), which is published annually. This directory includes an Events Calendar that usually lists the dates and city for the upcoming Winter Meetings.

Chapter 16

Measuring Performance: Calculating Baseball's Statistics

*B*aseball fans are amazing. Math may have given them nightmares as students, but let their favorite player make a hit or an out, and they have his slugging average computed before he takes a step from the batter's box. Statistics provide the game's followers with a context that allows them to compare players and eras. To hold your own in any conversation about the sport, you have to know what the numbers mean. So here's an introduction to baseball's primary stats.

Calculating a Batter's Abilities

Mention the numbers 755, 4,256, and 73 to avid baseball fans, and they'll probably rattle off the famous baseball records that correspond to them. (Just for the record, Hank Aaron hit 755 homers in his career, Pete Rose had 4,256 hits in his career, and Barry Bonds hit 73 home runs in 2001.) Even if you don't feel compelled to memorize baseball's legendary numerical feats, this section helps you make some sense out of the many ways that players and fans track and measure offensive ability.

Batting average

A batting average is the statistic used to measure what percentage of a player's at-bats results in a base hit. This statistic made its first appearance in 1864. To calculate it, divide the batter's total hits by his official times at bat:

Barry Bonds, San Francisco, 2002

$$\frac{149 \text{ hits}}{403 \text{ at-bats}} = .370 \text{ batting average}$$

(Yes, you might say Mr. Bonds can hit a little.)

A hitter's at-bats do not include walks, sacrifice bunts, sacrifice flies, obstruction calls, catcher's interference, or being hit by a pitch. These events count as plate appearances but not as at-bats, so they aren't used to calculate the batting average. When the hitter is safe on an error, you credit him with an at-bat, but not a hit.

To qualify for a major-league batting championship (which means leading the league in batting average over the course of a season), a player must have 3.1 plate appearances (not at-bats) for every game his team plays. In a regulation 162-game season, a hitter needs at least 502 plate appearances to qualify for his league's batting title. (Bonds met these requirements in 2002 by adding a major-league record-setting 198 walks to his 403 at-bats.)

On-base percentage

Branch Rickey and Brooklyn Dodger statistician Allen Roth created this statistic during the 1950s. On-base percentage tells you what percentage of a hitter's at-bats results in his getting on base by any means other than an error, interference, or fielder's choice. To calculate this figure, add a batter's hits, walks, and hit-by-pitch (hbp) totals and divide by his at-bats plus walks plus hit-by-pitch plus sacrifice flies.

$$\frac{100 \text{ hits} + 100 \text{ walks} + 10 \text{ hpb} = 210}{500 \text{ at-bats} + 100 \text{ walks} + 10 \text{ hbp} + 10 \text{ sacrifice flies} = 620}$$
$$= .3387 \text{ on-base average}$$

In this case, the on-base percentage rounds out to .339. The average major-league hitter is right around that number. Ideally, the first two hitters in your lineup, the players who jump-start your offense by getting on base any way they can, should produce on-base percentages of .375 or better.

Slugging average

You derive a player's slugging average by calculating how many bases he averages with each at-bat. To do so, divide the total bases he accumulated with hits by his at-bats. A single equals *one* base, a double *two* bases, a triple *three* bases, and a home run *four* bases. For example, in 2001, Sammy Sosa of the Cubs had 86 singles (86 bases), 34 doubles (68 bases), 5 triples (15 bases), and (gulp!) 64 home runs (256 bases) for a hefty total of 425 bases in 577 at-bats:

$$\frac{425 \text{ total bases}}{577 \text{ at-bats}} = .737 \text{ slugging percentage}$$

The average major leaguer slugs around .420. A hitter with a .450 slugging average has good power; the elite sluggers are at .490 or better. Now you can see why players refer to Sosa as "Slammin' Sammy."

OPS

The two most important things a hitter can do are getting on base and smacking the ball for power. OPS measures both these elements by combining on-base percentage and slugging average. This hybrid stat provides a much better gauge of a player's production than mere batting average. For example, in 2003, injuries limited New York Yankees first baseman Jason Giambi to a .250 batting average, a figure 18 points below the American League average. But Giambi's .412 on-base percentage (thanks to his 129 walks) and his .529 slugging average combined to give the first baseman a .939 OPS, the seventh best figure in the league. That high OPS largely explains why Giambi finished fifth in the AL in runs created.

Runs created

Bill James originally formulated this statistic to measure total offensive production. It measure's a player's ability to reach base and move around base runners. There are at least 15 versions of the stat, each more complex than the other. This represents the basic formula:

$$\frac{(\text{Hits} + \text{Walks})(\text{Total Bases})}{\text{At-Bats} + \text{Walks}}$$

Isolated power average (IPA)

Another Rickey-Roth creation, this stat measures a player's power by revealing how often he reaches a base on extra-base hits. Award the player 0 points for singles, 1 point for doubles, 2 points for triples, and 3 points for home runs. Total his points and divide by his number of at-bats. Let's use Barry Bonds's numbers from 2001:

$$32 \text{ doubles } (32) + 2 \text{ triples } (4) + 73 \text{ homeruns } (219)$$

$$= \frac{255 \text{ IP points}}{476 \text{ at-bats}} = .536 \text{ Isolated Power Average}$$

Know what the isolated power average was for the average National League hitter in 2001? It was .172, which makes Barry's IPA other-worldly.

Measuring a Pitcher's Performance

Not to be outdone by the hitters, pitchers also have a whole slew of stats to measure pitching performance. The stats covered in this section help you determine how effectively pitchers get out opposing hitters. Although dozens of pitching statistics exist, the critical indicator for any pitcher is wins. Flashy statistics are nice, but the name of the game for any pitcher is winning.

Earned run average (ERA)

This statistic measures how many earned runs (runs that score without benefit of an error) a pitcher surrenders every nine innings. To calculate, multiply the number of earned runs on a pitcher's record by 9 and then divide the result by his innings pitched:

Roger Clemens, Toronto Blue Jays, 1997

$$\frac{60 \text{ earned runs allowed} \times 9 = 540}{264 \text{ innings pitched}} = 2.05 \text{ earned run average}$$

Clemens's 2.05 ERA led the American League in 1997 and helped him win his fourth Cy Young Award.

Earned run averages have fluctuated widely over the years. When I played, an ERA under 3.50 was considered good. With all the offensive pyrotechnics in baseball today, a pitcher is doing well if he has an ERA of around 4.00. Because of the designated hitter rule, ERAs are usually 30 to 50 points higher in the American League than in the National League. (See Chapter 3 for information on the designated hitter rule.)

Getting a decision: The pitcher's dilemma

To earn a victory, a starting pitcher must pitch at least five innings (or four if the game goes less than six innings), and his team must have the lead at the time he leaves the game. If that lead is never relinquished, he gets the win. If the game is tied when a pitcher who has pitched at least five innings is removed for a pinch hitter, and his team goes ahead to stay during the inning in which he is pulled, he gets the win.

When the starter cannot get the win, the victory can go to any relief pitcher who is the pitcher of record at the time his team gains a lead it never loses. Credit a pitcher with a loss if he's charged with the run that beats his team.

If a reliever is the finishing pitcher for the winning team and does not qualify for the victory, credit the pitcher with a save in these situations:

✔ The pitcher gets the final three outs of a game that he entered with his team leading by three runs or less.

✔ The pitcher gets the final out (or more) when he inherits a situation in which the tying run is in the on-deck circle.

✔ The pitcher pitches the game's final three innings regardless of the score. (However, his pitching must be effective in the judgment of the official scorer.)

Cracking the WHIP

This stat tells you how many base runners a pitcher surrenders for every inning pitched. Simply add the number of hits and walks a pitcher allows and divide the total by the number of innings he throws. For example, in 2004, National League Cy Young Award winner Eric Gagne was one stingy moundsman:

$$\frac{37 \text{ hits allowed} + 20 \text{ walks}}{82.33 \text{ innings pitched}} = 0.69 \text{ WHIP}$$

A WHIP below 1.50 is outstanding in these heavy-hitting days, so you can see why the Dodger closer was able to save 55 games without blowing a single lead.

Determining a Fielder's Reliability

Fielding average reveals what percentage of attempted plays a fielder successfully completes. To calculate this percentage, add the fielder's putouts and assists, and then divide that number by his total chances for fielding a play (putouts, assists, and errors). Fielding average measures surehandedness, not range. Players who don't reach a lot of balls have fewer chances to make errors.

If you know how many innings a player has played at a position, you can determine his *range factor* by adding his putouts and assists, multiplying by 9, then dividing by his defensive innings played. In 2003, Phillies shortstop Jimmy Rollins played 1,386 innings in the field while recording 204 putouts and 463 assists. His range factor was 4.33, which means he reached slightly more balls than the average shortstop.

Crunching Your Team's Winning Percentage

You determine winning percentage by dividing a team's wins by the number of games played. Want to see a mind-boggling won-lost percentage? Check out the 1906 Chicago Cubs:

$$\frac{116 \text{ wins}}{152 \text{ games played}} = .763 \text{ won-lost percentage}$$

Would you believe they lost the World Series that year? Every team wants to play at least .500 ball. Usually, a .550 winning percentage makes you a playoff contender. However, you can win a weak division with a relatively low won-lost percentage. In 1973, The New York Mets won the NL East with a .509 won-lost percentage and then went to the World Series by beating the — oh, must I relive this memory? — Cincinnati Reds in the league championship series.

Team Stat: Rob Neyer's Beane Count

There are any number of stats that measure a team's performance, but one of the better ones was devised by crack baseball analyst Rob Neyer, Joe's colleague at ESPN.com. We're not half as bright as Rob, so we'll let him explain how his Beane Count (named after Oakland A's general manager Billy Beane) works:

"Beane Count was intended as something of a joke (which explains why the name itself is something of a joke). During the 2000 season, the Oakland Athletics were on their way to winning a division title. Oakland's hitters didn't hit for a high batting average, and they struck out more than any other team in the American League. But they ranked second in walks and second in home runs. And when I checked, I discovered that their pitchers were adept at *preventing* walks and (especially) home runs.

"These are related things. Hits, the batters and (especially) the pitchers can't control as much as they'd like. But home runs and walks are events the pitchers and hitters certainly *do* control. What's more, it's home runs and walks that, more often than not, the best teams have mastered.

"To figure Beane Count, I simply added together each team's league rank in home runs, walks, home runs allowed, and walks allowed. In 2000, the A's finished second in walks (2 points), second in home runs (2), first in fewest home runs allowed (1), and eighth in fewest walks allowed (8). Those combined totals left the A's first in the American League with a 13 Beane Count. Over the next four seasons they finished No. 1, No. 2 (behind the Yankees), and No. 3 (behind the Yankees and Red Sox). If you happened to notice that all these teams reached the postseason in those years, you get a shiny gold star."

If you can only own one baseball reference work, Lee Sinins's Sabermetric Baseball Encyclopedia should be your choice. Sinins has collected the complete statistical history of every major-league player and team on one CD-ROM that features a search engine you can use to analyze stats and create your own fun projects. When you call up a player's statistics, the encyclopedia provides his numbers in the context of league averages, so you can see how a player performed compared to his peers. We asked the search engine to compile a list of the all-time stolen base leaders among right-hand hitting third basemen under 5'10" and born in Delaware (it was a slow writing day). In a matter of moments, the list — which would have taken over a hundred hours to research manually — popped up with Hans Lobert sitting atop it (and we bet even ol' Hans wouldn't have known the lofty position he held unless he had the Encyclopedia loaded on his hard drive). You can order the CD-ROM by visiting Lee Sinins's Web site at www.baseball-encyclopedia.com.

The lowdown on statistics

Statistics are often misleading. Everyone believes that a .300 hitter is a good player and that a pitcher with a low ERA is a good pitcher. That belief is not necessarily the case. To be a good player, you have to either drive in runs or score runs (depending on where you hit in the batting order), and the great players do both. A .300 hitter makes seven outs for every ten at-bats, and if his seven outs come with men on base and his three hits come with no one on base, these hits are not very productive. Run production is crucial. Likewise, many pitchers pitch just good enough to lose. Pitchers will tell you that it's just as tough to win a 5–4 game as it is a 1–0 game, because they have to pitch out of more jams.

Run production is how you measure hitters. Wins and losses are how you measure pitchers. Batting averages and ERAs are personal stats.

Chapter 17

Going All the Way: Postseason Play and the World Series

· ·

In This Chapter

▶ Getting the World Series off the ground

▶ Expanding the postseason

▶ Introducing wild card teams

· ·

*G*etting to the World Series — that's the ultimate fantasy for every base-ball player, manager, owner, or fan. At least it ought to be.

I've participated in four World Series (including the Boston-Cincinnati classic in 1975, which many people have called the greatest World Series of all time) and seven National League Championship Series (NLCS). The moment I stepped on the field to play the Eastern Division champion Pittsburgh Pirates for the 1972 National League pennant in my first NLCS, I knew that the postseason is what baseball is all about. The stadiums are packed to bursting, and the spectators are continually on their feet or the edge of their seats. Adrenaline is running high in both dugouts, and the media is everywhere. It feels as if the whole world is watching. Every pitch, every at-bat, every play assumes ten times as much significance as it held during the regular season.

If you can't get excited about postseason baseball, you'd better check for a pulse. To understand what all the hoopla is about, we offer you a bit of the history of postseason play and examine the difficult path teams must tread to reach it.

The Humble Beginnings of the World Series

People who watch very little baseball during the regular season often find themselves riveted to the television when the World Series is broadcast in late October. At its finest, this best-of-seven confrontation between the champions of the American and National leagues has a gradual, dramatic build that makes the series the most compelling event in sports.

The series was not always quite so compelling. Baseball's earliest "world series" took place in 1882 and consisted of two informal postseason games between Cincinnati of the American Association and Chicago of the National League. The teams split these contests, which received scant press coverage and were seen as little more than exhibitions. In fact, the National League chose not to see them at all. At that time, the National League refused to consider the American Association as a legitimate major league. A standing edict forbade National League clubs from participating in contests against American Association teams. To defy that order without risking expulsion from the league, Chicago had to release all its players from their contracts before it could face Cincinnati. (The players re-signed with their club as soon as the games ended.)

The National Agreement of 1883 brought peace between the two leagues. One year after the pact was signed, the National League champion Providence Grays met the American Association champion New York Metropolitans for a three-game set. It was billed as a battle for the baseball championship of the United States. However, after the Grays won, the media hailed them as world champions. Subsequently, the phrase World Series began slipping into the baseball lexicon, though the Major Leagues would not officially embrace the name until the early 1900s.

Series setbacks

From 1885 to 1890, the American Association and National League pennant winners faced each other in series whose lengths varied from 6 games to 15. The National League won five of these six events. But friction between the two leagues forced the cancellation of the championship series in 1891, and shortly after that, the American Association folded.

In 1892, the National League expanded to 12 teams when it absorbed four AA franchises — Washington, Baltimore, St. Louis, and Louisville. The league then divided its season into two halves. Boston, the winner of the first half-season, played Cleveland, owner of the second half's best record, for the league championship and "baseball's world title." The best-of-nine series was less than a sensation. Fans generally abhorred the split-season concept (it was abandoned after this one season), so they were unable to muster much enthusiasm for the confrontation it produced. A series packed with suspense may have won them over, but it was not to be. Boston shellacked Cleveland five games to none (there was one tie). Due to the disappointing response to the matchup, no championship series of any kind took place during the following season.

Postseason blues

William C. Temple, a noted Pittsburgh sportsman, tried to revive postseason play in 1894 by offering a prize cup to the winner of a best-of-seven series between the National League's top two finishers. For the next four years, baseball hailed the winners of the Temple Cup as world champions. Again, fans failed to embrace this concept and the trophy went back to its original donor.

In 1900, a Pittsburgh newspaper, the *Chronicle-Telegraph,* offered a silver loving cup to the winner of a best-of-five series between the National League's first-place finisher, the Brooklyn Superbas, and the second place Pittsburgh Pirates. Brooklyn won the set, three games to one, but the sparse attendance (the four games attracted fewer than 11,000 fans) convinced the National League owners to once again abandon postseason play.

Success at last

Fortunately, baseball owners gave postseason play one last chance in 1903 after a new National Agreement recognized the recently formed American League as a major league. Barney Dreyfuss, owner of the National League champion Pittsburgh Pirates, challenged the American League champion Boston Pilgrims to a best-of-nine confrontation. Boston established the American League's credibility by winning the series, five games to three. More important, the series generated enthusiastic fan interest.

When the National League champion New York Giants declined to meet the American League champion Boston Pilgrims in 1904, the public outcry persuaded baseball's ruling body, the National Commission, to officially establish the World Series for the following season. The 1905 series between the New York Giants and Philadelphia Athletics officially established the best-of-seven format, which is still followed today. (The leagues experimented with a best-of-nine format from 1919 to 1921, but deemed a nine-game series too long to hold the public's attention.)

The All-Star Game

Since 1933, the stars of the American and National Leagues have competed against each other in the All-Star Game, a midseason *exhibition game* (which means it's not counted as part of the regular season records) played in a different major-league stadium each year. The managers of the previous season's pennant winners lead the AL and NL squads. Fans participate in a nationwide poll to choose the starting lineups (with the exception of the pitchers) for both clubs. Japanese baseball fans can also participate via the Internet. The managers' own picks fill out the rest of their 28-player rosters. Each major-league club must have at least one All-Star representative. The National League has a 41–32 lead in this "series," but much of that bulge was built from 1965 to 1985, when the NL teams — which were then much deeper in middle infield talent and power pitchers than their American League rivals — won 18 of 20 All-Star Games. Since then, however, the AL has prevailed in most of the meetings.

Except for 1994 when a players strike canceled the event, both leagues have participated in the World Series — or, to use its more elegant nomenclature, the *Fall Classic* — in every season since 1905. The series has endured to become an American cultural icon.

To find out more about World Series records, history, and heroes, check out these titles:

- *The Complete Baseball Record Book,* published annually by *The Sporting News,* contains all the essential records from both the playoffs and World Series.

- Donald Honig's *October Heroes* is an oral history of the World Series as told by such players as Tom Seaver, Gene Tenace, Johnny Podres, and Lloyd Waner.

- *Eight Men Out* by Eliot Asinof is the best book ever written about the appalling scandal that occurred in 1919 when gamblers bribed members of the Chicago White Sox to lose that year's World Series against the Cincinnati Reds. The fallout nearly destroyed baseball's credibility. Director John Sayles later transformed Asinof's masterpiece into a compelling film of the same name starring John Cusack and David Strathairn. This movie is currently available on video and DVD.

The Ever-Changing Road to the Series

Before 1969, to qualify for the World Series, a team only had to be the last team standing when its league's schedule came to a close. If your team finished the season with the league's best won-lost record, you were on your

way to the World Series. If you were tied with another team after playing all
your regular season games, a playoff determined the league champion. (In the
National League, a best-two-out-of-three-game series broke the tie; the American
League used a one-game, winner-take-all playoff.)

Expansion and change

Major-league baseball's 1969 expansion forever altered the postseason.
Franchise owners voted to divide both the American League and National
League — each of which had been a single league of ten franchises — into
two six-team divisions. Intradivisional opponents played each other 18 times
during the season and met teams from its league's other division 12 times
per year.

Both leagues also introduced a playoff format (since named the *League Championship Series* or LCS), which required the teams that ended the season with the
best records in their divisions to meet each other in a best three-out-of-five
series. The winner of each playoff was declared league champion and went on
to the World Series. If the season ended with two teams tied for a division lead,
they met in a sudden-death, one-game playoff. Whichever club won that contest went on to the LCS. The survivors of those events represented their
respective leagues in the World Series. Baseball tinkered with that format in
1985 when it expanded the playoffs to a best-of-seven game format.

Divisional championships and wild card teams

A more startling alteration to postseason play came in 1994 when the two
leagues adopted their present alignment (see Chapter 14 for more details) of
three divisions each. The addition of third divisions necessitated the creation
of a second tier of playoffs — a three-out-of-five game series followed by a
four-out-of-seven playoff to determine a league champion.

The division change also required the inclusion of a *wild card* (an additional
playoff qualifier) team in the postseason mix. The rules governing the wild
card team may seem a bit complex. To qualify for the wild card, a club must
post the best record among its league's second-place finishers. If two teams
tie for the division lead, but their records also qualify for a wild card berth,
both teams make the playoffs. Whichever of the two teams holds the edge
in its season series goes into the playoffs as the division champion. If the
two are tied for the division lead, but neither team qualifies for the wild card
(because a second-place team in another division has a better record than
either of the two tied for the lead), the division championship is decided by a
one-game playoff.

In case of a tie, scream!

What happens if two teams end the season tied for both the division title and the wild card spot? Three formulas are used to determine which team enters the playoffs as a division leader:

1. The team with the better record of the two in head-to-head matchups is automatically declared the division champion; the other club enters the playoffs as the wild card.

2. If the two teams split their season series, the club with the better record within its division takes the title.

3. If both clubs have identical intradivisional records, the team with the better record over the season's final 81 games is declared the winner. If those records match, the criterion is extended to the final 82 games, then 83, and so on until it produces a clear-cut winner.

The club with the best overall record in its league retains the home field advantage throughout the playoffs. For example, after winning a record-setting 116 regular season games in 2001, the Seattle Mariners hosted three out of five games during the first round of playoffs against Cleveland and would have hosted four out of seven games during the second round against New York (but the Yankees upset the Mariners in five games).

Which teams oppose each other in the first round of playoffs varies from year to year depending on the identity of the wild card. Usually, the wild card team faces the club with the best regular season record in the first round of the playoffs. However, for whatever silly reason, the wild card team currently cannot play its division leader in round one. Florida earned the wild card in 2003 by finishing second in its division to the Atlanta Braves, which boasted the best winning percentage in the National League. Instead of playing Atlanta in the first tier of the playoffs, manager Jack McKeon and his crew met and defeated the San Francisco Giants, the team with the NL's second-best record. The Marlins went on to win the World Series.

Part IV

We Don't Care if We Ever Get Back: A Spectator's Guide

The 5th Wave   By Rich Tennant

"The pitcher's having a little trouble with his inside curve and I'm trying to help him out."

In this part . . .

*I*t's time for our surgeon general's warning to baseball spectators: Once you're hooked on baseball, you won't be able to get enough of it.

In this part, we show you how to watch the game, where to sit, and how to keep score. As you become a diehard baseball fan, you'll undoubtedly want as much information as you can get on your favorite teams or players as soon as it's available. So this part covers where to get the most up-to-date baseball information. If you're on the Internet, we also tell you about a number of nifty Web sites to surf. Finally, we give you a brief introduction to the growing phenomenon known as "fantasy baseball."

Time to go to the park.

Chapter 18

Following the Bouncing Baseball

As a spectator, if you haven't experienced a baseball game live, well, you haven't experienced baseball. A ball field functions as more than a mere backdrop; by juxtaposing speed against distance, it provides a context for athletic miracles. Richie Sexson's latest 450-foot home run is merely a ball hit a long way when seen on television. But when viewed from a stadium seat, it turns majestic, almost unsettling in its celebration of raw, human power.

Baseball is a sport of nuance, and nowhere but the ballpark can these subtleties be explored and appreciated. Is the shortstop cheating toward second to gain a step on the double play? Is the hitter choking up with a two-strike count? How will the left fielder shade this right-handed pull hitter? Sitting in the stands, you can get an immediate answer to all these questions by simply looking out at the field.

A visit to your local ballpark is also a healthful experience. You get to bond with fellow humans, soak up the sun's vitamin D (if you go during the day), fill your lungs with air made fragrant by freshly trimmed grass, and escape life's anxieties. It's sort of like going to an outdoor consciousness-raising group — only vastly more entertaining.

Picking the Best Seat (For What You Want to See)

Given the emphasis stadium architects put on unobstructed sight lines, nearly every seat in a modern baseball park (one built or refurbished in the last 30 years) is a good one. As you move around the stadium, you may find that each section offers a different, often contrasting perspective of the game on the field (see Figure 18-1).

Which perspective is best? It depends on what interests you.

✔ For the best view of the pitcher-hitter confrontation, camp out behind home plate.

✔ Want to watch the double play unfold while observing the interaction between pitcher and runner? Head for the first-base side — a seat here also grants you a bird's-eye view of most of the game's putouts.

✔ From behind third, you can watch the relay and cutoff plays evolve as the runner races toward third or home against the right fielder's throw.

✔ Visit the upper deck and you can see the field as a giant chessboard with ever-changing defensive alignments.

✔ You can form an appreciation for the various angles fly balls assume by sitting in the bleachers (if your park has them), which are located directly behind the outfield fence.

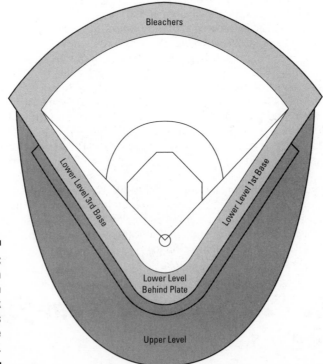

Figure 18-1: Each section in a ballpark has its own unique perspective.

Looking for a Souvenir?

Almost everybody who attends a ballgame fantasizes about catching a foul ball or (even better) a home run. Foul-ball hunters have their best opportunities in the upper deck or lower boxes on the first- or third-base side of the park. If you want to add a home-run ball to your trophy case, sit near the end of the foul lines (just look for the foul poles to find out where those sections are) or in the bleachers (unless you're at Coors Field, where you can just wait out in the parking lot). Figure 18-2 shows you some of the best places to sit if you want to get your hands on a baseball.

You're free to do whatever you want with any ball you catch, but you should know that in many ballparks, such as Chicago's Wrigley Field, hometown fans expect you to throw any home runs hit by the visiting team back onto the field.

You should never attempt to catch any ball while it remains in play.

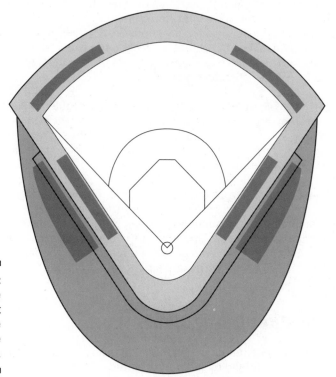

Figure 18-2:
Where
to await
a chance
for a free
souvenir.

Ballpark etiquette

When you visit a stadium, have fun and get loose — but not too loose.

✔ Refrain from using foul language (because children are usually nearby).

✔ Don't drink to excess. (In fact, why drink at all?)

✔ Never, ever throw an object onto the field, run onto the diamond, or do anything that interferes with play.

✔ Don't block the view of the folks sitting behind you.

Real Fans Keep Score

Nothing focuses your full concentration on a baseball game like keeping score. You can purchase *scorecards* from stadium vendors (who sell cards for each game) or at almost any sporting goods store (where they are sold by the book). Or you can make your own. For every game you score, you need two cards — one for the home team, another for its opponent. Figure 18-3 shows what a typical, blank scorecard looks like.

To score like a professional, the first thing that you should do is write the date, the weather, and whether the game is a day or night game (or the first game of a doubleheader, and so on) on the top of your scorecard, along with the names of the teams competing. Many fans keep their scorecards (and ticket stubs) for a lifetime of memories.

The numbers running across the top of the grid represent innings. Spaces on the left-hand side of the grid are reserved for the players' names, positions, and uniform numbers. You summarize a team's output of hits and runs for each half-inning in the spaces provided at the bottom of the scoring columns. When the game ends, record the player and team totals (at-bats, runs, hits, runs batted in, and errors) in the grid's right-hand columns.

The scorekeeper's codes

The first time you encounter a completed scorecard, it may look as if some ancient sage has scribbled on it in hieroglyphics. Don't be intimidated. The scribbling becomes decipherable after you learn the basic symbols. Position players are represented by numbers (not to be confused with their uniform numbers), as shown in Table 18-1.

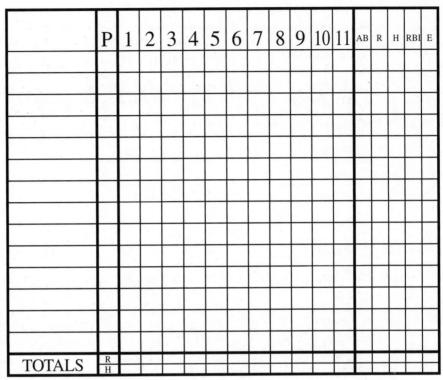

	P	1	2	3	4	5	6	7	8	9	10	11	AB	R	H	RBI	E
TOTALS	R H																

Figure 18-3:
A blank
baseball
scorecard.

Table 18-1	The Numbers Assigned to Each Player
Player	*Number*
Pitcher	1
Catcher	2
First baseman	3
Second baseman	4
Third baseman	5
Shortstop	6
Left fielder	7
Center fielder	8
Right fielder	9

All scoring systems adhere to this numerical code. The symbols and abbreviations used to record the outcome of each at-bat, however, can vary from scorer to scorer. Novice scorers should stick to the basic abbreviations shown in Table 18-2.

Table 18-2	Baseball Scoring Abbreviations
Event	*Abbreviation*
Single	1B
Double	2B
Triple	3B
Home run	HR
Base on balls	BB
Intentional base on balls	IBB
Balk	BLK
Caught stealing	CS
Double play	DP
Error	E
Fielder's choice	FC
Force-out	FO
Fly out	F
Ground out	G
Hit by pitcher	HBP
Interference	I
Strikeout	K
Line drive	LD
Passed ball	PB
Stolen base	SB
Sacrifice hit	SH
Sacrifice fly	SF
Triple play	TP
Wild pitch	WP

Combine the position numbers and abbreviations to record the sequence of an out — which tells you who got the *assist* (a throw by a fielder that leads to an out), if anyone, and who made the putout. You can also pinpoint the location of a hit or assign blame for an error. For example, if a pitcher retires a game's leadoff hitter on a fly ball to left field, mark F-7 in the first inning grid alongside the batter's name. If that ball drops just in front of the left fielder for a single, the proper notation is 1B-7. However, if the official scorer deems the ball catchable, enter an E-7. A double-play ball that is fielded first by the second baseman who throws it to the shortstop for the relay throw to the first baseman is scored 4-6-3 DP (second-to-short-to-first double play).

Tracking the runner

Most scorecards have tiny diamonds within the scoring blocks. (If yours doesn't, you can draw them.) Use the diamonds to record the progress of the base runners. Treat the lower point of the diamond as home plate and work around the box counter-clockwise.

For example, if a batter singles to center field, darken the line of the diamond leading from home to first while recording the circumstances that put him on base in the lower right-hand corner.

If the same player then advances one base on a wild pitch, darken the line from first to second and put the abbreviation WP in the upper right-hand corner.

When a short single to right moves this player up one more base, darken the line from second to third and note 1B-9 in the upper left-hand corner.

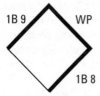

After a sacrifice fly to left field scores the runner, darken the line from third to home, fill in the diamond (to signify a run scored), and put a dot in the box of the batter who drove in the run. The result is a snapshot of a batter's entire one-inning history.

When the half-inning ends, draw a slash across the lower right-hand corner of the scoring block for any batter who makes the last out of a team's turn at-bat.

After mastering the rudiments of scoring, you can adopt such advanced techniques as color coding — which requires you to record walks in green, strikeouts in red, and hits in blue. (You'd better own one of those multi-barreled pens, or you may need an extra seat at the ballpark just for your office supplies.)

Many books explain the various scoring systems. But if you're looking for one that entertains as well as informs you, purchase Paul Dickson's gracefully written *The Joy of Keeping Score* (Harcourt Brace).

The Stadiums

We think of the player who hits 40 home runs while playing half his games in Coors Field as a fearsome slugger. But would we hold him in such high regard if his club's home address was Pac Bell Park and he struggled to hit 25 home runs a season? Conversely, the Colorado Rockies pitcher whose *earned run average* (ERA) hovers near 5.00 appears to be one step away from his release. However, let him pitch half his games in Atlanta's Turner Field, and he may find himself among the league's ERA leaders. (See Chapter 16 for more information on ERAs.) Ballparks matter. They not only provide a pleasant setting to watch a game, they also profoundly affect run scoring and our assessment of a player's ability. In this chapter, I examine the impact each major-league stadium has on performance and perception.

The National League stadiums

For years, National League stadiums tended to be a bit larger than their American League counterparts. These NL parks were built with pitching and defense in mind. But many of the newer parks in this league — Coors Field, Miller Park, and Bank One Ballpark — favor hitters.

Bank One Ballpark: Arizona Diamondbacks

When I first saw the model for this new park, its dimensions suggested a neutral field with perhaps a slight bias toward the pitcher. Forget it. This is another hitter's paradise. When Bank One's retractable roof is open — which is most of the time — long balls positively soar through Arizona's warm desert air. Bank One's deep outfield features a lot of quirky angles so triples come relatively easy here. Center field is large, and the overhangs can produce some challenging caroms. When the roof is closed, the sod in the outfield loosens and breaks away in clumps that can make running treacherous. Management equipped the stadium with a family-friendly play area that features a swimming pool. By the way, the Diamondbacks' retractable dome is a state-of-the-art affair that supposedly opens and closes much faster than any dome in either league.

Turner Field: Atlanta Braves

Prior to 1997, the Braves played in Atlanta–Fulton County Stadium, nicknamed "The Launching Pad." If parents did not want their kids to grow up to be pitchers, they took them here for discouragement. Season after season, Atlanta-Fulton was the best slugger's park in baseball.

However, pitchers love working in the Braves' new home digs, Turner Field. The park's spacious foul territory allows fielders ample room to convert lazy pops into outs before they drop beyond reach into the stands. During the spring, the strong cool wind blowing in from center field often stops fly balls that will rocket out of the park when the temperature rises. In recent seasons, the Braves and their opponents have hit more home runs on the road than at Turner. And players have been less likely to hit doubles on this field (although having the nonpareil Andruw Jones chasing down the ball in center field partially accounts for that).

Turner will increase the batting averages for players who can consistently drive the ball into the vast expanse of right field. Playing a strong-armed speedster in right field is practically a must in the ballpark. If your right fielder fails to cut off a base hit on the first or second hop, the ball can roll behind him forever.

Wrigley Field: Chicago Cubs

I hit my first major-league home run in this park. Since its opening, Wrigley has been considered a hitter's paradise, but the park is deceptive. When the wind blows in early in the season, this stadium favors pitchers, particularly those who are adept at inducing batters to hit ground balls. And during the late innings of day games, hitters can have a tough time picking up pitches coming out of the shadows.

However, when the wind shifts outward from late June on, scoring rises nearly 40 percent, and a batter's chances of hitting a home run double. One of the smallest foul territories in the Major Leagues also aids the hitters by allowing fielders less room to convert foul balls into outs, thus prolonging at-bats.

Right-handed sluggers tend to do well in Wrigley, but pull hitters can struggle here; their best shots often end up as harmless fly balls to the deepest parts of the park. On the other hand, batters who go with the pitch to drive the ball into the short alleys usually thrive in this environment.

Wrigley's tall infield grass slows all but the hardest hit groundballs and prevents many of them from going through for base hits. Rumors suggest that the Chicago grounds crew has built up the mound to give an advantage to the Cubs' young, hard-throwing pitching staff.

Great American Ballpark: Cincinnati Reds

And the hits just keep on coming. The Reds' new ballpark is a delight for hitters of every stripe. Sluggers, line-drive hitters, and players who hit the ball on the ground all excel in this stadium built with offense in mind. Routine fly balls can carry into the seats in both straight-away left and right, and the strong prevailing winds will blow the ball over the fence even in dead center field. However, triples are hard to come by in Great American; the park yielded only 11 three-baggers to the Reds and their opponents in 2003.

Grounders shoot through this hard-packed infield; any second baseman or shortstop playing here must demonstrate a quick first step. Players must deaden the ball to successfully bunt on this surface.

Coors Field: Colorado Rockies

Coors Field is baseball's black hole for hurlers. Pitchers who visit Coors are often never heard from again. This is the greatest hitter's park of all time. In 2003, the Rockies scored 6.35 runs per game at home, but only 4.15 runs per game on the road. Coors has increased Colorado's run production by at least 50 percent in every season since the field opened in 1995. Because it favors hitters, the park's dimensions often surprise people. They expect Coors to be a bandbox, but its playing field is actually slightly larger than average. Home runs launch themselves into orbit thanks to the thin, mile-high atmosphere.

And this isn't just a home-run park. Because the visibility at Coors is excellent, you can get a good read on a pitcher's offerings. The spacious playing field inflates extra-base hit totals and batting averages. Teams whose outfielders possess below-average speed and weak throwing arms are at a particular disadvantage here.

Coors Field also features two defensive quirks. First, the thin, arid atmosphere retards grass growth; hard hit grounders zoom past even the quickest infielders. And second, during the mid-summer months, the setting sun shines directly into the first baseman's eyes, at times making it difficult to pick up throws.

You will rarely witness a complete game at Coors. Few pitchers dare throw anything near the heart of the plate, and all that "nibbling" at the corners results in deep pitch counts. Pitching up in the strike zone at Coors invites disaster because every fly ball is a candidate for the seats. The thin Colorado atmosphere also robs the bite from many a pitcher's best curveball. When he's healthy, young Rockies right-hander Jason Jennings may be the prototypical Coors pitcher. He has enjoyed some success at home during his brief career by featuring a sinker that burrows in on hitters and a late-breaking slider that he keeps low. Any Rockies pitcher who maintains an earned run average (ERA) under 5.00 should be congratulated. In 2003, Colorado's Darren Oliver (another pitcher who deals the ball low) led his team in wins with 13 while compiling a 5.04 ERA. He didn't receive any Cy Young Award votes — one has to wonder if any Rockies pitcher ever will — but someone should have given him an Honorable Mention.

Miller Park: Milwaukee Brewers

Any hitter who puts the ball in the air in Miller Park has an excellent shot at an extra-base hit. The corners are deep, the power alleys are short, and the fielders have a lot of ground to cover in what looks like the widest outfield in major-league baseball. Anyone patrolling center field can rob enemy base hits by playing shallow, but he must possess excellent lateral range or the sky will start raining doubles. The ball carries well to right field, so left-handed sluggers pose a particular danger in this stadium.

However, pitchers also gain advantages at Miller. Brewers ace Ben Sheets learned to neutralize left-handed hitters by developing a groundball-inducing changeup in 2003; Milwaukee's slow infield renders many hard hit grounders into outs. A sharp glare also hampers hitters' visibility during day games, making it difficult for them to track the ball out of the pitcher's hand.

Pro Player Stadium: Florida Marlins

This stadium has two deep power alleys, so if you want to see baseball's most exciting hit — the triple — this is the park to visit. However, Pro Player suppresses the long ball. Any club that calls it home must feature an offense manned by players who can pressure defenses by taking the extra base. It's no coincidence that the Marlins won their second World Series title in 2003 after management committed to building the team around racehorses like National League stolen base champ Juan Pierre and his partner in baseball larceny, Luis Castillo.

Most home-run hitters grit their teeth whenever they visit Pro Player. The out-of-town scoreboard, known as the "Teal Tower," looms nearly 27 feet high in the outfield and has kept many a home run out of the box score. The gaps in right- and left-center field are among the most spacious in baseball; Pierre appears to be wearing jet packs when he chases down balls hit to either side of him. Deep left-center field is a graveyard for doubles. A batter can drive a pitch over 425 feet and walk away from home plate with nothing to show for his efforts but a long out.

Minute Maid Park: The Houston Astros

Want to see a major-league hitter salivate? Just drop him off in Minute Maid Park and place a bat in his hands. This stadium is the anti-Pro Player. The left field fence sits only 315 feet from home plate, and 326 feet to right field represents little more than a chip shot for an average left-handed slugger. Even though these dimensions make Minute Maid a home-run haven, pitchers can survive in these confines by inducing batters to hit the ball to the wide, deep piece of real estate called center field.

Left fielders must stay alert in this ballpark. Balls often carom at eccentric angles off the seats jutting out along the left field line, one reason why the 'Stros have hit nearly twice as many triples at home as on the road during the last three seasons. Center fielders must contend with the steep grade at their backs; to understand what they're up against, try staying on your feet while tracking down a fly ball as you race up the side of a hill. Obviously, pitchers are best served by keeping the ball down in this stadium, which is why the Astros were so eager to sign Roger Clemens, one of the rare power pitchers who records more outs on the ground than in the air.

Dodger Stadium: Los Angeles Dodgers

One of the reasons the Dodgers seem to have great pitching year-in and year-out is their ballpark. (Signing talented pitchers like Sandy Koufax, Fernando Valenzuela, and Eric Gagne is another reason.) The park does not appear cavernous, but at night, the dense, moist air floating in from the Pacific Ocean prevents hard hit balls from traveling far.

Hitters don't see the ball well here even during the day when glare and smog are often factors to contend with. As the summer wears on, bad hops abound after the intense heat hardens the infield; even the best fielders become error-prone on this surface. They also must cover an unusually large foul territory.

Fly-ball hitters languish in Dodger Stadium, though the stiff breezes that often blow out in right field provide some relief for left-handed sluggers. Dodgers batters usually hit 10 to 30 points higher on the road with much higher power numbers.

RFK Stadium: Washington, D.C.

The Montreal Expos are scheduled to move to Washington for the 2005 season. The franchise will remain in the National League, but a new team name has yet to be chosen as we go to press. RFK Stadium served as home to the now-defunct Washington Senators of the American League, from 1962 to 1971. During that time, RFK earned a reputation as a pitcher's park with a commodious outfield that devoured homeruns.

For the 2005 season, the stadium will undergo renovations that will cost at least $14 million. Those renovations will include a new dugout, clubhouse, and press box plus a modern major league scoreboard. Plans also call for retractable seats in the lower deck. Washington will call RFK home for three seasons and then move to a new 41,000 seat ballpark that the city will construct along the Anacostia River, less than a mile from the capitol.

Shea Stadium: New York Mets

Shea is a tough park for home-run hitters. In the park's first 40 seasons, only two Mets — catchers Mike Piazza and Todd Hundley — have hit 40 or more home runs in a season. By contrast, six Colorado Rockies have topped the 40-homer mark a combined 11 times since that team entered the National League in 1994. Visibility poses a problem for hitters at Shea. As the ball leaves the pitcher's hand, it momentarily gets lost in the background and can be difficult to track. Pitchers are doubly tough at night. The field is relatively poorly lit and the air seems to thicken, making it hard to drive the ball. The poor visibility impairs strike zone judgment as well. Many hitters see their strikeout rates rise and their walk rates shrink after coming to the Mets.

Strikeout pitchers — who don't give the hitter much time to see the ball anyway — can swagger as they take the mound at Shea. However, ground-ball pitchers who rely on brains rather than brawn don't usually fare as well, particularly during the day.

The Shea infield isn't in great shape, so ground balls are an adventure on this surface. And the strong winds off Flushing Bay knock down many fly balls before they can leave the park.

Citizens Bank Park: Philadelphia Phillies

The new Phillies stadium is just opening as we go to press. The early word indicates this will be a balanced park that might offer some advantage to home-run hitters; the plans call for an unusually low fence in the outfield — only six-feet high in some spots. The Phillies' old park, Veteran Stadium, featured artificial turf, but the team will play on grass at CBP. The Philadelphia pitchers should benefit with rangy infielders like shortstop Jimmy Rollins, second baseman Placido Polanco, and third baseman David Bell devouring ground-balls behind them.

PNC Park: Pittsburgh Pirates

The Pirates' park is only three years old and doesn't seem to favor hitters or pitchers. Left-handed sluggers love it because a shot down the right field line clears the fence at only 320 feet. But the right field fence angles off as far as 410 feet in left center, making it difficult for right-handed hitters to smack home runs, though they will get their share of doubles in the gaps. Infielders complain that the dirt infield has no give; the surface is hard on the knees and produces an inordinate number of bad hops.

Busch Stadium: St. Louis Cardinals

Busch Stadium used to be an atrocious park for home-run hitters. The Cardinals won National League pennants in 1985 and 1987 with only one batter (outfielder/first baseman Jack Clark) hitting as many as 20 home runs. They also captured a world championship in 1982 without a single 20-home-run man. Busch Stadium was carpeted in AstroTurf in those days, and the Cardinals's game was built around speed.

Team management has moved in the fences a tad since then, so it's a bit easier to hit home runs. They've also torn up the turf and returned to natural grass. Despite these alterations, Busch is still a below-average power park; the ball gets no help in the still air. But Busch is a great place if you're a connoisseur of defense. The Cardinals's grounds crew maintains a superb infield, and you rarely see any bad hops in this park.

Petco Park: San Diego Padres

Another stadium that opens just as we go to press, Petco may be the ultimate fan-friendly park. The Padres have promised to give their followers a cutting-edge venue with all its seats angled toward the pitchers mound to provide optimum sight lines. Some boxes will feature computers so that patrons can surf the Internet, check stats and out-of-town game scores, or order concessions without leaving the comfort of their seats. In an unusual move, Padres management has designated an area just beyond center field for lawn seating. Fans will be able to watch games from there for free. The customers aren't the only ones who will enjoy these confines. Pull hitters should love Petco with its short porches (fences) down both lines.

SBC Park: San Francisco Giants

How extraordinary is Barry Bonds? This baseball generation's überslugger accomplishes his unprecedented Homeric feats while playing half his games in the worst hitter's park in all of baseball: SBC Park. Left-handed hitters (other than Barry) find the place especially daunting. Though the fence down the right field line is only 309 feet from home plate, the wall is high and gale-force winds usually blow in over it from left to right. For this reason, power pitchers who induce fly balls thrive in SBC; Giants ace Jason Schmidt has recorded a 2.31 ERA on his home field the last two seasons, nearly a run better than his mark in other stadiums.

Just beyond the fence in SBC is the body of water known as McCovey Cove. Fans float out there in rowboats and kayaks, hoping to retrieve home runs that soar from the park. As we go to press, 38 balls have plunked into the cove since the stadium opened. (Twenty-nine of those have been hit by the remarkable Mr. Bonds. We told you he was good.)

The American League stadiums

Edison International Field: The Anaheim Angels

For years, Edison International was a pitcher's park. Then in 1979, the Angels erected three-tier seating behind the outfield walls. That construction enclosed the stadium, cutting off the wind. As a result, the ball started flying out of there. From 1994 to1997, the Angels played in the best home-run hitter's park in the American League. It was especially hospitable to left-handed power hitters like Anaheim center fielder Jim Edmonds. However, in 1997, management started a second renovation that opened up the center field area. The wind once again became a factor as home-run totals dropped, particularly for left-handed hitters. However, winds gusting about in right-center field still aided some right-handed sluggers. Edison International also depresses batting averages because visibility is poor.

For a long while, the infield of this stadium was notoriously rocky. You were more likely to see an infield error occur in this park than in any other American League stadium. Since the renovations, however, players say it's a much fairer infield.

Oriole Park at Camden Yards: The Baltimore Orioles

When Camden Yards first opened, the Orioles scored so many runs there that the stadium earned a reputation as an extreme hitter's park. Turned out that the high-octane offense was due to all the power in the O's lineup rather than some home field advantage. This ball field suppresses run scoring. Home runs are plentiful at the Yard, but the park's configurations diminish a batter's chances of hitting a double or triple. Fly balls carry deep to left field during the warmer months. In the past, Orioles groundskeepers have kept the infield grass unusually high, reducing ground-ball hits by a substantial margin.

If you attend a game at Camden Yards, keep an eye on the right fielder. The ball can take any number of crazy hops off of that tall wall and scoreboard that stand behind him. Like Anaheim, left-handed power hitters flourish in this park.

Fenway Park: The Boston Red Sox

Think Fenway and you think of the Green Monster in left field, Ted Williams, Jim Rice, Carl Yastrzemski, and all those 10–9 slugfests. Great hitter's park, right? Not anymore. In 1989, Boston constructed 600 stadium club seats above the grandstand behind home plate. Broadcast booths and a press box were installed atop that. Fenway's home improvements altered the park's wind currents in favor of the pitcher. Scoring has decreased ever since. It's still a good place for enhancing your batting average (the small foul territory contributes to that), but it actually suppresses home-run totals. Outfielders have to be quick to cover the vast real estate in Fenway's right field. If you're playing shallow and a ball gets past you, it can roll into Triple City. Left fielders must contend with the crazy caroms balls take off of that Green Monster. (See Figure 18-4.)

Figure 18-4:
The Green Monster looms at Fenway.

U.S. Cellular Field: Chicago White Sox

This stadium should warm the heart of any second baseman. Groundskeeper Roger Bossard and his crew maintain the infield so meticulously that the ball rarely takes a bad hop. A pitcher's paradise until the 2001 season when management pulled in the fences, now it's one of the top home-run parks in the Major Leagues. From 2000 to 2003, White Sox first baseman Frank Thomas hit 117 home runs, 85 of them at home. Those short fences are a blessing and a curse for the White Sox. Some of the team's hitters fall into the habit of swinging for the long ball on every pitch only to see their batting average whittled down by a lot of harmless fly balls.

Jacobs Field: Cleveland Indians

If it's late or early in the season, bring an overcoat. The wind off the nearby lake can be frigid. Jacobs Field has a well-deserved reputation as a hitter's park; visiting batters love to take their cuts here. However, the Jake can be hospitable to pitchers, too, during those cold spring and fall evenings. Many make the mistake of calling Jacobs Field a home-run hitter's park. It really isn't. Balls don't carry well to left field under any conditions, and the 19-foot high left field wall prevents many long drives from reaching the seats. A row of white buildings located beyond the center field fence makes it difficult for hitters to pick up certain pitches, another factor that diminishes offense. However, a jet stream blowing out to right field will help left-handed hitters like Cleveland outfielder Jody Gerut pop a ball out. Gerut hit 13 of his 22 home runs at the Jake in 2003.

Comerica Park: Detroit Tigers

Comerica was such an extreme pitcher's park when it first opened in 2001 that the Tigers front office was afraid hitters would be wary of signing with the team. So, the left field wall came in more than 20 feet just prior to the 2003 season, and the home-run totals ticked upward. And smart hitters are learning to drive extra-base hits into the long, wide gaps in left- and right-center field. With most of the fences so far back, you can't hide any slow, weak-armed hitters in the outfield when your team plays in Detroit. Fly-ball pitchers can challenge sluggers with impunity here.

Kauffman Stadium: Kansas City Royals

Line-drive hitters who can drive the ball into the gap for doubles and triples fare best in this ballpark. George Brett, who hit nearly everything on the line, almost hit .400 while playing here. His teammate Hal McRae, a similar hitter, won the American League Runs Batted In (RBI) crown at the age of 37. The excellent hitting background at Kauffman reduces strikeouts by about 10 percent while increasing batting averages. Management plans to move back the fences by 10 to 15 feet for the 2004 season, so home-run totals may decline, but doubles and triples should be even more plentiful in the expansive outfield. Balls will often hug the wall down the lines and scoot past outfielders.

Kauffman Stadium's grounds crew is considered the crème de la crème of the American League. They keep the Royals' infield in immaculate condition, so the infielders usually get true hops. In the past, this stadium has favored ground-ball pitchers, but with the fences moved back, members of the current Royals staff may be able to pitch up in the strike zone more often.

Hubert H. Humphrey Metrodome: Minnesota Twins

They called it the Homerdome when it first opened in 1982, but that was a misnomer. Left-handed sluggers can pull the ball over the short porch in right, but most right-handed hitters who want to reach the wall in left should call a cab. Home runs are hit here at a rate right around the league average. It is, however, a great park for doubles and triples. The right field wall resembles a large, dark, vinyl baggie; fly balls thud against it and die, allowing hitters ample time to take an extra base.

You won't see a lot of infield errors in the Metrodome. On the fastest artificial turf in the game, the ball either scoots right to you for an out or zips past you for a hit. Ground-ball pitchers have a tough time plying their trade in this stadium.

Visiting outfielders hate this place. If you aren't used to it, tracking a fly ball against the off-white backdrop of the Metrodome's Teflon-coated ceiling can be an imposing task. Balls seem to drop from out of nowhere, and then they play hopscotch on the turf. This quirk contributes to Minnesota's enormous home field advantage. In 12 postseason games played in the Dome, the Twins are 11–1, including 8–0 in the World Series. The park has fond memories for me because I got my 2,500th major-league hit here.

Yankee Stadium: New York Yankees

The myth is that Yankee Stadium favors left-handed power hitters. Actually it's a boon for left-handed pull hitters. If you can jack the ball down the line, you'll get some extra short-porch home runs. Left-handed Yankees sluggers who often hit the ball to the opposite field — Babe Ruth, Lou Gehrig, and Reggie Jackson come to mind here — usually stroked more home runs on the road than at home. The park aided hitters like Oscar Gamble and Tino Martinez, though they were powerful enough to hit the ball out of any park. Yankee first baseman Jason Giambi, who is bigger, stronger, and just as left-handed as Martinez or Gamble, hits the ball to all fields, so the park deprives him of a few home runs. With its expansive center field and generous foul territory, Yankee Stadium, despite the long-ball heroics that helped make it famous, is a pitcher's park. After appearing on the mound here, Dodger mound great Don Drysdale likened it to pitching in an airport.

Networks Associates Coliseum: Oakland Athletics

The Coliseum was the American League's premier pitcher's park until management enclosed center field and shut out the jet stream that thwarted so many long balls. Now the ball flies out of here in warm, clear climes. Because the outfield gaps are wide, speedy slap hitters can serve the ball to either side of the field and run all day. Groundskeepers maintain the infield and outfield in a neat buzz-cut; groundballs scoot past any lead-footed fielders for base hits.

Safeco Field: Seattle Mariners

One tough park to hit in. The glare in center field can blind hitters. In 2003, the Mariners heeded that old Rolling Stones song and painted the wall behind center black to remedy the problem. The dark backdrop helped somewhat, but it remains difficult to pick up pitches during day games. Sluggers find it difficult to pound the ball through Seattle's cool, damp atmosphere. Pitchers will challenge hitters with high fastballs, knowing that even the hardest hit fly balls rarely leave the field.

Safeco features a three-paneled retractable roof; it doesn't seal the stadium, but it covers it like a gigantic umbrella so that an open-air environment is sustained even during inclement weather.

Opposing teams never relish visiting the Mariner's home field. Seattle's fans are the most raucous in baseball. They can electrify their team with their cheering while taking the opposition out of the game.

The Ballpark At Arlington: Texas Rangers

Teams seldom win in this stadium without playing long ball. Doubles and triples flourish in the roomy power alleys, and home runs are practically a long bunt down the short right field line for most left-handed hitters.

Players call the rock-hard infield the worst in baseball; grounders that would be outs in most stadiums rush past infielders for singles or down the line for doubles. When the sun resides in the gap between the Ballpark's upper and lower decks, outfielders can easily lose sight of the ball. Arlington's error rate is 25 percent above the league average, even though the Rangers have been a team of sure-handed fielders over recent seasons.

SkyDome: Toronto Blue Jays

Right-handed hitters who spray the ball around thrive here; left-handed sluggers don't. When the retractable dome is open, the wind giveth and the wind taketh away. Balls can ride the currents well over the fence in right-center, but the unforgiving gusts will slap down line drives and flies hit to left. When the dome is closed, hitters gain a slight advantage, and you see a few more homers. SkyDome's artificial-turf infield may be the truest in baseball. (Probably because it's held together by Velcro rather than the zippers used to bond other turfs.) You get the feeling that customs officials turn away bad-bounce base hits at the border.

Tropicana Field: Tampa Bay Devil Rays

Tropicana Field features one of the smaller outfields in all of baseball. Pitchers who induce fly balls may have trouble here. Hitters who can drive the ball into the gap benefit. The park's asymmetrical design doesn't favor righties or lefties. And Tropicana's dome is non-retractable. Outfielders can lose balls in the stadium lights or against the background of the ivory roof. And those balls that wildly carom off the catwalk above the field remain in play. Though Tropicana's infield does feature all-dirt paths, the Devil Rays play on artificial turf. This means that ground balls that fielders might easily glove on grass, often shoot through the infield for base hits.

Stadium Statistics

Table 18-3 gives you the lowdown on all the major-league stadiums. (Because of space limitations, all these dimensions are in feet. If you want to talk meters, just divide the feet by 3.28.)

Table 18-3			Major-League Stadium Statistics				
Park	*LF Line*	*Left CF*	*Center*	*Right CF*	*RF Line*	*Surface*	*Capacity*
Bank One	330	374	407	374	334	Grass	49,033
Turner	335	380	401	390	330	Grass	50,091
Wrigley	355	368	400	368	353	Grass	39,241
Great American	328	379	404	370	325	Grass	42,263
Coors	347	390	415	375	350	Grass	50,449
Miller	344	371	400	374	345	Grass	41,900
Pro Player	330	385	404	385	345	Grass	36,331
Minute Maid	315	362	435	373	326	Grass	40,950
Dodger	330	385	395	385	330	Grass	56,000
RFK	335	385	410	385	335	Grass	45,016

Park	LF Line	Left CF	Center	Right CF	RF Line	Surface	Capacity
Shea	338	378	410	371	338	Grass	57,393
*Citizens Bank	329	369	401	369	330	Grass	43,000
PNC Park	335	389	399	375	320	Grass	37,898
Busch	330	372	402	372	330	Grass	50,354
Petco Park	334	367	396	387	322	Grass	42,000
SBC Park	339	364	399	421	309	Grass	41,503
Edison Field	330	387	400	370	330	Grass	45,030
Camden Yards	333	364	410	373	318	Grass	48,190
Fenway	310	379	420	380	302	Grass	33,991
U.S. Cellular	330	377	400	372	335	Grass	47,098
Jacobs Field	325	370	405	375	325	Grass	42,368
Comerica	345	370	420	365	330	Grass	40,120
Kauffman	330	375	400	375	330	Grass	40,785
Metrodome	343	385	408	367	327	Artificial	48,678
Yankee	318	399	408	385	314	Grass	57,478
Network Associates	330	362	400	362	330	Grass	43,662
Safeco	331	390	405	387	327	Grass	47,447
Arlington	332	390	400	381	325	Grass	49,115
SkyDome	328	375	400	375	328	Artificial	50,516
Tropicana	315	370	404	370	322	Artificial	43,772

* Indicates new stadium; dimensions are estimated.

When You Can't Get to the Park

If you're like most fans, you see the majority of your baseball on television, which is a terrific way to learn about the sport. When you watch games on the tube, you don't have to do any work. The camera people direct your attention to all the important action. If you miss a critical event — a fielding gem, a clutch hit, or dramatic strikeout — replays give you multiple chances to view it. Stop-action and slow-motion shots help you to dissect a play from a variety of angles.

All the major networks use computer graphics to analyze pitch locations, *hit spreads* (those places on the field where a batter's hits are most likely to fall), defensive alignments, and batter-pitcher matchups. The latest technological gizmos will reveal pitch location as well as velocity and bat speed. Cool, huh? You don't have to look at a single scouting report. The announcers always have a wealth of data at their disposal, so you get information you can't find anywhere else. And, best of all, if there's a rainout, you're already home.

Be sure to check out Chapter 19 for information on where and when you can catch a game on TV (and on the radio, too).

Chapter 19

Keeping Up with the Show: Baseball Online, on the Air, and on the Newsstand

In This Chapter

▶ Surfing for baseball on the Web

▶ Finding baseball on TV

▶ Reading about baseball the old-fashioned way

*T*he enormous amount of media coverage devoted to baseball reflects the sport's enduring popularity. And the coverage doesn't end with the regular major-league baseball season. You can lounge in front of the fire in the dead of winter and still enjoy plenty of baseball action — without leaving the comforts of your living room.

Baseball in Cyberspace

Back in the old days (last year, for some of us), you had to travel to your nearest newsstand to get the latest baseball scores and updates. Now you can get scores, news, and a wealth of other information at the click of a mouse. Thousands of baseball Web sites abound on the Internet. This section highlights some of the most popular ones. Flip to Table 19-1 for a list of additional sites to check out.

Baseball Prospectus

Baseball zealots should subscribe to this site and then bookmark it as their home page. Here you'll find many of the best young analysts in the game sharing their cutting-edge insights on everything from the myth of clutch hitting (it's not a skill you can count on from one season to the next) to the effects ballparks have on player performance (something we touch on in Chapter 18).

Will Carroll's "Under the Knife" column, in which the author analyzes players' injuries and physical vulnerabilities, is worth the subscription price alone. At times, you would swear Carroll has a crystal ball hidden somewhere. On March 4, 2003, he wrote in his pre-season prognosis of the San Diego Padres: ". . . I expect (Padres left fielder Phil) Nevin to have some sort of season-ending injury in the early stages of this season." Three days later, Nevin separated his shoulder while making a diving catch in a spring training game. He did not play again until July 23. Not quite season-ending, but whenever we recall Will's prognostication, the Classics Four start crooning *Spooky* in the background. You can access the Prospectus at www.baseballprospectus.com.

MLB.com

In 1995, baseball became the first major-league sport to go on the Internet (and the Seattle Mariners was the first team to have its own Web site). All 30 major-league franchises now boast Web sites. To keep up with your favorite team's latest doings, you only have to access www.mlb.com and pick a club from its pull-down menu. Then get ready to dive into a treasure trove of base-ball delights.

During the regular season, you can enjoy such goodies as the latest standings, league leader boards, up-to-the-moment scores, great play highlight reels, and live broadcasts of games you can't see anywhere else. You can also access sta-dium seating charts, check the schedules of every major-league team, and purchase tickets for select games. When we recently ventured onto this site, we even stumbled upon a live conference call between all 30 major-league managers.

Come here during the off-season if you want to get the facts behind the latest trade or check the results from one of the winter leagues. The site also lets you play general manager by offering one of the best fantasy baseball games in cyberspace.

The Negro Baseball Leagues

James A. Riley, director of research for the Negro Leagues Baseball Museum, is the editor of this Web site at www.blackbaseball.com. The site is an archival resource that acquaints you with the rich history of the various Negro leagues, their players, managers, owners, and teams. This site also serves as a link to sites that sell Negro League books, merchandise, and memorabilia such as jackets, caps, and autographs.

The National Baseball Hall of Fame and Museum

The National Baseball Hall of Fame Web site at www.baseballhalloffame.org can't give you the same thrills as an actual visit to Cooperstown, but it's the next best thing. This site offers users an online tour of the Hall of Fame, its museum, famed bronze player plaques, and library. You can purchase baseball books, prints, videos, and other merchandise through the Museum Shop. If you're curious to see how your favorite players fared in past Hall of Fame elections, spend a few hours poring over the comprehensive voting archives. A new feature lets site visitors fill out a sample Hall of Fame ballot, so they can compare their choices with the experts' picks in the next election.

Baseball Reference

Who holds the record for home runs by a National League switch hitter? How many games did Babe Ruth win as a pitcher? The best place to find out is this Web site (www.baseballreference.com), an online encyclopedia that contains the records for every player who ever pulled on a pair of major-league spikes. When you access a player's stats, you not only find his regular season numbers, you also discover how he fared in postseason play. Each player profile includes his fielding stats as well as a comprehensive list of where he finished in the voting for any major awards. (By the way, the answers to our trivia questions are Howard Johnson, who hit most of those homers as a third baseman for the New York Mets, and 96 wins for the Babe.)

Ballparks by Munsey & Suppes

Are you a ballpark buff? Does just a glimpse of Wrigley Field's near-mythic ivy-covered walls set you to swooning? Have we got a Web site for you! Ballparks by Munsey & Suppes (www.ballparks.com/baseball/index.htm) has all the information you could ever want about major-league ballparks present, past, and future — including seating plans, field dimensions, interior and exterior photos, turf type (for example, the Baltimore Orioles play on Maryland Bluegrass in Camden Yards), and historical summaries. Looking for the ideal gift for that Red Sox fanatic in your life? You can purchase a scale model replica of Fenway Park (complete with Green Monster) from a catalogue of great baseball venues past and present.

Skilton's Baseball Links

This Web site, accessed at www.baseball-links.com, links fans to over 10,000 baseball sites and updates. Talk about a baseball cornucopia! Visit this site when you want to find out whether your favorite team in the Federation de Baseball du Luxembourg won its big game last night.

MLBTV

Concerned relatives may have to pry you from your laptop or PC after you add this to your Internet Favorites list. The cybernetwork streams over 280 live games every month, and you can choose from a monthly or seasonal subscription plan. A 350K+ broadband connection is required to view the broadcasts, and all live games are subject to local blackout restrictions. You can order the service through www.mlb.com or call 888-800-1275.

Table 19-1	Other Baseball Web Sites	
Name	*Address*	*Neat Features*
Baseball Almanac	www.baseball-almanac.com	This site contains legendary lists compiled by many of baseball's greatest players, articles by writers and analysts including Ted Williams's top three batting tips ("Swing only at strikes" is number one), and the Total Baseball Encyclopedia's rankings for the 400 greatest baseball figures of all time.
Baseball Primer	www.baseballprimer.com	In "The Transactions Oracle," columnist Dan Szyborski analyzes the latest trades, signings, and other transactions, then invites readers to post their comments. The chats are often exhilarating.

Name	Address	Neat Features
Baseball Cube	www.sports-wired.com	Find complete listings of the amateur drafts dating back to 1965 and comprehensive player records, including hard-to-find minor-league statistics.
Baseball Newsstand	www.baseballnewsstand.com	Jim Furtado provides you with links to the top baseball writers in every major-league city every day.
Baseball Plays	www.jes-soft.com	You'll find training drills to improve the performance of any team, from Little League to the majors. Coaches can download a free baseball playbook featuring color graphics and animated plays.
ESPN	www.espn.com	This site is full of info, including Jayson Stark's Rumblings and Ramblings covering all 30 major-league teams; Rob Neyer's statistical analyses; John Sickels's Down on the Farm scouting reports on minor-league prospects; and, oh yeah, a wide-ranging baseball column by some fellow named Morgan.
The Exploratorium	www.exploratorium.edu	Consider this Baseball Science 101. This site contains thoughtful essays that explain, in layman's language, what makes a curveball curve, a slider slide, and a home run, uh, run.
Minor League Baseball	www.minorleaguebaseball.com	This site features a list of the top 100 minor-league teams of all time as compiled by the Sports Ticker, plus comprehensive histories (including rare player photographs) and statistics for each club.

(continued)

Table 19-1 *(continued)*

Name	Address	Neat Features
Pitching Coach Services	www.drmikemarshall.com	Former L.A. Dodgers reliever Mike Marshall, who set a major-league record by pitching 106 games in 1974, shares his secrets for pitching durability. You can download this baseball brainiac's (Dr. Marshall has a PhD in physiology) primer on pitching mechanics free of charge.
Web Ball	www.webball.com	You'll find a weightless training center, a guide to conditioning exercises for the pre-adolescent set. Fear Factor offers advice on how coaches can help kids to overcome fear and build confidence on the ball field. Our favorite tip: Learn to duck!
The Baseball Page	www.ericenders.com/ baseball.htm	Site offers a one-of-a-kind international timeline of important baseball events in the United States, Japan, Cuba, Mexico, Italy, Australia, Korea, and other countries, from 1847 to the present. The anecdotes often assume a strange-but-true quality, such as the story of the American soldiers who played the first baseball game in Mexico while using the wooden leg of Generalissimo Santa Ana (that's right, Billy Bob Thornton's nemesis from the Alamo) as a bat.
High School Baseball Web	www.hsbaseballweb.com	Top high school coaches share tips on how to enhance your chances of making the team, while college scouts reveal what you have to do off the field to merit a baseball scholarship.
Major League Baseball Graphs	www.baseballgraphs.com	This site offers the season-to-season history of baseball from 1901 to yesterday, all in a glance at a graph.

Name	Address	Neat Features
Player Contracts	www.bluemanc.demon.co.uk	Want to figure out how much A-Rod earns per hour? Grab your calculator then visit this site, which breaks down the annual salaries, including bonuses, for every major-league player.
Retrosheet	www.retrosheet.org	For baseball researchers, this is what the Field of Dreams resembles. It's a resource for box scores, rosters, play-by-play accounts, schedules, and game logs for major-league games dating back as far back as 1871.
Road Side Photos	roadsidephotos.com/baseball/index.htm	Doug Pappas, the chairman of the Society of Baseball Research's Business of Baseball committee, explains the dollars, cents, and nonsense of modern baseball economics in prose that's frequently as entertaining as it is illuminating.

Baseball on the Tube

Who said that baseball on television was boring? This is your chance to prove that person wrong. Following is a guide to get you pointed in the right direction — toward your television screen.

ESPN

This cable network, based in Bristol, Connecticut, begins its regular-season baseball coverage on opening day. ESPN and its younger sibling ESPN2 broadcast Sunday night games as well as games during the week, while ESPN *Deportes* carries a regular slate of games broadcast in Spanish. You can access the schedule for each of these networks at www.espn.com.

Fans can get the latest scores and game gossip on *Baseball Tonight,* which airs every evening throughout the baseball season. The ESPN sports ticker runs during the station's broadcasts of other sports, offering you up-to-the-minute game scores, transactions, and additional bits of news. The network carries divisional playoff games for both leagues during the postseason.

ESPN also affords baseball wide coverage all year round on its flagship news program, *Sportscenter.* The show appears at regular intervals throughout each day. ESPN2 covers some off-field baseball events, such as the expansion draft and the Baseball Hall of Fame induction ceremonies. Both networks also broadcast college baseball games. Consult your schedule to find out who plays and when.

Forgive us for mixing our media, but ESPN Sports Radio — a network with over 375 affiliates around the country — broadcasts all postseason games (including the World Series), the All-Star Game, and a selection of regular season contests. Its All-Star coverage includes two events that take place the day before the game: the popular Home Run Derby and the All-Star Game Gala.

ESPN's Classic Sports Network

Even when the snow is piled up to your rooftop, you can still watch baseball. Tuning in to the Classic Sports Network is like stepping into a time machine. The cable network doesn't carry any live baseball telecasts, but it does bring you some of the greatest games ever played, in their entirety. You'll see the Brooklyn Dodgers win their first and only world championship, Nolan Ryan pitch a no-hitter, the storied sixth game of the 1975 World Series between the Red Sox and Reds, and much more. Check your cable listings to see if your carrier provides the network.

Fox Sports

Rupert Murdoch's Fox Sports brings you 18 regular-season Saturday games starting in late May. The network designates the final two Saturdays of the regular season as "wild card" dates, during which it can broadcast as many as four games that may affect divisional races. In addition to the network's regular-season coverage, Fox Sports broadcasts the All-Star Game, select Division Series matchups, the National and American League Championship Series, and the World Series.

Other telecasts

Super-stations like TBS (Atlanta Braves) and WGN (Chicago Cubs) transmit broadcasts of their local team's games across the United States. Many Spanish-speaking networks carry baseball from the Caribbean leagues during the winter months. You can watch players like Juan Gonzalez, Bernie Williams, and Ivan Rodriguez strut their stuff while you wrap Christmas presents. Consult your local TV listings for times and schedules.

Baseball in Print

If you don't want to play or watch baseball (or look for it on the Web), perhaps you'd like to read about it. This section describes some great starting points for you. (You can find contact information for these publications in Appendix B.)

- ✔ *USA Today* provides fans with excellent daily coverage of national baseball. Unlike many local papers, it rarely brings a hometown slant to a game or story. *USA Today Sports Weekly* is an excellent source of week-to-week coverage, particularly during the off-season. You can call the paper's fine back-issues department to research any articles you may have missed on the stands.

- ✔ *The Sporting News* is a weekly magazine/newspaper that covers all the major-league teams throughout the year, as well as other sports.

- ✔ *Sports Illustrated* provides comprehensive coverage of particular baseball news stories or events.

- ✔ *Baseball America* publishes every two weeks; therefore, many of its major-league stories are old news by the time a copy reaches your hands. However, no publication can surpass its coverage of minor-league and college baseball. If you're in a fantasy league and want to chart the progress of an up-and-coming prospect, a subscription to this magazine is a shrewd investment. (See Chapter 20 for more information on fantasy leagues.)

Other publications for your baseball reading pleasure include:

- ✔ *Baseball Digest:* A monthly compendium of baseball articles written by leading sportswriters from around the country.

- ✔ *ESPN, The Magazine:* A sports fanzine (published every two weeks) whose mesmerizing graphics and illuminating sidebars pull the reader into the text.

✔ *Street & Smith's Baseball:* The most respected of the pre-season baseball annuals.

✔ *Street & Smith's Sports Business Journal:* Gives you the story of the game off the field while offering a glimpse of the economic hardball played in front offices throughout both leagues.

✔ *Who's Who In Baseball:* This annually updated publication contains the complete minor- and major-league records of nearly every current major-league player.

✔ *Beckett's Baseball Card Magazine:* A guide to the fluctuating baseball card market (the Dow Jones often exhibits less volatility) by the leaders in the industry. Beckett produces several publications that establish the market for cards and other baseball collectibles. The company's *Baseball Card Price Guide* sets the value for over 500,000 cards. The *Beckett Almanac* annually prices over 750,000 items, including autographs and team yearbooks. If you want to buy, sell, or trade baseball memorabilia, these guides are indispensable.

Chapter 20

Fantasy Baseball

. . . .

In This Chapter

▶ Understanding the appeal of fantasy baseball

▶ Drafting, playing, and scoring

▶ Excelling as a fantasy team manager

▶ Playing computer ball

. . . .

Millions of people play fantasy baseball every year. "What's the big deal?" you ask. Fantasy leagues let you act as general manager for a team of major leaguers in a baseball universe of your own creation. You get to pit your executive skills against an entire league of virtual general managers who try to guide their teams to the pennant. After scouting and signing players, you spend the entire season modifying your club through trades, free agent drafts, and other transactions. If you win a championship, you get to take home a little prize money, bask in the applause of family and friends, and have a bottle of Yoo-Hoo poured over your head (one of fantasy baseball's more endearing rituals).

Daniel Okrent — whose contributions to baseball literature include the aptly named *Ultimate Baseball Book* (Houghton-Mifflin) — created the first fantasy league in 1980 while dining in the Manhattan bistro La Rotisserie Française with several other devotees of the national pastime. The originators named the game *rotisserie baseball* after the restaurant. (Many participants today often use the terms rotisserie baseball and fantasy baseball interchangeably.)

What the Heck Is Fantasy Baseball?

Fantasy baseball is a game you play with 10 to 12 people. Each team selects 23 major-league players who compete against other teams of 23 players; all players are based on real-life players and their regular-season statistics. The week before the start of the major-league season, you gather with the other "owners" in your league and hold an auction-style draft in which each owner purchases players. After each of you fills his roster of players, the competition begins. Your team battles against the other teams based on the real-life statistics of the players drafted. You don't play individual games in fantasy baseball; instead, you try to accumulate the best totals possible in each statistical category.

What baseball statistics do you use? Most fantasy leagues use the eight categories (four hitting, four pitching) shown in Table 20-1.

Table 20-1	Fantasy Baseball Scoring Categories
Offense	*Pitching*
Total runs batted in (RBI)	Team ERA (See Chapter 16 for information on calculating ERA)
Total home runs	Total wins
Team batting average	Total saves
Total stolen bases	Walks plus hits divided by innings pitched ratio (WHIP)

The goal is to select players who will amass the highest totals in the categories (except for ERA and WHIP, where the lowest total wins). You're not restricted to using these stats; some of the more sophisticated leagues are replacing team batting average with team on-base percentage, and many leagues use more than a dozen categories to decide their championships.

Find out more about scoring in the section "Figuring your point total and winning," later in this chapter.

How Do I Play?

Covering all the nuances of fantasy baseball in a single chapter is impossible, so you get only the general stuff here. Check out Glen Waggoner's *Rotisserie League Baseball* (Little, Brown) to find out more and help you establish the official rules for your league.

Starting a league

Starting a league is easy. Here's what you do:

1. **Recruit 11 friends.**

   Twelve is the usual number of teams for a fantasy league, but you can play with fewer. If you can round up more than 12 participants, you may have to open the bidding to include players from both leagues.

2. **Select a date to hold your annual player draft.**

   Most leagues hold the draft the weekend before the major-league season begins. If this date doesn't work for your busy schedule, try to hold the draft two weeks before the start of the season or the weekend after baseball's Opening Day.

3. **Choose to play with either National League or American League players.** (See Chapter 14 for more information on the two leagues.)

   Limit your fantasy league to selecting players from only National League teams or only American League teams. Nearly all fantasy leagues choose only one league.

4. **Agree on an entry fee.**

   This dollar amount can be as high or low as you like. Pool the entry fees together to form the pot — the cash paid out to the winners at the end of the season.

That's it. Start gathering information on your favorite players and get ready to draft!

Drafting a team

Before you start drafting your team, set a salary cap for your fantasy league. For example, you and your fellow owners may decide to limit each team's payroll to $260 (or some other affordable sum). You don't have to play with actual money, however; you may credit an imaginary $260 to each team. But you must keep the $260-to-23-players ratio. (See the next section, "Filling out your roster," for the position-by-position breakdown of the 23-player roster.)

Although the league can't require any team to spend its entire $260 budget, spending less isn't wise. Always try to spend all your money on draft day to maximize your chances of getting all the players you want.

Assign a drafting order for calling up players to the auction block. Picking first does not ensure that your club will acquire the player of your choice. Team A may start the draft by saying, "Miguel Cabrera for $1." The other owners begin calling out bids, always upping the bid in increments of at least $1. When the bidding slows, the owner who started the bidding, in this case Team A, gives fair warning. ("Cabrera going once, going twice. . . .") If no other owner ups the bid, the last bidder wins the Florida Marlins' phenom. Team B then calls up a player, and then Team C, and so on until all teams have drafted 23 players. Setting up a draft order ensures fairness because all owners get equal opportunity to call up players for auction.

Designate two people as official secretaries to record all the players, dollar amounts paid for each player, and remaining dollar amounts for each team. Accurate records help to resolve any potential conflicts.

Filling out your roster

Your roster should consist of the following:

- Two catchers
- One first baseman (first and third basemen are also known as corners)
- One second baseman
- One shortstop
- One third baseman
- A back-up second baseman or shortstop
- A back-up first or third baseman
- Five outfielders
- Nine pitchers

If you're playing with American League rules, you need to also draft a designated hitter. (See Chapter 3 if you don't know what a designated hitter is.) If you play by National League rules, draft a utility player (an extra outfielder, infielder, or catcher).

A player qualifies at a certain position by playing at least 20 games at that position during the previous year. If a player appeared in at least 20 games each at second base and shortstop last year, you may play him at either position. If a player played 125 games at catcher and 15 at first base, you may only draft him as a catcher. The position-qualifying rule varies widely from league to league; for example, in 2003, Álex Rodríguez played all his games for the Texas Rangers at shortstop, but he started 2004 as the New York Yankees' third baseman. Many leagues would allow you to put Rodríguez at short or third during the 2004 season, but you might be limited to using A-Rod at third in 2005. Refer to Glen Waggoner's *Rotisserie League Baseball* for more information on the position-qualifying rule.

Nearly all leagues also draft a group of reserves. Use these players to fill in for injured or traded players. Because so many leagues treat the reserve list differently, refer to the book *Rotisserie League Baseball* to help you formulate a reserve list policy for your league.

Managing your team after the draft

After the draft, you can kick back, relax, and watch your team in action. Or, to really have some fun, you can start calling fellow owners to make trades. Trading players with other owners adds spice to any league and can help you improve your team in the process. For every player you trade to a team, you must get a player in return. After completing a trade, all teams involved (yes, you can negotiate multiteam deals) must have 23 players on their rosters.

Your league may decide to charge a nominal fee ($1 is the usual tariff) for every trade transaction. These fees can be added to any prize money your league awards at the end of the season.

When a flesh-and-blood major-league player is traded out of his league, released, put on the disabled list, or dispatched to the minors during the actual season, you can replace him in your lineup. For example, if Mets' left fielder Cliff Floyd breaks his leg in April and misses the entire season, you can replace him with a player from your reserves or acquire a new player. That new addition would not necessarily have to play Floyd's position; if your roster is deep with left field candidates, you can draft a player who mans a different spot, provided he keeps you within your league's position requirements. In the case of the Floyd injury, if your team employed Albert Pujols at first base, your league might allow you to switch him to left (one of five positions Albert has played during his major-league career) so you can sign a first baseman to replace Floyd.

Once again, thousands of rule variations exist for handling player movement during the season. Refer to the book *Rotisserie League Baseball* to help your league adopt a policy for picking up new players during the season.

Taking care of administrative tasks

As you may have guessed, running your own fantasy league involves some work. Here are some tips for minimizing the work and maximizing the fun:

- ✔ Adopt a written set of rules. Absolutely, positively do this or you'll face dozens of arguments throughout the season. Take an existing set of rules, such as the ones in *Rotisserie League Baseball,* and use them exactly the way they are or modify them to meet your league needs.

  Don't be afraid to tweak the so-called traditional rules of fantasy baseball. Create whatever rules you think will make the game as fun as possible.

- ✔ Appoint a commissioner. Choose someone, preferably the most ethical owner in your league, to wear the commissioner's hat and enforce rules and arbitrate all disputes.

- ✔ Buy a good statistics software package or pay for a stats service. A good software package allows you to download stats via computer and prepare detailed weekly reports and standings for each team. Appoint a statistician (preferably the computer guru in your league) to oversee the operation. If you don't have a computer or want to offload the work, subscribe to a statistics service, which, for a fee, calculates all your statistics and standings and mails the weekly results to each owner.

  Check the classifieds in Baseball Weekly or search the Internet under "Fantasy Baseball" to see what's available in both stats software and services. Stats services usually charge a yearly fee per player; you can purchase the software for a one-time fee. A service definitely costs more but is convenient and involves almost no work on your part.

Figuring your point total and winning

Rank teams throughout the season from first to last in each of the scoring categories. In a typical 12-team league, you award 12 points for every first place finish, 11 for second, 10 for third, and so on down to 1 point for 12th place. For example, say your team has the rankings shown in Table 20-2 in a 12-team league.

Table 20-2	A Scoring Example	
Category	*Place*	*Points*
Total Home Runs	1st	12
Total RBI	3rd	10
Batting Average	6th	7

Category	Place	Points
Stolen Bases	5th	8
Pitching Wins	2nd	11
Pitching Saves	10th	3
ERA	8th	5
WHIP ratio	12th	1
Total		**57**

You then compare your 57 total points to the other teams' total points. At season's end, the club with the most points finishes first. If you play for cash, award the prize money as follows (or create your own prize money distribution plan):

- ✔ 50 percent of the total prize money pool for the pennant winner
- ✔ 20 percent for second place
- ✔ 15 percent for third
- ✔ 10 percent for fourth
- ✔ 5 percent for fifth

Some Tips for Fantasy Baseball Success

Use the following information to keep your team near the top of the standings and your sanity on an even keel:

- ✔ **Gather info, more info, and even more info.** Gather as much information on players as you possibly can. Information gathering is the key to drafting success.

- ✔ **Check out as many pre-season publications as you can.** *Sporting News,* available online or at the newsstand, is an excellent source of fantasy baseball info. You should also read John Sickels' "Down on the Farm" column featured on ESPN.com to get the latest skinny on up-and-coming minor leaguers.

- ✔ **Carefully monitor your money during the draft.** Remember, you have only $260 to spend on 23 players. Plan wisely.

- ✔ **Choose players who stay healthy.** Injuries can destroy even the strongest team. Try to avoid the injury-prone and aging players.

Economics 101: Supply and demand in fantasy baseball

Here's where you finally find a practical use for that high school or college economics course you took years ago. Just as a scarcity of oil in Saudi Arabia causes gasoline prices to rise in the United States, supply and demand of players dictates the prices paid in fantasy baseball drafts. A short supply of certain types of players sends bids soaring through the roof. For example, each team in the majors typically includes a closer (a relief pitcher who finishes off games). Because closers accumulate most of the saves (one of the scoring categories in fantasy baseball), most drafts place a premium on the short supply of each league's outstanding closers. (Count on paying $25–$35 for each closer.) Similarly, demand rages for four-category players — offensive players who excel in all

four scoring categories: batting average, home runs, RBIs, and stolen bases. For example, in 1999, Chipper Jones hit .319 with 45 homers, 110 RBIs, and 25 stolen bases — the type of season that fantasy owners drool over. Expect to pay around $35–$45 for scarce, four-category players like Jones.

Unique events during your draft may cause player values to fluctuate as well. For example, if three teams still need a first baseman and only one good first baseman remains available, you'll pay a pretty penny for him or else get stuck with a lousy first baseman. Also, watch out for the favorite team factor: If most of your league's owners follow the Cubs, for example, expect a high demand and overbidding for Cubs players.

✔ **Beware of Spring Training phenoms.** Just because a rookie has a great Spring Training (baseball's pre-season) doesn't necessarily mean his success will carry over into the regular season. Don't overbid for a player based solely on his success in the pre-season. Put a premium on consistency, players who come close to replicating their performances season after season.

✔ **Watch out for the World Series factor.** If a player had a great World Series the year before, chances are owners will overbid for him in the next year's draft. World Series heroes usually remain fresh in everyone's mind on draft day. Don't get suckered into overbidding for them.

✔ **Remember, there's always next year.** Is your team mired in last place? Don't worry, hope springs eternal; next year could be the year you win it all.

Baseball on Your PC

Not content to draft a team of players and then follow their progress through the daily box scores? Want to know the thrill of managing your club to a World Series title? Computer baseball games put you right in the dugout, where you can watch the teams you draft and manage battle their way through a full season of competition. More than 100 such games are on the market today. The best of them include:

✔ **Diamond Mind Baseball:** You practically take a seat in a major-league dugout when you play this game. Easily the most sophisticated baseball simulation on the market, the game is surprisingly easy to master. Diamond Mind lets you utilize the most intricate strategy options while matching your managerial expertise against a human opponent or the computer.

Nearly anything that happens in a baseball game can occur in Diamond Mind. Umpires eject feisty players, home-plate collisions can leave players injured, and your fielders might blow a sure out by running into each other. Batters are rated for speed, production against righties and lefties (you can call up their stats with a click of the mouse), bunting ability, clutch-hitting production, injury vulnerability, and base-stealing (game designer Tom Tippett and his crew even rate what kind of jump a runner gets). Fielders are rated on range, fielding average, and throwing arm strength. Pitchers are rated for endurance (pitch counts matter here) as well as their ability to subdue right-handed and left-handed batters.

No matter how many talents your players possess, the decisions you make play a critical role in your team's success. For example, we blew one game against the computer when we forgot to properly warm up Eric Gagne before bringing him in for a save. Our opponents lit up the usually invincible Dodger closer like he was a cheap birthday candle. Ballparks also exert considerable impact on player performance in Diamond Mind competition. That pop fly that carries over the fence for a home run in Colorado's Mile High Stadium ain't nuthin' but a can o'corn in San Francisco's SBC Park.

Unlike other PC baseball games, Diamond Mind's rosters are deep enough to let each franchise carry more than 40 players (something that lets you wheel and deal like a big-league general manager). You can replay past seasons, order all-time all-star teams for nearly every franchise, or create your own leagues and teams and then dump the players into a talent pool for a draft. You can even play head-to-head against other gamers online. Our favorite Diamond Mind feature is the Projected Season Disk. It utilizes a complex rating system that allows you to play with current team rosters while the actual season is in progress. So we don't have to watch the World Series this year — we already know who won. To order, visit their Web site at www.diamond-mind.com.

✔ **Strat-O-Matic Computer Baseball:** Designer Hal Richman's baseball simulation offers an extensive range of managerial and general managing options. You can replay entire seasons dating back to the dead ball era of the 1900s or create a draft league. The Swap-O-Matic feature lets you match your trading skills against the computer (which told us, in so many words, to take a hike when we offered it a back-up catcher in exchange for Magglio Ordonez). Colorful pie charts help you manage by indicating who has the advantage in pitcher-batter matchups.

Playability remains one of Strat-O-Matic's most attractive features. First-time users can have their leagues up and running in less than half an hour. In just minutes, you can play a nine-inning game against a friend, the computer, or solo. Clicking the Quick Play option lets you replay a full day's schedule of games in seconds or an entire major-league season in less than ten minutes (depending on the speed of your computer). Want to abandon the dugout for the field? With the Create A Fringe Player option, you can put yourself on a team's roster and lead it to the pennant. An encyclopedia allows you to keep a permanent record of each player's seasonal and cumulative career performance. To order, visit their Web site at www.strat-o-matic.com.

✔ **Dynasty League:** Beautiful high-definition graphics represent a hallmark for creator Michael Cieslinksi's baseball simulation. Each stadium, from the golden oldies like Ebbets Field and the Polo Grounds to Cincinnati's recently opened Great American Ballpark, resembles an oil painting. Bang-bang calls at first, that shortstop's diving stop and throw, the deep drive bounding through the gap — Dynasty depicts all the heart-stop-ping plays (as well as the routine ones) with a verisimilitude that makes it the next best thing to an ESPN highlight reel. This game rates players on the usual skills, but it also takes into account intangible qualities such as team chemistry, clutch performance, a catcher's game-calling proficiency, and umpire judgment. Bizarre plays can also contribute to outcomes. Every now and again, a ball bounces off a player's head and into the stands for a home run. You can almost hear him cry, "Ouch!" Recent and past seasons are available, and the Greatest Teams discs give you an opportunity to match the best clubs and players of all time in league or tournament competition. To order, visit their Web site at www.designdepot.com.

Part V
The Part of Tens

The 5th Wave   By Rich Tennant

Idiot! I signaled for a SINKER!

In this part . . .

This part introduces you to Joe's picks of baseball's top players, pitchers, and fielders. One of our favorite chapters is the list of Joe's ten things to love about the national pastime. You can also read about ten legendary Negro League players who, though denied access to the major league stage by segregation, still managed to dazzle fans across the country during the first half of the 20th century. And we hope you get a hoot out of the list of player nicknames that have become a part of baseball lore.

Chapter 21

Joe Morgan's Top Ten Current Players and His All-Time All-Star Team

The Ten Best Current Players

Looking over this list, you immediately realize there's no talent drought in major-league baseball. Most of these players are under 30 years old and possess multidimensional skills. I won't be surprised if all of them reach the Hall of Fame. One thing you'll notice is that each of these men has demonstrated excellent strike zone discipline, offering further proof that if you swing at good pitches, you'll make good things happen.

Barry Bonds

Here's the deal: If you don't throw a strike to Barry, he doesn't swing. If you do throw a strike to Barry, he does swing. And he hits a home run. All right, we exaggerate. Barry doesn't always take bad pitches, and he doesn't always homer — it just seems that way. Baseball's King of Swing recently amazed me when he explained how he picks up the pitcher's arm angle, something he does faster than anyone in the game. He gives himself the maximum amount of time to look over a pitch by standing deep in the batter's box. His quick, compact swing betrays no wasted motion. When Barry connects, his body is perfectly balanced so he can drive his mass through the ball, which is why it travels so far.

A hitter's number one job is to get on base. Over the past few seasons, Barry has accomplished that better than anyone in baseball history. The astounding .582 on-base percentage he recorded in 2002 is the highest single-season mark in baseball history; the season before, he set the all-time single-season home-run record with a mind-boggling 73 big flies.

What I appreciate most about Barry is that he has always been a multidimensional player. In the field, this 40-year old former Gold Glover has lost some speed, but he is as baseball smart as he is talented. Bonds positions himself perfectly for most hitters and has enough arm to cut down runners attempting to grab an extra base. Barry can still swipe a bag when his team needs it; he is the only player in history with more than 500 homers and 500 steals.

A few years back, I predicted no one would ever break Hank Aaron's career home-run mark of 755. As we write this, Barry has 668 homers and shows no signs of decline. He is going to give Hank's mark a run. Barry has won six MVP awards, three more than anyone else. Is he the greatest player of all time? It may be too early to claim that, but he's definitely made himself part of the debate.

Albert Pujols

Albert displays a veteran's plate discipline even though he's only 24 years old. Young sluggers often pile up 100 or more strikeouts swinging wildly for the fences. Over his first three big-league seasons, Albert has steadily dropped his K (strikeout) total from 93 to 65, while his walks have climbed from 69 to 79. Albert waits on the ball extremely well, so breaking balls and off-speed pitches hold little mystery for him. And don't dare throw him a fastball unless it's in a great location; Albert can turn around any pitcher's best heater. He's one of only 15 players to top 110 homers before his 24th birthday.

Álex Rodríguez

This guy is probably the most complete player in the game today. There's no discernible pattern to his hitting approach. Álex powers the ball for base hits, yet he rarely pulls his homers. Instead, he hits the ball to the opposite field as if he were a slap hitter. A-Rod hits everything hard. He adjusts to pitchers as quickly as any major-league hitter. You might easily get him out with a fastball or breaking pitch in one plate appearance, but then he hits the very same pitch over the moon in his next at-bat. He's so good that he won the American League MVP award in 2003 while hitting .298 with 47 homers and 118 RBI — Hall of Fame numbers — in what was a comparatively off-year for him. He's an excellent high-percentage base stealer, and he played shortstop with enough skill to win two Gold Gloves. Had he stayed at that position, Álex might have eventually usurped Honus Wagner as everyone's all-time short-stop. But he switched to third after joining the Yankees, and it won't surprise me if he wins a Gold Glove at that position someday soon.

Vladimir Guerrero

You can often use breaking pitches to bury hitters with swings as long as Vlad's. But Guerrero's so quick and his wrists are so strong, you might fool him with a curve and he'll still hit the ball 400 feet. During his first four major-league seasons, Guerrero averaged over .300 even though he often swung at balls outside the strike zone. Over the past two years, however, Vlad has developed a keen batting eye, so — pitchers beware — he's probably just about to enter his prime.

Manny Ramirez

He's baseball's RBI man. Over the past six seasons, Manny has averaged nearly one run batted in per game. Pitchers can't expect success against Ramirez unless they vary their patterns. Manny displays phenomenal plate coverage, which is to say he can reach any pitch in the strike zone. He can pull anything you throw inside and goes the other way with authority on out-side pitches, unless he's in one of his rare "pull-happy" slumps. Those never last very long. Manny doesn't display much range in the outfield, but he has worked hard to cut down his errors, and he intimidates base runners with his strong, accurate throwing arm.

Sammy Sosa

Some thought it was a fluke when Sammy hit 66 homers to finish right behind Mark McGwire in their historic 1998 home-run race. Slammin' Sammy had never hit more than 40 homers in any season before that. Now he stands alone in the record books as the only player to top 60 home runs in three different seasons. When Sammy first entered the majors, pitchers overpowered him with inside fastballs. Cubs coach Billy Williams — a former batting champ and Hall of Famer — moved Sosa back and off the plate, leaving him better positioned to turn on anything thrown inside. I have long admired the way Sammy puts the team ahead of himself. With a runner on second and his club down a run, Sammy doesn't try to pull every ball. Pitch him on the out-side part of the plate and he'll slap a single into the opposite field for a game-tying single. However, if you leave that pitch hanging too long, Sammy will muscle it over the fence. He has as much opposite field power as anyone in the majors.

Gary Sheffield

He may own the quickest wrists in baseball. Gary's so fast he can flick out his bat at the very last moment to practically snatch the ball out of the catcher's mitt and drive it through the outfield for a double. He has one of the best batting eyes around, a leading reason why his lifetime on-base percentage stands at .401. In my mind, Sheffield doesn't get enough credit for being a complete player. He's an excellent right fielder, blessed with deceptive speed that helps him intercept balls in the gap. His throwing arm is top shelf, and he knows how to play his position. You rarely see him throw to the wrong base or commit some other mental error. He's never been a big base stealer, but he's a high-percentage thief. In 2002 and 2003, Gary swiped 30 bases in 36 attempts.

Jim Thome

Jim is a throwback to the prototypical slugger. This left-handed batter is more of a pull hitter than anyone else on our list, though he can whack the ball the opposite way. I like the way he combines patience with power. Jim annually draws over 100 walks; his lifetime OBP stands at .411, and he has hit 30 or more homers in eight consecutive seasons. In 2003, I was impressed by how quickly he adjusted to playing in the National League for the first time. He spent the entire season learning to read pitchers he hadn't seen before, yet he still managed to lead the league in home runs with 47 while finishing third in runs batted in. Jim has topped the 100 mark in RBI and runs scored seven times.

Mike Piazza

This is the best-hitting catcher of all time. Mike has maintained a career .319 batting average, remarkable when you consider all the wear and tear he sustains working behind the plate. He can pull a pitch if you come inside on him, but he can also pelt the ball to all fields for base hits. On the all-time list of receivers with at least 3,500 plate appearances, Mike ranks second in batting average, third in on-base percentage (.388), first in slugging (.572), and first, by a wide spread, in OPS (.959). On May 5, 2004, he broke Carlton Fisk's major-league record for most home runs by a catcher. Shortly after reaching that milestone, Mike started playing first base more regularly, though he still dons the face mask and shinguards on occasion.

Ken Griffey, Jr.

Injuries have prevented us from seeing the real Junior Griffey for the last several seasons. Happily, he regained his health in 2004 and has resumed his place among baseball's top sluggers. Ken hits the ball hard to all fields; when a pitch collides with his bat, it sounds like a gunshot. His home runs are usually long line drives rather than arching fly balls. Griffey hit his 500th career home run during the 2004 season. He just turned 35, so he remains a good bet to pass the 600 home-run mark. At his peak, Junior was one of the best center fielders in baseball history. He roamed all over the outfield, crashing into walls and climbing fences to make breathtaking catches.

Final thoughts

I also wish we could have found a slot for **Derek Jeter,** a complete team player who knows how to win, as well as four of the most productive hitters in baseball: **Todd Helton, Jason Giambi, Jeff Bagwell,** and **Rafael Palmeiro.**

Joe Morgan's All-Time All-Star Team

Oh, talk about a challenge! I argued with myself for days before trimming this list. I finally had to restrict the team to stars whose performances I have personally experienced as a player, teammate, spectator, or opponent (which is why you won't find Babe Ruth, Ty Cobb, Jackie Robinson, or many other deserving Hall of Famers in my lineup).

Catcher: Johnny Bench

My teammate with the Cincinnati Reds is the greatest all-around catcher ever to don a face mask. John had all the gifts a catcher needs: great footwork, a quick release, and a powerful, accurate arm. No one was better at blocking pitches in the dirt. His arm was so feared that he stopped running games cold.

John is the only receiver ever to lead his league in home runs, something he accomplished twice. He was one of those rare hitters who combined quickness with strength. Had John chosen to hit to the opposite field more often a la Mike Piazza, he might have won several batting championships. But his role in our lineup was to plate runs, so he sacrificed average to drive the ball. Bench led the league in RBI three times, drove in 100 or more runs on three other occasions, earned two MVP trophies, and copped ten consecutive Gold Glove awards.

First base: Willie McCovey and Mark McGwire

How's this for a platoon? I couldn't choose between them. The left-handed McCovey was the Barry Bonds of his day. Pitchers were loath to pitch to him. His 248 intentional career walks put him second in that category to Bonds, and he swatted 521 career home runs. Right-handed Mark McGwire is the career leader at first base in home runs (580) and home-run percentage (9.8 percent). With the possible exception of Mickey Mantle, no one has ever consistently hit the ball farther than Big Mac. Here's how outfielder Larry Walker once described a home run McGwire hit against his team: "When the ball came down, it had moon dust all over it." Both Willie and Mark were adroit fielders until their knees gave out. (It was difficult to leave Eddie Murray off this list. He won Gold Gloves and ranked among the steadiest players of the 1980's. During that decade he drove in 261 more runs than any other first baseman.)

Second base: Roberto Alomar

In his prime, Robbie Alomar displayed so much range, he could race deep into right field to intercept a hard-hit grounder and convert it into a double play. His quickness to either side continually put him in position to firmly plant his right foot and unleash rocket throws. Robbie scored 100 or more runs in six seasons and drove in more than 100 twice, quite a feat for someone who usually batted second in the lineup. Among second basemen who have appeared in the Major Leagues since 1950, Robbie ranks first in career batting average (.301), hits (2,679), and doubles (498).

Shortstop: Álex Rodríguez

A batting champion at 20, he looked like he was riding the express to Cooperstown then and has done nothing to diminish that impression since. You can refer to my comments on A-Rod in the Ten Best Current Players list earlier in this chapter. He has displayed the greatest combination of power, speed, hitting acumen, and defensive excellence I have ever witnessed in a shortstop.

(I also want to mention **Derek Jeter.** He's a great player during the regular season, but in October, when teams play for championships, he consistently elevates his game to Hall of Fame levels. That's something special.)

Third base: Mike Schmidt

Schmidt is a three-time MVP and the all-time leader among third basemen in home runs (515), extra-base hits (986), OPS (.908), slugging (.527), and RBI (1502). He even stole 174 bases and was the best fielding third baseman I've ever seen. Mike coupled great range to either side with a strong, accurate throwing arm. Blessed with acute hand-eye coordination and a panther's reflexes, Schmidt could have played anywhere, which is why he won ten Gold Gloves at the hot corner. In terms of pure athleticism, Mike probably possessed more pure physical ability than anyone I ever played with or against.

Left field: Barry Bonds

You already know my feelings about Mr. Bonds. Good thing I restricted this list to players I have seen. Imagine trying to pick a left fielder from among Ted Williams, Babe Ruth, and Barry? Bonds might still be my choice. He can just about match both the Splendid Splinter and the Bambino on offense and, in his prime, he was a far superior fielder and base runner.

Center field: Willie Mays

I always think of Willie in a hurry — dashing around the bases or scurrying out from under his cap to make another heart-stopping catch. He's the only man to win four home-run titles and four stolen-base crowns, demonstrating what a complete offensive package he was. I admired his baserunning skills; you couldn't stop him whenever he chose to take the extra base.

(**Mickey Mantle,** who perhaps represents the greatest merger of speed with power in baseball history, is a close second here.)

Right field: Henry Aaron

Mr. Everything. We think of Hank mainly for his 755 career home runs, but he was an outstanding right fielder with a strong, accurate throwing arm and enough range to start in center. I never saw him throw to the wrong base. I think people forget that Hank was also a great base stealer as a young player. He was successful about 80 percent of the time and usually stole his bags in close games when his team needed a run.

(I'd love to have **Frank Robinson,** one of the game's fiercest competitors, and **Roberto Clemente,** a perennial batting champion and defensive genius as back-ups at this position.)

Starting pitcher: My ace by committee

I can't name only one pitcher. If I had to pick the ideal ace, he would have Sandy Koufax's overpowering stuff, Bob Gibson's competitiveness, Juan Marichal's pitching assortment, Steve Carlton's focus, Tom Seaver's mechanics, Warren Spahn's control, and Roger Clemens's dedication. And he'd never lose a single game.

Relief pitcher: Rollie Fingers

Batting against his slider was like trying to hit a greased frisbee. Rollie was an "old-school" reliever who would pitch as many as three innings to ice a win. He led his league in saves three times and is the only relief pitcher to win the Cy Young and MVP awards in the same season (1981). He also earned the 1974 World Series MVP while playing for the Oakland A's. With 341 career saves — most of them earned in an era when saves were much harder to earn than they are today — Rollie is the only pure reliever in the Hall of Fame. (Hoyt Wilhelm and Dennis Eckersley, two other spectacular Hall of Fame firemen, both enjoyed successful careers as starters.)

Final thoughts

If I had room for a super-utility man, the all-time hit king **Pete Rose** would sit on my bench right next to manager Sparky Anderson. Pete starred in the Major Leagues at every position but catcher and shortstop. He won the Rookie of the Year Award playing second base, won Gold Gloves in right field, captured an MVP award as a left fielder, played on World Series champions at third and first, and showed enough range to start 70 games in center field. He hustled on defense no matter where he played and never let a position switch affect his hitting.

Chapter 22

Joe Morgan's Top Ten Current Pitchers

In This Chapter

▶ Crowning baseball's Kings of the Hill

*T*oday's hitters are bigger and stronger than ever. Fans expect every game to be a slugfest — except when the men listed in this chapter take the mound. The following ten pitchers seemingly turn back the clock to the dead ball era of the 1900s, a time when teams were grateful for any runs they scored. Throughout this chapter, I refer to the pitches each of these artists employs. You can learn more about how these pitches work by flipping back to Chapter 6. In making this list, I restricted my choices to pitchers who have demonstrated consistency over a number of years, guys whom their team-mates think of as "money in the bank."

(**Josh Beckett** and **Mark Prior,** two young pitchers who established themselves in 2004, did not make this list yet. Their times will come.)

Pedro Martínez

Martínez has lost some durability and velocity in recent years; you might have to restrict him to a tight pitch count or allow him an extra day's rest. But his lethal mix of speed (he still registers in the low 90s on the radar gun), control, movement, and guile puts him among the game's Top Guns. Pedro keeps batters guessing with a wide assortment of pitches. His curve breaks down at an angle like a hard slider, while his cutter bores in on lefties until it saws off their bat handles. The Martínez change-up replicates the action of a screwball and gently fades away from hitters as it passes over the plate — a baffling pitch from someone who still throws as hard as Pedro. Martínez has won three Cy Young Awards.

Randy Johnson

Five Cy Young Awards reside in this left-hander's trophy case. Randy throws a backbreaking slider, the kind that starts in a hitter's eyes like a way-too-high heater (see the Glossary in Appendix A) then careens downward through the strike zone. You can almost hear the screaming during its descent. Or maybe that's the hitter who just took another K (strikeout) after flailing at it. Johnson's change-up is a splitter that also breaks downward but with less velocity than the slider. Oh, and he throws a fastball deluxe — a 98-mph model that's difficult to track because a) it moves so fast and b) it moves so unpredictably. Nasty stuff. Johnson started 2004 in fourth place on the all-time strikeout list with 3,871. On May 18 of that season, the 40-year-old Johnson became the oldest major-league pitcher ever to pitch a perfect game in a 2–0 victory over the Atlanta Braves.

Greg Maddux

Greg has compiled a 2.89 ERA during an era when the league average has consistently topped 4.00. He entered 2004 with 289 wins, including a major-league record 16 consecutive seasons with at least 15 or more victories. A four-time Cy Young Award winner, Maddux has proven that you don't need great speed to win in the Major Leagues. His fastball rarely travels above the high 80s, but he retires hitters by changing speeds and throwing strikes. When Greg's two-seam fastball leaves his hand, it appears as if it will reach the batter outside the strike zone. But then it jumps at the last moment to nip the edge of home plate. I like how Greg works on every aspect of his game. Maddux has been one of the best fielding pitchers in baseball history (his National League record-setting 13 Gold Glove awards attest to that). He is also a competent hitter who can move runners over with a well-placed bunt.

Tom Glavine

Consider Glavine the left-handed Maddux. Greg's former teammate underwhelms batters into submission by throwing one of the best change-ups in the Major Leagues. He can throw the pitch for a strike at any point in the count, and the contrast in velocity makes his midspeed fastball appear that much livelier. Glavine constantly works the outside of the plate, away from the hitter's power. He displays an admirable stubbornness on the mound. Tom won't give in to a batter, preferring to walk someone rather than serve up a pitch they can hit for distance. When right, he keeps the ball low in the strike zone and annually finishes among the leaders in inducing ground balls and double plays. Tommy has won two Cy Young Awards, seven years apart (1991 and 1998).

Roger Clemens

Power pitchers tend to mix in a lot of fly-ball outs with their strikeouts. When you watch the Rocket pitch, notice the high number of groundouts he notches. His rising fastball accounts for most of his Ks, but his hard sinker and drop-off-the-table splitter forces batters to beat the ball into the ground. Clemens has demonstrated remarkable control throughout his career; among pitchers with 3,000 strikeouts, Roger ranks behind only Randy Johnson in his strikeout-to-walk ratio. His career record entering 2004 was pure Cooperstown: 310 career wins, 4,099 strikeouts, six 20-win seasons, and a major-league-record six Cy Young Awards.

Curt Schilling

A pitcher who understands the importance of pacing himself, Curt cruises through a ballgame, throwing in the low- to mid-90s, then ratchets up that heater to 98 when he needs crucial outs. He surprises batters by serving up a slow curve when they least expect it. The fun starts when Schilling reaches two strikes in the count. He can finish the hitter off with a split-fingered fastball that dives out of the strike zone or a four-seam fastball that stays up but veers away as it passes over home plate. Both pitches look the same out of his hand, making it tough for batters to adjust.

Barry Zito

Hitters never know what to expect when this left-hander arrives at work. He comes at them with the conventional pitches — fastball, slider, change, and curve — but he rarely throws two consecutive balls at the same speed or in the same spot. His best pitch is a curveball that doesn't break until the very last moment, when it drops in for a strike. Batters often give up on that pitch. Barry won the Cy Young Award in 2002 when he went 23–5 with a 2.75 ERA.

Mark Mulder

Another Oakland lefty, Mulder is one of the few pitchers who throws his slider as well as his curveball, and the subtle differences between the two pitches in speed and angle often dismay hitters. Mulder works economically. He forces batters to swing early in the count by throwing strikes that usually end up as weak grounders. Because he doesn't throw many pitches, Mulder can last deep into a ballgame; he annually ranks among the American League leaders in innings pitched and complete games.

Tim Hudson

Hudson is the right-handed ace of Oakland's Big Three. He doesn't throw any one great pitch; Hudson retires hitters with a grab bag of nasty stuff. He features a low-90s fastball, a change-up, a slider, and a splitter, each delivered at varying speeds. All these pitches move late, and Tim throws them with the same motion, so it's difficult for hitters to read his pitches until the ball is on top of home plate. Hudson tends to work low in the strike zone; he keeps his infielders busy with ground balls. This is one right-hander that base stealers fear. Tim has developed an excellent pickoff move. In 2003, he nailed six runners while allowing only seven steals.

Jason Schmidt

Schmidt is an impressive combination of power and poise. In 2003, he struck out 206 in 207 innings while walking only 46, numbers that gave him the third-best strikeout-to-walk ratio in the National League. He throws a 96-mph fastball coupled with a slider that deceives batters with its late, downward break. It's a difficult pitch to elevate, and that's one of the reasons Schmidt rarely surrenders home runs. Besides his physical gifts, Jason has developed the mental toughness you want to see in a staff ace. He responded to the pressure of starting Game 1 of the National League Division Series in 2003 by pitching a three-hit shutout for the Giants.

Final Thoughts

I also want to mention one of my favorite left-handers, **Jamie Moyer.** He doesn't throw hard, but Jamie changes speeds and hits locations with such mastery that he has posted nine consecutive winning seasons, including two 20-win campaigns. No pitcher accomplishes more with less pure velocity.

Chapter 23

Joe Morgan's Top Ten Current Fielders

In This Chapter

▶ Picking out the men with gold in their gloves

*Y*ou can't win baseball championships without superior fielding. Getting leather on the ball (defense) is just as important as getting wood on it (offense). Great fielders are exuberant; their pursuit of every batted ball is a dance of joy. When they take the field, these top ten fielders aren't merely playing a position; they're playing out their passions.

(This is another list a healthy Ken Griffey, Jr. could join. Before his spate of injuries, Junior set the standard for center field play.)

Andruw Jones

Andruw won his sixth consecutive Gold Glove in 2003. He may be the best center fielder since the prime time Willie Mays patrolled National League lawns. Andruw displays an almost preternatural sense of where the batter will hit the ball; he often takes his first step while the hitter is still in midswing. The jump Andruw gets allows him to run down hard-hit balls in the gap, robbing the opposition of extra-base hits. Jones has no weakness. He comes in on the ball as well as he goes back, and no one can match his lateral range to either side. Andruw's arm is among the strongest and most accurate in the game; runners hesitate to take the extra base against him. He once told me that he started playing baseball as a shortstop, which accounts for his unsurpassed footwork.

Mike Cameron

I put Mike Cameron on this list right behind Andruw Jones for a reason. Cameron covers nearly as much ground as Jones, and no outfielder equals him at robbing enemy home runs. Mike doesn't throw quite as well as Andruw — few center fielders do — but his arm is well above average. A two-time Gold Glove winner, he may be better than anyone at catching balls hit over his head. Cameron tracks those long flies with barely a glance over his shoulder. This skill allows him to run deep into the outfield and reach the wall with plenty of time to position for a leaping grab — a big reason why he has pulled so many balls back into the park.

Ichiro Suzuki

Flash floods don't cover ground as quickly as Ichiro. Suzuki is that rare right fielder who has a center fielder's swiftness. He is so rangy that any center fielder he plays alongside can cheat to his right, which means the left fielder has less ground to cover. This setup makes the entire outfield more effective. Ichiro's specialty is playing balls pulled down the right field line. His speed lets him cut off many of them before they reach the corner. If a shot does bound past him, he usually plays the carom perfectly, and few base runners ever challenge his great throwing arm. Suzuki has won three Gold Gloves in his three major-league seasons.

Scott Rolen

At 6'4" and 240 pounds, third baseman Scott Rolen resembles a plodding slugger until he slips on a glove. Then he reveals the nimbleness of a streamlined shortstop. Since becoming a full-time player in 1997, Rolen has led all major-league third basemen in assists, putouts, and range factor while finishing second (to Jeff Cirillo) in fielding percentage. Translation: Scott not only gets to more balls than any other third sacker, but he usually converts them into outs. This five-time Gold Glove winner plays an aggressive hot corner; he charges bunts so proficiently that he practically neutralizes that weapon for many teams. With his howitzer arm, Scott can throw out runners even when he doesn't have time to properly set himself.

Derek Lee

When Derek mans first base, he's all arms; Lee saves his teammates countless errors (and runs) by intercepting the wildest throws made to either side of him. His quick footwork and strong, accurate throwing arm make him a master of the difficult 3-6-3 double play. Derek is so flexible he can drop into a split to catch low throws from his teammates, a nifty play few first basemen can execute (without being unable to stand up and walk again afterwards, that is). He plays aggressively and will often nail the lead runner for an assist when other first basemen might opt for the easy putout (Keith Hernandez talks about the importance of aggressive play at first base in Chapter 7). Lee won his first Gold Glove in 2003.

Eric Chávez

As a third baseman, Eric has proven himself equally adept at executing diving plays to his left or right. He makes the bare-handed catch-and-toss as well as any third sacker around, and his arm is so powerful that he can put mustard on a throw even from his knees. Chávez will chase fly balls down the line a long way; he makes the over-the-shoulder grab or sliding catch with the aplomb of a center fielder. And Eric's sheer athleticism makes the most difficult plays look easy. He won his third straight Gold Glove in 2003.

Iván Rodríguez

Defensively, Iván (nicknamed "Pudge") is the closest thing to Johnny Bench I've ever seen. In his heyday, Iván threw out more than 45 percent of all would-be base stealers (thirty percent is about average). Time and injury have stolen some of his arm strength, yet he still ranks among the league leaders in nabbing base thieves, and most players remain reluctant to run on him. When a player reaches base with Iván behind the plate, he must stay alert; Rodríguez will pick off a runner with a snap throw if he strays too far from the bag. Pudge is an expert plate-blocker, and his game-calling skills helped guide a young Florida Marlins pitching staff to a world championship in 2003. He has won ten consecutive Gold Gloves from 1993 to 2002, reaching a major-league record (one he shares with Mr. Bench).

Pokey Reese

Pokey's hand-eye coordination is so prodigious that I'm surprised he doesn't hit for a higher batting average. As it is, he uses his glove to steal a truckload of runs every season. No second baseman reaches as many balls as Reese. He first came up in the Cincinnati Reds' farm system as a shortstop, and he's retained the powerful throwing arm needed to play that position. That cannon lets him throw out runners at any base from short right field. A two-time Gold

Glove winner, Pokey also gets rid of the ball quickly, making it almost a rare event whenever a runner upends him on the double play.

Luis Castillo

At second base, Luis blends excellent range with quickness and an encyclopedic knowledge of where to play hitters; he often makes routine catches on balls most fielders would have to dive after. When Castillo initiates the double play, he dishes the ball to his shortstop in a spot that makes it easy to handle. As the DP pivot man, Luis removes the ball from his glove quickly so his first baseman has ample opportunity to gauge the incoming throw's velocity and trajectory.

I love how Castillo played under pressure in 2003. During the final two months of the season, with the Marlins competing for the wild card they ultimately won, Castillo displayed his usual aggressiveness on the field without making a single error. That performance earned him his first Gold Glove.

Torii Hunter

During the 2003 All-Star Game, Torii brought the crowd to its feet by racing across endless acres of territory before leaping into space to snatch away a home run from Barry Bonds. It was the sort of audacious play that has made this center fielder's reputation. Hunter fears nothing. He will run over or through outfield walls in pursuit of enemy fly balls. Like Andruw Jones, Hunter can range far in any direction, but he's particularly adept at coming in to intercept low line drives — sure base hits when they leave the bat — before they touch the ground. He won his second Gold Glove in 2003.

Chapter 24

Joe Morgan's Top Ten Current Relievers

In This Chapter

▶ Highlighting the top closing acts

These are my picks as the ten best closing acts in baseball, the relievers who have proven they have the stomach and the stuff to get the biggest outs in any ballgame.

Eric Gagne

Eric is the toughest reliever for hitters to figure out because they never know what his best pitch will be on any given night. The right-hander produces unusual action on his change-up by holding the ball against his palm while gripping it between two fingers. Because he twists the pitch as if throwing a screwball, the ball soars toward home plate at 85 mph looking like a high slider, and then suddenly drops below the batter's sight line. No other pitch is quite like it. Gagne's fastball giddyups as high as 98 mph, and he delivers it with the same motion as his curve; that pitch is so slow it practically crawls to home plate. The abrupt change in speeds between all three pitches confounds hitters who always expect Gagne to attack them with something hard. Eric's command is excellent, particularly for someone whose pitches move so much. He established a major-league record in 2003 by successfully converting all 55 of his save opportunities.

Mariano Rivera

The new Mr. October. In 96 post-season innings, Mariano has surrendered only 70 hits while striking out 77 and walking only 12. His ERA in those outings is a miniscule 0.75, which is downright insane. The Yankees' Sandman sends hitters off to sleep with a slashing cutter that seems to hop away from bats. He started mixing in four-seam fastballs in 2003, just to give batters a different look, and the result was the lowest ERA (1.66) of his career. But when Rivera is at his best, that cutter moves so much he doesn't need anything else to put away opponents. In an age where closers have become one-inning specialists, Mariano will work two innings in big games without losing his stuff at the end. The bad news for hitters is that Mariano's control is improving. Mighty Mo averaged nearly three walks per nine innings from 1996 to 2001 but has cut that number in half since 2001. He's been the MVP for the Yankees since their postseason run began in 1996.

Billy Wagner

Explosive. Batters are fortunate they can see the ball when they face this left-hander. Billy throws in excess of 100 mph, and he can spot that blazer on both sides of the plate. Wagner doesn't throw a change-up per se; he keeps hitters off-balance with a sharp breaking slider that arrives 10 mph slower than his fastball. He fields his position well and uses a deceptive pickoff move to keep runners close. With all that heat, Wagner challenges any hitter, including Barry Bonds.

John Smoltz

Before switching to the bullpen, John was a standout starter during the regular season as well as the postseason. He might have the best pure stuff in baseball. Smoltz's fastball crackles in the high 90s, his splitter swoops down through the strike zone, and his curve often fools hitters by breaking late. But his nastiest weapon is an alligator-toothed slider that takes huge bites out of batting averages. Smoltz throws that pitch so hard, it arrives at the plate resembling a fastball until it abruptly plunges through the strike zone. When John takes his full windup, he's virtually unhittable; he's more vulnerable pitching from the stretch. But to get him to pitch from the stretch, you have to get hits against him while he's pitching from that full windup. That's the kind of paradox that transforms many batters into shoe salesmen.

Troy Percival

Percival occasionally throws a curveball or change to keep hitters off-stride, but most of the time he relies on pure smoke to blow opponents away. He consistently throws 98 mph, and when his heater passes across the top of the strike zone, batters have little chance of catching up to it. Percival has been one of baseball's most consistent closers. He has recorded eight consecutive seasons of 25 or more saves. Troy might also be the most feared reliever in the majors because his roving fastball is hard to pick up out of his delivery; he's just wild enough to keep batters loose.

Keith Foulke

Foulke doesn't throw exceptionally hard — his fastball peaks in the low 90s — but he has become a master at pitching to batters' weaknesses. His change-up is among baseball's best pitches and makes him particularly effective against left-handed hitters. Keith helps himself (and his team) with his glove; from 2000 to 2003 he didn't commit a single error. And he gets better every season.

Ugueth Urbina

Urbina varies his attack depending on which side of the plate you swing from. His slider, a pitch that sweeps low across home plate, sends right-handed batters back to the dugout moaning. He stymies lefties with his wicked change-up and splitter. And he can knock the bat from the hand of any hitter with his four-seamed fastball. Since becoming a full-time closer in 1997, Ugueth has saved over 200 games, an impressive total when you consider he has spent most of his career pitching on losing teams.

Eddie Guardado

Sportswriters and fans know him as "Everyday Eddie," because he's one of the few relievers who can pitch three or even four days in a row without losing his effectiveness. Eddie comes at the hitter with a fastball, curve, slider, splitter, and change. You get the idea — everything but the kitchen sink. And he mixes speeds and angles with such artistry that it looks as if he has 20 pitches in his repertoire. You want your closer to maintain or restore order. Eddie demonstrated a knack for that in 2003; the first batters he faced in each appearance batted .136 against him.

Robb Nen

Two of baseball's top relievers suffered career-threatening injuries in 2003. Both were still attempting comebacks when I compiled this list, but they have been so dominant in the recent past, I couldn't exclude them from any discussion of the game's top closers. Before he went down to a torn labrum in his pitching shoulder, Robb Nen saved at least 35 games in every season from

1996 to 2002. Another hard-thrower, his extraordinary control of an elusive slider accounts for much of his effectiveness. He entered 2004 as one of only 15 pitchers in major-league history to notch 300 or more saves.

Trevor Hoffman

Trevor Hoffman throws baseball's supreme change-up, a pitch that practically saunters up to home plate begging to be hit, only to vanish under the batter's swing. I've seen him throw it to the same hitter three times in a row, something few pitchers can get away with. His fastball is barely above average, but pin-point control allows him to consistently hit spots with it. Trevor's 352 saves rank him fifth on the all-time list.

Chapter 25

Joe Morgan's Ten Negro League Legends

· ·

In This Chapter

▶ Making a mark despite the color line

· ·

*B*aseball drew its color line during the mid-1880s when all-white professional teams, such as the powerful Chicago White Stockings, refused to take the field against integrated clubs. By 1899, baseball owners did not allow a single African American to play in the major or minor leagues. But African Americans continued to play on independent teams, and in 1920 Rube Foster created the Negro National League.

Major-league baseball's unofficial policy of segregation (team owners never publicly acknowledged the color line's existence) remained in effect until Jackie Robinson joined the Brooklyn Dodgers in 1947. Up to that time, baseball's deplorable shortsightedness not only deprived African Americans of the right to compete at baseball's highest level, it also robbed major-league fans of the opportunity to see some of the game's most amazing talents. Many Negro League players would have been starters in the Major Leagues had they been given the chance. A number of them would have rewritten the game's record books. The ten men listed here — all Hall of Famers — would have been all-stars in any league, during any era.

Josh Gibson

(Homestead Grays, Pittsburgh Crawfords)

Many sportswriters and major leaguers who played against Gibson believe he was the greatest all-around catcher ever. Gibson was a superb defensive receiver. Hall of Fame pitcher Walter Johnson once said, "He catches so easily, he might as well be in a rocking chair, and he throws like a bullet." Gibson was also a power hitter with few peers; Negro League and semi-pro box scores credit him with 75 home runs in 1931 and 69 in 1934. During a 17-season career, he batted .354 and topped .400 on two occasions. Gibson was also considered a leader, both on the field and off, of a powerful Homestead Grays team that won nine consecutive pennants from 1937 to 1945. Johnson said Gibson would have fetched $200,000 in an open major-league market. Sadly, Gibson never found out what he would have earned in the white major leagues. The catcher died of a brain hemorrhage at the age of 33 in January 1947, only months before Jackie Robinson broke the color line.

Satchel Paige

(Chattanooga Black Lookouts, Birmingham Black Barons, Cleveland Cubs, Pittsburgh Crawfords, Kansas City Monarchs, New York Black Yankees, Satchel Paige's All-Stars, Philadelphia Stars, Cleveland Indians, St. Louis Browns, Kansas City A's)

The color line lifted just in time for this 42-year-old pitching legend — Paige was the Negro League's biggest drawing card — to join the Cleveland Indians in the midst of a grueling pennant race. All Paige did for the Indians was go 6–1 with a 2.47 ERA. He even pitched two shutouts. It has been estimated that the rubber-armed Paige won as many as 600 games during his 30-year Negro League and barnstorming career.

A showman, Paige once reportedly made his entire outfield sit down while he pitched to Josh Gibson with the bases loaded. He struck Gibson out on four pitches. In 1952, 46-year-old Paige pitched out of the bullpen for the St. Louis Browns; he won 12 games and saved 10 more. The following season, he was among the league leaders in saves with 11. Satchel made one last major-league appearance when he pitched three innings for the Kansas City A's in 1965. He struck out one while allowing only one base runner and no runs. He was 59 years old. One can only imagine the big-league records Satch would have set had only the owners let this baseball marvel play in his prime. Ted Williams and Robin Roberts, two Hall of Famers, told me that Gibson and Paige were as talented as any players they had ever seen. Both of them should have been on baseball's All-Century Team in 1999.

Oscar Charleston

(Indianapolis ABCs, Lincoln Stars, Chicago American Giants, St. Louis Giants, Homestead Grays, Philadelphia Stars, Brooklyn Brown Dodgers, and other teams)

Many of his contemporaries cite Charleston as the greatest player in Negro League history. At least one sportswriter, who saw both players in their prime, told me he would rate Charleston over Willie Mays! Blessed with great speed, Charleston played a shallow center field because he was confident in his ability to race back to catch anything hit over his head. He had so much lateral range that his other two outfield mates usually played right next to the foul lines. A powerful hitter, Oscar won at least four batting titles and several home-run crowns. (Negro League records are sketchy and incomplete.) He's credited with a .353 lifetime batting average. Charleston, who also successfully managed in the Negro Leagues, was known as an astute judge of talent. When Brooklyn Dodgers general manager Branch Rickey wanted to break major-league baseball's color line, he hired Charleston as a scout. Charleston brought both Jackie Robinson and Roy Campanella to Rickey's attention.

John Henry Lloyd

(Macon Acmes, Cuban-X Giants, Philadelphia Giants, Columbus Buckeyes, New York Black Yankees, and other teams)

Many baseball historians cite Honus Wagner as the greatest shortstop — some even say the greatest player — of all time. Wagner considered Lloyd his equal. John Henry was in his early thirties when the Negro Leagues were founded; he spent his early career playing for independent black and Cuban teams. Yet he played in the Negro Leagues for a dozen years while compiling a career batting average of .344. In 1928, the 44-year old shortstop put together one of baseball's most remarkable seasons. He batted a league-leading .564 (no, that's not a typo) and led all comers in home runs.

Walter "Buck" Leonard

(Brooklyn Royal Giants, Homestead Grays)

This left-handed, power-hitting first baseman combined with Josh Gibson to give the Homestead Grays one of baseball's great home-run tandems. Leonard helped Gibson power the Grays to nine straight pennants. More than just a slugger, Buck won three batting titles. In 1939, he enjoyed his best season as he led the Negro Leagues in hitting with a .492 batting average. Leonard was also considered a Gold Glove–quality first baseman, able to range far to his right to steal base hits headed for the hole.

Willie Wells

(St. Louis Stars, Detroit Wolves, Homestead Grays, Kansas City Monarchs, Newark Eagles, Baltimore Elite Giants, New York Black Yankees, Indianapolis Clowns, Memphis Red Sox)

Players who opposed Willie's teams used to tell each other, "Don't hit the ball to shortstop because the Devil is playing there." Throughout the 1930's, "Devil"

Wells ruled the Negro Leagues as the king of shortstops. He was noted for his wall-to-wall range and coolness under pressure. Teammate Monte Irvin remembered Wells for "always coming up with the big play." When Willie wasn't stealing enemy hits, he was gathering enough knocks of his own in Negro League competition to compile a career .364 batting average. He won consecutive batting titles for the St. Louis Stars by hitting .368 in 1929, followed by a .404 average in 1930. Wells also played winter ball in Cuba and won an MVP award when he batted .328 for the champion Almendares club in 1939. Pitchers hated the way Willie crowded the plate and made him a frequent beanball target. Wells answered their assaults by becoming one of the first professional players to wear a batting helmet. He earned spots on eight Negro League all-star teams and the Veterans Committee elected him to the Baseball Hall of Fame in 1997.

Cool Papa Bell

(St. Louis Stars, Pittsburgh Crawfords, Detroit Wolves, Kansas City Monarchs, Chicago American Giants, Memphis Red Sox, Homestead Grays)

The story is as oft-told as it is apocryphal: Cool Papa Bell was so fast he could turn off a light switch and slip under the covers before the room got dark. That never happened, but there's no doubt that Bell was one of the fastest men ever to play baseball. He was once clocked circling all four bases in an astounding 12 seconds. Cool Papa often went from first to third on bunts and scored from second on sacrifice flies. On at least three occasions, he stole two bases on a single pitch. A line-hitter who was an inside-the-park home-run threat any time the ball got past an outfielder, Bell hit .341 over a 25-season career.

Ray Dandridge

(Detroit Stars, Newark Dodgers, Newark Eagles, New York Cubans, Milwaukee Millers)

Willie Mays has said that Dandridge was the best fielding third baseman he ever saw. Panther-quick with a missile launcher for an arm, Dandridge could range to either side to subtract enemy base hits from the box score. A career .330 plus line-drive hitter, Ray batted .370 in 1944 and led the Mexican League with a .368 average in 1948. That performance earned him a minor-league contract with the Milwaukee Millers, a New York Giants American Association farm team. Though already 36 years old, Dandridge was the American Association Rookie of the Year in 1949 and its MVP in 1950. Despite these awards, he never got called to the big leagues.

Smokey Joe Williams

(San Antonio Bronchos, Leland Giants, Chicago Giants, Lincoln Giants, Chicago American Giants, Bacharach Giants, Brooklyn Royal Giants, Homestead Grays)

Ty Cobb, not the most generous of men, once said that Williams would have been a sure 30-game winner had he been allowed to pitch in the Major Leagues. Williams may have been the fastest pitcher of his time, regardless of league. Chicago Giants owner Frank Leland would boast, "If you've ever seen the speed of a pebble thrown in a storm, you have not yet seen speed the equal of this wonderful giant from Texas." In 1914, he went 41–3. Sixteen years later, his fastball was still smoking as he struck out 27 Kansas City Monarchs in a 12-inning game.

Rube Foster

(Chicago Union Giants, Cuban Giants, Cuban X Giants, Philadelphia Giants, Chicago Leland Giants, Chicago American Giants)

You'll notice that every team Rube Foster played for was known as the Giants. That was appropriate because he was a giant personality, the most dominant figure in Negro League baseball for the first quarter of the twentieth century. Foster did not throw nearly as hard as Satchel Paige or Smokey Joe Williams, but he won just as often. He was a crafty pitcher who kept hitters off-stride with the twisting, "fadeaway" screwball he later passed on to New York Giants ace Christy Mathewson.

Foster joined the professional ranks in 1902 when he won 51 games, including 44 in a row, while pitching for the Cuban Giants. The following season he topped that performance by going 54–1. A shrewd baseball tactician, Foster assumed the role of pitcher-manager for the Chicago Leland Giants in 1907. He guided that team to a remarkable 110–10 record. Three years later, Foster's Giants won national fame by winning 123 games and losing only six. He offered to match his squad against any white major-league club in a best-of-seven series for the "true baseball championship of the world." No one responded to his challenge. In 1920, Foster founded the Negro National League, which is widely regarded as baseball's first viable black major league.

Chapter 26

Ten Things to Love about Baseball

In This Chapter

▶ Going one-on-one: The pitcher-hitter confrontation

▶ Bringing families together

▶ Reveling in the thrill of a close play

*I*f we wanted to reveal all the reasons we love this great game, we could fill this entire book. But we wanted to cover a lot of other topics as well, so we had to keep this list manageable. Here are ten things about the national pastime that keep us coming back to the ballpark game after game, season after season.

Those Magic 90 Feet

Daniel Adams must have been a genius. According to John Thorn, the estimable co-editor of *Total Baseball,* Dr. Adams is the man who fixed the bases at 90 feet. Just think what a difference 12 inches would have made either way. Had Adams set the bases 91 feet apart, pitchers would dominate low-scoring contests that would lull fans to sleep. At 89 feet, hitters would unleash a mind-numbing barrage of runs that fans would eventually find equally off-putting. But 90 feet is just right. This distance maintains the balance between offense and defense while giving baseball a sense of continuity. A runner out by a step 100 years ago would be out by that same step today.

The Perfect Diamond

Yankee Stadium's outfield configuration gives it a short right field for lefty sluggers to take aim at. In Fenway, hitters try to knock the ball over the Green Monster in left field. Each stadium has a dimension that makes it unique. But the diamond, composed of four bases arranged around the pitcher's mound, remains the one constant in every park. Some infields may be harder or faster than others, but the layout of the game's core structure never favors one team over another.

National League Chess Matches

American League contests don't require as much strategy as those in the National League; the former's designated hitter rule removes many of a manager's late-inning decisions, such as choosing a pinch hitter for a pitcher late in a ball game. I like the way managers' wheels start spinning from the sixth inning on in a close National League contest. We saw a good example of that in the 1999 National League Championship Series between the Mets and the Braves. Every time Bobby Valentine made a move, Bobby Cox would counter it, and vice versa. They both showed the difference a manager can make in a tight ballgame. American League managers can't make a similar impact because of the DH rule.

Showdown: The Pitcher-Hitter Confrontation

This is baseball's version of High Noon: Two gunslingers stare down each other's barrels, and only one can come away victorious. The pitcher controls the speed and location of the ball; the batter has only tenths of a second to adjust to whatever the hurler serves up. But the batter can set up a pitcher by working him into an advantageous count, such as two balls, no strikes, or three balls, no strikes. This game within a game continues to hold our fascination.

All in the Family

A ballpark is a great place for bonding. Parents and their children can go to a game and yell themselves hoarse together as they root for the home team. Then they talk for months about everything they saw that day. Every game is a shared gift that they store in the warmest folds of their memories. Put simply, baseball brings people together.

Larceny on the Base Paths

When a great base stealer like Alex Sanchez or Carl Crawford reaches first in the late innings of a close game, the entire park is electrified. We assume the runner is going to try to swipe second; the only question is when he will take off. Tension builds as the pitcher and runner engage in a game of cat-and-mouse, with the pitcher trying to hold his adversary close to the bag with side-steps and numerous throws. The top base thieves can take a pitcher out of his pattern by forcing him to abandon the change-up and slow curve. They change the entire pace and tone of the game.

6-4-3

Maybe this is an infielder's bias, but I think few things are prettier than a perfectly turned 6-4-3 (short-to-second-to-first) double play. Twin killings require perfect synchronization between the shortstop and second baseman. The shortstop has to get the ball to his double-play partner so that he has enough time to step on second and nip the runner at first. And the second baseman often has to get the ball to first with 200 pounds or more of raging base runner bearing down on him. When you see two masters — like Alex Gonzalez and Luis Castillo — turn this trick, it's the closest thing baseball has to ballet.

Going for Three

The triple is the most exciting hit in baseball. When a hitter drives a ball into the gap in right or left center, we watch a mini-drama unfold: The runner revs into high gallop on the base paths, while the outfielder dashes to the ball and his teammates set up for what they hope will be a perfect relay to third. Ball and runner converge on third simultaneously, and only one can get there first. We hold our collective breath waiting for the umpire's call: safe or out!

Size Doesn't Matter

Baseball is a game that places emphasis on skill and hand-eye coordination rather than muscle. You can excel no matter how big or small you are. In the mid-1970s, a wire service photo showed Washington Senators first baseman Frank Howard towering over Kansas City Royals shortstop Freddie Patek as he held Patek at first base. Frank was 6'7", 255 pounds; Freddie was 5'4", 145 pounds. Yet they were both all-stars. That's the beauty of the sport.

Going Deep for a Win

The *walk-off home run* — any homer that ends a ballgame — is baseball's exclamation point. The player who hits it — always a member of the home team — circles the bases while the visiting club walks off the field. We saw a perfect example of this dramatic blow in Game Seven of the 2003 American League Championship Series when New York Yankees third baseman Aaron Boone's 10th-inning blast crushed the Boston Red Sox. That night, Aaron was like a great matador who had just executed a swift kill. He brought the crowd to its feet before sending it to the exits.

Chapter 27

Ten Baseball Nicknames That Hit the Mark

*E*ver since some sportswriter from the 1880s christened Chicago White Stockings superstar Mike "King" Kelly with his royal moniker, nicknames have been entrenched in the baseball lexicon. Following are ten of our favorites.

Bob "Death to Flying Things" Ferguson

Yes, it's a tad wordy, but as nicknames go, you will rarely find one more evocative. Ferguson played for a number of teams, including the Troy Trojans, from 1876 to 1884. Baseball historians credit him with being the first switch hitter ever to appear in a major-league box score, though his plate work won him little fame. You would think someone came up with Ferguson's sobriquet as a tribute to his fielding prowess. Ferguson was, by all accounts, a slick glove, but he spent most of his career manning second base, a position that rarely required him to chase down difficult fly balls. Teammates hung the moniker on Ferguson after observing his deadly proficiency for swatting houseflies in a hotel lobby. Houseflies weren't all he swatted. After retiring as a player, Ferguson became a professional umpire and once settled an on-field dispute by breaking a player's arm with a baseball bat. That incident and several other confrontations won him another nickname: "Fighting Bob."

Walter "The Big Train" Johnson

The Washington Senators signed this Hall of Fame pitcher after a traveling salesman sent them a letter lauding Johnson's power and control. "He knows where he's throwing," the peddler supposedly wrote, "because if he didn't, there'd be dead bodies strewn all over Idaho." From 1907 to 1927, Johnson won 417 games, notched 3,509 strikeouts, and recorded a major-league record 110 shutouts.

The right-hander might also hold the major-league record for most nicknames. Sportswriter Grantland Rice tagged him "The Big Train," when he heard a batter describe Johnson's fastball as "roaring like an express train as it passes by." After Johnson treated some teammates to a few hair-raising spins in his new automobile, they took to calling their ace "Barney," an homage to legendary race car driver Barney Oldfield. Umpires paid tribute to Johnson's integrity and sportsmanship by referring to him as "Sir Walter" and "The White Knight." And sportswriters who watched Johnson pitch during his semi-pro career knew him as "The Coffeyville Express" (he called Coffeyville home for several years), "The Kansas Cyclone," and "The Humboldt Thunderbolt" (Humboldt, Kansas being his birthplace).

Al "The Mad Hungarian" Hrabosky

The closer for the St. Louis Cardinals in the mid-1970s, Hrabosky would stalk in from the bullpen wearing a sinister Fu Manchu mustache, wild shoulder-length hair worthy of Rasputin, and an ornate silver ring he called The Gypsy Rose of Death (which he once described as "a family heirloom from Dracula"). Before throwing his first pitch, Hrabosky would stomp off the mound toward second base, turn his back to the hitter at home plate, and work himself into a rage. As soon as he was ready, the left-hander would pound his glove, whirl around, and toe the pitching rubber with lava seeping out of his ears. Then, more times than not, he'd pour a white-hot fastball past the hitter. The theatrics were meant to intimidate opposing players, who were never quite sure just how crazy Hrabosky really was.

Mickey "The Commerce Comet" Mantle

When Mickey Mantle joined the New York Yankees for rookie camp in 1951, several coaches asked him to participate in a footrace. As teammate Tom Sturdivant once told me (Richard), "It was a joke for anyone to race against him, the guy could outrun Kentucky Derby racehorses. Why, he made us look like we were standing still. I'm not kidding. Mickey beat us by so much, the coaches were positive he was leaving early. So they had us race again. Same result. Okay, we're going to go one more time. Man, they would have had us out there all day. I was running next to Mick and I finally told them, 'He's not jumping the gun. Mickey's leaving when we're on the first step. It's just that he's a half a block away on the second step.' They didn't have stopwatches fast enough to time him. I think that's when they hung the nickname 'The Commerce Comet' on him, except he was faster than a comet. Fastest thing I ever saw."

Jim "The Toy Cannon" Wynn

Jim Wynn was tagged "The Toy Cannon" because he generated so much power for his size (5'10" and 160 pounds). Jim and I played together with the Astros from 1963 to 1971. Pound-for-pound, he may have been the greatest slugger ever. Jim had hands as strong as any blacksmith's. Though he swung a relatively heavy piece of lumber (36 ounces), he was able to snap it through the strike zone rather than push it. The ball exploded off his bat. Jim played most of his career in the Astrodome when it was the worst home-run hitters park in the majors. Had he played on any other home field, he would have hit 40 or more homers every year. In 1967, Henry Aaron nipped Jimmie for the National League home-run title by only two dingers. Afterwards, the ever-gracious Aaron said, "As far as I'm concerned, Jim Wynn is the home-run champion this season because of the place he plays in."

Tony "Doggie" Perez

Perez was one of the finest clutch hitters I've ever seen. On the Big Red Machine (Cincinnati Reds), we called him "Doggie" or "Big Dog" because any time he came to the plate with runners on base, you expected him to take a large bite out of the pitcher. He was able to do that because, unlike some sluggers, he understood what he faced in any given situation. With the bases loaded, if the pitcher gave him something to pull, Tony jacked it hard to the left, often for extra bases. But throw him a difficult outside pitch under the same circumstances, and Doggie would slash it to right field for a two-run base hit. He drove in 100 or more runs seven times and had five other seasons of 90 or more RBIs.

Bill "Spaceman" Lee

Before games with the Boston Red Sox, this wacky left-handed pitcher would hit fungos (see Appendix A for a definition) to himself in the outfield. Lee once publicly admitted to throwing two spitballs to Tony Taylor, one of which Taylor belted for a homer. When a reporter asked him how a singles hitter like Taylor could jerk out a spitter, Bill replied, "I guess he hit the dry side." If you asked him why he threw a certain pitch, Bill would do five minutes on Einstein's theory of curved space. Lee earned his nickname when a visitor to the Red Sox clubhouse asked his teammate, utility infielder John Kennedy, if he had seen a NASA launch that afternoon. Pointing to Bill's locker, Kennedy replied, "We don't need to look at anyone going up in rockets on TV; we have our own spaceman right here." Lee was a character, but he knew how to pitch. He had a funky moving sinker, a good slow curve, and pinpoint control.

Rusty "Le Grande Orange" Staub

Staub and I came up together with the Houston Astros. Rusty's dedication to hard work made him a star. He was not a good hitter when Houston first signed him; he was just a big guy who could handle only the high fastball. But he studied the pitchers and spent hundreds of hours in the batting cage honing his swing. Rusty became such a formidable player that he made the All-Star team six times. In 1967, his best season, he batted .333 to finish fifth in the NL batting race and had a league-leading four doubles. I played with him that season, and almost every pitch he made contact with — including the outs — was hit hard. The 6'3", 210-pounder earned the nickname "Le Grande Orange" (meaning, of course, the big redhead) when the Astros traded him to the Montreal Expos in 1969. With his star presence and booming bat, Rusty became an instant fan favorite as he brought the expansion franchise some much needed on-field credibility.

Frank "The Washington Monument" Howard

When Howard starred with the Washington Senators, the 6'7" 255-pound player was called "The Washington Monument" not only because he appeared to be as big as that landmark but because he looked as if he could hit a baseball over it. Frank was one of the strongest men ever to play the game. After Ted Williams became manager for the Senators in 1969, he told Frank that he had seen only three men who could hit the ball harder than he could: Babe Ruth, Jimmy Foxx, and Mickey Mantle. Because Ruth once reportedly hit a ball 600 feet in an exhibition game and the Mick still holds the record for the longest regular season home run (565 feet), Frank's in mighty august company. Frank was the first player I ever saw who made the bat look like a toothpick in his hands. Nearly every pitcher who faced him was terrified that he might hit a line drive back through the box.

Dick "The Monster" Radatz

Facing Radatz was a real horror show for a lot of batters. This was the original Terminator. When this 6'5", 250-pound behemoth stomped in from the Boston Red Sox bullpen, hitters started considering early retirement. He threw close to 100 mph, and whenever he took his warm-up tosses, he'd throw the first pitch all the way to the backstop. The idea that a guy who throws pitches you can barely see might be a little wild that day gets the hitter's attention in a hurry. When Radatz pitched in the early 1960s, most relievers alternated good and bad years. "The Monster" was a rarity because he strung together four seasons of all-star quality (1962–1965). During that period, he registered 49 wins and 100 saves (when saves were much harder to come by than they are today) for Red Sox teams that never topped .500.

Chapter 28

Joe Morgan's Top Ten Future Stars

In This Chapter

▶ Lighting up the baseball galaxy with stars in the making

As baseball moves through the twenty-first century, the future looks bright, as you can see just by studying this list of talented wunderkind players.

Mark Prior

Prior is a 24-year-old right-handed phenom. During the second half of the 2004 season, Mark went 10–1 with a 1.52 ERA while his Chicago Cubs fought for the division lead. He is one of only five pitchers in major-league history to strike out more than ten batters per nine innings in a season before turning 24 (and a tip of the hat to the *Sabermetric Baseball Encyclopedia* for supplying that tidbit). Prior doesn't throw quite as hard as Beckett, but he has demonstrated greater command. He looks as if he can deliver his mid-90s fastball, curve, and change-up for strikes at will. Mark is also an excellent fielder, athletic enough to spring off the mound to pounce on bunts.

Miguel Cabrera

He turned 21 shortly after opening day in 2004. Cabrera only played 87 games in 2003, yet he finished second among National League rookies in home runs (12) and RBI (62). I like how he demonstrates a veteran's presence at the plate with men on base. His batting average with runners in scoring position was the fourth highest in the National League, and he batted .500 with the bases full. With his short, quick stroke, Miguel can blister anyone's fastball, something he demonstrated when he re-launched one of Roger Clemens's rockets for a home run in the 2003 World Series. Slow-breaking stuff still bedevils him, but that's a common weakness for rookies. In his first major-league season,

Cabrera revealed acumen for playing right field, a new position for him. He doesn't run fast enough to have great range, but he played the hitters expertly and curtailed reckless base runners with his powerful throwing arm. However, he's a natural third baseman, sure-handed and nimble whether diving to his left or right.

Vernon Wells

If he played in New York or Los Angeles, Wells would already be a household name. In 2003, Vernon led the Major Leagues with 215 hits while hitting 33 homers and compiling a .550 slugging average. His 373 total bases and 49 doubles led the American League. That total base mark impresses me. In major-league history, only two 24-year-old center fielders have gathered more bases in a season. One was Willie Mays and the other was Mickey Mantle. Not bad company. Despite his obvious power, Wells doesn't come to the plate looking to hit pitches out. He's a line-drive hitter who often powers the ball into the gaps. His defense in center is Gold Glove caliber. Vernon doesn't attempt many steals, but he is so swift I have no doubt he could swipe 40 bases — and hit 40 homers — after he learns how to read pitchers' motions and commits to running more often.

Carlos Beltran

In 2003, Carlos notched 100 RBI, 100 runs scored, and 30 stolen bases for the third straight season. Beltran is a switch-hitter who does an excellent job of maintaining a compact swing from both sides of the plate; his stats from either side of the plate look nearly identical, as opposed to left-handers or right-handers. Carlos provides fans with a model of the selective-aggressive hitter. He will earn his walks, but if you serve him a fastball he can reach, he pounces early in the count. This is one of the most valuable base-stealers in the game. Carlos filches his bag more than 90 percent of the time; it usually takes a perfect throw to nail him. In the outfield, he reads the ball well immediately off the bat, the secret to getting an excellent jump. Carlos's arm is slightly above average, but he compensates with accuracy and a quick release.

Hank Blalock

Hank is only 23 as we write this, yet he already knows how to hit to all fields with power. He's an intelligent hitter, content to let the home runs come while he smacks line drives with one of the sweetest swings in baseball. When

Blalock learns to wait out pitchers longer — he tends to swing at the first or second pitch in each at-bat — he will have the stuff to win batting titles while popping 40 or more homers.

Francisco Rodríguez

Special K-Rod. This 22-year-old reliever can turn up the thermostat in the batter's box in a hurry. Francisco guns his fastball in the high-90s, but that pitch alone isn't what makes us think he will become the game's next great closer. K-Rod may very well throw the deadliest slider in baseball, a high-velocity missile that break dances as it passes home plate. That pitch is so difficult to track that Rodríguez gave up only 50 base hits in 86 innings during the 2003 season. Yet despite the slider's unpredictable movement, he showed excellent control by walking only 35 while striking out 95. K-Rod will occasionally suffer wild spells, but when he gets his stuff over, he's as unhittable as any reliever you can find.

C.C. Sabathia

A left-handed power pitcher, Sabathia routinely hits 97 mph on the radar gun, and his fastball has excellent late movement. He won 43 games with a laudable .632 winning percentage in his first three big-league seasons while playing for the sub-.500 Cleveland Indians. I like how he has improved some facet of his game every year. In 2003, he perfected his change-up and breaking pitches while cutting his walks by 25 percent. As a result, he finished tenth in the American League with a career low 3.60 ERA and earned a spot on his first All-Star team.

Jose Reyes

Hamstring woes have hampered this 20-year-old second baseman's progress. With wheels intact, Jose scoots around the bases like someone wearing spikes flambé. Reyes slashes line drives, often to the opposite field, with good pop. He can also bunt his way on base or beat out slowly hit grounders for singles. When Jose first entered the Major Leagues, there was some concern about his plate discipline; he walked only twice in his first 100 at-bats and got himself out too many times by swinging at balls wide of the strike zone. After he learned to take those pitches, he picked up 11 walks in his next 185 plate appearances. That's still not what you want from a leadoff hitter, but the improvement is something Jose can build on with experience. He has enough speed and smarts to hit .300 and steal 50 or more bases every year.

Dontrelle Willis

This left-hander started the 2003 season in Double-A ball, and he was pitching in the World Series before the year ended. Dontrelle throws a dead-red fastball in the mid-90s and a wicked swerving slider, both from behind a preposterously high leg kick that hides the ball from the batter until the very last moment. Willis's unusual delivery makes it tough for hitters to identify his pitches or gauge their velocity. He throws everything hard and should join the ranks of the pitching elite when he learns to change speeds. Every time I see Dontrelle perform, he impresses me with his athleticism. He fields his position well, hold runners close with one of baseball's better pickoff moves, and looks like a dangerous hitter.

Michael Young

Talk about responding to pressure. The Rangers moved Michael from second base to shortstop to replace All-World Álex Rodríguez. Young responded by transforming himself into one of the top shortstops in baseball. Michael has superior range to either side and uses one of the best infield arms around to nip even the fastest base runners on close plays. He's an excellent line drive hitter who has added enough muscle over recent seasons to make him a legitimate power threat.

Final Thoughts

I can't close this chapter without mentioning **Josh Beckett,** who dominated the New York Yankees with a five-hit shutout in the Game Six clincher of the World Series. He throws a 97-mph heater, a deadly forkball that acts as a change-up, and a sweeping curveball. Injuries have slowed his progress, but if his arm is sound, his name belongs somewhere on this list.

Part VI
Appendixes

The 5th Wave   By Rich Tennant

"I hate to break this to you, but as far as I can figure, you have a negative slugging percentage."

In this part . . .

Around the horn . . . bang-bang play . . . high heat. . . .
Baseball has a rich, colorful lexicon, and you must
understand it if you want to follow the action. We provide a
list of key phrases, slang words, and terms in Appendix A.
Appendix B gives you contact information for the world's
major baseball organizations, from major league franchises
to youth and senior leagues.

Appendix A

Baseball Speak: A Glossary

• •

In this appendix, you discover the most common baseball terms (as well as a few uncommon terms here and there!) to help you in any baseball-lingo jam.

Ace: The top card in a deck, the top gun on a pitching staff. Strikeout kings and 20-game winners like Mark Prior, Javier Vazquez, and Bartolo Colon are all considered aces. Teams can have more than one. The 1997 Atlanta Braves staff featured a fistful of aces: Cy Young Award winner Greg Maddux, Tom Glavine, John Smoltz, and 20-game winner Danny Neagle.

Across the letters: Any pitch that passes the batter chest high.

Activate: To return an injured or suspended player to your team's active roster (in the majors, a 25-man squad).

Adjudged: Any judgment call made by the umpire, such as declaring a runner out at second base on a close play.

Advance: For a runner, to move along the base paths. ("Jeter advanced from first to third on Rodríguez's single to right.") For a hitter, to move the runner at least one base. ("Cabrera's groundout to Vidro advanced Pierre from second to third.")

Advance sale: The number of seats sold before game day.

Advance scout: A scout who follows opposing teams, trying to spot their strengths and, more importantly, their weaknesses.

Ahead in the count: If you're a pitcher, you have more strikes than balls on the hitter you're facing. If you're the hitter at the plate, the count contains more balls than strikes.

Alive: An inning that is extended by the offense after two outs. ("Base hits by Ellis and Chavez kept the inning alive.")

Alley: The section of outfield real estate between the center fielder and the left or right fielders. It is also called the *power alley* (where hits go to become doubles or triples) or the *gap*.

Alley hitter: A batter who is an expert at driving the ball into the alleys for extra base hits. Among current players, Ichiro Suzuki has been one of the better alley hitters.

Alligator mouth: A braggart. In his best-selling baseball diary *Ball Four*, Jim Bouton describes one player who couldn't back up his talk as having "an alligator mouth with a hummingbird [behind]." (You can probably guess what he used in place of "behind.")

Allow: To surrender hits or runs. ("Kerry Wood allowed three runs on five hits in the first.")

All-Star: Any player voted by the fans or chosen by the manager to appear in an All-Star Game.

All-Star break: A three-day hiatus in the major-league schedule; break occurs in mid-July and coincides with the All-Star Game.

All-Star Game: The annual interleague contest between players representing the American League and National League. The league that wins the game earns home field advantage in the World Series come October. Fans wishing to choose the starting lineup for both teams can vote in major-league ballparks or online at www.mlb.com.

Alphonse and Gaston act: Two fielders charging after the same ball suddenly pull up short when they each think that the other is going to make the catch. The ball drops or goes through for a base hit. They just pulled the old Alphonse and Gaston act. The name comes from two turn-of-the-century cartoon characters, Alphonse and Gaston, whose deference to each other was so extreme, simple tasks like getting through a doorway took an eternity. ("After you, my dear Gaston." "No, after you my dear Alphonse." "No, I insist.")

Ancient mariner: A fielder who lacks wide range. The term comes from the poem *The Ancient Mariner* ("who stoppeth one in three") and was originally said of shortstop Joe Cronin during the twilight of his Hall of Fame career.

Appeal: When a player who has been fined or is subject to some other disciplinary action asks to plead his case to the league president or commissioner's office.

Appeal play: The defensive team's attempt to reverse a safe call by contending that a runner missed a base or left a base too early on a fly ball. An appeal must be called for immediately following a disputed play and before the pitcher throws another pitch toward home plate. Major-league protocol requires the pitcher to step off the mound and throw to the base in question. The umpire at that base then rules if the runner was indeed safe or out.

Appearance: Taking part in a baseball game, either as a pitcher, fielder, or hitter.

Apple: A baseball. ("Pujols really rocked that apple into the upper deck.")

Arbiter: Little-used term for an umpire, particularly the umpire working behind home plate.

Around the horn: A double play that goes from third base to second to first. The phrase comes from a time before the opening of the Panama Canal when ships had to sail around South America's Cape Horn to reach the Pacific from the Atlantic.

Arson squad: A bullpen that routinely allows the opposition to score. The relief pitchers are said to "throw gasoline on the fire."

Artificial turf: Any playing field surface that is not made of grass.

Ash: A baseball bat made from northern white ash.

Ash handle: The bottom portion of the bat.

Aspirin: A pitch thrown so fast that the ball appears to be smaller than it actually is. ("Billy Wagner was bringing it so hard today, the baseball looked like an aspirin.")

Assist: A throw from one fielder to another that puts out the batter or a base runner.

At 'em ball: A ball that is hit directly at a fielder.

At-bat: Any time the batter gets a hit, makes an out, or reaches base on an error or fielder's choice. If the batter draws a walk, is hit by a pitch, completes a sacrifice, or reaches base on catcher's interference, he is credited with a plate appearance but not an at-bat.

Attempt: The act of trying to steal a base. ("Tony Womack has 55 steals in only 61 attempts.")

Automatic out: A weak batter who has such a poor sense of the strike zone that he rarely hits or walks. Most pitchers are automatic outs when they come to the plate.

Away game: When your team plays on your opponent's home field.

Babe Ruth's curse: The jinx that supposedly haunts the Boston Red Sox, who haven't won a world championship since the team sold Babe Ruth to the dreaded New York Yankees in 1920.

Back through the box: A ball hit sharply through the pitcher's mound.

Backdoor slide: A difficult maneuver in which the runner reaches out to touch the base with his finger or hand as his body slides past the bag. Roberto Alomar is a master of the backdoor slide and used it to elude a home plate tag against the Boston Red Sox during a nationally televised game in 1999.

Backdoor slider: A pitch that appears to be out of the strike zone as it approaches the batter, but then breaks over the plate.

Backstop: The screen that sits behind and extends over the home plate area. It protects fans from foul balls. Major-league backstops must stand at least 60 feet from home plate.

Backup: When one fielder runs behind another who is about to field a ball or receive a throw in order to catch the ball if it eludes the fielder.

Bad ball: A pitch thrown out of the strike zone, but just close enough to invite the batter to swing.

Bad bounce or bad hop: A batted ball that eludes the fielder when it takes an unexpected hop, usually because it has struck an object on the field such as a pebble.

Bad call: A call that the umpire misses.

Bad hands: An affliction attributed to poor fielders.

Bad hose: A sore throwing arm.

Bad-ball hitter: A batter who is adept at hitting pitches outside the strike zone. New York Yankee catcher Yogi Berra used to get base hits on balls thrown nearly over his head.

Bag: A term often used in place of *base*.

Bail out: What a hitter does when he falls away from a pitch that appears to be coming toward his body.

Balk: A pitcher's motion that is deemed deceptive by the umpire. Runners who are on base when a balk is called get to advance one base.

Ball: A pitch out of the strike zone that the batter doesn't swing at and the umpire does not call as a strike.

Ball boy or ball girl: The person who retrieves foul balls.

Ball club: A baseball team.

Baltimore chop: A batted ball that bounces so high it cannot be fielded before the hitter reaches first base. Wee Willie Keeler, John McGraw, and the cagey Baltimore Orioles popularized it during the 1890s.

Bandbox: A small ballpark, which favors hitters. The Baker Bowl, which was home to the Philadelphia Phillies until 1938, was a notorious bandbox. Only 280½ feet separated home plate from the right field wall.

Bang-bang play: The base runner and ball reach a base or home plate at nearly the same moment.

Banjo hitter: A batter who hits mostly singles.

Barber: A pitcher who throws close to the batter's chin and "gives him a shave."

Barrel: The thickest part of a bat.

Base: The 15-inch (38-centimeter) square white marker found at three of a baseball infield's four corners. (Home plate is five-sided.) Bases are placed 90 feet (27.5 meters) apart from each other.

Base on balls: What a pitcher surrenders whenever the umpire calls four of his pitches out of the strike zone (balls) during a hitter's time at bat. The batter takes first base, the errant hurler's manager takes a Maalox, and, if the pitcher allows very many of these, he takes a trip to the showers. Also known as a *walk*.

Base runner interference: The act of a base runner deliberately preventing a fielder from completing a play by making bodily contact, deflecting the ball, or blocking the fielder's vision. If an umpire calls the play, the runner is ruled out.

Baseball: The white, red-stitched sphere that pitchers throw, fielders catch, and hitters whack during a baseball game. It is composed of a cork core under layers of rubber, yarn, and cowhide.

Baseball mud: Umpires rub this auburn mud into new baseballs to remove the sheen from the leather. Why? So that pitchers can get a better grip on the ball. Also known as rubbing mud.

Basket catch: A catch made with your glove at belt level. Coaches frown on the practice, but Willie Mays won 12 consecutive Gold Gloves with his signature catch.

Bat: The sculpted, wooden implement (usually fashioned from pine or ash) that hitters use to assault a baseball.

Bat around: What a team does when its entire lineup bats during an inning.

Bat boy or bat girl: The players' valet during the game. The bat boy or bat girl picks up the hitter's bat and helmet when the hitter's turn at bat ends. He or she also brings new balls to the umpires between innings.

Bat check: When an umpire inspects a player's bat, usually upon the request of an opposing manager, to verify that it meets major-league specifications.

Bat speed: The time it takes a hitter to get his bat through the hitting zone.

Batter: What a player becomes when he steps into the batter's box to take his swings.

Batter's box: The rectangle, marked by chalk, on both sides of home plate. The batter must stay within that box when hitting.

Battery: A team's pitcher-catcher combination for any given game.

Batting cage: A metal cage placed behind home plate during batting practice. It protects bystanders from being hit by foul balls.

Batting eye: A player's ability to judge the strike zone. Batters who average 100 or more walks per season (Barry Bonds, Jason Giambi, and Jim Thome) have excellent batting eyes.

Batting glove: Batters usually wear this soft leather glove on their bottom hand (right for left-handed hitters, left for righties), though some batters wear them on both hands. Batting gloves prevent blisters and give the hitter a better grip on the bat handle. Some fielders wear batting gloves underneath their fielding gloves to soften the impact of hard-hit balls.

Batting helmet: Hard plastic helmet that protects a hitter's cranium from errant pitches.

Batting order: The sequence in which a team's hitters appear at home plate during a game.

Beanball: A pitch that is deliberately thrown to hit the batter.

Beat out: When a runner reaches base just ahead of a throw, as in "Baldelli beat out that grounder to short for a base hit."

Bees: The sting a batter feels when he hits a pitch off-center (usually felt in cold weather).

Bench: What players sit on while they are in the dugout. Players who are *benched,* are *grabbing some bench,* or have been forced to *ride the pines,* have been indefinitely removed from a team's starting lineup.

Bench jockey: A player, usually a sub who rarely appears in games, who hurls insults from the dugout at opposing players on the field to break their concentration.

Bereavement list: A team can place a player whose family member or friend has died on the bereavement list and fill his roster spot with another player. The grieving player must stay on the list for at least three days and his team must reactivate him within ten days.

Big bill: A ground ball's final hop. (It bounces as high as the bill on a crouched fielder's cap.)

Big leagues: The Major Leagues.

Bingle: A softly hit single.

Bird dog: A part-time baseball scout.

Black Seats: Seats located behind center field that management keeps empty so batters can see the white ball better against the dark background.

Black, The: The outer edges of home plate. Balls that are *on the black* are strikes and difficult to hit squarely. Control pitchers like Greg Maddux or Jamie Moyer are often said to *paint the black* with their pitches.

Bleachers: The least expensive seats in the park. Located behind the outfields of most major-league parks.

Bleeder: A base hit — usually one that barely makes it through the infield. It can also be a weak pop fly that falls in front of an outfielder.

Block the plate: When a catcher positions his body in front of home plate to prevent a runner from scoring. The catcher must have the ball in his position when he starts the play in order for it to be legal.

Bloop: Or blooper. A weakly-hit fly ball that just makes it over the infield. Also known as a *dying quail* or *Texas Leaguer.*

Blown Save: Any time a pitcher enters the game with his team leading by three runs or fewer and allows the opposition to tie the score or go ahead.

Bonehead play: A mental error. A typical error by a player who rarely made one: Babe Ruth made the final out of the 1926 World Series when he was caught trying to steal second with the score 3–2.

Bonus baby: A young prospect, usually a college player, who signs for a large bonus before proving himself as a professional.

Book, The: A mythical compendium of traditional baseball strategies. Managers who *go by the book* play to tie in the ninth at home, bring in left-handed relievers to get out left-handed hitters, and have their pitchers bunt with none (and often one) out and runners on base. The best managers often go against The Book.

Boot: A fielding error. Also known as a *muff.*

Bottom of the inning: The second half of an inning.

Box score: The statistical record of a baseball game.

Breaking pitch: Any ball that curves.

Brushback: A pitch aimed at a batter, not to hit him (though they sometimes do, often to the pitcher's chagrin) but to move him off the plate. Also known as a *purpose pitch* or *chin music.*

Bug on the rug: A ball that eludes outfielders by bouncing about on the turf (artificial grass).

Bullpen: The area where pitchers warm up before entering a game. In most stadiums, it is located behind the outfield fence. In other parks, the bullpens can be found in foul territory along the left and right field lines. The term is also used to refer to the collection of relievers on a club. ("The New York Mets have a deep bullpen.")

Bunt: An offensive weapon in which the hitter holds his bat in the hitting zone and lets the ball make contact with it. If he is bunting for a hit, the batter tries to get to first before an infielder fields the softly hit ball and throws him out. If he is bunting to move a base runner up a base, the hitter only needs to push the ball to a spot where a play at first base is the infielder's sole option.

Bush: Any amateurish action or behavior. Publicly criticizing a teammate for a failed but honest effort is considered *bush.*

Butcher: A poor fielder.

Caddy: A substitute — generally an excellent fielder who takes the place of a mediocre fielder in the late innings of a ball game.

Cadillac trot (or Cadillacing): A slugger's trot around the bases after hitting a home run. From a quote by Ralph Kiner, a homer king of the late 1940s and early '50s: "Singles hitters drive jalopies, home-run hitters drive Cadillacs."

Call: The umpire's declaration of safe or out, ball or strike, fair or foul. The term also refers to the official score's ruling on a play (hit or error, wild pitch or passed ball, and so on).

Call up: Summoning a minor leaguer to the majors.

Called game: A game that has been terminated by the umpire-in-chief before its completion. Umpires usually call games due to inclement weather or curfews.

Called out looking: What is said to have happened to a batter when he takes strike three without attempting to swing at it.

Camp under: What an outfielder does when he positions himself under a fly ball.

Can of corn: An easy fly-ball out.

Career year: The best season of a player's career.

Carry a club: To be the leading force behind your team's victories over an extended period. ("Bench's home-run splurge has carried the Reds for the last ten days.")

Castoff: A player cut from a team.

Catch: The act of a fielder getting secure possession of the ball in his glove or hand. Whether you have secure possession is sometimes obvious, but it is often a subjective call by an umpire.

Catcher's box: The area behind home plate where the catcher must stand until the pitcher delivers the ball.

Cellar: Last place in your division or league.

Cellar dweller: The team in last place in the league.

Challenge the hitter: To throw your best pitch, usually a fastball, to the hitter, daring him to make contact.

Challenge the outfielder: To test an outfielder's throwing arm by trying to advance to the next base.

Chance: Any opportunity for a fielder to catch a ball.

Change-up: A slow-pitch thrown with the same motion as a fastball, meant to throw off a hitter's timing.

Cheat (shade): When a fielder sets up a few steps to the left or right of his normal fielding position in anticipation of where the batter is mostly likely to hit the ball.

Checked swing: A swing that is terminated before a batter *breaks his wrists* (brings his top hand over the bottom hand while taking his swing). Whether the hitter went around too far is the umpire's subjective call.

Choke hitter: A hitter who grips the bat at least an inch or two from the bottom of its handle. Using an extreme version of this grip (four inches or more) sacrifices power for contact.

Choose-up sides: A method for determining the rosters for teams in an informal baseball game. Two team captains alternate picks from among the available players.

Circus catch: A spectacular, unusually acrobatic fielding play.

Cleanup hitter: The number four hitter in a lineup. He is expected to *clean* the bases by driving in runs.

Closed stance: A hitting stance in which the batter's front foot is nearer to the plate than the back one.

Closer: The relief pitcher who finishes games, usually in *save* situations. Mariano Rivera, Keith Foulke, Eric Gagne, and Jason Isringhausen are all considered premier closers.

Clubhouse lawyer: A player who is outspoken and critical about club, league, or union policy.

Clutch: A situation when the outcome of a game or series is on the line. It often occurs in the late innings of an important ballgame.

Collar: From *horse collar* (which resembles a large 0). A batter who doesn't get a hit in a game is *wearing the collar*. Collars come in all sizes — size three when the batter is hitless in three at-bats, size four when he suffers a quartet of failures, and so on.

Come-backer: A ball hit back to the pitcher.

Conceding the run: What a team does when its manager orders his infielders to remain in their normal fielding positions with a runner on third and less than two outs, rather than move in close to home plate. This maneuver makes it easier for the runner to score on a ground ball while enhancing the defensive team's chances of turning a double play.

Corked bat: A bat with a deep hole drilled into the center of its barrel. The perpetrator (corked bats are illegal) fills the hole with cork, shredded rubber, or mercury, and then plugs it with glue and sawdust to make the bat appear normal. Bats filled with these substances propel the ball faster and farther than those made strictly from wood.

Count: The numbers of balls and strikes called on a hitter during a time at bat. The balls are always listed first. A 2–1 count means the batter has two balls and one strike.

Cousin: A pitcher who can't get a particular hitter out with any regularity, as in "Enrique Wilson hits Pedro Martinez as if he were his cousin."

Cup of coffee: A brief stay in the Major Leagues. A minor-league player who fills in for an injured major leaguer for a few weeks and is then sent back down has been up for *a cup of coffee.*

Curtain call: What a player takes when he comes out of the dugout to bow or wave to the crowd; it usually occurs after a player hits a home run in front of the hometown crowd.

Cutoff: When an infielder or pitcher intercepts an outfielder's throw.

Cutter: A fastball that breaks late, often to the side.

Cycle: When a hitter hits a single, double, triple, and home run in the same game. Of these four, the triple is the hardest to collect (unless you're a hitter like former major-league outfielder Lance Johnson, who rarely homered but annually led his league in triples).

Dead ball: A ball that the umpire has ruled is no longer in play because play has been suspended. (A base runner is *dead* when a fielder throws him out.)

Dead fish: An off-speed pitch.

Dead from the neck up: A phrase used to describe a player who is gifted physically but is intellectually challenged.

Deep in the count: Two balls and two strikes or three balls and two strikes against a batter.

Defense: The team in the field.

Defensive indifference: An undefended stolen base. The defensive team makes no attempt to throw out the base stealer.

Defensive interference: Any act by a fielder that interferes with a batter's swinging at a pitch.

Designated for assignment: When a team designates a player for assignment, management has ten days to decide to return him to the active roster, demote him to the minors, trade him to another team, or give him his outright release. A player may only be designated for assignment when the team wants to add a player to the 40-man roster that is already full.

Designated hitter (DH): The hitter in the American League lineup who bats without having to take the field. He always bats in place of the pitcher, though the rules state he may bat in any position in the batting order.

Diamond: A baseball field (more correctly, the *infield*).

Dig out: To successfully field an inaccurate throw.

Dinger: A home run.

Disabled list: Teams can place an injured player on this list only after receiving a medical doctor's diagnosis. Players placed on the disabled list must remain inactive for 15 to 60 days. Players on the 60-day DL do not count against the 40-man roster. A team can place a player on the DL retroactive to any date after the last date he appeared in game.

Dish: Home plate.

Doctored ball: A ball that the pitcher has scuffed, scratched, or coated with an illegal substance, such as petroleum jelly or saliva. Doctored balls tend to break erratically.

Domeball: Baseball games played in enclosed stadiums.

Double: A two-base hit.

Double play: A single defensive play that produces two outs; it usually occurs in the infield. In an unassisted double play, one fielder records both outs.

Double steal: Two base runners attempting to steal on the same pitch.

Double-header: Two consecutive games played between the same teams on the same day.

Down the line: A hit that closely follows the foul line.

Downtown: The place where Petula Clark hangs out and where deeply hit home runs are said to land. During the late 1960s, a San Diego Padres outfielder was known as "Downtown" Ollie Brown.

Ducks on the pond: Base runners.

Earned run: Any run charged to the record of the pitcher. These runs can develop as the result of a hit, a sacrifice fly, a fielder's choice, a walk, a hit batsman, a wild pitch, or a balk. Runs that develop as the result of an error, passed ball, or catcher's interference are *unearned*. (See Chapter 16 for how to figure a pitcher's earned run average, or ERA.)

Ejection: Banishment from the field of a player, manager, or coach by an umpire.

Error: A defensive misplay.

Even count: One ball and one strike or two balls and two strikes against a batter.

Even stance: A hitting stance in which both of the batter's feet are equidistant from the plate.

Everyday player: A player who appears in his team's starting lineup for most of its games.

Exhibition games: Any game that does not count in the season's standings. All spring training games are exhibition games.

Expansion: Adding new franchises to a league. The first major-league expansion in the twentieth century occurred in 1961, when the Los Angeles Angels and new Washington Senators (the old Senators had moved to Minnesota) joined the American League. During the last major-league baseball expansion in 1998, Tampa Bay joined the American League, and the Arizona Diamondbacks joined the National League.

Extra-base hit: Any base hit other than a single.

Fadeaway: The original term used for what we now call a screwball. Hall of Famer Christy Mathewson reportedly created the appellation.

Fair ball: A batted ball that: 1) Settles in fair territory between the foul lines; 2) Remains in fair territory until it passes first or third base; or 3) Stays within the foul lines while it passes over the outfield fence for a home run.

Fair territory: The part of the playing field between and including the first and third base lines, from home base to the outfield fences.

Farm system: A major-league team's system of minor-league clubs.

Fielder's choice: When a fielder handles a ground ball and attempts to throw out a base runner other than the hitter.

Finding the handle: Getting a firm grip on the ball before throwing it.

Finesse pitcher: A hurler who gets hitters out more with guile and control than speed. Greg Maddux is arguably the greatest finesse pitcher in baseball history.

Fireballer: The opposite of a finesse pitcher, this stud overpowers hitters with a blazing fastball. Randy Johnson has been the king fireballer of the past decade.

Fireman: A relief pitcher, usually one who is brought into a precarious situation. He is there to put out the fire.

First ball hitter: A batter who usually swings at the first pitch. Such hitters rarely walk and usually have low on-base percentages.

Five o'clock hitter: A low-average hitter who hits his best shots during batting practice.

Five-tool player: A player who runs the bases quickly, fields his position expertly, demonstrates a strong, accurate throwing arm, and hits for both power and average. Alex Rodriguez, Vladimir Guerrero, and Carlos Beltran are five-tool players.

Flake: Any player who behaves eccentrically. Reliever Turk Wendell, who brushes his teeth between every inning, is said to be a flake.

Flare: A looping fly ball hit to the opposite field, just beyond the infield. It usually plunks in for a base hit.

Fly ball: A ball hit into the air on an arc.

Force-out: When a batted ball forces a runner to advance to another base and the fielder possessing the ball tags that base before the runner reaches it.

Forfeit: A game terminated by the umpire upon the violation of a rule, with the victory going to the offended team.

40-40 club: That group of rare players who have hit 40 home runs while stealing 40 bases in the same season. Oakland's Jose Canseco became the first 40-40 man in 1988. As of 2004, Barry Bonds and Álex Rodríguez were the only other two members of this select group.

Foul pole: The yellow poles along the outfield walls that mark the end of the foul lines. They indicate whether a ball hit into the seats is foul or a home run. Balls hit to the left of the left field foul pole are foul, as are balls hit to the right of the right field pole. A ball that hits either pole is, for reasons no one understands, called fair. (That being the case, why don't they call it the fair pole?)

Foul strike: A strike charge to the batter when he hits a foul ball that is not caught with less than two strikes. After two strikes a hitter can foul off as many balls as he wants without the umpire calling strike three.

Foul territory: The section of the playing field outside the first and third base lines.

Foul tip: A batted ball that careens sharply toward the catcher's mitt and is caught. It is a foul tip only if it is caught. Any foul tip is also a strike. The ball is in play. If the catcher catches a foul tip with two strikes on the batter, the batter has struck out. If a foul tip is not caught (in which case it remains a foul ball), the pitch is called a strike if the batter has less than two strikes. With two strikes on the batter, the count holds and the at-bat continues.

Franchise player: A star player, usually young, around whom management can build a team. St. Louis's Albert Pujols and Oakland's Eric Chavez are both franchise players. When the young Tom Seaver was leading the New York Mets out of oblivion in the '60s, he was nicknamed "The Franchise."

Free agent: A player who is not contracted to play for any team. He is free to negotiate with any club interested in his services.

Full count: When the pitcher has three balls and two strikes on the batter.

Fungo: A long, thin bat used by a coach or player to hit grounders or flies during fielding practice. The hitter tosses the ball into the air before striking it.

Game face: A look that tells you a player is all business. ("When Kevin Brown wears his game face, his glare penetrates the hitter like a laser.")

Gamer: A player who thrives in pressure situations, handles adversity well, or has a high threshold of pain. Also, the bat a hitter uses during a game. Out of every dozen bats he orders, the average major leaguer usually finds three or four gamers. He uses the other bats during batting practice or gives them away as souvenirs.

Games back: The number of games your team is out of first place.

Gap: The area between the left fielder and center fielder or the right fielder and center fielder. See *alley*.

Gap shot: An extra-base hit that lands in the gap and usually rolls or bounces to the wall. Also called a *tweener* or *gapper*.

Get a piece of the ball: When a hitter is just trying to make contact with a pitch, usually with two strikes on him.

Getaway game: The final game in a series for the visiting team.

Glove: The padded leather covering that protects a fielder's hand and makes it easier for him to catch a baseball. All fielders use gloves except the catcher and first baseman, who wear *mitts*. (The difference between a mitt and a glove? Mitts have more padding.)

Glove man: An expert fielder. Often used to describe a weak hitter whose fielding prowess keeps him in the lineup.

Go deep: To hit a home run.

Go yard: To pitch a complete game (something that is becoming increasingly rare in modern baseball).

Goat: A player who makes a glaring mistake that contributes to a defeat. It's a term used almost exclusively by reporters and fans. Most professional players will tell you that no one play ever costs a team a game.

Gold Glove: The annual award given in the Major Leagues (AL and NL) to the best fielding player at each position.

Goose egg: A scoreless inning. ("Josh Beckett has put up nothing but goose eggs through seven.")

Gopher ball: A pitch that is hit for a home run.

Grand slam: A home run with the bases loaded. (Note: The popular phrase "grand slam home run" is a redundancy.) Also known as a *grand salami* (a term popularized by broadcaster Tim McCarver).

Green light: Not an actual sign. When a player has the green light, his manager has told him he can steal a base whenever he chooses, or he can swing away on 3–0 and 3–1 counts.

Ground ball: A batted ball that rolls or bounces on the ground. Also known as a *grounder*.

Ground-rule double: A fair ball that goes over the outfield fence on a bounce. The runners take two bases.

Guarding the lines: When an infielder positions himself close to the first- or third-base line to stop fair balls from shooting into the corners for extra-base hits.

Gun: A fielder's strong throwing arm. The term is usually applied to an outfielder or catcher. ("Texas catcher Ivan Rodriguez has a gun behind home plate.")

Gun shy: Being fearful of getting hit by a pitch.

Hack: To swing at a pitch ("take a hack").

Handcuffed: What an infielder becomes when a ball is hit so hard that he can't handle it, even though it was hit right at him.

Handle: The end of the bat gripped by the hitter. It is the thinnest part of the bat.

Hanging curve: A curveball that breaks little except a pitcher's heart. Hanging curves don't hang for very long; hitters usually quickly deposit them into the upper decks for home runs.

Happy zone: The portion of the strike zone where a batter is most likely to hit a pitch hard, which makes it the unhappy zone if you are a pitcher.

Headhunter: A pitcher who throws at hitter's heads.

Heads-up play: A smart maneuver on the base paths or in the field.

Heat: An above-average fastball. Also known as *cheese, high cheese, smoke, gas, high heat,* and *hummer.* Dennis Eckersley used to call his fastball a *yakker.* Want to flash some retro-cool? Try on a term popularized by the Cincinnati Reds pitchers during the mid-1960s. That hard-throwing lot — they led the National League in strikeouts four times in five years — measured their fastballs by how much *hair* they had. The faster the pitcher, the more hair he had on the ball. ("Did I have much hair out there today?" "You were positively shaggy, son.")

Hill: The pitcher's mound.

Hit: A ball batted into fair territory, which allows the hitter to reach base safely without benefit of a fielding error or a fielder's choice.

Hit behind the runner: When the batter hits the ball to the right of a runner advancing to first base.

Hit by pitch: A plate appearance that results in the batter being hit by a pitch. The batter is awarded first base. It's also known as *taking one for the team.*

Hit-and-run: An offensive strategy called by a manager with a runner on first. As the pitcher winds up, the runner takes off for second base. The batter must make contact so that the runner can safely take second on an out or go for extra bases on a hit.

Hitch: The term used to describe a hitter's habit of dropping his hands just prior to swinging his bat. It disrupts the timing of most batters, though for some players (like former slugger Cecil Fielder), a hitch is part of their timing mechanism.

Hitter's count: A ball-strike count that favors the hitter by forcing the pitcher to throw a fastball over the plate. 3–0, 3–1, and 2–0 are all considered hitter's counts.

Hole: In fielding, the term refers to an area deep and to the far right of the shortstop or deep and to the far left of the second baseman. In hitting, when a pitcher has a ball-strike advantage over a hitter, the batter is said to be *in a hole.* ("Lowe has Glaus in an 0–2 hole.") Also, a batter who doesn't make contact often is said to have a lot of holes in his swing.

Home plate: Home plate is a 17-inch (43 centimeter) square with two of its corners removed to leave a 17-inch-long edge, two 8½-inch (21.5 centimeter) adjacent sides, and two 12-inch-long (30.5 centimeter) sides angled to a point. The result is a five-sided slab of white rubber with black borders. A runner scores by safely rounding all bases and touching home plate.

Home run: A fair fly ball that travels over the outfield fence. An inside-the-park home run doesn't leave the playing field; it is a fair ball that eludes fielders for so long that the hitter is able to circle the bases before a play can be made on him. Other terms for the home run include *homer, dinger, jack, going yard, dial 8, long-ball, round-tripper, 'tater, four-bagger, going downtown,* and *clout.*

Home team: The host team in a baseball game. Mutual agreement determines who will be the home team when a game is played on neutral ground.

Homestretch: The final month of a season.

Hoover: An expert infielder who fields or "vacuums" ground balls. Hoover was also the nickname of third baseman Brooks Robinson, a perennial Gold Glove winner.

Hot corner: Third base.

Hot dog: A player who shows off. (For example, a hitter who stands at home plate admiring his own home run.) Players who field their positions with flamboyance are often said to be *hot-dogging* or *cutting the pie.*

Human rain delay: A hitter who takes a long time settling in the batter's box.

Ice cream cone: A ball caught in the top of a glove's webbing so that the top half is visible.

In his kitchen: A pitch that jams a hitter on the bat handle. Yankee outfielder Lou Piniella once hit such an offering from Red Sox left-hander Bill Lee for a game-winning double. Afterwards Piniella told Lee, "Bill, you can come into my kitchen, but don't sit down to eat."

In jeopardy: A term that indicates the ball is in play and the offensive player can be put out.

Incentive clause: A clause in a player's contract that awards him for achieving certain goals.

Incomplete game: Any game that ends before the visiting team finishes batting in the fifth inning.

Indifference: Allowing an opposing base runner to advance a base without attempting to stop him.

Infield fly rule: With less than two outs, a fair fly ball (that is neither a line drive nor an attempted bunt) that can be caught with ordinary effort by one of the infielders when first base and second base are occupied by runners (or when runners are on all the bases). The umpires call this rule. The batter is automatically out even if the fielder misses the ball. (This rule is designed to keep infielders from missing fly balls on purpose in order to make an unfair double play — with less than two outs, runners don't try to advance if they think a ball is going to be caught!)

Inning: A unit of a baseball game consisting of a turn at-bat and three outs for each team. Regulation games consist of nine innings. A game can have fewer innings if it is called (canceled) by the umpire (due to inclement weather or some other circumstance) or more innings if the game is tied after the regulation nine.

Inside baseball: Strategy such as the hit-and-run, stealing, bunting for base hits, squeeze plays, sacrifices, hitting the cutoff man, and defensive positioning. All involve a degree of savvy and teamwork. Also known as *little ball.*

Inside-the-park home run: A home run that does not leave the playing field. To achieve it, a batter must race around all four bases before the fielder's throw beats him to home plate. During the last game of the 1999 season, Tampa Bay's Randy Winn smacked a genuine rarity against the New York Yankees: an inside-the-park grand slam.

Insurance runs: Any runs scored in the late innings by the team that is already ahead.

Jamming: When a pitcher throws the ball inside and near the batter's hands, he is *jamming* the batter.

Journeyman: A serviceable player, rarely a star, who bounces around from club to club. The prototypical journeyman: right-handed pitcher Robert Miller, who was traded or sold 12 times to ten different teams.

Juggle: To mishandle a throw or a fielding chance.

Junk: Off-speed pitches such as the change-up, the slow curve, the palmball, and the knuckle ball. Relief pitcher Stu Miller was a renowned junkballer during the 1960s. He was said to throw at three speeds: slow, slower, and slowest.

K: Another term for a *strikeout.*

Keystone: Second base. A team's shortstop and second baseman are known as the *keystone combination* for their double-play collaboration.

Knock: A base hit. ("Magglio Ordonez had five knocks today.")

Laugher: A lopsided victory, as in "The Braves won an 11–1 laugher." Also known as a *blowout.*

Launching pad: A ballpark where home runs are plentiful. Modern players consider Colorado's Coors Field the ultimate launching pad.

Lead: The distance between a runner and a base.

Leadoff hitter: The hitter who bats first in the batting order.

Left-handed specialist: A relief pitcher who is usually brought in solely to get out one to three tough left-handed hitters.

Leg hit: What a hitter earns when he gets a single on a batted ball that doesn't travel beyond the infield. Also, an *infield hit.*

Let the ball play him: Said of a fielder who waits for a batted ball to reach him rather than aggressively charging it.

Line drive: A ball that is hit, usually hard, on a straight line. Also known as a *bullet* or *frozen rope.*

Lineup: The nine players (or ten if you are using a designated hitter) who start a game.

Live ball: A ball that is in play.

Long reliever: A relief pitcher who enters in the early innings after a starter has been bombed or injured. Also known as the *long man,* he usually pitches three innings or more.

Looper: A fly ball that carries just over the infield for a base hit.

Lord Charles: Uncle Charlie has long been a nickname for the curveball. Lord Charles is the *curveball maximus.* It doesn't merely break; it dives and is as fast as most pitchers' sliders. The phrase was first used during the early 1980's to describe New York Mets pitching ace Doc Gooden's phenomenal curveball.

Loud foul: A ball that is hit hard and far, but foul.

Lumber: A baseball bat.

Magic number: You hear this term mentioned frequently as the season winds down. The number represents any combination of wins and losses by the first- and second-place teams that clinches the top spot in the standings for the first-place club. For example, the Atlanta Braves lead the National League East with a record of 100–60; the Florida Marlins are in second at 99–61. With only two games left in

the 162-game season, Florida cannot possibly win more than 101 games. Therefore, the magic number for the Braves is two; if Atlanta wins both of its remaining games, it will have 102 wins, a total Florida cannot reach. Atlanta can also clinch by winning one game while Florida loses once because the Braves would have 101 victories while the Marlins could not win more than 100.

Make-up game: A game that has been rescheduled due to inclement weather or some other postponement.

Men in blue: Umpires.

Mendoza line: A batting average in the vicinity of .200. Kansas City Royals third baseman George Brett is said to have coined the term in "honor" of Mario Mendoza, a light-hitting shortstop with the Seattle Mariners who compiled a career batting average of .215.

Mental error: A mistake made by a distracted player, such as forgetting the number of outs.

Middle reliever: A relief pitcher who enters (usually) in the fifth or sixth inning of a close game.

Money player: A player who performs his best in critical games.

Mop-up man: You don't want to see him pitching too often for your favorite team. Mop-up men pitch when their team is losing by a lopsided score.

Mr. October: A player who excels during postseason play. The nickname was first hung on Yankee right fielder Reggie Jackson after he clouted three successive home runs in the final game of the 1977 World Series.

Must-win: A game a team must win to stay alive in the pennant race or postseason play.

Nab: To throw out a runner, usually on a close play.

National pastime: Another name for the sport of baseball.

Nightcap: The second game of a double-header.

No man's land: An area on the base paths so far from any base that the runner is usually tagged out when he hazards into it.

No-hitter: A nine-inning complete game in which a pitcher does not allow a hit to the opposing team. The opposition can have base runners through fielding errors or walks. See *Perfect game.*

Non-roster invitee: A player who is invited to spring training by a team, without any guarantee of a roster spot.

No-pitch: The umpire's call whenever he rules that a pitch is neither a ball nor a strike, usually because the pitcher released the ball after the umpire called timeout.

Obstruction: A call made by the umpire when a fielder, who neither possesses the ball nor is about to field the ball, impedes the progress of the runner.

Offensive interference: Any act by the offensive team that interferes with or confuses a fielder attempting to make a play, such as if a base runner deliberately runs into the second baseman while he is fielding a ground ball.

Oh-fer: What a batter takes when he fails to hit in a game or series. ("Jones took an oh-fer last night when he went 0-for-five.")

On-deck circle: The circle between the dugout and home plate where a player awaits his turn at-bat.

Open stance: A hitting stance in which the front foot is farther away from the plate than the back foot.

Opposite field: That side of the field that is opposite the batter's hitting side. For example, left field is the opposite field for a left-handed hitter like Barry Bonds who bats from the right side of home plate.

Out: One of the three required retirements of an offensive team during its half-inning turn at bat.

Out pitch: A pitcher's best pitch; the one he is most likely to throw to get an out or finish off a hitter.

Outright: To sever a player from a team's major-league roster, either by sending him to the minors or releasing him.

Overslide: The act of a base runner sliding past and losing contact with a base.

Passed ball: Any ball that eludes a catcher, which, in the official scorer's opinion, he should have controlled with ordinary effort.

Payoff pitch: A pitch thrown on a full count (three balls, two strikes).

Peg: A fielder's throw.

Pennant: The flag awarded to the champion of each league.

Pepper: A fast-moving (soft) hitting and fielding game designed to improve a player's reflexes. The fielder and hitter stand 20 feet apart. The hitter hits the ball to the fielder, who catches it and immediately pitches it back. The hitter hits that offering, and play continues.

Perfect game: A complete game in which the pitcher does not hit any batter with the ball and does not allow any hits, walks, or errors.

Phantom double play: A double play called by the umpire, even though the second baseman or shortstop did not step on second base for the force-out.

Phenom: An ultra-talented rookie. In 2004, Florida Marlins pitcher Dontrelle Willis was a National League phenom. Also spelled *pheenom.*

Pick it: To catch a ball. Players who can really pick it are good fielders.

Pickoff: A throw by a pitcher or catcher to nab a runner off base.

Pinch hitter: A hitter who substitutes for a teammate in the batting order. Managers often ask this hitter to come through in a pinch (a crucial situation).

Pinch runner: A runner who substitutes for a teammate on the bases.

Pine tar: A dark, viscous substance spread on the bat handle so that a hitter can get a better grip.

Pitch around: Refusing to throw a pitch into the strike zone of a dangerous hitter.

Pitcher of record: A game's winning or losing pitcher. You must throw at least five innings in a game to qualify for a win.

Pitcher's duel: A low-scoring game usually decided in the late innings.

Pitching rotation: The order in which a team's starting pitchers start games. Most modern teams employ five-man rotations, allowing each starter at least four day's rest in between starts.

Pitchout: When a pitcher intentionally throws the ball outside the strike zone so that his catcher has a better chance to catch a base runner trying to steal.

Plate appearance: Any trip to the plate by a hitter. Plate appearances include at-bats, walks, sacrifices, interference calls, and hit-by-pitches.

Platoon: A system in which players are alternated at a position, usually based on what side of the plate batters swing from. Left-handed platoon hitters generally start against right-handers; their right-handed counterparts usually take the field against lefties.

"Play!" or "Play Ball!": The umpire's order to start the game or to resume play following a dead ball.

Play-by-play: Any verbal or written account of every play that occurs in a given game. Also, a broadcaster's verbal description of a ballgame broadcast on TV or radio.

Player to be named later: The term applied to any player ineligible to be traded at the time a trade is consummated, such as a player who is on the disabled list or a recently drafted player who cannot be swapped until a year after his signing. The term is also used when a team submits a list of players for its trading partner to choose from at some future date. In 1984, the St. Louis Cardinals traded shortstop Jose Gonzalez to the San Francisco Giants. Upon joining his new team, Gonzalez legally changed his surname to Uribe, inspiring baseball curmudgeon Don Zimmer to quip, "I guess he really is the player to be named later."

Player-manager: A player who also acts as his team's manager. No one has held that title in the Major Leagues since the Cincinnati Reds' Pete Rose in 1986.

Pop fly: A high but weakly hit fly ball that rarely goes beyond the infield.

Portsider: A left-handed pitcher.

Productive out: Some define this as any out that advances a runner, or even better, scores a run. Others believe a batter can make a productive out only when his team is behind by a run, tied, or in the lead. But a third school of thought holds that the term "productive out" is a misnomer because any out that does not result in a run reduces your team's chances of scoring. Outs that move base runners along without scoring are merely less damaging than outs that do not advance runners.

Protest: Managers play games *under protest* when they believe an umpire has made a call that contradicts the rule book. No one can protest an umpire's judgment call. Managers must announce their protests to the umpire immediately following the disputed action, before the next play begins. The league office is the arbiter of all protests. Protests are rarely allowed.

Pull: To hit the ball early enough so that the bat meets the ball in front of the hitter. Right-handed hitters pull the ball to the left side; left-handers pull to the right. Pull hitters usually hit for power.

Pull the string: To throw an off-speed pitch.

Punch-and-Judy hitter: A batter who sprays softly batted hits to all fields; also known as a *spray hitter.*

Punchout: A strikeout. Also called a *whiff* or a *K.*

Purpose pitch: A pitch thrown close to the batter with the purpose of moving him off home plate.

Putout: A fielder is credited with a putout when he possesses the ball that retires a runner or hitter.

Quality start: Any game in which the starting pitcher works six or more innings while allowing three or fewer runs.

Question mark: A player whose status with a team is uncertain because of injury, a recent poor season, or a general decline in skills.

Quick pitch (or quick return): A pitch made before the batter is set. An umpire must judge whether the batter was set. A quick pitch is illegal. If the umpire rules that the pitcher threw the ball before the hitter was set in the batter's box, he can declare the pitch a ball (if no runners are on base) or a balk (if a runner is on base).

Rabbit ears: Any player, manager, or umpire who is hypersensitive to criticism.

Radar gun: The device used by baseball scouts to measure the speed of pitches, also know as the *JUGS gun.* Scouts refer to these guns as either fast or slow, depending on their make and how they record ball speed.

Rain check: The detachable portion of a ticket that guarantees you admission to another game in case the contest you're attending is rained out or postponed.

Regular season: In the Major Leagues, the 162-game season that determines each division's final standings and playoff participants.

Regulation game: A baseball game that is played to its completion.

Release: A pink slip. What a player reluctantly obtains when he is permanently cut from a team's roster.

Release point: The point at which the ball leaves a pitcher's hand. Good pitchers consistently release the ball from the same point.

Relief pitcher (reliever): Any pitcher who enters a game after the *starter* (the starting pitcher) has been removed.

Retired number: A uniform number worn by some baseball immortal that is no longer available to current players.

Retiring the side in order: When a pitcher retires three batters in an inning without surrendering a base runner.

Retouch: The act of a runner returning to a base.

Rifle: A powerful throwing arm.

Rookie: A first-year player. For the purpose of picking its Rookie of the Year award winner, the Baseball Writers Association of America has deemed that a player will retain his rookie status as long as he has not pitched 50 innings or accumulated 130 at-bats or 45 days of service time (excluding September call-ups) before a particular season.

Rosin bag: A cloth bag containing a powder called rosin. Kept at the side of the mound, it is used by pitchers to dry their fingers to improve their grip on the ball. Applying rosin directly to the ball is illegal.

Rubber: A 6-x-24-inch (15.5-x-61-centimeter) rubber slab on top of the pitcher's mound.

Rubber game: The third game of a three-game series in which the opposing teams have split the first two contests.

Rule 5 draft: Any player is eligible for the Rule 5 draft provided his team does not carry him on its 40-man roster and 1) He was 18 or younger when he signed his first pro contract and three Rule 5 drafts have occurred since his signing; or 2) He was at least 19 when he signed his first pro contract and two Rule 5 drafts have occurred since that signing. When a team drafts a Rule 5 player, it must keep him on its 25-man roster or the disabled list for the entire following season or offer him back to his original team.

Run: A scoring unit posted by an offensive player who touches first, second, third, and home plate in that order.

Run Batted In (RBI): A batter is credited with a run batted in when he drives a runner home (helps him score a run) via a hit, a sacrifice bunt or fly, a walk, a hit batsman, a fielder's choice, or on an error if the official scorer rules the run would have scored had the error not been made. (For example, a runner scores from third with less than two out on a long, catchable fly ball that is dropped by the center fielder. The center fielder is charged with the error. However, the official scorer credits the batter with a run batted in after deciding that the runner would have scored on a sacrifice fly had the ball been caught. Had the ball been hit to shallow center, and the scorer ruled it was not hit far enough to score the runner without the error, the batter would not receive an RBI.) You also credit a batter with an RBI if he drives himself in with a home run. Batters do not get ribbies when they drive runners in while grounding into double plays.

Rundown: Members of the defense chase a runner back and forth on the base paths in an attempt to put out the runner.

Runner: An offensive player who is advancing toward, returning to, or occupying a base.

Sacrifice bunt: When the hitter willingly bunts into an out in order to advance a base runner. Also known as "giving yourself up."

Sacrifice fly: A ball hit deep enough to score a runner from third base with less than two outs.

Save: The statistical credit awarded to a relief pitcher who finishes a game on the victorious side but does not get the win. (To discover how saves are calculated, see Chapter 16.)

Scatter arm: A pitcher or fielder who throws wildly.

Scorecard: The graph that allows you to track every play in a game, inning by inning.

Scoring position: A runner on second or third base, where he can score on almost any hit to the outfield. (Sluggers like Barry Bonds, Albert Pujols, and Alex Rodriguez seem to be in scoring position the minute they step in the batter's box.)

Scout: The person who evaluates talent for a professional baseball organization. Most scouts scour high schools, colleges, and minor leagues for players. *Advance scouts* monitor other major-league clubs to pinpoint opposing players' strengths and weaknesses.

Scratch run: A run produced by a sacrifice grounder, an infield hit, or ground-ball out.

Season tickets: Tickets for an entire season of home games.

Seeing-eye grounder: A ground ball that barely eludes an infielder for a base hit.

Set position: The position the pitcher takes on the pitching rubber just before going into the windup.

Set the table: To get on base for the power hitters in your team's lineup.

Set-up man: A relief pitcher who usually arrives in the seventh or eighth inning, preferably when his team is winning. He sets up the ninth inning for the closer.

Seventh-inning stretch: A brief pause in the action between the top and bottom of the seventh inning. It allows time for fans to stand and stretch their legs. One story, perhaps apocryphal, claims that the practice began in 1910 when President William H. Taft stood up to stretch in the seventh inning of a Pittsburgh Pirates game. The rest of the crowd stood up with the president out of respect. However, research has uncovered numerous earlier references to the ritual.

Shoestring catch: A running catch made at the top of a fielder's shoes.

Show, The: The Major Leagues. A term popularized in the film *Bull Durham,* starring Kevin Costner.

Shutout: A pitcher's complete game victory in which the opposition doesn't score.

Signs: Managers, coaches, and players use these coded signals to pass information to each other during a game. The term is also used to describe the hand signals catchers use to call pitches.

Single: A one-base hit. Also known as a *knock.*

Slugfest: A high-scoring game.

Slugger: A hitter who is usually among the home-run leaders. Babe Ruth, who led the American League in home runs 12 times, was the quintessential slugger.

Solo homer: A home run with the bases empty.

Southpaw: A left-handed pitcher.

Spectator interference: What an umpire should call when a fan reaches out of the stands or enters the playing field and touches a ball that's still in play.

Split-fingered fastball: A pitch thrown by placing the ball between the first two fingers. When thrown by a master like Roger Clemens, the pitch approaches home plate on a high plane then dives precipitously.

Squeeze play: When a hitter attempts to score a runner from third with a bunt. If the runner leaves third before the hitter makes contact with the ball, it is called a *suicide squeeze;* if the hitter misses the pitch, the runner is dead. In the *safety squeeze,* the runner waits for the hitter to make contact before racing toward home.

Starting rotation: A team's group of regular starting pitchers who pitch in sequence.

Strawberry: A pinkish abrasion on the hip or leg, usually caused by sliding.

Stretch drive: The final lap of a horse race, or the final weeks of a season when teams are driving toward the pennant.

Strike: What occurs when a) a batter swings and misses the ball; b) the batter hits a foul ball (unless he already has two strikes on him); c) the ball crosses the plate in the strike zone and the batter doesn't swing; or d) the players' union and the major-league baseball owners can't reach an agreement and the players refuse to come to work.

Strike zone: The area a ball must pass through to be called a strike by an umpire. According to the rules, this zone is the width of home plate and extends from the bottom of the kneecap to the uniform letters across a player's chest. In practice, it varies, sometimes widely, from umpire to umpire.

Strikeout: An out made by a batter who accumulates three strikes during an at-bat. Also known as a *K* or a *whiff.*

Striking out the side: Perhaps the most misused phrase in baseball. To strike out the side, a pitcher must strike out every batter he faces in an inning rather than merely strike out three batters in an inning. If the pitcher allows a base runner of any kind during the inning, the phrase does not apply.

Suspended game: A game that is called but is scheduled to be completed at some future date.

Sweet spot: The best part of the bat to hit the ball. The sweet spot is a few inches from the end of the barrel.

Switch-hitter: A batter who hits from both sides of the plate.

Tag: The act by which a fielder retires a base runner. The fielder either touches a base with his body or the ball before the runner arrives, or the fielder touches the runner with the ball (which can be in the fielder's glove or hand) before the runner reaches the bag.

Take: To let a pitch go by without swinging.

Tape-measure home run: A long home run, usually one that travels 450 feet or more. Barry Bonds and Sammy Sosa regularly hit tape-measure shots. The term was first applied to the long home runs hit by Mickey Mantle in the 1950s.

Ten-and-five rule: Any player who has ten years of major-league service time and has spent the previous five years with the same team has the right to veto any trade. Teams will often try to trade players before they achieve this status.

"Time": The umpire's declaration that interrupts play. The ball is dead.

Tools of ignorance: The catcher's equipment. The term implies that one has to be lacking intelligence to want to wear them. Actually, the converse is true. A good catcher is usually one of the smartest people on a team.

Trade: An exchange of players between two or more teams.

Trading deadline: Major-league baseball imposes two trading deadlines during the regular season. July 31 is the last day teams can transact a talent swap without passing the players through waivers. The second deadline occurs at midnight on August 31 when teams must set their postseason rosters. Any players acquired after that date are ineligible for postseason play.

Triple: A three-base hit.

Triple play: Any defensive play that produces three outs on the same batted ball. In an *unassisted triple play,* one fielder records all three outs.

Triple-double: When a player attains at least ten doubles, triples, and home runs in the same season.

Twin killing: A double play.

Umpire: The on-field baseball official who declares whether a batter is safe or out, a pitch is a ball or a strike, or a batted ball is foul or fair. He also interprets the rule book on all plays.

Umpire's interference: An act by the umpire that obstructs a catcher as he's attempting to throw out a base stealer. This call is also made when a fair ball strikes an umpire in fair territory before passing a fielder. The ball is dead.

Uniforms: What players wear on the field.

Utility player: A player, usually a substitute, who has the versatility to play more than one position. Though it rarely happens, utility players can get enough plate appearances at their various positions to qualify as regulars. Billy Goodman started at six different positions for the 1950 Boston Red Sox and won an American League batting title.

Walk: When a hitter receives four balls during a plate appearance, he is entitled to take first base. All other base runners advance if they are forced in by the walk. See *base on balls.*

Walk-off homer: A home run that ends the ballgame; it can only be hit by a home team player. In May 2003, Chicago Cubs shortstop Alex Gonzalez accomplished a rare feat by hitting two tenth-inning walk-off homers within six days of each other.

Warning track: A dirt path in front of the outfield fences, which warns the outfielders of their proximity to the walls.

Waste pitch: A pitch deliberately thrown outside the strike zone in the hope that the batter will chase it. Pitchers usually throw them if they are ahead of the batter in the count (on 0–2 or 1–2 counts). This pitch really is a waste if you throw it to a *bad-ball hitter* who hammers it for extra bases.

Wheelhouse: A hitter's power zone — an area that is usually waist-high and over the heart of home plate.

Wheels: A player's legs.

Whiff: A strikeout.

Whitewash: A shutout.

Wild pitch: A pitched ball that is thrown so far from the target that it gets past the catcher. If the official scorer decides the catcher should have caught the pitch, he can rule it a *passed ball.* Wild pitches and passed balls are charged only when they advance a base runner or allow a batter to reach base safely on a third strike.

Winter league: A baseball league that plays during the winter months. Most winter leagues are based in Florida, Arizona, or Latin America. Many Latin American big leaguers play winter ball for their hometown teams as a matter of local pride. American major leaguers usually play in these leagues to sharpen their skills after an injury-plagued season or to learn a new position.

Worm-burner (worm-killer): A ground ball that rolls over the infield without taking a bounce.

Appendix B

Baseball Organizations

● ●

The Major Leagues

Major League Advanced Media
75 Ninth Avenue
New York, New York 10011
Phone: 212-485-3444

Major League Alumni Association
1631 Mesa Avenue, Suite B
Colorado Springs, Colorado 80906
Phone: 719-477-1870

Major League Players Association
12 East 49th Street
New York, New York 10017
Phone: 212-826-0808
Web site: www.bigleaguers.com

Major League Umpires Association
1735 Market Street
Suite 3420
Philadelphia, Pennsylvania 19103
Phone: 215-979-3200

National Baseball Hall of Fame and Museum
25 Main Street
Cooperstown, New York 13326
Phone: 607-547-7200
Web site: www.baseballhalloffame.org

Negro Leagues Baseball Museum
1616 East 18th Street
Kansas City, Missouri 64108
Phone: 816-221-1920
Web site: www.nlbm.com

Office of Major League Baseball
245 Park Avenue South
31st Floor
New York, New York 10167
Phone: 212-931-7800
Web site: www.mlb.com

Media

Baseball Writers Association of America
78 Olive Street
Lake Grove, New York 11755
Phone: 631-981-7938

Bloomberg Sports News
400 College Road East
Princeton, New Jersey 08540
Phone: 609-750-4691

ESPN
ESPN Plaza
935 Middle Street
Bristol, Connecticut 06010
Phone: 860-766-2000
Web site: www.espn.com

Fox Sports
1201 West Pico Boulevard
Los Angeles, California 90035
Phone: 310-369-6000
Web site: www.foxsports.com

National Collegiate Baseball Writers
Association
2201 Stemmons Freeway
Dallas, Texas 75207
Web site: www.ncbwa.com

Publications

Athlon Sports Baseball
220 25th Avenue
Nashville, Tennessee 37203
Phone: 615-327-0747
Web site: www.athlonsports.com

Baseball America
201 West Main Street
Suite 201
Durham, North Carolina -27702
Phone: 919-682-9635
Web site: www.baseballamerica.com

Baseball Digest
990 Grove Street
Evanston, Illinois 60201
Phone: 847-491-6440

Beckett Baseball Card Monthly
15850 Dallas Parkway
Dallas, Texas 75248
Phone: 972-991-6657
Web site: www.beckett.com/estore

ESPN The Magazine
19 East 34th Street
7th Floor
New York, New York 10016
Phone: 212-515-1000
Web site: www.espnmag.com

Junior Baseball Magazine
22026 Gault Street
Canoga Park, California 91303
Phone: 818-710-1234
Web site: www.juniorbaseball.com

The Sporting News
10176 Corporate Square Drive
St. Louis, Missouri 63132
Phone: 800-777-6785
Web site: www.sportingnews.com

Sports Illustrated
Service Division General Offices
135 West 50th Street
New York, New York 10020
Phone: 212-522-1212
Web site: www.si.com

Sports Illustrated For Women
135 West 50th Street
New York, New York 10020
Phone: 212-522-1212
Web site: www.siwomen.com

Spring Training Baseball
107 Poplar Avenue
Carrboro, North Carolina 27510
Phone: 919-967-2420
Web site: www.springtrainingmagazine.com

Street and Smith's Sports Annuals
120 West Morehead Street
Suite 230
Charlotte, North Carolina 28202
Phone: 704-973-1575
Web site: www.streetandsmiths.com

Total Baseball
21 Carlaw Avenue
Toronto, Ontario M4M 2R6
Phone: 416-466-0418
Web site: www.totalbaseball.ab.ca

USA Today Sports Weekly
7950 Jones Branch Drive
Arlington, Virginia 22229
Phone: 800-872-1415

Statistics and Research

Elias Sports Bureau
500 Fifth Avenue
Suite 2140
New York, New York 10110
Phone: 212-869-1530
Web site: www.elias.com

Society for American Baseball Research
812 Huron Road
Suite 719
Cleveland, Ohio 44115
Phone: 216-575-0500
Web site: www.sabr.org

Sports Network
2200 Byberry Road
Suite 200
Hatboro, Pennsylvania 19040
Phone: 212-441-8844
Web site: www.sportsnetwork.com

Sportsticker Boston
Boston Fish Pier
West Building #1, Suite 302
Boston, Massachusetts 02210
Phone: 617-951-0070
Web site: www.sportsticker.com/ticker

STATS, Inc.
8130 Lehigh Avenue
Morton Grove, Illinois 60053
Phone: 847-583-2100
Web site: www.stats.com

American League Teams

Anaheim Angels
2000 Gene Autry Way
Anaheim, California 92806
Phone: 888-796-4856
Web site: www.angelsbaseball.com

Baltimore Orioles
333 West Camden Street
Baltimore, Maryland 21201
Phone: 888-848-8473
Web site: www.theorioles.com

Boston Red Sox
4 Yawkey Way
Boston, Massachusetts 02215
Phone: 617-267-9440
Web site: www.redsox.com

Chicago White Sox
333 West 35th Street
Chicago, Illinois 60616
Phone: 312-674-1000
Web site: www.chisox.com

Cleveland Indians
2401 Ontario Street
Cleveland, Ohio 44115
Phone: 216-420-4200
Web site: www.clevelandindians.com

Detroit Tigers
2100 Woodward Avenue
Detroit, Michigan 48201
Phone: 313-962-4000
Web site: www.detroittigers.com

Kansas City Royals
P.O. Box 419969
Kansas City, Missouri 64141
Phone: 816-921-8000
Web site: www.kcroyals.com

Minnesota Twins
34 Kirby Puckett Place
Minneapolis, Minnesota 55415
Phone: 612-375-1366
Web site: www.twinsbaseball.com

New York Yankees
161st Street and River Avenue
Bronx, New York 10452
Phone: 718-293-4300
Web site: www.yankees.com

Oakland Athletics
7000 Coliseum Way
Oakland, California 94621
Phone: 510-638-0500
Web site: www.oaklandathletics.com

Seattle Mariners
1250 First Avenue South
Seattle, Washington 98134
Phone: 206-346-4000
Web site: www.mariners.org

Tampa Bay Devil Rays
One Tropicana Drive
St. Petersburg, Florida 33705
Phone: 727-825-3137
Web site: www.devilrays.com

Texas Rangers
1000 Ballpark Way #400
Arlington, Texas 76011
Phone: 817-273-5222
Web site: www.texasrangers.com

Toronto Blue Jays
One Blue Jays Way
Suite 3200
Toronto, Ontario M5V 1J1
Phone: 416-341-1000
Web site: www.bluejays.ca

National League Teams

Arizona Diamondbacks
P.O. Box 2095
Phoenix, Arizona 85001
Phone: 602-462-6500
Web site: www.azdiamondbacks.com

Atlanta Braves
P.O. Box 4064
Atlanta, Georgia 30302
Phone: 404-522-7630
Web site: www.atlantabraves.com

Chicago Cubs
1060 West Addison Street
Chicago, Illinois 60613
Phone: 773-404-2827
Web site: www.cubs.com

Cincinnati Reds
100 Main Street
Cincinnati, Ohio 45202
Phone: 513-765-7000
Web site: www.cincinnatireds.com

Colorado Rockies
2001 Blake Street
Denver, Colorado 80205
Phone: 303-292-0200
Web site: www.coloradorockies.com

Florida Marlins
2267 Dan Marino Boulevard
Miami, Florida 33056
Phone: 305-626-7378
Web site: www.flamarlins.com

Houston Astros
P.O. Box 228
Houston, Texas 77001
Phone: 713-259-8000
Web site: www.astros.com

Los Angeles Dodgers
1000 Elysian Park Avenue
Los Angeles, California 90012
Phone: 213-224-1500
Web site: www.dodgers.com

Milwaukee Brewers
One Brewers Way
Milwaukee, Wisconsin 53214
Phone: 414-902-4400
Web site: www.milwaukeebrewers.com

New York Mets
123-01 Roosevelt Avenue
Flushing, New York 11368
Phone: 718-507-6387
Web site: www.mets.com

Philadelphia Phillies
One Citizens Bank Way
Philadelphia, Pennsylvania 19148
Phone: 215-463-6000
Web site: www.phillies.com

Pittsburgh Pirates
115 Federal Street
Pittsburgh, Pennsylvania 15212
Phone: 412-323-5000
Web site: www.pittsburghpirates.com

St. Louis Cardinals
250 Stadium Plaza
St. Louis, Missouri 63102
Phone: 314-421-3060
Web site: www.stlcardinals.com

San Diego Padres
P.O. Box 122000
San Diego, California 92112
Phone: 888-MY-PADRES or 619-881-6500
Web site: www.padres.com

San Francisco Giants
24 Willie Mays Plaza
San Francisco, California 94107
Phone: 415-972-2000
Web site: www.sfgiants.com

Washington (Expos)
As we went to press, the Washington franchise of the National League had yet to construct its official Web site. However, once the site is up, you can gain access by going to www.MLB.com and pulling down the Teams menu.

The Minor Leagues

Appalachian League
283 Deerchase Circle
Statesville, North Carolina 28625
Phone: 704-873-5300
Web site: www.appyleague.com

Arizona Fall League
10202 South 51st Street
Suite 230
Phoenix, Arizona 85044
Phone: 480-496-6700

Arizona League
P.O. Box 1645
Boise, Idaho 83701
Phone: 208-429-1511

California League
2380 South Bascom Avenue #200
Campbell, California 95008
Phone: 408-369-8038
Web site: www.californialeague.com

Carolina League
P.O. Box 9503
Greensboro, North Carolina 27429
Phone: 336-691-9030
Web site: www.carolinaleague.com

Dominican Summer League
Calle Segundo No. 64 Reparto Antilla
Santo Domingo, Dominican Republic
Phone: 809-532-3619
Web site: www.dominicansummerleague.com

Eastern League
511 Congress Street
7th Floor
Portland, Maine 04104
Phone: 207-761-2700
Web site: www.easternleague.com

Florida State League
103 East Orange Avenue
Daytona Beach, Florida 32114
Phone: 386-252-7479
Web site: www.fslbaseball.com

Gulf Coast League
1503 Clower Creek Drive
Suite H-262
Sarasota, Florida 34231
Phone: 941-966-6407

International League
55 South High Street
Suite 202
Dublin, Ohio 43017
Phone: 614-791-9300
Web site: www.ilbaseball.com

Mexican League
Angel Pola #16
Col. Periodista, Mexico D.F. 11220
Phone: 011-525-557-1007
Web site: www.lmb.com.mx

Midwest League
1118 Cranston Road
Beloit, Wisconsin 53511
Phone: 608-364-1188
Web site: www.midwestleague.com

National Association of Professional Baseball Leagues, Inc.
210 Bayshore Drive SE
St. Petersburg, Florida 33731
Phone: 727-822-6937
Web site: www.minorleaguebaseball.com

New York-Penn League
9410 International Court North
St. Petersburg, Florida 33716
Phone: 727-576-6300
Web site: www.nypennleague.com

Northwest League
P.O. Box 1645
Boise, Idaho 83701
Phone: 208-429-1511
Web site: www.northwestleague.com

Pacific Coast League
1631 Mesa Avenue
Suite A
Colorado Springs, Colorado 80906
Phone: 719-636-3399
Web site: www.pclbaseball.com

Pioneer League
157 South Lincoln Street
Spokane, Washington 99201
Phone: 509-456-7615
Web site: www.pioneerleague.com

South Atlantic League
504 Crescent Hill
Kings Mountain, North Carolina 28086
Phone: 704-739-3466
Web site: www.southatlanticleague.com

Southern League
2551 Roswell Road
Suite 330
Marietta, Georgia 30062
Phone: 770-321-0400
Web site: www.southernleague.com

Texas League
2442 Facet Oak
San Antonio, Texas 78232
Phone: 210-545-5297
Web site: www.texas-league.com

Venezuelan Summer League
C.C. Caribbean Plaza
Modulo 8 Local 173-174
Valencia, Carabobo, Venezuela
Phone: 011-58-241-8240980
Web site: www.venezuelansummerleague.com

Independent Leagues

Atlantic League
401 North Delaware Avenue
Camden, New Jersey 08102
Phone: 856-541-9400
Web site: www.atlanticleague.com

Central League
1415 Highway 54 West
Suite 210
Durham, North Carolina 27707
Phone: 719-520-0060
Web site: www.centralleaguebaseball.com

Frontier League
P.O. Box 62
Troy, Illinois 62294
Phone: 618-667-8000
Web site: www.frontierleague.com

Northeast League
1415 Highway 54 West
Suite 210
Durham, North Carolina 27707
Phone: 919-401-8150
Web site: www.northeastleague.com

Northern League
306 West Seventh Street
Suite 400
Fort Worth, Texas 76102
Phone: 817-378-9898
Web site: www.northernleague.com

Southwestern League
525 East Madrid
Las Cruces, New Mexico 88001
Phone: 505-523-4165
Web site: www.swlbaseball.com

Foreign Leagues

Caribbean Baseball Confederation
Frank Feliz Miranda No. 1 Naco
P.O. Box 21070 y 21416
Santo Domingo, Dominican Republic
Phone: 809-562-4737 or 809-562-4715

Central League (Japan)
Asahi Building 3F
6-6-7, Ginza
Chuo-ku Tokyo 104-0061, Japan
Phone: 03-3572-1673

Chinese Professional Baseball League
5, Tiyuguan Road, Beijing, 100763
People's Republic of China
Phone: 011-86-10-858-26002

Chinese Professional Baseball League of Taiwan
2F, No. 32, Pateh Road, Sec. 3
Taipei, Taiwan
Phone: 886-2-2577-6992

Dominican League
Estadio Quisqueya
Santo Domingo, Dominican Republic
Phone: 809-567-6371

Dutch Major Leagues
Perkinsbaan 15, 3439 ND
Nieuwegein, Holland
Phone: 31-030-607-6070

Japanese League
Imperial Tower 10 F
1-1-1 Uchisaiwai-cho
Chiyoda-ku Tokyo 100-0011, Japan
Phone: 03-3502-0022

Korean Baseball Organization
946-16 Dogok-Dong, Kangnam-Ku
Seoul, South Korea
Phone: 02-3460-4643

Mexican Pacific League
Av. Insurgenttes No. 847
Sur Interior 402, Edificio San Carlos
Col Centro, CP 80120
Culiacan, Sinaloa
Phone: 011-52-667-761-25-70

Pacific League (Japan)
Asahi Building 9F
6-6-7, Ginza,
Chuo-ku Tokyo 104-0061, Japan
Phone: 03-3573-1551

Puerto Rican League
Avenida Munoz Rivera 1056
Edificio first Federal
Rio iedra, Puerto Rico 00925
Phone: 787-765-6285

Venezuelan League
Avenida Casanova Central Comercial El Recreo
Torre Sur, Pico 3, Oficinas 6 y 7
Sabana Grande
Caracas, Venezuela
Phone: 011-58-212-761-7661

College Baseball

Alaska League (Summer College League)
601 South Main Street
Kenai, Alaska 99611
Phone: 508-432-1774
Web site: www.goldpanners.com/abl

Allegheny Mountain Collegiate League
508 Lacebark Court
Gibsonia, Pennsylvania 15044
Phone: 724-934-1978
Web site: www.amcconf.org

American Baseball Coaches Association
108 South University Avenue
Suite 3
Mount Pleasant, Michigan 48858
Phone: 989-775-3300
Web site: www.abca.org

Atlantic Collegiate Baseball League
401 Timber Drive
Berkeley Heights, New Jersey 07922
Phone: 908-464-8042
Web site: www.acbl-online.com

California Community College Commission on Athletics
2017 O Street
Sacramento, California 95814
Phone: 916-444-1600
Web site: www.coasports.org

Cape Cod Baseball League
7 Nottingham Drive
Harwich, Massachusetts 02645
Phone: 508-432-6909
Web site: www.capecodbaseball.org

Central Illinois Collegiate League
RR 13, Box 369
Bloomington, Illinois 61704
Phone: 309-828-4429
Web site: www.ciclbaseball.com

Coastal Plain League
4900 Waters Edge Drive
Suite 201
Raleigh, North Carolina 27606
Phone: 919-852-1960
Web site: www.coastalplain.com

Great Lakes League
7575 Tyler Boulevard
Mentor, Ohio 44060
Phone: 440-954-9400
Web site: www.greatlakesleague.org

National Association of Intercollegiate Athletics
23500 West 105th Street
Olathe, Kansas 66051
Phone: 913-791-0044
Web site: www.naia.org

The National Collegiate Athletic Association
P.O. Box 6222
Indianapolis, Indiana 46206
Phone: 317-917-6222
Web site: www.ncaa.org

National Jr. College Athletic Association
P.O. Box 7305
Colorado Springs, Colorado 80933
Phone: 719-590-9788
Web site: www.njcaa.org

New England Collegiate Baseball League
P.O. Box 415
Jamestown, Rhode Island 02835
Phone: 860-285-0133
Web site: www.necbl.com

New York Collegiate Baseball League
28 Dunbridge Heights
Fairport, New York 14450
Phone: 585-223-3528
Web site: www.nycbl.com

Northwoods League
P.O. Box 12
Rochester, Minnesota 55903
Phone: 507-536-4579
Web site: www.northwoodsleague.com

Pacific International League
504 Yale Avenue
Seattle, Washington 98109
Phone: 206-623-8844
Web site: www.pacificinternational
league.com

Shenandoah Valley League
Route 1, Box 189J
Staunton, Virginia 24401
Phone: 540-886-1748
Web site: www.valleyleaguebaseball.com

Texas Collegiate League
P.O. Box 200988
Arlington, Texas 76006
Phone: 214-333-5340
Web site: www.texascollegiateleague.com

High School Baseball

Champions Baseball Academy
10701 Plantside Drive
Louisville, Kentucky 40299
Phone: 502-261-9200
Web site: www.championsbaseball.com

National Classic High School Tournament
El Dorado High School
1651 North Valencia Avenue
Placentia, California 92870
Phone: 714-993-5350

National Federation of State High School
Associations
750 West Washington Street
Indianapolis, Indiana 46204
Phone: 317-972-6900
Web site: www.nfhs.org

National High School Baseball Coaches
Association
P.O. Box 5128
Bella Vista, Arkansas 72714
Phone: 479-876-2591
Web site: www.baseballcoaches.org

Sunbelt Classic Baseball Series
505 North Boulevard
Edmond, Oklahoma 73034
Phone: 405-348-3839
Web site:
www.geocities.com/Baja/Ravine/1976

Westminster National Classic
Westminster Academy
5601 North Federal Highway
Fort Lauderdale, Florida 33308
Phone: 954-735-1841
Web site: www.wacad.edu

Senior Leagues

Men's Adult Baseball League/Men's Senior
Baseball League
One Huntington Quadrangle
Suite 3N07
Melville, New York 11747
Phone: 631-753-6725
Web site: www.msblnational.com

National Adult Baseball Association
3609 South Wadsworth Boulevard
Suite 135
Lakewood, Colorado 80235
Phone: 303-639-9955
Web site: www.dugout.org

Youth Baseball

All American Amateur Baseball Association
331 Parkway Drive
Zanesville, Ohio 43701
Phone: 740-453-8531
Web site: www.aaaba.net

Amateur Athletic Union
1910 Hotel Plaza Boulevard
Lake Buena Vista, Florida 32830
Phone: 407-934-7200
Web site: www.aausports.org, www.
aaubaseball.org

American Amateur Baseball Congress
118-119 Redfield Plaza
P.O. Box 467
Marshall, Michigan 49068
Phone: 269-781-2002
Web site: www.aabc.us

American Amateur Youth Baseball Alliance
3851 Iris Lane
Bonne Terre, Missouri 63628
Phone: 573-518-0319
Web site: www.aayba.com

American Legion Baseball
700 North Pennsylvania Street
Indianapolis, Indiana 46204
Phone: 317-630-1213
Web site: www.baseball.legion.org

Babe Ruth League
P.O. Box 5000
Trenton, New Jersey 08638
Phone: 609-695-1434
Web site: www.baberuthleague.org

Continental Amateur Baseball Association
82 University Street
Westerville, Ohio 43081
Phone: 740-382-4620
Web site: www.cababaseball.com

Dixie Youth Baseball
P.O. Box 877
Marshall, Texas 75671
Phone: 903-927-2255
Web site: www.dixie.org

Dizzy Dean Baseball
P.O. Box 856
Hernando, Mississippi 38632
Phone: 662-429-4365
Web site: www.dizzydeanbbinc.org

Hap Dumont Youth Baseball
1325 N. Westlink
Witchita, Kansas 67212
Phone: 316-721-1779
Web site: www.hapdumontbaseball.com

Jayhawk Baseball Camps
1651 Naismith Drive
Lawrence, Kansas 66041
Phone: 785-864-7907
Web site: www.kuathletics.com/
baseball/camp

Little League Baseball
P.O. Box 3485
Williamsport, Pennsylvania 17701
Phone: 570-326-1921
Web site: www.littleleague.org

National Amateur Baseball Federation
P.O. Box 705
Bowie, Maryland 20715
Phone: 301-464-5460
Web site: www.nabf.com

National Association of Police Athletic Leagues
(PAL)
618 U.S. Highway 1
Suite 201
North Palm Beach, Florida 33408
Phone: 561-844-1823
Web site: www.nationalpal.org

PONY Baseball
P.O. Box 225
Washington, Pennsylvania 15301
Phone: 724-225-1060
Web site: www.pony.org

Reviving Baseball in Inner Cities (RBI)
245 Park Avenue
New York, New York 10167
Phone: 212-931-7897

Riverside Amateur Baseball Association
P.O. Box 31663
Riverside, OH 45437
Phone: 937-256-6370
Web site: www.eteamz.com/riverside
baseball

T-Ball USA Association
2499 Main Street
Stratford, Connecticut 06615
Phone: 203-381-1440
Web site: www.teeballusa.org

U.S. Amateur Baseball Association
P.O. Box 55633
Seattle, Washington 98155
Phone: 425-776-7130
Web site: www.usaba.com

U.S. Amateur Baseball Federation
911 Stonegate Court
Chula Vista, California 91913
Phone: 619-934-2551
Web site: www.usabf.com

USA Baseball
4825 Creekstone Drive
Suite 200
Durham, North Carolina 27703
Phone: 919-474-8721
Web site: www.usabaseball.com

USA Junior Olympic Baseball Championships
4825 Creekstone Drive
Suite 200
Durham, North Carolina 27703
Phone: 919-474-8721
Web site: www.usabaseball.com/
jr_olympics

Index

FOR DUMMIES

The easy way to get more done and have more fun

PERSONAL FINANCE

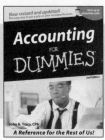

0-7645-5231-7

0-7645-2431-3

0-7645-5331-3

Also available:

Estate Planning For Dummies
(0-7645-5501-4)

401(k)s For Dummies
(0-7645-5468-9)

Frugal Living For Dummies
(0-7645-5403-4)

Microsoft Money "X" For
Dummies
(0-7645-1689-2)

Mutual Funds For Dummies
(0-7645-5329-1)

Personal Bankruptcy For
Dummies
(0-7645-5498-0)

Quicken "X" For Dummies
(0-7645-1666-3)

Stock Investing For Dummies
(0-7645-5411-5)

Taxes For Dummies 2003
(0-7645-5475-1)

BUSINESS & CAREERS

0-7645-5314-3

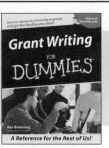

0-7645-5307-0

0-7645-5471-9

Also available:

Business Plans Kit For
Dummies
(0-7645-5365-8)

Consulting For Dummies
(0-7645-5034-9)

Cool Careers For Dummies
(0-7645-5345-3)

Human Resources Kit For
Dummies
(0-7645-5131-0)

Managing For Dummies
(1-5688-4858-7)

QuickBooks All-in-One Desk
Reference For Dummies
(0-7645-1963-8)

Selling For Dummies
(0-7645-5363-1)

Small Business Kit For
Dummies
(0-7645-5093-4)

Starting an eBay Business For
Dummies
(0-7645-1547-0)

HEALTH, SPORTS & FITNESS

0-7645-5167-1

0-7645-5146-9

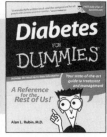

0-7645-5154-X

Also available:

Controlling Cholesterol For
Dummies
(0-7645-5440-9)

Dieting For Dummies
(0-7645-5126-4)

High Blood Pressure For
Dummies
(0-7645-5424-7)

Martial Arts For Dummies
(0-7645-5358-5)

Menopause For Dummies
(0-7645-5458-1)

Nutrition For Dummies
(0-7645-5180-9)

Power Yoga For Dummies
(0-7645-5342-9)

Thyroid For Dummies
(0-7645-5385-2)

Weight Training For Dummies
(0-7645-5168-X)

Yoga For Dummies
(0-7645-5117-5)

Available wherever books are sold.
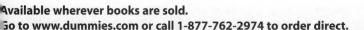
Go to www.dummies.com or call 1-877-762-2974 to order direct.